The Life
and Work of

William
Salesbury

A RARE SCHOLAR

I bawb sy'n caru'r iaith Gymraeg

The Life
and Work of
William
Salesbury
A RARE SCHOLAR

JAMES PIERCE

First impression: 2016
© James Pierce & Y Lolfa Cyf., 2016

The publishers wish to acknowledge the support of
Cyngor Llyfrau Cymru

Cover design: Y Lolfa
Cover photograph: © Martin Crampin

ISBN: 978 1 78461 272 6

Published and printed in Wales
on paper from well-maintained forests by
Y Lolfa Cyf., Talybont, Ceredigion SY24 5HE
e-mail ylolfa@ylolfa.com
website www.ylolfa.com
tel 01970 832 304
fax 832 782

Contents

List of abbreviations   7

Salusbury Family Tree   8

1   *Ad fontes*, his family and background   10

2   Erasmus; a life-long influence   21

3   Oxford   31

4   London; Thavies Inn, Germans and Hebrew   40

5   *Lesclarcissement de la langue francoyse*   49

6   Early career, marriage and literary interests   55

7   Death and discord   68

8   Literary beginnings   78

9   A dictionary   89

10   Proverbs, hope and further conflict   105

11   Building bridges   118

12   1550; the year of four books   128

13   A prayer book by any other name   152

14   A book in manuscript   166

15   A Catholic Queen   177

16   Campaigning re-joined   195

17 The Act of 1563   208

18 The translation   216

19 A Godly enterprise   234

20 The New Testament   246

21 Salesbury's last book   261

22 Salesbury's successors   276

23 Post mortem   289

24 Decline and fall   304

    Epilogue   317

    Endnotes   327

    Appendix   372

    Bibliography   381

    Index   392

List of abbreviations

ALMA	*Additional Letters of the Morrises of Anglesey*
BBCS	*Bulletin of the Board of Celtic Studies*
CCHA	*The Canadian Catholic Historical Association*
CMCS	*Cambrian Medieval Celtic Studies*
DNB	The Dictionary of National Biography
DWB	The Dictionary of Welsh Biography
GGH	*Gwaith Gruffudd Hiraethog*
HGF	*The History of the Gwydir Family*
HP	*The History of Parliament (1509–1558, Bindoff, 1558–1603, Hasler)*
JEBS	*Journal of the Early Book Society*
JHSCW	*Journal of the Historical Society of the Church in Wales*
JWBS	*Journal of the Welsh Biographical Society*
KLlB	*Kynniver Llith a Ban*
Llysieulyfr	*Llysieulyfr Salesbury*
LPFDH	*Letters and Papers, Foreign and Domestic, Henry VIII*
NLWJ	*Journal of the National Library of Wales*
OBWV	*The Oxford Book of Welsh Verse*
PACF	*Pedigrees of Anglesey and Carnarvonshire Families*
RST	*The Radnorshire Society Transactions*
TDHS	*Transactions of the Denbighshire Historical Society*
TBS	*The Bibliography Society*
WR	*Wales and the Reformation*
NA	National Archives
NLW	National Library of Wales

Salusbury Family Tree

The five sons of Thomas Salusbury (Salbri Hen), founder of the Salusbury dynasty, reputedly killed at the Battle of Barnet, 1471.

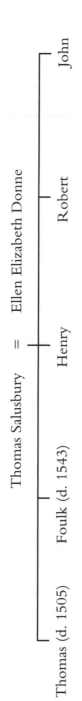

Thomas Salusbury = Ellen Elizabeth Donne

Thomas (d. 1505)   Foulk (d. 1543)   Henry   Robert   John

The family tree of Robert Salusbury (senior) of Plas Isa, fourth son of Thomas Salusbury.

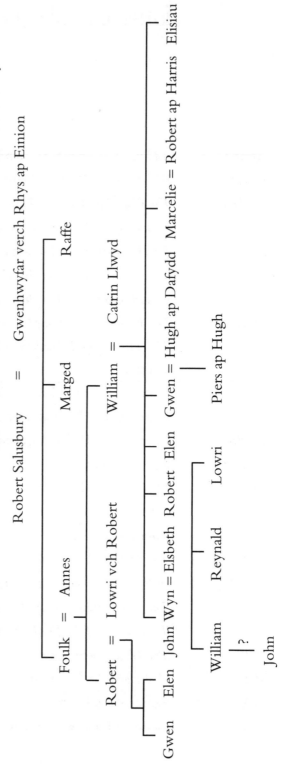

Robert Salusbury = Gwenhwyfar verch Rhys ap Einion

Foulk = Annes   Marged   Raffe

Robert = Lowri vch Robert   William = Catrin Llwyd

Gwen   Elen   John Wyn = Elsbeth   Robert   Elen   Gwen = Hugh ap Dafydd   Marcelie = Robert ap Harris   Elisiau

William   Reynald   Lowri   Piers ap Hugh

?

John

Whilst the family tree of Robert Salusbury (senior) and Gwenhwyfar is presented with a fair degree of confidence, I am less sure of the accuracy of that of Thomas and Ellen Salusbury. The year of Foulk's death (1543) leads me to suspect that some of Thomas's sons were the product of a later marriage. Either that or there is an error somewhere.

Salesbury's aunt, Marged, married Pirs ap Huw ap Ieuan Llwyd of the Llwyd family of Foxhall, Humphrey Llwyd's clan.

Salesbury's uncle, Raffe, had a son, Piers. His will of 1548, a rare survival, mentions another son, Thomas. There might have been other children, but the document is largely indecipherable.

Details of the husbands and children of his nieces, Gwen and Elen, can be found in Chapter Fifteen.

Of his own children, Robert and Elyn are named in the arbitration settlement of 1546, but I have found no further trace of them, though it is possible that Robert is the Robert Salesbury named in E 134/38&39Eliz/Mich33 (1594).

Gwen's husband died in 1567; I have not found a record of her re-marrying. Her son, Piers, Salesbury's grandson, died in 1586, when he would have been in his early twenties and before he is likely to have married.

Salesbury's youngest child, Elisau, died in 1572. There is no mention of a wife or a child in the will, but he mentions a sister, Marcelie and her husband, Robert. I have not found evidence of their having any children.

Salesbury's heir, John Wyn, is the only one of his children to have provided his father with a great-grandchild, John Salesbury. The evidence is in the will of his widow, Elsbeth. Unfortunately, it is not possible to tell from the will which of his two sons, William or Reynald, was the father. That a third, unknown son, by then deceased, was the father is possible.

There is a poem (see Cefn Coch MS. A) to 'Sion Salbri o Llanrwst ag iw ferch Lwlen' (John Salesbury of Llanrwst and to his daughter Lwlen) by Tomas Prys, Elis Price's son. Perhaps Lwlen is a familiar form of Lowri, though I have not seen it elsewhere. (Depressingly, the poem shows that the bullying of the Salesburys by the Prices continued into the next generation; it is full of sarcasm and derisory comments.)

Chapter One

Ad fontes, his family and background

The year of his birth

William Salesbury was born around 1507 in Llansannan, Denbighshire. Although no record of the birth survives, Salesbury made a passing reference to the parish in a herbal that he compiled towards the end of his life. Writing about marshmallow, he noted that it could be found in Llansannan in the field below the mansion of Maredudd ap Grono and added as an afterthought, 'sef yn y plwy y ganwyt vi' [that is, in the parish where I was born].[1]

Regarding the year of his birth, there are four key pieces of evidence that point to it being 1507 or thereabouts. The first is the will of his father-in-law, Robert ap Rhys,[2] drafted shortly before his death in 1535, which refers to the forthcoming marriage of his daughter, Catrin, to Salesbury. If Salesbury was in his mid to late twenties, an appropriate age for a Tudor gentleman to marry, it would confirm the year of birth.

A court case from the early 1530s[3] mentions 'William Salesbury'. Although not unique, the name is not common, and with there being a Welsh connection to the dispute, the likelihood is that this is Salesbury. His involvement suggests that he had completed his training as a lawyer, which would place him in his early or mid twenties.

There is a reference in a document[4] of around 1574 to Salesbury to being an old man. To qualify as such, his birth needs to before 1510 (making him in his sixties or seventies) rather than around 1520,[5] which would place him in his fifties.

Finally, there is the date of his first published work, his dictionary of 1547. To win the royal permission necessary for such a book[6] required a huge amount of political nous, involving diplomatic lobbying and what today is called 'networking'. The experience needed to achieve these skills and connections could only be garnered by years of work as a lawyer and by operating on the fringes of government, placing Salesbury as someone approaching early middle age.

Cae Du and Plas Isa

Far more can be discovered, and discovered with some certainty, about where he grew up. Llansannan is a small, isolated village with a pleasant church which is dedicated, unsurprisingly, to Saint Sannan. The most likely site of Salesbury's birthplace is Cae Du, a farm that lies a mile or so to the south, outside the main settlement on a road that leads up to moorland. It is mentioned in a sixteenth-century document[7] and five centuries later the present day farm, which lies to the left (east) of the road, still bears that name, though the family that works it lives in a twentieth-century house, the original now lying in ruins, its surviving stones hidden by nettles. Nearby runs a stream which might well have been the original water supply and some of the older farm buildings may contain stones recycled from the fifteenth-century dwelling. The land slopes steeply away down to the river Aled, which flows past the furthest end of the village.

The house was in a much better condition at the beginning of the twentieth century, when a survey was made of it and published in *Hanes hen furddynod plwyf Llansannan* [A History of the Ruins of Llansannan Parish][8] in 1910:

> The old house stands with its gable to the lane, and its wall on that side deep in the earth, while the lower gable, because of the slope, well above the ground-level, and its floor high enough to form a cellar at that end. The old house had three rooms on the ground floor and two up, as well as the cellar already mentioned, and the famous little room in the chimney, where Salesbury is said to have translated the New Testament. (tr.)

Unfortunately, though it is widely reported and accepted that Salesbury lived there, such reports date from no earlier than the eighteenth century.[9] No doubt they truthfully reflect local traditions and beliefs, but there are no contemporary documents to confirm them, though there are many that show that he and his family had extensive holdings in the parish and many local connections: his uncle, Raffe, lived there, for example.[10]

At one stage, Cae Du was owned by Margaret ferch (daughter of) John Pigot of Llanfair Talhaearn, who bequeathed it in her will of 1569 to her sons, Foulk and John Salusbury.[11]

During the nineteenth century Salesbury was a far more celebrated figure than he is today and the story of his translating the New Testament in secret during the reign of Queen Mary in the 'famous little room' mentioned above, although apocryphal, was widespread. Margaret's will, written eleven years after Mary's death, does not disprove the Cae Du connection. In fact, it comes tantalisingly close to confirming it. She had married into the clan to which Salesbury belonged and, if Cae Du had become surplus to the requirements of his estate, he might well have wished to sell it to someone within the extended family rather than a rival dynasty.

However, the main Salesbury home, Plas Isa, was some ten miles away to the south and west in the market town of Llanrwst. This was a much grander, more substantial building, as the word 'Plas' (mansion) indicates. This is the house with which Salesbury is usually associated; he is often referred to as 'William Salesbury of Plas Isa'.[12]

Though Cae Du was a house that most people in sixteenth-century Wales would have looked on with envy, it sheltered, like all longhouses, livestock and was very much a working farmhouse. Plas Isa, on the edge of a prosperous, busy town, was animal free and a home worthy of a country gentleman, the sort of man who might be appointed a justice of the peace or even be elected to parliament,[13] though Salesbury held neither of these positions.

The house stood a quarter of a mile from the town's church amidst the rich, flat meadows of the Conwy valley, whilst on the other side of the river rises the great, towering mass of Snowdonia. That wild, untamed scenery would not have been appreciated then as it was from the time of the Romantics, but Salesbury, as a herbalist, is sure to have adorned the immediate surroundings of the house with gardens, including a physic garden.

Sadly, nothing is left of Plas Isa. Descendants of Salesbury lived there until at least the 1660s.[14] In 1872, Mr J. Hughes of Plas Isa is recorded as having won first place for his cockerel and two hens in a local agricultural show.[15]

Photographs and drawings from around 1900 show a house in urgent need of restoration. The *Western Mail* of 31 October 1898 carried this appeal:

> Plas Isaf,[16] Llanrwst, the old house of William Salesbury, the first translator of the New Testament into the Welsh language, is fast falling into ruins; and unless some steps be speedily taken to stay the hand of Time a priceless and irrecoverable memorial will be forever lost to Wales ... we trust that to mention the present regrettable condition of Plas Isaf will be enough to arouse sufficient enthusiasm and support to preserve it from the ruthless havoc of time and weather.

It was not. In 1950 what was left of the house was demolished and levelled to become the Plas Isaf yard of Cawley Bros, Coal Merchants.

Despite their disappearance, far more is known about Salesbury's two houses than the early years of his life. It is not known why he was born in Llansannan rather than in Llanrwst. Details of his education are vague. It is known that he studied at Broadgates Hall, Oxford, and then at Thavies Inn, London, but not when and for how long. In fact no direct record of his life survives before 1546.

The Salusbury clan

Fortunately, a few details of the members of the family have survived. It is known that his mother's name was Annes (the Welsh form of Agnes);[17] her father was Wiliam ap Gruffudd ap Robin of Cochwillan, Caernarfonshire. Salesbury's father was Foulk Salesbury and the couple had one other surviving child, William's older brother, Robert.

Salesbury's family was a junior branch of an important and influential local dynasty, the Salusburys, which claimed to be descended from Adam, duke of Salzburg, whom Henry II had appointed as commanding officer of the garrison in Denbigh, but this is another apocryphal story, an example of the creative genealogy of which the Tudors were so fond.

The less grandiose reality is that the Salusburys were descended from incomers from Lancashire who prospered over the generations and acquired the language and culture of their new land. There is a town of Salesbury in Lancashire and Ekwall,[18] the leading expert on the history of place and personal names, noted the frequency of the surname in north Wales during the fourteenth century. (Why Salesbury's spelling of the surname differs from the version used by the rest of the clan is unknown.)

The first Salusbury to make a mark in history was Thomas Salusbury, who is reported to have been killed fighting for the Lancastrian cause at the Battle of Barnet (1471). He had five sons, Thomas, Foulk, Henry, John and Robert (William Salesbury's grandfather). The eldest son, Thomas, inherited the Lleweni estate and fought for the new, Lancastrian king, Henry VII, at the Battle of Blackheath (1497).

Thomas was knighted. The family had arrived. His grandson, John, was made a knight of the carpet at the coronation of Edward VI. The elder of John's two grandsons, Thomas, was executed in 1586 for his part in the Babington Plot, but his younger brother, John, restored the family's good name through his role in putting down the Essex revolt of 1601.

Though no one in the clan can rival Salesbury in intellectual achievement, two of them do find themselves in the footnotes of England's cultural history. Sir John Salusbury (Elizabeth knighted him following the revolt) is the first. He had married Ursula Stanley, the illegitimate but acknowledged daughter of the fourth earl of Derby. She was therefore the half-sister of Lord Strange (the fifth earl), who might well have been an early patron of William Shakespeare and who is believed by some academics to have been a member of the 'school of the night' gently satirised in *Love's Labour's Lost*.

Shakespeare's company had been paid handsomely by Essex's supporters to mount a production of *Richard II* shortly before the revolt. The play deals with the usurpation of a legitimate monarch, a dangerous subject at any time, but even more so when followed by an attempt to do exactly that in the real world. The company pleaded ignorance, but were suspected of complicity by the most powerful people in the land. It did not help that Shakespeare's chief patron, the earl of Southampton, had been an Essex supporter, had been arrested and sentenced to death (he was reprieved).

Shortly after the revolt Salusbury paid for a book of poetry featuring works by his protégé, Robert Chester, and others. Those others included Shakespeare, as it was in this book that *The Phoenix and the Turtle* first appeared. This helped Shakespeare distance himself from Essex and Southampton and was a very generous, perhaps life-saving, act on Salusbury's part.

The other Salusbury to leave a mark on English cultural history was Hester Lynch Piozzi, daughter of Hester Maria and John Salusbury of the Bachygraig sept. She is best known to the world as Mrs Hester Thrale, Doctor Johnson's friend of many years. The friendship cooled after her second marriage, but the connection made between the two of them meant that, on his tour of north Wales, Johnson stayed at Lleweni Hall,[19] the chief residence of the Salusbury clan.

(Interestingly, Virginia Woolf in *Dr Burney's Evening Party* has Mrs Thrale think to herself, 'Did not the blood of Adam of Salzburg run in her veins?', a clear reference to the myth of the Salusburys' aristocratic origins.)

More intriguing than these known connections to two of the great figures in the history of the English language is the rumoured royal connection of the Salusburys. It must be stressed that this is rumour, but many in north Wales believed that Roland de Velville, the constable of Beaumaris Castle from 1509 to 1535, was the illegitimate son of HenryVII. De Velville was Breton and Henry Tudor had spent time in exile in Brittany. De Velville's granddaughter, Katheryn of Berain, married into the Salusbury family, probably in 1557. (She was the mother of the Babington conspirator and his brother, the suppressor of the Essex revolt.)

Of the five sons of the Thomas Salusbury who was killed at the Battle of Barnet, two made a mark of sorts in history: Thomas, as the heir and through fighting at Blackheath, and Foulk,[20] as dean of Saint Asaph cathedral.

Thomas's other sons, Henry, Robert and John, achieved little of note, apart from acquiring impressive estates: Henry that of Bachymbyd, John's at Llanrhaeadr, whilst Robert made a fortuitous and very profitable marriage to Gwenhwyfar,[21] the daughter and heiress of Rhys ap Einion. It was through this marriage that Plas Isa, along with substantial land-holdings, passed into the family.

His father's imprisonment

Robert and Gwenhwyfar had two sons, Foulk and Raffe, and a daughter, Marged.[22] It is not known when Robert died, but it is reasonable to assume that he did not outlive Foulk who, in a document[23] produced in the 1570s, is recorded as having been buried on 3 January 1520:

> 'ffowk salbri mab ac aer Robert salbri hynaf o lann rrwst a gladdwy[d] [yn]*
> llannsanan dduw llun kynn gwyl vair y kynhwyllau pan oedd Krist 1519' [Foulk
> Salusbury son and heir of Robert Salusbury the older of Llanrwst who was buried
> in Llansannan the Monday before the feast day of Mary of the Candles when Christ
> was 1519 (which now that the year starts in January equates to 1520)]
>
> *An ink blot obscures what is assumed to be 'yn'.

The information is included in the family tree of another branch of the family. An earlier document,[24] written between 1536 and 1538, gives a little more detail. It is the case brought against Robert Salesbury (William's brother), heir of Foulk, for the recovery of the 'crown debt' for which the plaintiffs, Hugh Dryhurst and Robert Knowsley, two Denbighshire gentlemen, had stood surety. It reveals that the debt had led to Foulk spending two years in the Fleet prison.

None of his surviving relatives, Robert, William, Annes or Gwenhwyfar appear to have lived in straitened circumstances. The likely reason for this is that his death removed the debt that hung over the family. Indeed this is the defence that was entered on Robert's behalf, 'Alleged in the Answer that it was the custom of the country in the lordship of Denbigh for the widow to have the moiety of the goods and chattels of her husband.'

This 'answer' suggests that the two gentlemen had stood surety for Foulk, who was then released from prison only to die before reparations could be made. The conditions in the Fleet prison were truly appalling[25] and two years of incarceration are sure to have damaged Foulk's health and in all likelihood contributed to his early death.

The reference to 'the lordship of Denbigh' and the date of 1520 may explain why Dryhurst and Knowsley had taken so long to bring the case against Robert Salesbury. They might have explored legal or other avenues locally which seem not to have brought about a resolution of the problem, but then in 1536 the first Act of Union was passed, giving Welshmen full and unrestricted access to the English legal system, something that had previously been denied them. This might have been the plaintiffs' first opportunity to bring their case in London.

The outcome is not known, but continuing Salesbury prosperity and ownership of Plas Isa and other houses and land-holdings suggest that either Robert won or that a compromise was reached that did not greatly disadvantage him. The fact that William Salesbury went on to have an amicable, or at least non-hostile, relationship with Dryhurst[26] suggests the latter.

The case hinged on whether the traditional Denbigh custom 'for the widow to have the moiety of the goods and chattels of her husband' had been legal in 1520 and was still legal now in English law in the 1530s. Perhaps Robert won the case because the plaintiffs' legal team were incompetent, which is suggested by their elementary mistake of confusing the names of Robert's mother (Annes) and grandmother (Gwenhwyfar). (Annes appears, correctly named, in an arbitration document of November 1546.)[27]

Foulk Salesbury's death lifted a great burden from his family. Was that a deliberate sacrifice on his part? Had he been in a position to pay but had held back, enduring the physical and mental trauma of prison in order to keep his wife and sons from poverty? Had he intended to reimburse Dryhurst and Knowsley? The one thing that is certain is that young William was now able to study at university.[28]

Early education

University education required a high level of literacy and numeracy and, above all, fluency in Latin, which was the language of instruction. To negotiate his way through England to Oxford and to cope with life in town he would need a good command of English, which '… to me of late yeares [that is, in his childhood], was wholy to lerne'.[29] This leads to the questions, where did Salesbury receive his pre-university education and how could the family have afforded it?

Shrewsbury School had not yet been founded and there was not a single grammar school in Wales at that time. One possibility is that a nearby monastery might have provided tuition, but the monasteries of Wales, which had once been beacons of learning and culture, with prolific scriptoria and well-stocked libraries, had never recovered from the twin blows of the Black Death and the Glyndŵr revolt and were in terminal decline.

It is true that as recently as the early 1490s Guto'r Glyn, as he lay dying, composed a poem to Dafydd ab Ieuan, the abbot of Glyn Egwestl,[30] thanking him for the care he was receiving and praising his learning, but he was an exception to the age and by the 1530s only one Welsh abbey, Tintern,[31] had its full complement of twelve monks and the abbot of Valle Crucis was not caring for a dying bard but committing highway robbery. The level of education amongst the clergy at that time was so low that many priests could not understand the Latin lessons that they read out in church.

If there were no schools in Wales and the Marches and no religious institution capable of instruction, then private tuition appears to be a reasonable assumption. That requires money, of course, but there are examples of bright boys of modest means being educated alongside the sons of the wealthy. Bishop William Morgan, translator of the Bible of 1588, is one such example.[32] Perhaps another branch of the family stepped in to help the young Salesbury. Accepting charity can be demeaning, but the value of an education was becoming more and more widely recognised amongst the gentry, especially for younger sons who had no estate to inherit.

There is a further possibility suggested by another throwaway line in the herbal. Writing about garlic and where it can be found, Salesbury recalled its location in Lancashire: 'Ac yd y daw im cof a mi yn vachgen yn swydd Lancastr myfy a welais …' [And as I remember when I was a boy in Lancashire I saw …].[33]

Could he have been educated there, either at the private house of a kindly family or at a grammar school? The Queen Elizabeth Grammar School, Blackburn, co-incidentally just a few miles from the town of Salesbury, was founded in 1509. Was it in Lancashire that he perfected his Latin as well as his English?

It is nothing more than a possibility, of course, and the school roll from the early part of the sixteenth century has not survived to prove or disprove the theory,[34] but at a time of trauma the family might well have removed its youngest and most vulnerable member from the worries and troubles that plagued it. It could be argued that the removal of young William from the scene would have been beneficial for him and one less worry for the adults in an age when the relationship between parent and child tended to be less affectionate than it is today.

(It should be remembered that his aunt, Marged, had married into the Llwyd family who, like the Salusburys, had their origins in Lancashire. Their name, originally, had been Rossendale but they had abandoned it and adopted the Welsh system of naming. If the family still had connections in England, then they might have made the necessary arrangements and Rossendale is within easy travelling distance of Blackburn and its grammar school.)

A troubled homeland

Young Salesbury was likely to be safer in Lancashire than in Wales. That was not because England at that time was a haven of peaceful, law-abiding citizens, far from it, but that Wales was even more lawless and dangerous.[35] In many ways, though the comparison is a little exaggerated, the country was similar to a modern-day 'failed state'. There was territory under the control of the crown (the land that had been ruled by the royal house of Gwynedd before its destruction in 1282, plus later acquisitions) and a mishmash of Marcher lordships, which were little more than feudal dictatorships. The Welsh legal system, once the most advanced in Europe, had decayed to such a point that it gave more protection to criminals than to their victims; the same criminals could avoid the law by moving from one area of jurisdiction to another and the Marcher lords did not see their subjects as people whom they should protect, but as resources to exploit.

So alarming was the condition of Wales that in the early 1530s Thomas Cromwell, Henry VIII's effective, ruthless lieutenant, revived the dormant Council in the Marches of Wales, appointed the equally ruthless Rowland Lee as its president and gave him licence to be as merciless as he thought necessary to restore order. There was an improvement, but the great breakthrough in achieving law and order and good government was the Act of Union, 1536 and then again in 1543, which abolished the Marcher lordships, gave Wales's citizens the same legal rights and access to the law as those in England and established thirteen Welsh counties, each with the same constitution (a sheriff, justices of the peace and representation in Parliament) as their English counterparts.

There were huge cultural and economic differences between Wales and England, but Salesbury would have experienced few of them whilst he lived in Lancashire. England had the same north/south division then as now. Like Wales, the north was overwhelmingly rural and traditional with few towns, with their members of the professions, merchants and literate artisans to question and challenge the old ways of thinking. It would not be until he travelled to Oxford and London that the young Salesbury would discover just how different the world outside Llanrwst was and how it extended beyond the shores of England to Italy, the Netherlands, Germany and Geneva, where new ideas were bubbling up and making their way across the Channel.

In 1520 or 1521, still mourning his father's death as he made his way to university to take up his studies, Salesbury must have reflected on the irony that this opportunity had come about through his father's misfortune. He might also have contrasted his situation with that of his brother. Both had suffered the shame of their father's imprisonment and the difficulties it had caused. Usually it is the elder son, as heir, who is regarded as the favoured one and Robert had indeed inherited an estate, from which the shadow of debt had now been removed, but he was being left behind to run it, waking to the same views each day, the same unchanging routines and duties, the same people, awkward, boring and all too predictable. His younger brother, the unfortunate one, was going to study in Oxford[36] where he would live alongside the gentry and nobility, albeit in Spartan conditions, would exercise his mind daily and meet scholars from across Europe. Then he would be off to London, the seat of power, to study law in conditions that were not at all Spartan, returning as a sophisticated and educated gentleman who would travel around the courts of Wales and the Marches to follow his profession.

William was in no way responsible for the way things had turned out, but Robert would not have been human if he had not felt at times that life had not treated the brothers with equal fairness.

Chapter Two

Erasmus; a life-long influence

The challenge to Scholasticism

If, in the backwoods of north Wales or Lancashire, Salesbury's teacher or tutor had been young and not long out of university, it may be that he had heard mention of the man who dominated the intellectual world of the sixteenth century. On the other hand, if his teacher had been middle-aged or older he would have been taught by someone schooled in a curriculum unchanged since the establishment of universities in the twelfth century. If that was the case, it would not have been until his arrival at Oxford that Salesbury is likely to have made acquaintance with the teachings of Erasmus.

Today, the celebrity that he once enjoyed has shrunk to his name being used for a Europe-wide student programme and his image appearing on old banknotes. Art lovers will know of the Holbein portrait in the National Gallery[1] and some will have heard of his most famous book, *Praise of Folly*, though fewer will have read it. All that is in sharp contrast to the renown that this Colossus of academic life enjoyed at the time that Salesbury began his studies.

'Colossus' smacks of hyperbole, but it is difficult to convey his importance and influence without risking accusations of exaggeration. Put simply, he was the man who more than anyone ushered in the Humanist Revolution and put an end to the medieval system of education and its attendant world view. Moreover, that new way of thinking was not limited to the universities but filtered out to change the politics, religion, culture and understanding of every stratum of society.

All of those things were achieved by a man of humble background and quiet, modest demeanour. Erasmus never trumpeted his abilities or achievements, nor did he seek wealth or high office. He always sought reconciliation rather than conflict or schism. He did not court controversy, though in later life he was rarely able to avoid it. After 1526 his work was frequently criticised by conservative Catholic theologians, particularly those of Louvain, Paris and Spain and in 1529 radical Protestants caused him to flee Basel for Freiburg.

Erasmus was born in Rotterdam around 1467. His father, Gerard Helye, had been a scribe in Italy and his fluency in Latin and Greek was an inspiration to his son. When Erasmus was orphaned at sixteen, the brothers at his school in 's-Hertogenbosch pressed him to become a priest. He wished to go to university to continue his studies, but the monks prevailed and in 1492 he was ordained. It was around this time, though it was not published until 1518, that he wrote his first book, *Antibarbari*.

In 1495, he finally realised his ambition to attend university and moved to Paris where, to subsidise his studies, he gave private lessons. One of his pupils was William Blount, the fourth Lord Mountjoy, who in 1499 took him on an extended visit to England, where he befriended Thomas More, met the eight-year-old Prince Henry and, more importantly, John Colet, William Grocyn, William Latimer, Thomas Linacre, Cuthbert Tunstall, John Fisher, William Warham, Richard Fox, Richard Pace and John Clerk, all of whom were or would become men of influence in academic or ecclesiastical circles and would spread Humanist learning in England.

His return to Paris in 1500 coincided with the printing of his first published book, *Collectanea Adagiorum*, a best-seller. A stream of books followed that with the recent (post-Gutenberg) creation of a network of printers, bookshops, book-fairs and dealers disseminated his ideas with a speed and universality that had never before been possible.

He returned to England in 1505 and during this stay helped Colet to establish St Paul's School, which was founded on Humanist ideas and ideals.[2] From 1511 to 1514, at John Fisher's request (he was by then chancellor of the university), Erasmus gave lectures at Cambridge on theology and Greek. (As Latin was the language of instruction and the lingua franca of the educated, Erasmus's lack of English in no way impeded him.)

After that extended stay, Erasmus never revisited England, though he corresponded with his English Humanist colleagues, in particular with More.[3] In the early 1520s he settled in Basel and by 1536 the situation there was much improved and he was able to return, but within weeks of that return he had contracted dysentery, dying on 11 July.

Whilst there were other noted Humanists and other champions of the causes he espoused, it was Erasmus above all others who was responsible for the great changes that came about in European thinking and learning after 1500.[4]

His championing of Greek undermined then removed the dominance that Scholasticism, the medieval system of education, enjoyed throughout the universities of Europe. The change took place over several decades and was fiercely contested by many. At Oxford, the more conservative of England's two universities, those who opposed his ideas called themselves, rather pointedly, the Trojans. Open revolt broke out there in 1518 and it required the combined forces of More, Archbishop Warham (the chancellor of the university), Cardinal Wolsey and Henry VIII to face down the rebels.

The Scholastic curriculum consisted of seven subjects divided into two categories, the *trivium* (Grammar, Rhetoric and Logic) and the *quadrivium* (Arithmetic, Geometry, Astronomy and Music). In theory this should have provided a wide range of opportunities for study, speculation and investigation, but Scholasticism was innately conservative and restrictive. Innovation and challenges to accepted wisdom were not welcomed nor were additions to the curriculum. The philosophers and theologians studied were mainly the products of the Scholastic system: Thomas Aquinas, Duns Scotus and Peter Abelard, for example. Aristotle (who had been granted a special kind of licence whereby he was considered an honorary Christian) and some Neo-Platonist authors were studied, but through Latin translations of their work, never from the original Greek. Latin was the sole language of instruction, so that mathematicians such as Euclid were also studied in translation.

Lectures were listened to in silence and students were not allowed to ask questions, although during the *disputatio* which followed the *lectio* the students debated with one another in the presence of the lecturers, who commented on the validity or otherwise of the points made. However, the subject matter of these disputations was very limited and to the modern mind seems wildly esoteric, if not downright absurd. For example, questions such as:

'Could God have taken the form of a woman, or a devil, or a donkey, or a cucumber, or a lump of flint'

'Will it be possible to eat and drink after the resurrection'

and

'By what conduits was the contagion of sin channelled from one generation to another'[5]

dominated the lives of generations of students and academics.

The introduction of Greek led to the obvious question, why not read Aristotle in his original language? This led on to the dangerously rational thought that reading the work of other Greek writers such as Aeschylus, Sophocles, Herodotus and Thucydides would also be beneficial. These writers, philosophers and historians were of course pagan, but Erasmus's *Antibarbari* of 1518 had argued the case for the study of these non-Christian teachers and his arguments carried the day. The study of scientists and mathematicians such as Archimedes, Anaxagoras, Thales and Democritus helped broaden the curriculum further and led to the adoption of Greek words into the scientific lexicon of English.

What attracted so many minds, old and young but especially the young, to Erasmus was the rigour of his scholarship and investigation. Scholasticism never reached deep. It accepted what had gone before and added a little to the edifice of learning. It never questioned whether the whole system was a house built on sand that should be razed to the ground. Erasmus did. This investigative philosophy of his was called *ad fontes*, which can be translated as '[back] to the source[s]'. Nowhere was it applied more enthusiastically than to his study of the New Testament.

Erasmus and the Bible

The lessons from the Bible read out in Church were from the Latin translation completed in 405 by Saint Jerome. To all but the educated few, these words would have been meaningless. In effect, the Church owned and controlled the Bible and its teachings and it was determined to maintain its monopoly of that wisdom. There were lay people fluent in Latin, but they were overwhelmingly members of the establishment and until the cataclysm of the 1530s the interests of the church and the establishment (that is, the King) were broadly the same.

Jerome translated the Bible at a time when Latin was a language spoken by most of the inhabitants of the Roman (Western) empire. The irony that his Bible was called the Vulgate because he had intended it to be accessible to the ordinary people (the vulgar) was lost on the church hierarchy. Attempts to make the Bible available in vernacular translation, as the followers of John Wycliffe had done in the late fourteenth century, were ruthlessly repressed, but Erasmus was unequivocal in his support of this cause:

> I violently disagree with those who do not want to see the Scriptures translated into the language of the people and read by laymen … Would that these had been translated into all the languages of men so that they could be read and studied by Scots and Irishmen, by Turks and Saracens.[6]

There were weaknesses in Jerome's translation and a thousand years of slavish and uncritical copying from copies of copies of copies had meant that it had lost the validity it had once enjoyed. The most influential of all Erasmus's works was his *Novum Instrumentum* (1516), which consisted of his revised version of the Vulgate, with all the errors and accretions of centuries corrected or removed with, on the opposite page, the corresponding passages of the Greek New Testament. Such was the response of scholars that it went into 229 reprints in the sixteenth century alone.

Not even Erasmus's work was completely error free, but the meticulous nature and practice of his *ad fontes* doctrine of scholarship contrasted sharply with the second-hand knowledge and fallacious thinking of the medievalists and *Novum Instrumentum* was an inspiration and a great practical help to pioneers such as William Tyndale who wished to see the ordinary people read the Bible in their own language.

Proverbs and copiousness

His support for the translation of the Bible was not the only way in which Erasmus helped to democratise learning. Another of his best-selling books was *Collectanea Adagiorum*, which had been his first published work (in Paris in 1500). It consisted of 818 adages in Latin, some from the Greek. Erasmus expanded the work and in 1508 produced *Adagiorum chiliades*, which contained 3,260 sayings in Latin and Greek.

At first sight this does not appear democratic. The practice of starting a conversation with a well-judged Latin saying or sprinkling such sayings throughout a learned discourse survived well into the twentieth century. For most practitioners it was an innocent habit that they had grown up with or had acquired through their education. For others it was a means to mark themselves out as different from and, in their own minds no doubt superior to, ordinary people or 'the common herd'.

Paradoxically, the very words and phrases they were using were those of the 'common herd', the hoi polloi of Athens and the plebeians of Rome. This was the wisdom of the common man, but from a previous age. In the medieval age wisdom was the preserve of the church hierarchy, kings and a few approved Scholastic philosophers. Erasmus had elevated the words of the street to respectability and acceptance. It was as revolutionary a work as Beaumarchais's *Marriage of Figaro* two centuries later, in which a servant shows himself to be more intelligent than his master.

Where Erasmus led others followed. Across Europe vernacular collections of proverbs were made and published. The first collection to appear in English was John Heywood's in 1546.

The last of Erasmus's great bequests was language itself. Though a champion of Greek, the language in which he expressed himself as a lecturer and writer and in conversation with his university colleagues was Latin and it could be argued that Latin, rather than his native Dutch, was the language in which he felt most at home.

Expressing himself in a Latin that was stylish, elegant and mellifluous was essential for Erasmus. He purged Latin of its ponderous, medieval obfuscations and spellings and took the classical authors as his guide to re-introduce the biting wit, lightness of touch and the capacity to present sophisticated thinking in a language that was not daunting or overly complex. Those inspired by his words followed his example and scoured the classic authors, not just for the content of their work but to inform their style of writing. Books on rhetoric were published, at first in Latin but then in the major languages of Europe.

In 1512, Erasmus published *De copia verborum ac rerum* [Foundations of the abundant style].[7] The abundance referred to was in the armoury that should be at a writer's disposal. The greater the linguistic resources at your command, the more likely you are to choose the formulation that is the most nuanced and eloquent in expressing what it is you wish to say. Flaubert would have agreed with that. Knowing 150 ways of saying 'Thank you for your letter',[8] as one modern writer has presented Erasmus's advice, is not the same as using them all. It is not Erasmus's fault that some of his readers applied his dictum a little too literally. (In my reading of him, admittedly in translation, I found his prose entertaining and elegant.)

The influence wanes

Erasmus's influence was great throughout the sixteenth century. Though England became a Protestant country, Erasmus, as a 'proto-Protestant', was safe from censure. When, in 1559, Pope Paul IV placed all of Erasmus's publications on *Index Librorum Prohibitorum* [Index of Prohibited Books], that favourable English viewpoint was strengthened.

However, what was once seen as bold and iconoclastic no longer excites later generations. His innovations became such an unquestioned part of university education that the innovator himself was forgotten. What was once ground-breaking becomes the new orthodoxy. A style of writing once seen as liberating and original may seem stultifying and staid to those schooled in it from an early age by those with little flair for language.

The change in attitude to Erasmus is best demonstrated in Shakespeare's *Love's Labour's Lost* in which the main character is language itself. Shakespeare has great fun mocking the over rich, Euphuistic style that John Lyly and other playwrights had developed. It is the king and his friends who speak in this overblown manner in their clumsy attempts to impress the visiting ladies of the French court, but the character whose use of language is most lampooned is Holofernes who speaks in a grotesquely 'copious' manner:

> The deer was, as you know, *sanguis*, in blood; ripe as a pomewater, who now
> hangeth like a jewel in the ear of *caelo*, the sky, the welkin, the heaven; and anon
> falleth like a crab on the face of *terra*, the soil, the land, the earth ... Most barbarous
> intimation! yet a kind of insinuation, as it were, *in via*, in way, of explication; *facere*,

> as it were, replication, or, rather, *ostentare*, to show, as it were, his inclination, after his undressed, unpolished, uneducated, unpruned, untrained, or rather, unlettered, or, ratherest, unconfirmed fashion, to insert again my *haud credo* for a deer.

The irony is that Erasmus would have thoroughly enjoyed that mockery. It is very similar to what he had done in *Ciceronianus*, where he satirises his contemporaries' uncritical acceptance of and devotion to the writings of Cicero and its untoward effect on their writing style.

Erasmus had a wicked sense of humour, which he used as a method of self-defence. In *Praise of Folly* there are many targets for his criticism and mockery (alchemists, the aristocracy, schoolteachers, theologians, monks and friars, monarchs, bishops and cardinals), but he avoided the repercussions that such devastating attacks would undoubtedly have earned someone less wily by making the author of the criticisms the goddess Folly.

When Folly says, 'Tell me, what comedian, what itinerant salesman would you rather watch than the friars that show off their oratorical skills in preaching sermons? They make themselves totally ridiculous ...', the linguistic and philosophical nicety that Erasmus has adopted allows it to be interpreted as, 'It is folly to say that a preaching friar is ridiculous.'

Shakespeare might not have been aware of the debt he owed Erasmus. Many academics have commented on the range of vocabulary used in his works. As a hybrid language there was already a choice of French or Germanic vocabulary, 'aid' or 'abet', 'royal' or 'kingly', but in the sixteenth century the lexicon had been expanded by followers of Erasmus, who had set about coining new words from Latin and Greek to enrich it further, to give it copiousness. Some of these words fell by the wayside and withered. 'Nidulate' (to build a nest), 'fatigate' (to make tired), 'deruncinate' (to cut off) and 'illecebrous' (enticing) seem pompous and unnecessary to the modern reader, but hundreds, if not thousands, of other words (such as 'invention', 'anatomy', 'insane', 'dislocate', 'expensive', 'orbit', 'ultimate') slipped seamlessly into the fabric of English.

Each term for a similar concept has its own weight and nuance and the verbal armoury available to Shakespeare was greater than that enjoyed by any previous writer of English. This helped him choose the right word, not just for precise meaning or for its sound or the creation of mood, but also to fit the rhythm of iambic pentameter. And when there was not a word available that suited his purposes, Shakespeare could follow the example of Thomas Elyot, George Pettie and other disciples of Erasmus and create his own, as with 'invulnerable', 'incarnadine', 'countless', 'green-eyed', 'moonbeam', 'barefaced', 'blood-stained', 'madcap' and many others. In fact, Shakespeare did it over 1,500 times and the results are still on our lips.

Though Shakespeare might have derided Erasmus's influence and at other times not been aware of it,[9] there is one incontestable moment when that influence brought about the greatest sequence of poems in the English language. In the early 1590s, he wrote seventeen sonnets to a young man, urging him to fulfil his duty and provide the world with an heir. Those seventeen were followed by another 136 and the collection delights, astounds and intrigues to this day.

What inspired Shakespeare's initial poems? The starting point appears to be a letter in Erasmus's *De Conscribendis Epistolis* 'in which a young nobleman is urged to marry. Shakespeare apparently knew the epistle from Thomas Wilson's translation included in his *Art of Rhetoric* (1553): "If that man be punished who little heedeth the maintenance of his tillage ... what punishment is he worthy to suffer that refuseth to plough that land which, being tilled, yieldeth children."'[10]

If Erasmus was directly influencing creative minds at the end of the sixteenth century, fifty years after his death, how great would his influence have been at the beginning of that century on a young man with a talent for language? The answer is, enormous, and Salesbury readily acknowledged it in his praise for him, calling him, 'yr athro dyscecickaf huotlaf, ac awdurusaf yn cred oll'[11] [the most learned, eloquent and authoritative teacher in everybody's belief].

In many ways Erasmus was the father figure missing from Salesbury's life, influencing and guiding him and giving him the moral under-pinning essential for real, substantial success rather than the mere holding of office or temporary, superficial acclaim.

Erasmus's imprint is there for all to read and would be easily discerned from a study of Salesbury's writing even if he had not written the words above. Many would argue that it is chance rather than fate that determines life's course. For Salesbury that was certainly the case. It was Erasmus and Oxford that shaped him and as he travelled to university for the first time he must have been aware that, had his father not died, the opportunity to study might never have come his way.

Chapter Three

Oxford

Broadgates Hall

In 1691, Anthony Wood[1] wrote of Salesbury:

> ... a most exact critic in British antiquities, was born of an ancient and genteel
> family in Denbighshire, spent several years in academical learning either in St
> Alban's or Broadgate's Hall or both. Thence he went to an Inn of Chancery in
> Holbourn near London, called Thavies Inn, where he studied and made sufficient
> progress in the common law; and thence, as 'tis probable, to Lincolns Inn.

This is the earliest record, in English, of his attending Oxford University
and, though it was written a century after Salesbury's death, Wood's position as
the first chronicler of the university and its students gives it some authority.

However, a poem of praise to Salesbury written by his friend and
colleague, Gruffudd Hiraethog (d. 1564), gives definitive proof:

> Fo ŵyr dy gorff, wrda, i gyd,
> Foddion y Saith Gelfyddyd;
> Ystryw holl soffestri hen
> Yw'r dichell o Rydychen.

> [Your body knows, good sir, all
> Of the seven arts' physic;
> Ancient sophistry's cunning
> Is the Oxford stratagem.][2]

Before 1485, a Welshman at Oxford would have been a rare phenomenon.
The lack of clear and fair government in the country, combined with specific
laws (not always enforced) restricting the movements of the Welsh and a

simmering resentment and suspicion between the two peoples meant that travel or migration to England was uncommon.

Henry Tudor's victory at Bosworth changed all that. The grandson of Owain ap Maredudd ap Tudur (Owen Tudor) from Anglesey (whose illegal marriage to Henry V's widow had produced several children), Henry's claim to the throne was weak, but he had taken it by force and that force to a great extent consisted of Welshmen who had been paid in promises of preferment. Though the government of Wales remained in chaos, punitive laws were no longer enforced and whole sections of the Welsh gentry started to settle in England to make good on the promises they had been given.

A huge psychological and cultural barrier had been broken, at least among the gentry, some of whom, most notably the Seisyllt (Cecil) family, rose from relatively humble Welsh beginnings to achieve great wealth and considerable power. As a Welshman at Oxford, Salesbury would not have been regarded as an object of curiosity as he certainly would have been half a century earlier.

The choice of Broadgates Hall makes it almost certain that Salesbury left Wales already determined on a career in law. 'The said Hall was always for the most part a nursery for Students in the Civil and Canon Law, as from our Registers and other places is apparent.'[3] (Although Wood mentions the possibility of St Albans Hall, which was owned by the convent of Littlemore and was purchased by Merton College after the convent's dissolution, it is generally assumed that Salesbury went to Broadgates.)

At the time of his arrival, the principal of the hall was John Noble, a noted lawyer, and throughout its history its principals were usually eminent members of the legal profession, most notably, in the early seventeenth century, John Budden, who was Regius Professor of Civil Law at the university.

By the sixteenth century the college system was well advanced in its evolution and the number of halls had declined from about seventy in 1450 to eighteen in 1513.[4] Only three of those halls survived to become colleges: Brasenose, St Edmund Hall and Broadgates, which in 1624 was re-named Pembroke College. 'Legally a college was a corporation enjoying its privileges by charter from the crown, a hall was a kind of tutorial lodging house, licensed or at least ultimately regulated by the university.'[5]

When Salesbury embarked on his journey to Oxford, he is most likely to have done so in the company of others. Travel, difficult and uncomfortable, especially in winter, was also dangerous and there was safety in numbers. Travellers with little in common would have journeyed together to the benefit of all. One cannot help thinking of a party of wayfarers who looked very much like Chaucer's Canterbury pilgrims and though Salesbury's purpose in travelling was secular, England was very much a Catholic country as it had been for nearly a thousand years.

Henry VIII was married to his Spanish queen and the Pope would soon award him the title of 'Defender of the Faith' for his book attacking Luther. Henry had delegated the everyday running of his kingdom to a cardinal. The schism between Rome and Avignon was over. Troublemakers such as Wycliffe or Jan Hus had either died or been executed. The church had never been so united. Apart from the foul-mouthed heresies of a German monk, there was little to concern anyone.

In fact, so unchanged and unchallenged was England in its acceptance of Catholicism that Salesbury and his travelling companions are likely to have made some of their overnight stops at hospitals attached to monastic houses. This would not have posed a moral dilemma for Salesbury; at that time he, too, was unquestioningly Catholic, 'And as I was thus tangeled and abhominablye deceived, and trained, and brought up in tender age, in the Popes holilyke Religion before Christes second byrthe here in Englande…',[6] as he later recalled.

Social change

However, there were changes in the life of England that Salesbury would have noticed, as well as very obvious differences between England and Wales.

Differences in the pattern of land settlement would have been immediately apparent. Wales was more sparsely populated, with many isolated settlements and fewer and generally smaller towns. Though it would not be until the nineteenth century that England became an urban country, towns and large villages in England tended to be the focus of social and cultural life. In Wales the tendency was for such life to be centred on ties of kinship: towns had been a Norman innovation. This, coupled with the existence in the more heavily populated English towns of a significant number of professional people (lawyers, teachers, merchants, physicians and apothecaries) and literate artisans may explain why Protestantism spread so much more rapidly in England than in Wales, where it struggled to gain ground.

The farmland of England (then as now) was generally sweeter and richer than that of Wales, though, ironically, it was England that was famous for its vast numbers of sheep.

It was the profitability of sheep that was leading to a major change to the English landscape, enclosure. Though it was nowhere on the scale of the enclosures of the nineteenth century, the social injustice it caused and represented aroused great criticism from prominent figures as diverse as Hugh Latimer and Thomas More: enclosure could only come about through the eviction of tenants and their families and so the numbers of the rural poor were swollen.[7]

Rural and urban poverty would have been apparent to any traveller in England. The country's population had recovered from the catastrophe of the Black Death, but the feudal system of agriculture which had been able to provide employment for so large a population had itself been killed off. As a result 'sturdy beggars'[8] loitered in market squares and on the highways and street corners of every part of England, provoking censure and anxiety amongst those whose financial positions were more comfortable.

At the same time, and for the first time since the Peasants' Revolt, a growing number of people were questioning the great disparity in wealth within the kingdom. These commentators, concerned with the concept of the 'Commonweal', included Thomas Smith, Henry Brinkelow, Hugh Latimer, Thomas Beccon, Thomas Lever and John Hales. Though a few of them would be involved, briefly and ineffectively, in government during the reign of Edward VI,[9] it would not be until the civil war that their ideas would be widely debated.

Another prominent feature of England at that time was the disrepair of its town walls. Modern warfare had rendered these medieval defences redundant and so they had been left unmaintained. Their demise was hastened by those who looted them for good-quality building stone. Similarly, large houses that incorporated defensive features were either being abandoned or modified to current tastes.

Finally, Salesbury would have noticed that most moderately-sized English towns through which he passed had a grammar school. These were providing boys from ordinary backgrounds with an education that could lead to university and to opportunities previously undreamt of, so that a butcher's son from Ipswich, Thomas Wolsey, could rise to be the most powerful man in the country after the king. (At the time of Salesbury's birth, Wales had no grammar school. By the time of his death there would be half a dozen or so.)[10]

The perception of the Middle Ages is that there was little or no change from one generation to another. However, Salesbury was a member of a generation that was moving into a new era, but it would be foolhardy to attribute to him an overall awareness and understanding of all that was happening.

What can be said is that by the time he had ended his journey to university he would have become familiar with at least some of the following English towns: Chester, Shrewsbury, Ludlow and Worcester[11] and that as a result Oxford, a middling-sized market town, would not have particularly impressed the now slightly less naïve country boy.

It is impossible to know whether the young Salesbury had a wild, reckless side or an adolescent curiosity that might have led him to the more disreputable parts of town, but what would have undoubtedly attracted him, whenever the (considerable) demands of his studies allowed, were the bookshops, of which Dorne's was the most famous.

Salesbury was a bibliophile throughout his life and this was his first opportunity to indulge his passion for the book. Some of the English border towns had bookshops and others had annual book fairs, but Wales had none. Oxford had bookshops aplenty and its first printing press had been established by Theoderic Rood as long ago as the 1480s.

It is likely that Salesbury had far more freedom to visit bookshops and the town generally than many of his fellow students. The fact that he was not ordained, did not take a degree (intentionally so) and went on to study law in London all point to his being a gentleman commoner.

Gentlemen commoners paid for their accommodation and tuition and were an important source of revenue for the university, which gave them privileges not accorded to other students, particularly the boys who had to earn their position at university by carrying out menial tasks such as waiting at table and cleaning. As a gentleman scholar he was less tied to his hall and he was not subject to corporal punishment, as other students were.

Sparta

Not that his life in Oxford could in any way be described as comfortable. In winter the halls and colleges were freezing:

> The moste part of this winter my hands were so swellynge with colde that I
> coulde nother holde my penn for to wryth nother my knyff for to cut my mete
> at the table, and my fete also their wo so arayde with kybblayns [chilblains] that it
> grevyde me to go enywhere.[12]

That was written in the late fifteenth century, but conditions were unchanged in 1550, when Cambridge students were, 'fayne to walk or runne up and downe halfe an hour to gette a heate on their feete when they go to bed.'[13]

There were two meals a day, dinner at about 11 a.m. (beef or mutton, bread and butter, cheese and beer) and supper at 5 or 6 p.m., which was a smaller version of dinner, but possibly supplemented by pottage. It was not the plain and repetitive nature of the food that pained the students but its lack of quantity.[14] It never delivered 'fulness of Bellie', though Salesbury would have been able to satisfy his appetite with purchases from the town, not an option open to other scholars, especially the plebeians.

Students slept four to a room, rose at four in the morning to attend mass and morning prayers in an unheated chapel, then worked for two or three hours prior to lectures. After dinner there would be more study, which might involve 'repetitions', that is students being made to expound on the morning's lectures, then after supper, disputations or other lessons, before retiring to bed at nine or ten o'clock. 'Of more than 1,300 scholars admitted to New College between 1386 and 1540 one in ten died in their first four years before taking a degree.'[15]

If it was not the Spartan conditions despatching the students to an early grave, it was outbreaks of the plague (during which the university would close), influenza, the sweating sickness, malaria and typhus. In addition to those dangers was that of falling into a Thames that was grossly polluted by the offal from the towns' slaughterhouses. The river often flooded in winter.

However, there were lighter moments to leaven the academic year. Feasts (to celebrate saints' days) were common and there were revels at Christmas, at which there would be entertainments. As well as introducing Greek into the universities, the Humanists were also responsible for plays becoming common in colleges and halls for schooling in the art of rhetoric. Exercise was encouraged and there are records from 1508 of 'tenys playes' and 'bowlinge allies'.[16]

Tradition and reform

The curriculum that Salesbury followed would have been little changed from that followed for centuries, consisting of the *trivium* and *quadrivium*, the 'seven arts' to which Gruffudd Hiraethog had referred. The one innovation was the introduction of Greek. Had he gone to Cambridge, Salesbury might have had access to a broader curriculum and have enjoyed a more adventurous, less timorous and reactionary attitude to new ideas than that prevalent in Oxford.

At the end of the fourteenth century Oxford had been a hotbed of Lollardism and other challenges to conventional thinking. As a result Archbishop Thomas Arundel, a murderously repressive traditionalist, imposed a stultifying conformity upon the university from which it had yet to recover. At the beginning of the sixteenth century, Oxford tended towards acceptance of the status quo, whilst Cambridge was more vibrant and less cautious in its approach to learning. This is reflected in the number of major figures in the English Reformation who were Cambridge rather than Oxford educated. The 'Oxford Martyrs', Cranmer, Latimer and Ridley, were all Cambridge men (Jesus, Clare and Pembroke Colleges).

A Humanist innovation that was most definitely not yet on the Oxford curriculum was Hebrew. 'For a sixteenth century Oxford college to have a Hebrew lecturer or a fellow who was a competent Hebraist was the exception rather than the rule.'[17] Yet Salesbury was to become a noted Hebraist, 'for he was a rare scholar, & especially an Hebrician, whereof there was not many in those days.'[18]

However, the process of acquiring the third of the classical languages could well have started at Oxford. Printing was giving access to knowledge in a way that half a century earlier would have been unimaginable. It was not just the quantity of material available, but its cost. In 1494 a manuscript cost between 6s and 8d and 27 shillings.[19] In the 1520s many text books could be bought for less than a shilling. Within a term Salesbury could have bought a private library that Chaucer's clerk of Oxenford would not have acquired in a lifetime.

Through good fortune, Dorne's accounts for the year 1520 have survived.[20] They show what the students and townsfolk of Oxford were buying: 44 copies of Terence, 30 of Virgil and smaller numbers of Ovid, Lucan, Horace, Martial and Plautus. Erasmus's works and Gaza's Greek Grammar were also good sellers. One of the books sold that year was the *Alphabetum*, one of the two books necessary for learning Hebrew, the other being the *Primarium*. In this new age of readily available material (in monastery libraries the manuscripts, many huge and unwieldy, were chained to the shelves) there was nothing to stop Salesbury making a similar purchase and establishing his own, private curriculum, tailored to his own interests.

Amongst the books on Dorne's lists was one that would have turned a traditional Catholic apoplectic, and just a few years later would have got Dorne into very serious trouble, *Opera Luteri* [The Works of Luther].[21] Printing allowed all ideas, including the 'dangerous' ones, to circulate rapidly. It had been easy to seize and destroy copies of the Lollard Bible, when each one required months of work by a scribe using traditional, expensive materials. It was much, much more difficult to suppress a book or broadsheet that was cheaply and quickly produced in an edition of hundreds. No wonder Roland Phillips (*c*.1465–1538), the vicar of Croydon, said, 'We must root out printing, or printing will root out us.'[22]

Despite these hints of things to come, Oxford was firmly Catholic and fundamentally unchanged. Amongst the halls and colleges were Canterbury, Gloucester, Durham and St Bernard's and Salesbury would have shared his daily experience of Oxford with Benedictines, Franciscans, Cistercians,

Dominicans, Carmelites, Austin Canons and Austin Friars. Thomas More had been a student at Canterbury College, taking the same career path as Salesbury, in his case it had been four years, with no degree taken, followed by law at Lincoln's Inn.

Monastic Oxford was swept away in the 1530s and most of the town and university that Salesbury knew has gone, but St Frideswide's church (close to where Broadgates Hall stood), Christ Church meadow, Merton College and substantial parts of Magdalen, Lincoln and New College are much as they were in his day.

During his studentship he would have witnessed the building of Cardinal College, the first sign of the re-invigoration of the university for some time. Following the political downfall and demise of its benefactor, Wolsey, the development was abandoned, but then salvaged, with the college opening in 1532 as King Henry VIII's College before being re-established as Christ Church College in 1546.

Nothing is known of the friendships that Salesbury made during his days there or of the influences on him, apart from Erasmus, nor of the impression that he made on his lecturers and peers. He survived the early rising, the repetitive and inadequate diet, the cold of the dormitory and the ever present threat of contagion and after two or three years of such hardships moved to London to study law.

The development of his religious thinking is also unknown. Was he still a Catholic? Had his admiration for Erasmus led him to favour reform within the church or was he already a fully-fledged Protestant ready to follow in Luther's footsteps?

Chapter Four

London; Thavies Inn, Germans and Hebrew

Magni clarique, important and distinguished

The choice of Broadgates Hall as Salesbury's place of study strongly suggests that a career in law had been decided upon before his departure to Oxford.

William's great-uncle, Foulk Salusbury, had entered the church and had become dean of St Asaph. (In 1535, his attempt to become bishop by offering Cromwell a bribe of 100 marks a year was unsuccessful.[1]) A more distant kinsman in the church was the Robert Salusbury who combined the abbotship of Valle Crucis with the extra-curricular activity of highway robbery.[2]

The church was a distinct possibility. A military career much less so, as there was no standing army. In the fourteenth and fifteenth centuries English mercenaries could make a fortune abroad; Sir John Hawkwood, who died 1394, being the most famous example. There were some examples of adventurers crossing the channel for military employment, including William Herbert and a young Thomas Cromwell, but the rewards were no longer immense and in Herbert's case the motive was flight from the law: he had killed a man in a brawl in Bristol.

An academic career was a possibility, but not a well-paid or luxurious one; when the King needed to appoint an administrator, he tended to look to the Church rather than Oxbridge. In the last one hundred years, only one layman had held the post of Lord Chancellor.

Medicine was not an option. Doctors had some respectability, but the fact that from 1540 to 1745 surgeons belonged to the Company of Barber-Surgeons is an indication of their modest status.

Why, then, choose the law over the church? Not only did it guarantee Salesbury a lifetime of well-remunerated work, it also gave the family a degree of much needed security. A Tudor family whose members did not include a lawyer was vulnerable to external threats. 'In that litigious era, a squire had need to know the law to preserve his property.'[3]

The gentry and nobility were accumulating larger and larger estates with such naked aggression and fervour that their acquisitiveness and cynicism was a match for the worst excesses of unregulated capitalism. This was not an age when a man could say, 'My word is my bond' and be taken seriously. No method of land grab was considered inappropriate: force, guile, outright deception, enclosure, intrigue, wardship, advantageous marriages, altered wills, the patronage of a noble family. There was no place for morality or ethics: every form of chicanery was seen as legitimate.

It was not just defenceless peasants who could lose their land. Anyone, irrespective of wealth or social rank, could be a victim. Being on the right side of a legal argument did not guarantee protection, but without recourse to an able lawyer an innocent party had little hope of justice.

The situation in north Wales was no better than in the rest of the kingdom. In fact, it appears to have been worse, with several predatory families (the Wynns, the Bulkeleys, Pennants, Breretons and Prices being the most notable, with the Salusburys of Llewenni not far behind) constantly stalking their territory for prey. In fact, Great-uncle Foulk appears to have been complicit in Sir John Salusbury's forging of church leases.[4] It seems that the more criminal or outrageous the tactic, the greater its chance of success.

It was not just the Salusburys of Llewenni who used well-placed relatives in the church to further their ends. In 1536, Richard Bulkeley offered Thomas Cromwell a bribe of £100 to make David Owen the abbot of Aberconwy. Owen would then have been in a position to lease out the monastic land to Bulkeley's relatives, which with the forthcoming Dissolution would almost certainly make the acquisition permanent. Bulkeley was outbid or outmanoeuvred by the Price family, whose leading representative, Dr Elis

Price, again displeased Bulkeley by locking up the prior of Penmon, a Bulkeley place-man, in an attempt to have him removed.[5]

Little wonder, then, that in the early or mid-1520s, Salesbury found himself travelling from Oxford to London to start his legal studies at Thavies Inn. Named after its original owner, John Thavie, it had been founded in 1348 and was situated in Shoe Lane, backing onto the cemetery of St Andrew's, Holborn. Until the nineteenth century there was a window in the church that commemorated Thavie.[6] Although the church survived the Fire of London and the Blitz, the window did not survive the enthusiasm of Victorian renovators.

Thavies Inn was an Inn of Chancery. These had long co-existed with the Inns of Court, but were soon to be superseded by them. (Lincoln's Inn acquired the lease of Thavies Inn in 1549.) Fellow alumni of Thavies Inn included John Donne and John Fletcher, who succeeded Shakespeare as The Globe's chief playwright.

Lincoln's Inn has no surviving records of Thavies Inn, so the only contemporary evidence for Salesbury being a student there is his own. In the introduction to a publication[7] of 1550 he gave 'Thavies Inne in Houlborne' as his address. It was the custom of 'old boys' to lodge at the inn whenever they were in London and that is what Salesbury was doing.

If he had been staying in Oxford and a similar arrangement had been in place for Broadgates Hall, he would not have availed himself of it, unless his circumstances were particularly straitened. That a prosperous, middle-aged gentleman considered his old student lodgings as a comfortable place to stay is testimony to the privileged world he had entered. Oxford hardship had gone.

Erasmus, observing the position and authority of English lawyers, declared that they were '*magni clarique*' (important and distinguished).[8] England's Inns of Court and Chancery could be regarded as its third university, 'an university or schoole of all commendable qualities requisite for Noblemen.'[9]

Lectures were given by senior barristers (readers), followed by discussions. Students would listen to 'pleadings' in the courts in Westminster Hall and afterwards debate the issues and points of law raised. After dinner two junior barristers were required to argue the opposite sides of a theoretical case.

There would be detailed study of writs, liability, covenants, rights and other key facets of the law. English was the language of the court, Latin the language of statutes, and writs and formal pleadings were executed in what was called 'Law French'. In addition, history, dancing and music were taught so that students were suitably fitted to their future roles in the upper strata of society. Qualifying took between six to eight years.

Salesbury was entering a profession whose expectation was one of entitlement. In fact, he was entering two new worlds, that of Thavies Inn and, all around it, the great cosmopolitan city of London, with a population of approximately 40,000. It would have made an immediate impression on him. Dominating the skyline was the spire of the old, Gothic St Paul's, which would not be surpassed in height until the construction of the Post Office Tower in the 1960s.

A walk of just over half a mile along Holborn Hill, right into Shoe Lane, then left along Fleet Street was all it took to transport Salesbury from his place of study to St Paul's. Around the cathedral, in Pater Noster and Fleet Street, were the printing presses and the many bookshops and book stalls to which Salesbury would have been irresistibly drawn.

He now found himself living within shouting distance of the Fleet prison in which his father had been locked away for two years, not a secret that he is likely to have shared with any of his new companions, though it is possible that his curiosity might have led him to visit the viewing gallery[10] in Farringdon Street from where members of the public could observe the inmates.

The River Fleet stank. So did the Thames. They were, in effect, open sewers, but unlike the prison inmates, Salesbury was able to make an easy escape to the sweet smelling countryside. Thavies Inn was at the edge of a London which, despite the growth in its population, had barely spread beyond its city walls. Within five to ten minutes he could be in open countryside, where farmers' wives spread their washing on bushes and hedges to dry, a detail that can be seen on the sixteenth-century Agas map.

To the north of the Inn, between Leather Lane and Farringdon Road, were the estate gardens of Ely Place, the London residence of the bishops of Ely. The gardens were renowned for their produce, fruit and saffron in particular.

Shakespeare refers to the gardens in *Richard III*, when Gloster (Richard) says:

> My lord of Ely, when I was last in Holborn
> I saw good strawberries in your garden there:
> I do beseech you send for some of them.[11]

Elizabeth I would give these gardens to one of her favourites, Christopher Hatton, whose name they now bear.

The Steelyard and Tyndale

If the nearby countryside and gardens gave relief from the smells and noise of the city, one can be sure that Salesbury would soon be drawn back to its many attractions. He had had a childhood of fresh air and open countryside, a city was new to him and London was truly cosmopolitan. In it he could meet and speak to people from all over Europe and beyond. Few of his fellow citizens of Llanrwst could have coped with such a culture shock, but for someone fascinated by language and new ideas it must have been a demi-paradise.

To his fluency in Welsh, English, Greek and Latin, Salesbury added French (not just the 'Law French' of his training), German and Hebrew.[12] Whilst it is possible to learn a language purely from written sources, the opportunity to converse with first-language speakers undoubtedly aids and speeds the process of acquisition and London had a large community of Hanseatic League traders based at the Steelyard, which was situated on the north bank of the Thames, where Cannon Street station now stands.

Salesbury also mastered Hebrew. As a 'dead' language (used for religious purposes only), it was not so important to practise it conversationally, but any guidance would have been gratefully received and the one place in England where he might have met a Hebrew speaker was London.

Edward I's law banning Jews from England was still in force and would not be repealed until the Commonwealth, but converts to Christianity were not covered by the ban and during the sixteenth century they played a leading role in the teaching of the subject. (During the 1540s Princess Elizabeth was taught Italian by Tremellius, a convert from Italy whose Protestantism caused him to flee when Mary acceded to the throne.)

There was, however, a reason other than language for Salesbury to visit the capital's foreign communities, the Germans in particular, and that was religion. Many of the traders were sympathetic to the new ideas originating in their home country. (The word 'Protestant' would not come into use until the end of the decade.) Some parts of Germany had already gone over to the Reformist cause and an English exile, William Tyndale, had found relative safety in Worms.

The Steelyard was a good place to discuss religion, particularly as it was easy for the merchants to smuggle in heretical texts amongst their legitimate imports. The authorities were well aware of this. They had also heard rumours that the exiled Tyndale, whom they were trying desperately to track down, was about to print his translation of the New Testament, ready for sale in England.

In January 1526, an alarmed and incensed Thomas More organised and led a raid on the Steelyard. Four of the traders were arrested. On Shrove Sunday they and the English heretic, William Barnes, were led in procession (sitting backwards on donkeys) to St Paul's Cross, where they recanted their heresies. (Recanting saved a heretic from the flames, just so long as he did not repeat his crime.) To remind them of the consequences should they fall to temptation a second time, a bonfire was made of the books and tracts that had been seized.

Shortly afterwards, the worst fears of the Catholic leadership were realised: copies of Tyndale's New Testament were being sold on street corners and alleyways in towns and villages throughout the south and east of England, but especially in London.

The furious and panicked authorities did all they could to stop the trade, but the coasts were difficult to police and there had been a long tradition of avoiding the duty payable on a wide range of goods, particularly wine and expensive fabrics, so that 'smugglers', mostly respected traders, had plenty of experience and local knowledge to outwit the authorities.

Some of the smugglers were religiously motivated. Many were motivated by profit. The books were small (octavo sized) and so were easy for owners to conceal. At an average price of three shillings, the book was not cheap, but it was not beyond the pocket of most ordinary people. So popular were they and such was the demand that pirated versions from Antwerp started to flood the market.

The limited number of printers in England and their location (overwhelmingly in one part of London) meant that it was easy to prevent a 'native' English New Testament being published. Those unfortunate enough to be caught in possession were easily dealt with, but stemming the flow of imports was proving impossible. At one stage the authorities resorted to buying as many copies as possible to stop innocent minds from being polluted.

Thomas More led the campaign to prevent Tyndale's Testament reaching its intended audience and had the full support of the leading church figures of the day: William Warham, archbishop of Canterbury, Cardinal Wolsey (the archbishop of York), Cuthbert Tunstall, bishop of London, and John Fisher, bishop of Rochester. As the leading layman of the day – he would be appointed Chancellor of the Duchy of Lancaster in 1528 and Lord Chancellor in 1529 – More could call upon the resources of the state, the church and his own private fortune to combat what he considered to be the greatest of heresies, but why a leading Humanist who was a close friend of Erasmus, a supporter of translating the Bible into vernacular languages, took such a reactionary and vicious standpoint on the subject is unfathomable to the contemporary mind.

Despite his efforts, the translation, accompanied by other works by Tyndale, continued to be trafficked, albeit with extreme caution, in London and throughout the south and east of the country.

In February 1528, Tunstall initiated a six-month-long campaign to arrest Lollards, Lutherans and all those who owned or had had read to them Tyndale's New Testament, but Tunstall, though a strict Catholic, was humane. The man to fear was More. He built up a network of spies, informers and agents provocateurs. He often led raids or was personally present at arrests, that of Humphrey Monmouth, Tyndale's friend and mentor, being one example. Nor did his personal involvement end there. He had a whipping post installed in his Chelsea garden, as well as stocks and fetters which he used enthusiastically in his interrogation of those arrested. Though a lawyer and the holder of the highest legal post in the kingdom, he regularly detained suspects illegally.

No one was safe, not even law students. In 1528, a student in Gray's Inn who distributed copies of the New Testament from his room was amongst those arrested.[13] Worse still, under More's direction in February 1530, the first of England's 'Protestant' martyrs, Thomas Hitton, was burnt at the stake.

It could be that Salesbury's path to Protestantism was long and gradual. It was not for another twenty years that he would write or do anything that betrayed his sympathies and not until 1550 that he would declare his faith outright.

He might already have become a fully committed Protestant, meeting regularly with fellow believers, German and English, but then taken fright at the punishments meted out to those who were caught by the authorities and decided to keep his thoughts to himself and concentrate on his legal studies and his passion for language.

Or perhaps he did not take fright, but enjoyed the thrill of taking risks and participating in clandestine activities. If he did, then he did so successfully.

Whichever of those three possibilities is nearest to the truth, there can be no doubt that Tyndale's actions made a deep impression on Salesbury and that he would have been fully aware of the religious conflicts that were being waged and of the key players on either side. He would also have been aware, as was everyone from 1528, that the King wished to divorce his wife of twenty years and marry an English commoner.

Anne Boleyn's religious sympathies would give hope to Protestants and Henry's infatuation with her would bring about the separation from Rome, but Wolsey's downfall and his replacement as Lord Chancellor by More, had made matters worse for reformers.

Around 1530 Salesbury qualified as a lawyer. A little over a decade earlier he had been a debtor's son with a faltering command of English and no experience beyond the backwoods of Wales and Lancashire. Now he was a professional man fluent in the major languages of Europe and the classical world, steeped in the new ideas of Humanism and the Renaissance and schooled, courtesy of Thavies Inn, in all the social niceties that allowed him to move easily not just in the company of scholars, but of the nobility, too.

The terms of his training meant that he was not allowed to practise law in Westminster for three years. Although he had qualified in English law, this would not be the law of the courts in his native Denbighshire until the first Act of Union in 1536. Despite that anomaly, it is assumed that within a relatively short time of qualifying, Salesbury returned to north Wales to establish a practice there and in the surrounding areas, including the Marches. There is no evidence to the contrary.

In Wales he would be able to find many gentlemen with whom he could discuss genealogy and Welsh poetry, the two interests he shared with his native peers. In England, there would be many who would share his love of Horace and Ovid, could flirt with young ladies in French, dance a *galliard* or a *volte* or discuss in guarded tones the subject of transubstantiation, but in Wales, there would be few. It is likely that his education had ensured a degree of isolation in Salesbury's life.

Chapter Five

Lesclarcissement de la langue francoyse

John Palsgrave

The third great influence in Salesbury's life was neither a great writer whose works were read and admired throughout Europe nor someone driven to devote his life to giving his countrymen the Bible in their own language, but a teacher and translator who did not find a financially secure position until well into his middle age.

John Palsgrave, born in London sometime in the 1480s, is first recorded in 1503 as a student at Cambridge. After graduating in 1504, he took his M.A. in Paris, where he acquired his fluency in French.

In January 1513, he was appointed schoolmaster to Princess Mary, Henry VIII's younger sister. In the August of the following year Mary, just eighteen years old, was betrothed to King Louis XII of France, who was fifty-two and already in ill health. Palsgrave accompanied the princess to France as her secretary. The wedding took place on 9 October 1514. Louis promptly dismissed all of his new wife's English servants.

Fortunately for Mary, she was widowed by New Year's Day 1515, leaving her free to marry the man she loved, Charles Brandon, duke of Suffolk.

The unemployed Palsgrave had not been so fortunate, but he must have made a good impression on the princess, as she wrote two letters of commendation on his behalf to Cardinal Wolsey, in November 1514 and April 1515.

Wolsey did not respond to the letters. The reasons are unknown, but

Wolsey held a grudge of some sort against him and his career was blighted for the rest of the cardinal's life.

In 1530 Palsgrave wrote: 'It is a great synne to hynder a man that standeth upon his promocyon upon malyce.'[1] Wolsey is not named, but there can be little doubt as to whom he was referring.

How Palsgrave survived is not known, but in 1516 he was in Louvain studying law and strengthening his command of Greek. By this time he had come to the attention of Thomas More, who had written to Erasmus, then at Louvain, to notify him of his arrival, 'I know, my dear Erasmus, I need waste few words in asking you to assist the studies of a man who is devoted to good literature, full of promise, known to be a hard worker, and his progress hitherto is already familiar to you: one moreover who is both my friend and yours, which means yours twice over.'

By 1517, he was back in England and held a variety of minor church offices, until in 1520 his prowess in French brought his inclusion in Henry VIII's entourage for the meeting with Francis I at Calais, the 'Field of the Cloth of Gold'.

Much of the 1520s was spent in tutoring the sons of the powerful including, from September 1525 to February 1526, Henry Fitzroy, the duke of Richmond, Henry VIII's illegitimate son. Other pupils were Lord Thomas Howard, Gregory Cromwell, son of Thomas, and Charles Blount, son of Lord Mountjoy, who had first brought Erasmus to England.

This was the most difficult time of Palsgrave's life. The post of tutor to the King's son (there would be rumours of the young Henry being legitimised and named as heir to the throne) should have been a career-crowning moment for him, but the six-year-old duke was surrounded by protectors whose priorities were hunting and hawking, not the learning of Latin. Palsgrave's position was made impossible and the appointment was soon over. (The same treatment was given to his successor.) In addition, the sons of the powerful were not always able pupils. Gregory Cromwell was noted for not having the sharpness of mind of his father. Worst of all, Palsgrave had been granted the benefice of Ashfordby in Leicestershire, which turned out to be in ruins, causing him severe financial problems.

The study of language

These were the conditions under which he laboured to complete *Lesclarcissement de la langue francoyse*, his grammar of the French language. He had first had the idea for the book in 1513 and in 1523 had negotiated a contract with Richard Pynson, 'Printer to the King', for its production. Pynson was able to start printing in 1530, but following his death partway through the task, 'The imprinting [was] fynysshed by Iohan Haukyns'.

The book was well received, though it is not likely to have made Palsgrave's fortune. However, with Wolsey's downfall and death he did not need it to be a financial success. In 1532 he took his M.A. at Oxford and the following year Cranmer appointed him to the living of St Dunstan-in-the-East. His salary as tutor to the duke of Richmond had been £13 6s 8d. At St Dunstan's, which he held for the rest of his life, it was £60 8s 3d.

Palsgrave published just one other work, a translation into English (from Latin) of *The Comedy of Acolastus* by William Fullonius.[2] Despite having been a protégé of More, he found no difficulty in accepting the Henrician Reformation, becoming a royal chaplain in 1540. He died in 1554.

Palsgrave's was not the first French grammar in the English language. It had been preceded by Alexander Barclay's *Introductory* (1521) and Pierre Valence's *Introduction* (1528), but at over a thousand pages of clearly presented, logically structured analysis of the language it was the 'most comprehensive and valuable of all the grammars published in the sixteenth century and constitutes a prime source for the study of French in the early modern period.'[3] Another academic calls it 'scholarly, thorough and exhaustive.'[4] (There is no lack of positive comments on the work.)

Despite its length, the only part of the book that is superfluous in any way is the letter of introduction, though it is revealing of the intellectual thinking of the day. Written in the copious style championed by Erasmus, it starts with the obligatory words of subservience to the King, whose permission ('privilege') had been needed before the book could be printed, followed by the Renaissance-influenced tropes of modesty, 'I shall assaye some small thing to adde to my poor diligence' and talk of his 'poore labours'.

He then mentions how his research has led him to seek out books in the French language, and the further influence of Erasmus can be seen in a passage where he says, 'except after their trewe pnunciation and arte Grammaticall ones knowen we might have plenty of frenche words also to expresse our myndes withal.' (Palsgrave had already added to the language, as it was in *Lesclarcissement* that terms such as 'article', 'adverb', 'interjection' and 'phrase' first appeared.)

Palsgrave does a fair amount of name-dropping (Princess Mary, the 'duke of Suffocke' and 'Thomas, late duke of Northfolke' amongst them) as part of his sales pitch, which also includes a letter of commendation from a former pupil, 'Andrewe Baynton'.

It is when he begins his introduction that Palsgrave shows the clinical mind that makes this work a masterpiece and it is not just the grammar that he outlines meticulously. He gives equal standing to the sound of the language. His contents include:

> To the soundyng of theyr vowels.
> To the sounding of theyr dipthongs [*sic*].
> To the sounding of theyr consonants.
> For the kepyng of trewe accent.
> Whan a vowel shalbe pronounced long or short.

Like a cartographer, he sets out to map the uncharted territory of a foreign tongue and by generalising from the particular and discerning the underlying patterns of language he banishes vagueness and ambiguity and reassures the reader by making the unfamiliar familiar.

A poor teacher confuses his pupils by giving too much information at a time and in a disorderly fashion. Palsgrave explains the terms of language succinctly in lucid, non-technical terms that do not assume prior knowledge. He explains conjugations, passives, articles, adjectives and 'the concords of grammar in the French tong'.

The list of contents is four pages long. (It ends with an acrostic poem, *Laucter en rendant mercis a maistre*, which spells Arundel, leading one to assume that Thomas Arundel was Palsgrave's patron: the Arundel family built up one of the great private libraries of the sixteenth century.)

After every major part of speech has been comprehensively covered Palsgrave gives a 'table'. 'The table of substantyves [nouns]' is followed by twelve pages of notes on adjectives and then 'The table of Adiectives'. 'Of the verbe' consists of thirty pages. 'The table of verbes' takes up half of the volume's thousand pages. There are tables of 'preposytions' (six pages), 'adverbs' (eighty-five pages), 'coniunctions' (twenty pages), a list of 'Numeralles' and 'chapiters of the pronowne' (five pages).

Though they are dispersed throughout the book and categorised under parts of speech, the 'tables' constitute a dictionary, a word yet to be invented. (Thomas Elyot in 1538 was the first to use it in print.) Palsgrave had provided a thorough summation (grammar, lexicon and pronunciation) of an entire language.

Milestones

The list of innovations and achievements in *Lesclarcissement* is phenomenal. They include: the first study of one vernacular language through the medium of another; the recognition and documentation of regional, social and other variations in language (for example between prose and poetry, spoken and written, contemporary and historic); entries illustrated by examples of their everyday use; a complete break from the mechanistic, rather turgid, means of recording classical languages to one based on the phenomena of a living language, studied as a zoologist might study and describe a newly-discovered species of animal; giving synonyms; distinguishing between homographs, e.g. the lid of the eye, *paulpiere*, and the lid of a cup, *covueleque*; clear and 'user friendly' cross referencing and the use of different fonts to present different types of linguistic information. (There are many more that could be listed.)

Many of these innovations were fed by Palsgrave's experiences as a teacher. He was aware of all the difficulties and misunderstandings that a pupil could encounter (many of which he would have experienced himself when he arrived in Paris with little or no command of the language) and took pains to avoid them.

Nor are his achievements restricted to French. Discovering and describing the regularities in French grammar required comparison with the mother tongue making Palsgrave 'a very early pioneer in the history of English grammar writing'. There are a whole host of English words and phrases that make their first appearances in print in *Lesclarcissement*, though some, like 'twenty to one', are misattributed to Shakespeare. His 'vocabulysts' of English words can be used as a monolingual English dictionary. Gabriele Stein, the leading authority on Palsgrave, regards him as an English lexicographer whose achievements are still 'unparalleled'.

It is estimated that about 750 copies of *Lesclarcissement* were printed. Though its virtues were immediately appreciated, there was no second edition. Its sheer size (Palsgrave had originally intended it to be 500 pages long) made it too expensive (Stein speculates a price of around nine shillings) to all but the wealthy. One cannot even be sure that Palsgrave wanted it to be a commercial success. Before his appointment to St Dunstan's the widespread circulation of his accumulated knowledge and analysis would have jeopardised his position as a language teacher to the wealthy. After the appointment he no longer needed the book to be commercially viable.

To many people a grammar book, no matter how accomplished it might be, is as stimulating as a telephone directory or the manual for an electric appliance, necessary but of no intrinsic interest, but for a lover of language such as Salesbury, Palsgrave's grammar would have been a cornucopia of wonders to be pored over with fascination.

He is known to have made use of it for his first book (1547)[5] and in all likelihood was influenced by Palsgrave's methods of explaining pronunciation for one of his works of 1550,[6] but the significance of Palsgrave is that throughout his life Salesbury aspired to the same high level of forensic analysis and description of language.

That Salesbury owned *Lesclarcissement* sometime by the mid–1540s is certain (the evidence will be given in a later chapter). It is quite likely that his passion for language led him to buy his copy soon after its publication. In fact, of the three men who influenced him most, Palsgrave is the one whom Salesbury may well have met. It is quite possible that their paths crossed in London, either in 1530 or during one of Salesbury's visits to the capital. It is even possible that the young Salesbury sought out Palsgrave to tell him of his admiration for his work.

Chapter Six

Early career, marriage and literary interests

Between 1530 and 1547 Salesbury's life comes more sharply into focus. A small but significant number of documents survive. To these can be added details gleaned from later events and references. A picture of the man and his life starts to take shape.

Richard Rich, Attorney General for Wales

Salesbury's working relationship with Richard Rich may date from as early as 1529, but it is not until 1550, when Rich was Lord Chancellor, that it is recorded. In the introductory letter to a book published that year, Salesbury describes himself as Rich's 'moste fayethfull and humble servaunte'.[1]

Working for the highest legal officer of the kingdom was a post that would have been sought by the ambitious and well qualified, not one that would have been given to a country lawyer with no experience beyond the assizes of Denbigh and Caernarfon. It suggests that Salesbury had established himself as a distinguished and experienced lawyer and was already known to Rich, who is chiefly remembered as the man whose perjured testimony sent Thomas More to the executioner's block.

In the play *A Man for All Seasons*, when More learns that Rich has been appointed Attorney General for Wales, he says, 'For Wales? Why Richard, it profits a man nothing to give his soul for the whole world... But for Wales...'

Betraying More was a shrewd career move. Rich was appointed to the post in May 1532 and did not relinquish it until 1558. In 1533 he became

(England's) Solicitor General. He held the Welsh post *in absentia*, so it would have been necessary to appoint a deputy to carry out the work and keep him informed of developments. In an essay[2] published in 1989 Dr Peter R. Roberts, one of Wales's leading historians, makes the case for Salesbury being the appointee.

There were few in Wales with Salesbury's education and legal qualifications and young Welshmen of his background usually sought preferment in England, where there were more opportunities.

The post required fluency in Welsh: even after the Act of Union of 1536, which made English the language of the courts, the fact that a large majority of the ordinary Welsh people could not speak English meant that the letter of the law was not strictly adhered to.

Salesbury had at least one kinsman at court, John Salusbury ('Siôn Y Bodiau'),[3] who might have used his influence to help him acquire the post. Another possibility is that Sir William Brereton, a more distant relative and by marriage rather than blood, was the man who secured him the appointment. There was no doubting his power:

> Using his place at court, William Brereton had secured a virtual monopoly of royal appointments in Cheshire and north Wales. He exploited this authority to further Brereton interests, was a nuisance to Cromwell's local agent, Bishop Rowland Lee, and promised to be an obstacle to plans then in their infancy to settle the Welsh border.[4]

(Brereton was certainly in contact with Salesbury's great-uncle, Foulk, the dean of St Asaph, in 1534, when Brereton loaned him and another kinsman – Robert Salusbury, the soon to be disgraced abbot of Valle Crucis – the sum of £1,000.)[5]

If Salesbury profited from his connection to Brereton around 1532, then the year of 1536 would have been an anxious and awkward one for him. Brereton's dominant position in Wales and the Marches and his kinship to the king through his marriage to Lady Elizabeth Savage, the widowed sister of the earl of Worcester, marked him as someone whom Thomas Cromwell was keen to remove. The situation was further exacerbated in 1534, when one of Brereton's servants was killed. He blamed John ap Gryffyth Eyton, a Flintshire gentleman, and, 'exploited his local muscle to arrest Eyton and sent him under armed guard to London. Although Eyton was acquitted, Brereton had him re-arrested, possibly with Anne Boleyn's help, returned him to Wales and, after a rigged trial, saw him hanged – and all this in defiance of Cromwell's efforts to save him.'[6]

When Anne Boleyn fell out of favour with Henry, Cromwell was able to exact revenge. Brereton was named as one of the Queen's lovers and executed. Salesbury was sufficiently distant from court to be unaffected by Brereton's downfall.

An interesting aspect of Salesbury's appointment as Rich's deputy was that, though he was born in Wales and spoke Welsh as his first language, he would not have been regarded as 'Welsh'. He belonged to the English settler class, who were seen as trustworthy. There were native Welshmen who held major posts in Wales (for example William Griffith of Penrhyn, who was Chamberlain and Deputy Justice of the Northern Principality) but, certainly before the Acts of Union, they were very much the exception. Griffith (c.1480–1531) held office 'on sufferance and by royal favour'.[7] (In the 1570s Bishop Whitgift (later to become Archbishop Whitgift), who acted as Lord President of the Council of the Marches in Sir Henry Sidney's absence, adopted the policy that officers 'neyther should be Welshmen nor dwelling within the Marches'.)[8]

There is, however, the intriguing possibility that Salesbury did not owe his position to Brereton or some other well-placed kinsman, but had made Rich's acquaintance during his time at Thavies Inn. A document in the National Archives (C 4/1/54) concerns the case brought by 'John Bosvel' against the abbot of Beaulieu and 'his commoners William Plymmouth, John Sydley, John Bover and William Salesbury'.

The name jumps out from the page, but 'Salesbury', though infrequent as a surname, was not unique and a William Salesbury[9] had been the almoner of Hyde Abbey, also in Hampshire, in 1501. An involvement with Beaulieu Abbey would seem unlikely for a north Wales lawyer trained in London, until it is remembered that the abbot, Thomas Skevington, was the bishop of Bangor and had been since 1509, though he rarely visited the diocese and only played an active role there in the last four years of his life, 1529–33.

(The everyday running of the diocese was 'entrusted to a resident official who in this case was Dr [John] Glyn', dean of Bangor from 1505 to his death in 1535.)[10]

The case could well date from these last years of Skevington's life, but there is no evidence to support this assumption. At that time, Salesbury would have been newly qualified as a lawyer and looking for work, any work. As the younger son, he had little to inherit, so building a legal career was essential for his survival and working for the abbot of Beaulieu, 'the richest monk in England'[11] would have been a prestigious first post.

Cited with Salesbury is John Sydley (also known as Sydly/Sedley). There are several surviving records in which he is referred to as an 'auditor of the exchequer'.[12] Sydley was a Londoner and held a government post, which meant that he might well have had useful connections. He certainly seems to have been seeking to make his fortune. One extant document reports his purchase of three houses in Bow Lane. He is just the sort of person a recently-qualified lawyer desperate for work would have tried to cultivate.

Sydley, who also died in 1533, was a generation older than Salesbury (born c.1507) and Richard Rich (born c.1496).[13] Interestingly, his first wife's name had been Elizabeth Ginkes (or Jenks), which was the same name as Rich's wife. Could the two women have been cousins or niece and aunt? Rich had spent much of his youth in London, in the parish of St Lawrence Jewry. (Thomas More, born and brought up in Milk Street, had been aware of the young Richard Rich and described him as 'light of tongue, a great dicer and not of commendable fame'.)

In the 1520s, Rich was desperately trying to carve out a career for himself. He briefly served Wolsey before his downfall, before attaching himself to Thomas Audley, who would succeed More as Lord Chancellor. Under Audley's mentorship his career blossomed. Within a few years he would become Speaker of the House of Commons and Solicitor General. At some time between 1520 and 1525, Rich was a reader (lecturer) at New Inn, one of the Inns of Chancery. In 1529 he was Autumn Reader at the Middle Temple. This work as a reader, especially the latter appointment, which would have coincided with Salesbury's final year (or years) at Thavies Inn, may explain how the two men met, if, that is, they did meet at this time.

Interestingly, it was not just Salesbury, Rich and Sydley who were near neighbours in London. In his will of 1535,[14] John Glyn refers to himself as a 'citizen and denizen of London' and requests that he be buried at the Church of the Holy Sepulchre without Newgate, which was just a short walk from Thavies Inn.

The friendship with Rich does not speak highly of Salesbury's judgement of character, but Rich was yet to commit the acts of treachery and cruelty that were to make him infamous.

If Sydley and Rich were related by marriage, it becomes easy to understand how a meeting with one would have led to Salesbury knowing both men. Add John Glyn, Skevington's lieutenant in Bangor, to the mixture and Sydley's and Salesbury's apparent connection to Beaulieu Abbey is no longer implausible. (It should also be noted that at least one source[15] gives Rich's birthplace as Basingstoke in Hampshire and that at the 1555 trial for heresy of John Philpot, archdeacon of Winchester and member of a prominent local family, Rich remarked that he was a kinsman of Philpot's father.) As Rich's career took off and he was appointed Attorney General for Wales, it would have been natural for him to enlist Salesbury, well qualified, talented, with local knowledge and Welsh-speaking, as his deputy. The appointment would have allowed Salesbury to return home, establish his career and marry, which is exactly what he did.

Though written reports might have sufficed in keeping Rich informed of all that was happening, Salesbury is likely to have taken advantage of any opportunity to travel to London to report in person. Such visits (with stops at Ludlow and Oxford) would have given him the opportunity to buy books, meet with old friends, keep up with events and enjoy the excitement of city life.

As to details of cases in which Salesbury was personally involved, only one (C 1/981/83) has survived from this period; Richard, grandson and heir of John Eton versus William Salesbury. It concerns a dispute over the 'manor of Bovy Pantelor,[16] within the parish of Llansannan'. Thomas Audley is named as Lord Chancellor, which dates the case to between 1532 – when Audley took office – and 1544, the year of his death. It looks very much as if 'Eton' is a variation of 'Eyton', which, if correct, means that the heir of Brereton's victim of rough justice was bringing a case against a man whose career he might have launched.

However, though the background to the action may be dramatic, the case itself is not. It is little more than a long-running dispute over the lease and tenure of a specific property and is typical of the thousands of such cases that clogged up the courts of the Tudor age.

Eton's case was brought in the Court of Chancery and would have required Salesbury's presence in London. Though the likelihood is that he made regular visits to the capital, only one is recorded in his own words. In a book of 1547,[17] he refers to travelling to the city three years earlier in the company of a friend. The Eton case would be a second proven visit and the case brought against Salesbury's brother, assuming that it was Salesbury who acted for the defence, would be a third.

Salesbury's marriage to Catrin Llwyd

Just as the details of Salesbury's legal career have to be pencilled in from a small number of fixed points, so too must his marriage to Catrin Llwyd (Katherine Lloyd), which most probably took place in late 1534 or sometime the following year.

Her father's will,[18] drafted in September 1534 and proved in January 1535, contains the following words, 'Item, to Katherine lloyd vz [verch] Robert xll [forty pounds] for her mariage monney and xij kyne and calves and vj oxen.'

He was then near to death. Was the marriage brought forward for his benefit or was he so ill that he died within days of making the will, meaning that the wedding ceremony, as a token of respect, is likely to have been postponed?

An arbitration document[19] of November 1546 records Catrin and William as having three children, Siôn (John) Wyn, the 'son and heir', another son, Robert, and a daughter, Elyn. Assuming an absence of twins amongst the three children and that the couple respected marital propriety, the very latest they could have married was early 1544 but, as will become apparent, a date prior to 1540 is much more likely.

One notable aspect of the marriage is that the Salesbury brothers,

William and Robert, had married sisters, Catrin and Lowri. Their father, Robert ap Rhys,[20] had entered the church and risen to be Chancellor of St Asaph, but his choice of career had not prevented him from marrying and fathering twelve sons and four daughters. Ap Rhys attached himself to Wolsey's rising star and profited greatly, amassing many benefices (eighteen, so his enemies alleged) and appropriating church land at Ysbyty Ifan and at the abbeys of Aberconwy and Strata Marcella. 'His pride and his dynastic ambitions… aroused in the clergy and the laity of the neighbourhood a profound resentment.'

His son, Elis ap Rhys or Elis Price,[21] frequently referred to as Dr Elis, has already been mentioned. It was he who had incarcerated the prior of Penmon, John Godfrey, to the great anger of the Bulkeleys of Anglesey, and manoeuvred his brother, Richard Price, into the abbotship of Aberconwy with the help of a massive bribe. That had occurred in 1535 whilst Price was working as one of Cromwell's commissioners, reporting on the economic and moral state of the religious houses. His behaviour in that post shocked his fellow commissioners, John Vaughan and Adam Becansaw, who reported him to Cromwell.

> Dr Elice ap Robert, son of Sir Robert ap Rice, is coming with a new commission, which I fear will be slanderous unto my [Becansaw's] visitation, as he rides about openly with his concubine, whom he took from her mother at Coventry. I would not take process against him till I heard from you. He showeth in taverns the king's commission to advance himself, which causeth the people to murmur. He does not regard my admonition to 'leave such young touches.' I should have sent to you at this time 60/- of the Bishop's goods more than I do, but Dr Elice gives them audacity to pay none.

Cromwell's deputy in Wales, Roland Lee, bishop of Coventry, tried to protect Price, 'I hear that ill reports have been made to you of Dr Ellis. I beg you will hear him, as he is young, and no tree grows to be an oak at the first day.' But his master had already dispensed with Price's services, as Salesbury's brother-in-law acknowledged in a letter sent the same day as Lee's:

> I received your letter commanding me to [cease] visiting within the limits of Wales: which I have done. The reason for this was my youth and 'progeny', as you

were informed by some who were not my friends. I am sorry I ever meddled with the office, especially if you are so displeased, and I am brought into ridicule.[22]

(It may well be that Robert ap Rhys, aware of the avarice of his sons, Elis and Cadwaladr in particular, felt it necessary to include Catrin's 'mariage monney' as an item in his will to ensure that her brothers did not take it and so ruin her prospects of a settled, prosperous life.)

Why did Salesbury marry Catrin? Marriage in Tudor times was for profit and for procreation; love was not a consideration. Though he was not the heir, Salesbury would have had some land and property, he belonged to a well-paid profession and he was the deputy Attorney General for Wales. Catrin belonged to a family of ruthless seekers of land, wealth and office, willing to bend or break the law in pursuit of their goals, but at that time, and not just in Wales, those faults would have been seen by many as virtues. There were members of the Salusbury clan who behaved in exactly the same manner. (Sir John Salusbury of Llewenni was Robert ap Rhys's greatest rival and bitterest enemy. In January 1533 he had acted on Cromwell's behalf and served indictments on ap Rhys and on Bishop Standish and by June of that year could report that he had 'proved the indictment against Robt. ap Rese for praemunire and extortion' and that 'the extortioner made use of the money to procure friends and bear them out.')[23]

With such animosity between the clans it is difficult to understand how the marriage came about, but there can be fault lines within families and a few years later when Salesbury's estate was vulnerable to attack, there were those who shared his surname who sided with his enemies.

Perhaps it was decided that it was better to have the Prices inside the tent rather than outside, but who decided? In the patriarchal society of the day it was the father who chose his offspring's spouse and negotiated the wedding contracts, but Salesbury was father-less and grandfather-less. Was his elder brother a domineering character who stepped in and took over that role? Did the betrothal date from early childhood? (Such arrangements were common at the time.)

It might have been that William's uncle, Raffe, or his great-uncle, Foulk, as his nearest surviving male relatives of an older generation, acted as negotiators. Foulk was dean of St Asaph cathedral and Robert ap Rhys[24] was the chancellor. Both men were of a Machiavellian disposition and each might have thought it to his family's advantage to bring about the union. (In the absence of the bishop (Henry Standish), ap Rhys, as vicar-general, is assumed to have had overall control of the diocese.)[25]

Another possibility is that Salesbury's grandmother was the negotiator. Married women were powerless, no more than their husbands' chattels and being beaten was an everyday hazard of married life, but widows, especially wealthy widows, could live independent lives and Salesbury's grandmother, Gwenhwyfar, had the status of one who had brought great wealth into the family. She might have chosen Catrin and negotiated the marriage terms.

The final possibility is that Salesbury asserted his right to make his own decisions, and examination of what evidence exists suggests that this is the most likely explanation for his choice, as Catrin was the 'natural',[26] that is illegitimate, daughter of Robert ap Rhys.

Though John Salusbury of Llewenni[27] would marry Ursula Stanley, who was illegitimate, she was the daughter of an earl who openly acknowledged and supported her and at the time of their marriage (1586) the family was suffering from the shame of its involvement in the Babington plot. Catrin was acknowledged by the Price (ap Rhys) family,[28] but generally the stigma of illegitimacy would have been a barrier to a respectable place in society and to securing a good marriage.

In the only poem written to him during his lifetime,[29] Salesbury is described as having a stubborn streak,

> Nid ai i fan ond a fynni,
> Ni chair ond a fynnoch chwi.
>
> [There's no going to a place unless you wish (to),
> No accepting what you do not wish (for).]

He was a young man with no father or grandfather to guide or overrule him. If he was smitten by an attractive woman, as is the tendency with young men, there was no one to stop him rushing into marriage; he was in a position to ignore any older, wiser voices from within his family.

Whatever the circumstances that led to the betrothal, there is no reason to presume that Salesbury's first five years of marriage were anything other than contented. In fact, life in general would have been very comfortable and satisfying. He had a wife and family, held a prestigious legal position, had a well-remunerated profession to follow and was able to cultivate his interests and friendships.

Poetry and manuscripts; Gruffudd Hiraethog, John Prise and John Leland

Salesbury's great interest was literature. He was an admirer of Erasmus and had a wide-ranging knowledge of the classical authors, whose poems and other writings were readily available in print. There was no bookshop in Wales at that time, but some of the border towns had them or held annual book fairs.[30] If there were visits to London (via Oxford), that gave him the opportunity to stock up on new editions.

He was also a great lover of his native literature. His closest friend was the bard, Gruffudd Hiraethog,[31] who wrote the poem to him that testified to his stubborn (or should that be determined?) nature. Gruffudd was a local man (he took his name from the moor that rises above Llansannan), of roughly the same age as Salesbury and is regarded as the finest bard of his generation.

A poem that Gruffudd wrote on behalf of Salesbury's sister-in-law, Lowri, fails to answer a key question, where did William and Catrin live during the first years of their marriage? It is a request poem, a popular form of the time, in which the bard asks an individual or group of people to give a particular object to another party. Gruffudd asks twelve men of Llansannan to give Lowri, Robert's wife, some bees.

Some of the names of the men can be found in surviving records, including Piers Salbri,[32] Salesbury's cousin, Ifan ap Siôn Pigod, who would leave him 'twentie shillinges' in his will of 1580 and Maredudd ap Gronw, who appears in Salesbury's herbal, but missing from the list is Salesbury. Was it thought inappropriate for the brother-in-law to be included in the list or does it mean that he was not living in Llansannan? If so, where was he? His brother Robert had inherited the estate, but documents refer to him as Robert Salusbury of Berthddu,[33] a fine house a short distance south of Llanrwst. Did Gwenhwyfar, as the 'dowager' Salesbury and the person who had brought such wealth to the family, maintain a matriarchal presence in Plas Isa, the grandest of all the houses owned by the family? If so, did Salesbury and his family live with her or had they settled in another estate property, Caemelwr perhaps?

The Salusburys had a long association with the bards and many of William's older relatives are present in the poems of Tudur Aled[34] (d. 1525), another leading literary figure. It would be another two centuries before Welsh poetry would appear in print. New poems were performed in the presence of the patrons to whom they were addressed. Older poems were preserved in manuscripts, ancient and modern, which circulated amongst the bards and the gentry and were copied and re-copied and there are four surviving manuscripts with a substantial number of poems in Salesbury's handwriting. Amongst his favourite poets were Tudur Aled, Dafydd ap Gwilym, Siôn Cent, Iolo Goch and Dafydd ab Edmwnd.[35]

It was not just poetry manuscripts that interested Salesbury. His interest in language in general, but especially his mother tongue, meant that any manuscript (charters, statutes, genealogies, chronicles or the lives of saints) was of interest. It was a phenomenon that had started in Florence with Poggio Bracciolini, who travelled the German and Italian-speaking areas of Europe unearthing works by Cicero, Quintilian, Vitruvius and others. After the Dissolution of the monasteries in 1538, there was an added urgency to the task in England and Wales, with libraries laid waste and literary, historical and illuminated masterpieces lost forever:

> Some to serve theyr iakes [toilets], some to scour theyr candelstyckes and some to rubbe their bootes. Some they solde to the grossers and sope sellers and some they sent over the see to the boke bynders, not in small nombre, but at tymes whole shyppes full, to the wonderynge of the foren nacions.[36]

Salesbury was amongst the first wave of those who salvaged what they could of the kingdom's heritage and was a colleague of the two most famous collectors of the age, John Leland and John Prise.[37]

Prise,[38] like Salesbury an Oxford-educated lawyer, Humanist and government functionary, had married Joan Williamson of Southwark, Thomas Cromwell's niece by marriage, and prospered accordingly. He examined Bishop John Fisher before his trial and execution, played a significant role in the Dissolution as an inspector of monasteries and acquired

St Guthlac's Priory, Hereford, which became the family home. He wrote abridgements of the confessions of some of those who had taken part in the Pilgrimage of Grace and was present at the resulting executions in Hull. Prise survived Cromwell's downfall, being appointed Secretary to the Council of the Marches two months after his mentor's execution, a post he held until his death in 1555.

N. R. Ker has listed over a hundred theological manuscripts that were saved by Prise, and estimates that one tenth of all existing manuscripts of English origin of Bede's theological works belonged to him. Some of his manuscripts can be seen in the chained library of Hereford Cathedral. (There is a rich, dark irony in the fact that so much of the monasteries' learning was salvaged by a man who played an active part in their destruction.) His friend, Leland, paid tribute to him, 'Ioannes Rhesus antiquitatis amator, atque idem sedulus illustrator.' (John Rhys lover of antiquities, and moreover a diligent illuminator.)[39]

A great deal of circumstantial evidence connects Salesbury to Prise, but the irrefutable link is his autograph in *Llyfr Du Caerfyrddin* [The Black Book of Carmarthen],[40] one of Prise's most prized manuscripts.

The most famous of all the Tudor manuscript collectors was John Leland, a faithful supporter of Henry, who was nevertheless appalled at the destruction visited on the monastic libraries. He had a great interest in 'British' (Welsh) history and culture and a good knowledge of the language. In his final years 'he fell besides his wits',[41] something that many attribute to the distress caused by the literary vandalism he witnessed.

There is evidence that Leland and Salesbury were colleagues. In his *Itinerary in England and Wales* Leland notes a visit to Salesbury's native 'paroche of Llan Sannan' and mentions in passing the Edwards family of Chirk, to whom Salesbury was related. (One of Salesbury's books is dedicated to John Edwards of Chirk, his 'cosen'.) Unfortunately, though Leland reports talking to 'Salisbyri, knight of Denbigh land',[42] he does not name Salesbury in his writings, but in a letter of 1565, Salesbury names him. Praising his good friend, Humphrey Llwyd, he says of him, 'This gentleman after J. Leland & Jo. Bale, of all that I knowe in thys Isle, is most universaly sene in Histories & most singerly skilled in rare Subtiltees'[43] which seems conclusive, but Leland was by then dead and Salesbury might have been speaking of what he had heard of him rather than from personal experience.

One reason for Salesbury's search for manuscripts was that at the back of his mind was the idea for a book, one that would require a great deal of research of his language in its one source of written material. To consider producing a book for a nation that had no printing press, bookshop, university or grammar school was hugely ambitious and the nature of the book envisaged made it all the more so. Lodged deeper still in the recesses of his mind was a project that verged on fantasy, one that at this stage he probably felt unable to divulge to anyone, even his closest friends.

However, his literary plans would not have been realistic at that time. Salesbury would have needed someone very high up at court to approach either the King or the Privy Council for permission, but since the death of Brereton there was no such person in his life and choosing the right moment would have been very, very difficult. The 1530s had been a decade of crises and dramatic events: the Pope's refusal of a divorce; the break with Rome; the unpopular marriage to Anne Boleyn and the executions of More and Fisher; the continuing disappointment of no male heir, the execution of Queen Anne; the Pilgrimage of Grace, which came so close to removing Henry as King; the joy of a male heir, Edward, followed so quickly by the death of his mother, Jane Seymour; the Dissolution of the monasteries; the farce of the failed marriage to Anne of Cleves; the downfall and execution of Cromwell and much, much more.

The kingdom was in turmoil. In contrast, Salesbury's life was peaceful and incident free but events in 1540 would change his life forever.

Chapter Seven

Death and discord

Robert's will

In 1540, Robert Salesbury, William's brother, died. There are no details of the illness or injury that befell him. He had already been widowed so his daughters, Gwen and Elen, were now orphans.

Those facts can be gleaned from an extract from Robert's will that was printed in a book of 1902[1] whose author, D. R. Thomas, as archdeacon of St Asaph cathedral, had access to the diocesan archive. Unfortunately, the will has since vanished. No one at St Asaph or at the National Library of Wales knows of its whereabouts.

Here is the extract, to which Thomas has added some explanatory details in brackets:

> ... to be buried in the Church of llanrwst : 2/- to reparacon of sayd church; 2/- to Sir Hugh Gruff to say a trentall for my wyffe's soule and mine : to my br. William Glyne my sword and buckler, to Robert ap Hugh my jacket and dowblett : to Morris Salusbury my stole, s'pleice and cotte of defence ; to my das. Gwen and Elen lands &c within Denbighland, Carnarvonshire, ruthin and Dyffryn Clwyd ; All my father's and Grandfather's purchased lands and that came to me by inheritance. Executors and Curators, Sir David Owen (Vicar of Eglwysfach) Sir John Gruff, my curate and gostly father, Ric : ap John and Robt. Wynn ap Robert (ap Rhys) ; the government of my daughters to be at the discretion of 'Doctor Elis (Prys) in whom ys alle my truste.' Overseers, Doctor Elis, Robert Salusburye Clerk (S.R. of Llanrwst and Llansannan) Ric. Price, Clerk ('Y Person Gwyn', Rector of Cerrigydrudion & late Abbot of Aberconwy) and Thomas Waghan Salusbury. Witnesses ... Robert ap Price Wyne, Peter Salusbury (guarantor),' &c

The request for a 'trentall' (a series of thirty masses) shows that Robert, unlike William, had retained his Catholic faith and not been attracted to the ideology of the Reformation. It also suggests that Lowri's death had been very recent. As death in childbirth was common, it might well be the explanation of Lowri's passing. The infant, too, might have died or it could be that Elen was a babe in arms and that her sister, Gwen, was just a year or so older. In a document[2] of 1554, the girls are referred to as being under twenty-one years of age, which would make them no more than twenty and nineteen. So the oldest they could have been when they were orphaned was six and five.

The details of the will raise several questions.

Why, when your brother is the leading lawyer in Wales, would you ask your brother-in-law to draft your will? And why, when your brother is married to your late wife's sister, has a family of his own, a comfortable home and ready access to your mother and grandmother to take in the girls, would you ask your bachelor brother-in-law, who had earned himself a reputation for riding around 'with his concubine'[3] and had fathered several illegitimate children, to look after your infant daughters?

If Robert's death had been sudden and unexpected, then Salesbury might have been absent on business, in which case it would have been reasonable for Elis Price to step in. However, there seems to be no credible explanation for the second question, other than that Robert disliked William's flirting with Protestantism[4] or was jealous of his success, but would he have let such matters outweigh the well-being of his daughters?

Dramatis personae

Five years later David Owen, a priest and one of the executors, purchased Aberconwy Abbey.[5] (He was, therefore, worldly enough to profit from the seizure of church property. Equally worldly was his non-adherence to the vow of celibacy.) He would later conspire with John Wyn ap Maredudd in the seizure of the Salesbury estate.[6] The presence of Elis Price's brothers, Richard and Robert, gives even greater cause for concern, though the appearance of three Salusburys amongst the guarantors and witnesses lends the document an air of balance and legitimacy.

Most commentators have assumed that the will is an attempt by Price to rob the Salesburys (William, his children, his mother and grandmother) of their inheritance. One historian has stated that it was 'difficult to think of an age in which unselfishness, devotion to an ideal, faithfulness to a master or a friend were rarer in public life, or one in which lust for material gain was greater.'[7] After considering those words alongside the character of Price (who had locked up the prior of Penmon in his battle with the Bulkeleys to profit from the Dissolution and then outmanoeuvred the same family to get his brother, Richard, appointed by Cromwell as abbot of Aberconwy) that would seem to be the correct conclusion.

Guardianship of the girls gave Price control of all the rents and income from their estate and the ability to sell off individual properties at whatever price and to whomsoever he wished. The potential for illicit gain was immense. Worse still, a married woman could not own property in her own right. Upon marriage ownership was transferred to her husband. The Salesbury estate would pass out of the hands of Gwen and Elen and it was Price, as guardian, who would oversee the choice of husbands.

As if that were not disastrous enough, it is more than likely that, included in the land and property listed in the will which was legitimately Robert's to pass on to his daughters, were elements of the Salesbury estate that indisputably belonged to Gwenhwyfar, Annes and William.

The historian who wrote that 'In that litigious era, a squire had need to know the law to preserve his property'[8] was accurate in his observation. It is not known how soon after Robert's funeral that Salesbury took defensive action, but evidence from later in the decade shows that the conflict soon became intense and hostile.

The perils of travel

If it is correct that Price had taken advantage of his brother-in-law's absence at the time of Robert's death, then Salesbury must bitterly have regretted it. After six years of marriage to Price's sister he must surely have been aware of his character, which suggests that on the last occasion that he had bid his brother farewell, he had had no reason to suspect that Robert's health was in any immediate danger. However, at the time a minor ailment or accident could soon become life-threatening.

Salesbury's everyday work as a lawyer would take him no further away than Caernarfon or Denbigh. As Deputy Attorney General for Wales he could have travelled as far as Carmarthen or Monmouth, or even to London to report directly to Rich. The return journey from these locations would have been measured in days, but what if he had ventured even further afield? As an educated man in his early thirties, with an interest in the new ideas coming from the continent and a facility with languages, it would be unlikely that he would turn down an opportunity to travel, if one arose.

A letter[9] dated 30 August 1539 suggests that on at least one occasion Salesbury had travelled as far as Paris. It was written by John Bekynsaw, a student at the university there, to Lady Lisle, wife of the Governor of Calais and contains the following sentence:

> I perceive that … ye had not received the box of crepyns [white linen caps] which I sent you from Guylyam le Gras by one Guyliam, my lord Wyllyam his servant, for the which I am very sorry, for when I delivered them to him Mr. Salysbery was present, and because he said he would depart before Mr. Salysbery and I know the man well because he had been here before with my Lord Wyllyam, willing ye should have had them by the first, I delivered them to him, I trust ye shall have them ere this letter come to your hands…

Unfortunately, no forename is attached to 'Mr. Salysbery'. There are just three other William Salesburys[10] recorded in the kingdom at that time. There is one 'Salysbery' (Nicholas) mentioned in the documents of the National Archives and four instances of a 'Salesbury' (three Roberts and a John).

However, Salesbury's interest in ideas from the continent, his fluency in French and his mastery of Greek (Bekynsaw's academic speciality) mark him out as a distinct possibility for being the visitor, as does the fact that their times at Oxford had overlapped.

More substance is given to the argument that this is Salesbury by the fact that his cousin, Foulke Lloyd, is described in a document of 1538–44[11] as 'Foulke Lloyd of Calais, servant to Lord Lisle'. 'Cousin' is not used here in the broad sense of 'kinsman', but very specifically; Foulke's mother, Marged (née Salesbury), was the sister of William's father. Having a well-placed relative in Calais would have made travelling easier. Another incentive to use Calais as the starting point of his journey abroad was the presence there of Elis Gruffudd,[12] the noted chronicler and translator. (In Salesbury's herbal, written during the 1570s, there is a reference to a particular plant, *ammi visnaga*, which 'In the gardens of the city of Paris in France [grows] abundantly.' (tr.))[13]

Bekynsaw (the name is most often spelt 'Bekinsau')[14] was a noted scholar (praised by Leland), who had studied at New College, Oxford, from 1518 to 1526, when he gained his M.A. He had been at the university in Paris since the late 1520s and had married a French woman, Audrey, with whom he had had a son. To finance his studies he acted as an agent for various English aristocrats resident in Calais, most importantly for Lady Lisle, for whom he purchased items such as caps, pearls, jewellery and furs, and he and the merchant named in the letter, Guillaume Le Gras, oversaw the education of Lady Lisle's son from her first marriage, the ten-year-old James Bassett, who lodged with Le Gras.

From the letter it can be assumed that Lady Lisle knew, or knew of, 'Salysbery' and that he had been about to return to Calais (but not as immediately as Lord William's servant). That does not necessarily mean a return to England. He may have wished to venture into the Low Countries, perhaps to Antwerp, one of the great mercantile ports, or to a university town such as Louvain.

All that can be deduced from the letter is that there is a possibility that Salesbury had been in Paris in August 1539, had previously been in Calais and that he returned there that month or in early September. If Salesbury was, indeed, a traveller, for which conjecture there is no further evidence, and had been abroad the following year, it could have taken a considerable time for him to be located by his family and just as long to return, allowing ample time for Price to wreak havoc.

Salesbury's cousin, Foulke, was made rudely aware of the dangers to one's property posed by being abroad for any length of time. It would appear that the case that he and his wife brought against Robert Fletcher of Denbigh, where he is described as 'servant to Lord Lisle' was due to Fletcher having taken advantage of their absence to encroach on land at Henllan.

A servant of Cromwell?

If it was Salesbury who was in France in 1539, what was the purpose of his visit to Bekynsaw? Had they met at Oxford and Salesbury was taking advantage of their friendship to enjoy a handy billet in Paris? Was it Bekynsaw's scholarship or a recommendation by Leland that drew him there or was there a darker motive?

Bekynsaw was believed to be Romanist in his sympathies and the rumours concerning his loyalty had reached London. In October 1538[15] he felt it necessary to write to the King denying that he had criticised him and stating unequivocally his support for the dissolution and for the royal supremacy. In October 1539, he returned briefly to England and gave a similar pledge to Cromwell, who granted him a payment of £10.[16] The factional and religious politics of court was a snake-pit. Was Salesbury's presence in Paris a coincidence or had he been sent by Cromwell to assess Bekynsaw's loyalty and report back?

His employer, Rich, worked closely with Cromwell; Salesbury's colleague and co-pioneer of Welsh printing, John Prise, was related to Cromwell through marriage and Elis Price, after his fall from grace in 1535, was back in his employment by 1538. (From 1540 the relationship between Prise and Salesbury would be intensely hostile, but it is possible that before that date they co-existed amicably.) Cromwell was the man responsible for the Great Bible, the first authorised edition of the Bible in English. Salesbury would have had no problem in working for a man who had done so much to advance the Reformist cause.

If Salesbury was in Paris on Cromwell's behalf, it was to no avail. By July of 1540 he had been removed from power and executed. Bekynsaw played no part in his downfall, but Cromwell had been right to suspect him. He is thought to have been involved in the 1543 'prebendaries' plot' to remove Cranmer from power. The plot failed and Bishop Gardiner's nephew, Germain Gardiner, was executed. In 1546, Bekynsaw published *De Supremo et Absoluto Regis Imperio*, which supported Henry's supremacy and won approval from Protestants such as John Bale, but when Mary came to the throne Bekynsaw was able to show his true allegiance and sat in four of her parliaments until ill-health brought his career to an end.

Salesbury's absence from Llanrwst at the time of Robert's death would have greatly facilitated Price's machinations. An absence abroad would have been even more of a boon to his brother-in-law. Wherever he had been, the campaign to protect what he regarded as his and his family's property would have started immediately on his return and he would have used his full and substantial legal armoury.

English law, Welsh law and arbitration

Traditionally, Wales and England had had different systems of inheritance. In Wales all legitimate sons had enjoyed equal shares, *cyfran* (gavelkind), whilst in England the eldest son acquired all (primogeniture). The Act of Union (1536) abolished the Welsh legal system, but 'lawdable Customes of the said Countrey' were allowed to continue. In any case, Foulk Salusbury had died in 1520 so, possibly, his sons had inherited equal shares of his estate, though in the case brought against Robert to recover the crown debt of his father, he is referred to as 'son and heir'.

This is just one example of the many complications and complexities in the case. Another is that *cyfran*, as a 'lawdable Custome' stayed in force until the feast day of St John the Baptist (24 June) 1541,[17] so that Robert, like his father, had died whilst the old law was in place. This was a remarkable stroke of luck for Salesbury: his position under Welsh law as the brother of a deceased man with no sons was much stronger than it would have been under English law.

(The original, uncorrupted, Welsh laws stated that the land of a man who died without male issue was to be inherited by his brothers, but by the late Middle Ages a more relaxed attitude had been taken and the tendency had been to recognise the rights of daughters to inherit. With their settler background and status, it is unlikely that Salesbury's family had followed the Welsh legal code, but the letter of the law, if interpreted as it had been originally intended, favoured William rather than his nieces and there is some evidence that in Dyffryn Clwyd and the lordship of Denbigh, the old Welsh law had remained in force. There were objections to be made and many fine points to be debated, but Salesbury had a potent weapon in his armoury.)

Arbitration

So little information has survived that detailed examination of the case is impossible. The exact date of Robert's death is unknown. The wills of Robert Salesbury (senior) and Foulk have not survived. (What had been left to Gwenhwyfar and Annes who, as widows, could own property in their own right? What had been left to William?) Were there clauses in Gwenhwyfar's inheritance settlement that stipulated who was to take control of them in the event of her death?

It can be assumed that Salesbury fought doggedly and over many years until it was agreed by both parties, Salesbury and Gwenhwyfar, widow of Robert Salusbury, senior, and Gwen and Elen, joint heiresses of Robert Salesbury, junior, to go to arbitration. The arbitration document,[18] dated 4 November 1546, has survived.

The arbiters were: John Salesbury the younger, John Wyn ap Mered', Elys Price, Hugh Salesbury and Robert Myddelton. Whilst the Salusburys and Myddelton would have been neutral (all parties involved were Salesburys), it is hard to understand Price's appointment as an arbiter. Presumably Salesbury objected but was overruled. Just as suspicious is the inclusion of John Wyn ap Maredudd of Gwydir. The Wynns were the most ruthless of all the land-grabbing families of north Wales. If Salesbury had doubts about John Wyn's trustworthiness, they were justified; he would later conspire successfully with Elis Price and David Owen (the clergyman) to marry Gwen and Elen to two of his sons, Gruffudd and Owain.[19]

The outcome of the arbitration offered Salesbury some (limited) satisfaction.

To William and his heirs were allocated:

Plas Isa and its land and all land that was in the ownership of Robert [senior] and Gwenhwyfar that is currently in his [William's] hands;

the land in Llanrwst called Caer Brychiaid that was once owned by Owen ap Raynold;

all the houses and lands inherited by Robert and Gwenhwyfar in the parishes of Llansannan, Llangernyw and Llanfair;

all the lands and smallholdings that were lately in the ownership of Robert Salesbury, senior, Foulk Salesbury and Robert Salesbury, junior, in the lordships of Ruthyn and Aberchwilar with some named exceptions [thirteen in all];

that all the above mentioned after William's day would descend without interference from Gwen and Elyn to John, William's eldest son, and to his heirs and, in the absence of heirs, to Robert, his second son, to Elyn his daughter, to the heirs of William from his present wife, Katherine Lloid, and to their heirs for ever.

Gwen and Elen were awarded:

the lands and smallholdings in the parish of Llanrwst and the commote of 'Istulas' that had been in the inheritance of Robert, Gwenhwyfar, Foulk and Robert their father, apart from those above already awarded to William Salesbury;

the land that had been in the inheritance of the same persons in the lordships of Ruthyn and Aberchwilar, apart from those awarded to William Salesbury;

and that William, Gwenhwyfar and Agnes Salesbury transfer the above lands together with every lease within the parishes of Llanrwst and Corwen, and Caernarfonshire to the satisfaction of Gwen and Elyn when they come of age;

and that the whole is kept clear of annuities to Gwenhwyfar or to Agnes, but that Gwen and Elyn pay an annuity to Gwenhwyfar of £6 8s 4d throughout her life.

Salesbury had secured for himself and his children a substantial part of the estate that his grandmother had brought into the family. His mother and grandmother had been saved from living their last years in penury; he was now assured of income other than that earned from his legal practice and Gwenhwyfar was spared the trauma of seeing Plas Isa, the pride of the Salesburys of Llanrwst, pass out of her hands and into the possession of strangers.

The 'putting away' of Catrin

There is another clause, unconnected to property, which shows the emotional damage that the dispute had caused:

That the said William Salesbury at the reasonable request of the said Elys Price or Kadwaladr ap Robert shall take hys wif Katheryn verch Robert to hym agayn and her to kepe and use as his wiff according to the lawes and as a man ought to do his wiff and not to put the said Katheryn from hym for matier cause or kinde of offence or displeasure heretofore committed or done by the said Katheryn nor shall put away ffrom hym the said Katheryn for eny cause matier kinde of offences heretofore comytted and done by the said Katheryn and we awarde that the said

William shall not in any wise ffrom henfurth put away his said wif Katheryn but by an ordre of a lawe.

It must be assumed that 'put away' means that Salesbury had caused Catrin to live apart from him, but there is no record of any relevant legal action. The whole affair was messy and destructive and the only ones involved who are free of suspicion of avarice are the daughters. It was natural and right for Salesbury to defend his position, but did he cross the line and try to claim what was morally and legally Gwen and Elen's? Is it possible that there was an element of protectiveness and benevolence in Elis Price's behaviour? Was his concern for his half-sister heartfelt or was it a case of overturning an insult to family honour?

Catrin, as a married woman, had no legal rights and was as powerless as the girls. She was torn between two families and two strong-willed men. A victory for Salesbury would mean that the inheritance of her three children would be assured. On the other hand she would have felt concern for the future of her sister's orphaned children and felt a pull of loyalty to a family that had recognised her and raised her as one of their own when they were not obliged to do so. Perhaps she had tried to mediate and that had been seen as disloyalty or she might have been unable to cut the strings of attachment that tied her to the Prices.

Whatever the answer, she lost more than anyone. Catrin suffered the humiliation of being 'put away', was expelled from the family home and separated from her children.

Chapter Eight

Literary beginnings

John Prise

Strangely, it was during this tumultuous time of marital strife and legal conflict that Salesbury laid the foundations for his literary career. There are several factors that may explain this. The first is that John Prise, Salesbury's colleague, had left London after the fall of his mentor, Cromwell. Now based at Ludlow, he was within easy reach of Salesbury. Their jobs are likely to have brought them together often and their shared background and interests (manuscripts, Welsh poetry, history and antiquarianism) would have been the catalyst for friendship, as is evident from Prise's loan of *Llyfr Du Caerfyrddin* to his companion and their mutual acquaintance with Gruffudd Hiraethog, who wrote a poem in praise of Prise.[1]

Prise had many cultural interests, but there was one that was dominant, his campaign to defend the good name of Geoffrey of Monmouth and his *Historia Regum Britanniae* [History of the Kings of Britain] from the literary and historical scepticism of Polydore Vergil. Vergil[2] was a Humanist scholar who had been brought to England by Henry VII and it was at the King's request that he had started work on *Anglica Historia*. It was printed in Basel in 1534 and cast serious doubt on the authenticity and accuracy of Geoffrey's work.

Many had been suspicious of Geoffrey's history since its appearance in 1136. The author claimed that it was a translation of a 'British' text that had been given him by Walter, Archdeacon of Oxford, but that the unnamed source had vanished. Despite this, its popularity grew. There was a Welsh translation, *Brut y Brenhinedd*, and Caxton had made extensive use of Geoffrey's work in his 1470 *Description of Britain*.

Wales had lost its independence, its legal system, its royal dynasties, but *Historia Regum Britanniae* gave it a status amongst the scholars of Europe, which is why, for men like Prise, it was so important. Nor was it Welshmen alone who were upset or angered by this undermining of the book. English antiquaries felt similarly agitated. Leland 'stormed against anyone who doubted the story of our Trojan founder, King Brutus: he raged against those who belittled our all-conquering King Arthur.'[3]

Prise did not rage. He was 'calm' and 'well-ordered'.[4] As any good lawyer would, he collected all the available evidence from the manuscripts of Gildas, Nennius and others to build what he saw as an overpowering case for the defence. The result was *Historiae Britannicae Defensio*, which was circulated in manuscript form amongst England's antiquaries from 1545.[5]

Though Geoffrey's history is obviously inaccurate and sometimes just fantastical, it fitted the mood of the moment. The break with Rome meant that it was de rigueur for those who sought power and influence to espouse the cause of English/British uniqueness and apartness from Europe. Henry was of Welsh (British) descent and so could trace his line back through the kings of Britain listed by Geoffrey to Brutus, the Trojan founder of the island kingdom to which he had given his name and whose language, British (that is, Welsh), was still spoken.

In Geoffrey's version of history Arthur is a warrior king who defeats Iceland and subdues Gaul. Caesar is twice defeated by the Britons and is only successful on his third attempt through the treachery of Androgeus of Kent. Supporters of Henry's break with Rome asserted the independence of the old Celtic (British) church. The cultural interests of England and Wales were aligning for the first time in centuries.

Sir William Herbert

Whilst Prise was objective and rational in his defence of Geoffrey, others felt no reluctance in resorting to bombast and jingoism. (Those who agreed with Vergil tended to keep a discreet silence.) Arthur Kelton wrote the following 'verse':

> We Welshemen saie for our defence[6]
> That ye Romayns, surmounting in pride

With your Imperiall magnificence,
Supposyng therby the hevens to devide,
Came long after our noble tribe:
So that we maie write of your estate,
Not ye of us: ye came all too late.

Kelton's patron was Sir William Herbert,[7] the most senior Welshman in the kingdom. He was a brash, hail-fellow-well-met sort of a man, a 'rough diamond' who could charm many, including Francis I of France and Philip II of Spain. Rumours abounded that he was illiterate, but they might have originated in his never being as articulate in English as he was in Welsh. He was certainly not an intellectual. He could be brutal and thuggish. He killed a man in a brawl in Bristol and cold-heartedly brought about the death of England's most able mathematician, Robert Recorde, by imprisoning him for debt. He was a wily, political operator who served four Tudor monarchs and whose sister-in-law, Catherine Parr, had become the Queen Consort of England.

Whilst Salesbury's signature in one of Prise's most prized manuscripts confirms that the two men were colleagues, for Salesbury and Herbert the evidence is not as strong, though a document[8] of 1553 to 1555 records a link between Herbert and the Salusbury clan. 'John Salysburye of Grays Inn, servant to the Earl of Pembroke' brought a case against two Welshmen concerning 'land in Creigiog and Criegiog Uwchllan, late of Robert Salysbury.'

Gruffudd Hiraethog's connection to Herbert can be seen in a request poem he wrote on behalf of Dafydd Ifans, Herbert's porter.[9] Herbert had a London home, Baynard's Castle, and a country house, Wilton. Gruffudd must have met Ifans at one of those houses. The poem dates from after 1551, but Gruffudd might have made Dafydd's acquaintance prior to that. In 1547 Salesbury refers to having visited London with Gruffudd three years previously and in a book of 1550[10] he makes a pun on the similarity of 'Salesbury' and 'Salisbury Plain', suggesting a familiarity with the landscape near Wilton. This might have been the occasion when Gruffudd met Dafydd for the first time.

It is not impossible that Salesbury would have taken his good friend Gruffudd to see the sights of London, but it is more likely that there was a very specific purpose to the visit. Besides being poets, the bards were the guardians of the nation's genealogy. Mention of a man's immediate family and of his illustrious ancestors was an essential part of any *cywydd moliant* (poem of praise) or *marwnad* (elegy) and so the keeping of detailed genealogical tables was essential. Not only was Gruffudd the leading poet of his generation, he was also the leading genealogist, an accomplishment that would see his appointment as Deputy Herald for Wales (Garter, Norroy and Clarenceux). Unfortunately, the date of his appointment is unknown, but a copy of the College of Arms' 'Instrucions ffor gryffyth yraethoc' survives.[11]

A meeting with the King

The most likely explanation for his visit of 1544 was that he had been asked to draw up a family tree for the King, which he would present with as much ceremony, flattery and humility as possible. Given the nature of the visit, the tree would have emphasised Henry's Welsh heritage and traced his line back through Arthur, Brennius, Leir and Ebraucus to Brutus, grandson of Aeneas.

Whilst fighting fiercely to preserve his family's fortune, it can be surmised that Salesbury had been co-operating with Prise on a plan to introduce their nation to the technology that Gutenberg had introduced to the world a century previously. From 1450 to 1550 twenty million printed volumes were produced in Europe.[12] At the time of the visit, not one had been in Welsh. Each man wished to publish a book, but the press was strictly controlled. Every book needed a licence, either from the King or the Privy Council. No commoner could address the King. It needed someone very senior at court to intercede on your part to put forward the proposition.

There was only one man who combined sufficient seniority of status with a desire to champion and promote Welsh culture and that was Sir William Herbert, a trusted courtier who would be named as an executor of the King's will.

Though lacking in education and taste, as seen by his patronage of Kelton, and not an articulate man, he was the means by which the highly cultured and linguistically gifted Prise and Salesbury could find their way into print.

Why was it that Salesbury set out on the literary path in the personally difficult 1540s rather than the peaceful 1530s? Robert's death had been a tragedy for all the Salesburys, most especially his daughters, and William had had to fight desperately to preserve the family's inheritance, but it is likely that he was now a much richer man than he had been before his brother's death, which meant that he had more time to devote to studying and writing.

Also, the 1540s were propitious to his project and the previous decade had not been. One of the marks of Salesbury's greatness is that he could recognise a historical opportunity and had the courage and determination to take advantage of it, persuading or cajoling others to help him do so, in this case John Prise, Gruffudd Hiraethog and Sir William Herbert.

The spirit of the age favoured Britishness. England had once controlled most of France, now there was just Calais and Boulogne. She had become an 'island' and isolated herself from Papal Europe. The story of Britain, of an independent British church free from 'Romish' corruption and of noble, warrior kings such as Arthur who could repel foreign invaders was powerful and necessary and the King was a Briton.

Henry, prematurely old and not far from death, might have remembered the many individuals from Wales who had served him faithfully and recalled that it was an army made up predominantly of Welshmen that had brought his father to the throne. Throughout his reign there had been dire predictions of revolt in Wales, which were passed on with anticipation from the Imperial ambassador, Chapuys, to Charles V, but none had materialised. The west of England and the north had rebelled against the Tudor kings, but not Wales.

There is no record of an audience with Henry. It could be argued that Salesbury and Prise could just as easily have approached the Privy Council, but there are several reasons for supposing that it was the King's specific permission that was sought and that he was likely to be more amenable than his council.

The men were seeking permission to print the first ever books in a language that eight years earlier had, in effect, been legally abolished by act of parliament. Not only did the language have no legal status, the act stated that it should be 'extirpd' (obliterated). Only the King had the authority to reverse such an injunction and Prise and Salesbury, as representatives of a nation that was different from England in language and religious adherence (the Welsh clung obstinately to the rituals and practices of the pre-Henrician

Reformation) offered him something he would value as a lasting achievement: religious and linguistic uniformity throughout his kingdom.

It is conjecture that the two men, accompanied by Herbert and Gruffudd Hiraethog, met the King, but it would seem to be the only explanation for the fact that less than three years later they had seen their books through the press and that, weeks before he died, Henry had signed a 'gracious Privilege' in which:

> we have graunted and geven… licence to our welbeloved subiectes William Salesbury and Jhon Waley to print or cause to be printed oure booke entitled a Dictionarie bothe in englyshe &welche, whereby our welbeloved subiects in Wales may the soner attayne and learne our mere englyshe tonge. and that no other person or persons of what estate degree or condicion so ever they be of, do prynte or cause the same Dictionary to be printed or any part therof, but only the sayd William and Jhon… duryng the space of seven yeres…[13]

Yny lhyvyr hwnn

In 1546, belatedly and modestly, the first printed book in Welsh was published. Just one copy survives. The front cover is missing, so the book is known by its opening words, *Yny lhyvyr hwnn* [In this book]. The printer, Edward Whitchurch, is not named, but can be identified by his colophon. The author is also anonymous, but a passing reference in a book of 1567[14] confirms that it was John Prise.

Its missing front cover, unassuming appearance and length (just thirty-three pages) make it a modest volume, but for Wales it could not have had greater cultural or symbolic significance.

A little over six months later the number of Welsh books would double with the appearance of Salesbury's *A Dictionary in Englyshe and Welshe*, whose stated aim, as can be seen in the privilege, was to help the Welsh acquire mastery of the English language.

The Acts of Union had been a success. The 'Problem of Wales' had been solved, but there was still a sense of unease about the country, fuelled perhaps by the fact that Henry's father had used it as his invasion base. In 1543, in *The King's Book*,[15] Henry had set out the tenets of his church. It would appear that Prise and Salesbury had played on his insecurity and persuaded him that the

Welsh needed to be given a pared down version of that book in their own language so that they could be obedient to his will. A dictionary would bring about a similar conformity in language and enable the Welsh to read the Bible that the King had so graciously permitted to be translated into English.

A royal proclamation of 8 July 1546 required every book to name its author and publisher. *Yny lhyvyr hwnn*[16] bears the date 1546, so the absence of names means it must have been published in the first part of that year. It opens with an address to the reader, 'Now our gracious king has no greater desire than to see that the words of God and the evangel are distributed amongst his people ...' (tr.)

Recognising that this is an official and formal statement of the Church's doctrine, Prise is careful to maintain his anonymity by using either the third person or the impersonal. It is only towards the end of the address that he starts to slip into the first person.

Orthography

Before setting out the doctrines and other information essential for the well-being of the soul, he outlines the principles and use of the Welsh alphabet, which gives the book something of the flavour of a school primer. As this was the first printed book in the language Prise, with his legal and Humanist education, thought it important to establish the ground rules of literacy.

However, constrained by space and the nature of his commission, he allows himself just a little more than two pages for his notes, which comprise two tables accompanied by seventeen and then twenty-eight lines of explanation, hardly an opportunity to emulate the achievements of Palsgrave. He gives the Welsh alphabet ('ch', 'ng', 'ph' and 'th' are omitted and 'lh' is used for the present day 'll' and 'δ' for 'dd'; both 'c' and 'k' and 'f' and 'v' are included) and goes on to explain accent, consonants and vowels with reference to English, Greek and Latin and where to place the stress in words. He touches briefly on mutation and states his preference for avoiding the doubling of letters at the end of words.

Another reason for this section of the book is that printing had affected the spelling of languages. English had lost several letters, such as thorn and yogh, from its alphabet. Now, belatedly, Welsh was facing similar challenges, the most immediate being the lack of a sufficient number of 'k's in Whitchurch's cases of type. 'C' did not appear in the Welsh alphabet but by page two of the book Whitchurch is already using 'c' for 'k', 'dywyssoc' for 'dywyssok'.

Prise mentions that there are some changes to the orthography, but does not go into detail apart from noting that he would not be using 'dd' or 'll'. As a last thought on spelling Prise comments that he would have preferred to have used the Greek alphabet as this had been the alphabet used by the ancient Britons, citing Caesar as his proof and, though he does not give the reference, in *De Bello Gallico* (6.13ff) these words can be found: 'They consider it wrong to commit all these things to writing, though in other matters, indeed both in public and private documents, they use the Greek alphabet.'

Pliny's *Naturalis Historia* (XVI, 95), with its description of the great learning of the Druids is also cited. This may now seem an incredible claim, but Prise's contemporaries would not have thought so: it was just one of the many strange ideas that were aired when linguistic matters were discussed. John Dee, for example, abandoned his position as England's most promising mathematician to search for the Adamic language and to indulge in other dubious activities, not least astrology.

Another linguistic theory then current was that Welsh (Cymraeg) was 'Cam-Groeg', that is 'errant Greek', and in the margins of Bede's *De natura rerum* Prise noted the similarity between the word 'galw' (to call) and the Greek καλω.[17]

Having rejected the extreme choice of using Greek letters, Prise also ignored more mainstream innovations that were common in England and settled on an orthography that was both cautious and conservative.

Astrology, maths and doctrine

The book proper starts with a calendar, Januarius-December (Ionawr-Rhagfyr), with saints' days (Welsh and 'European') and other significant religious festivals noted appropriately.

At the bottom of each page there is advice for farmers, varying in length from three to eight lines, on jobs to be done that month. The source of the advice seems to be Prise himself. What is very notable is how deeply embedded astrology was, despite its pagan origins, in the Christian mind-set. Each month is given its zodiacal sign, for example on 10 February it is recorded that the sun is in Pisces ('Yr haul yn y pysc'), and the advice is accompanied by the most propitious time to sow according to the moon, such as 'yn y lhawnlhoer' (in the full moon) or 'oddyvewn pedwar nywarnod y ddiwedd y lheyad' (within four days of the end of the moon).

There is an almanac for twenty years, starting 1547, and the rule for calculating Easter 'forever'. Prise explains the length of the year, 365 and a quarter days, and the phenomenon of the leap year. The orbit of the moon is given as 27 days 8 hours and the movement of the sun [*sic*] and the moon through the zodiac is also explained.

To complete this part of the book Prise sets out a table of the numbers so that readers can record the year. He names them and gives them their Roman and Arabic symbols, accompanying the latter with an explanation of 0 and of place value. This is noteworthy, as Arabic numbers had only recently appeared in print in England (in Robert Recorde's *The Grounde of Artes*, 1543). It may point to Prise and Salesbury being colleagues of Recorde, a fellow Welshman.

After these secular pages, which give valuable insights into the workings of the mind of a well-educated Tudor gentleman, come those in which the beliefs of Henry's new church are stated.

There are no surprises in these pages. (Any deviation from the King's beliefs would have had unfortunate consequences for Prise; in the last months of his life Henry's temper was at its most volatile.) They consist of the Credo, the Lord's Prayer, the Ten Commandments,[18] the Seven Sacraments, the virtues to be practised and the vices to be shunned and are set out by a loyal servant with a well-trained legal mind who ensures that everything is in order, in both senses of the word.

Significantly these pages contain the first printed translations of the scriptures into Welsh. There is nothing that did not exist in manuscript form and even the most hardline Catholics had not opposed vernacular versions of the Ten Commandments and the Lord's Prayer, but the symbolism is immense. Just ten years earlier Tyndale had been executed for translating the Bible into English; now, here, for the first time and with the King's blessing, the Welsh people could read the Bible's most sacred words printed in their own language.

The great paradox is that in taking active steps to achieve religious uniformity between the two lands, Henry was granting official and cultural status to the prime cause of that lack of uniformity, the Welsh language.

Historians of theology may wish to pore over the words for small but significant shifts in belief (some commentators suggest that Henry was inching towards Protestantism during his last days), but for the general reader the book's significance is that it marks Wales's entry into the modern world.

For that achievement Prise deserves recognition and praise, but it is important to realise his limitations and those of the book he produced. *Yny lhyvyr hwnn* is significant in its own right, but leads nowhere.

For his translations Prise did not use Erasmus's Greek New Testament, but relied on existing translations from the Latin that could be found in Welsh manuscripts such as *Gwassanaeth Meir*.[19]

It does not carry an impulse for further works in Welsh and Prise had no such plans. He had adopted the trappings of Humanism; the acquisition of Greek, the use of italic handwriting and the Italian spelling of Latin, 'quum' for 'cum', for example. His championing of Arabic numbers was remarkable, but apart from the last point, there is nothing in *Yny lhyvyr hwnn* that is innovative. As noted, it is a cautious and conservative book, though that is partly due to the nature of the task Prise had undertaken. Having rejected the extreme option of using the Greek alphabet, his orthography is that of the late Middle Ages, the only changes being those necessitated by the process of printing. There is no hint of the Latinisation of spelling and vocabulary that was taking place in England.

If Prise really was steeped in Humanism, he lacked the leap of imagination to introduce its benefits into his own culture. His two great passions were collecting manuscripts and defending Geoffrey of Monmouth. In matters of religion he had a flexible conscience. He was Catholic but anti-papal under Henry, Protestant under Edward VI, then about-turned and produced a report on coinage for Mary, who returned England to the Roman fold.

Yny lhyvyr hwnn is a unique and isolated work, a judgement that in no way should diminish it, but if Welsh was to take its place in the company of the powerful vernacular languages of Europe it needed someone possessed, just as Tyndale was, of a deep and unwavering religious conviction and whose eye was ever focused on the latest developments in international learning, not on the acquisition of Anglo-Saxon manuscripts.

Chapter Nine

A dictionary

Court politics; anxiety and haste

A Dictionary in Englyshe and Welshe was printed in January 1547. It opens with a dedication to the King which combines fulsome praise, gratitude for the Act of Union and the case for the two peoples of the kingdom being able to speak to each other in a shared language:

> Where as emongeste other sondrye and manifolde good and godlye ordinaunces bothe mooste wyselye inuestede and mooste effectuously performede and put in use by your grace moste noble and Redoubtede Prynce
>
> —
>
> your excellent wysdome (as you haue an eye to euery parte and membre of your Dominion) hath causede to be enactede and stablyshede by your moste cheffe and highest counsayl of the parlyament, that there shal herafter be no difference in lawes and language bytwyxte youre subiectes of youre principalytye of Wales and your other subiectes of your Royalme of Englande
>
> —
>
> it is moost conueniente and mete that they be[ing] under dominion of one most gracious Hedde and Kynge shal use also one language and that euen as theyr hertes agree in loue and obedience to your grace so may also theyr tongues agree in one kynd of speche and language…

Henry died on the 28th of that month, which means that it is likely that the dictionary's pages were coming off the press as the King lay dying and that it was being collated and bound as the funeral preparations were being made.

The privilege[1] for printing, as opposed to the general approval granted in 1544, was signed on 13 December 1546. Salesbury must have had real concern that the project to which he had dedicated the previous two years would come to nothing. The first fear was that the King would die before the book appeared in print and that the new regime (no one could know who would hold power) would cancel the permission. The second was that the King himself would change his mind and that Salesbury's best laid plans would come to naught.

In those last months, Henry was a wreck of a man; in constant pain, his body bloated, his legs heavily ulcerated and suppurating. Yet he had never been so volatile and vindictive. He came close to having his last wife executed, but fortunately Catherine Parr's direct appeal and statement of loyalty was met with a volte-face and warm expressions of his love and trust. Others were not so fortunate: the duke of Norfolk and his son, the earl of Surrey, were arrested and sentenced to death (he believed they were plotting to murder his son). Surrey's execution was carried out on 19 January. Norfolk's was scheduled for the 29th: Henry's death brought about his reprieve.

Whoever approached the King for his signature on 13 December would have needed wisdom and diplomacy and to have mastered the art of timing. Fortunately for Salesbury, the courtier responsible was blessed either with good judgement or good fortune and the privilege was granted.

The atmosphere at court was poisonous. With the King's death imminent, all manner of scheming and subterfuge was taking place to gain positions of authority to influence Henry's plans for the succession and to win a place on the council that would be established to guide his nine-year-old son and heir. The manoeuvring was not just between individuals and factions but between the two religious camps and at times it was murderous.

The reformers had been gaining ground at court. Cranmer, archbishop of Canterbury, had discreetly done all he could to move religious thought towards Protestantism, Prince Edward had been tutored predominantly by reformist scholars, such as Roger Ascham and William Grindall, and Queen Catherine's sympathies also lay in that direction. She had published a well-received book, *Prayers Stirring the Mind unto Heavenly Meditation* in which she prudently avoided aligning herself with the new religion, but that did not deter her enemies.[2]

There was a whispering campaign against the Queen, orchestrated by Stephen Gardiner, bishop of Winchester, and Lord Wriothesley, the Lord Chancellor, questioning her loyalty to the King, which led to a warrant for her arrest being issued, but Wriothesley and his ally Rich, Salesbury's employer, motivated by religion and personal ambition, were prepared to use methods more deadly than whispers.

Working in alliance with Edmund Bonner, bishop of London, and the duke of Norfolk, they arrested Anne Askew, a twenty-five-year-old apostle of the new religion, and ordered her to be tortured, expecting to extract a confession that she had conspired with the Queen[3] and others at court, such as Cranmer and Anne Parr, the Queen's sister and Herbert's wife, in spreading the doctrines of Protestantism. When the Constable of the Tower, Sir Anthony Kingston, refused to continue the torture, Rich and Wriothesley took up the task themselves.

Askew's body was broken, but not her spirit. The Queen was not betrayed. Anne died in the flames, a Protestant heroine. The following year, 1547, John Bale published her account of the torture and the beliefs for which she had died and Foxe included her in his *Actes and Monumentes*.

The intrigue and uncertainty bred anxiety. Salesbury was right to fear that a new regime would not sanction his dictionary, even though it was a totally secular work.

The greatest potential threat was Stephen Gardiner. For hardline defenders of the Catholic Church, the use and promotion of vernacular languages had now become anathema. In 1559 Erasmus's books would be placed on the Vatican's *Index Librorum Prohibitorum*, but already anything that carried the taint of his influence, even something secular, was treated with suspicion. This may explain why, as chancellor of Cambridge University, Gardiner had quashed new ideas on Greek pronunciation put forward by John Cheke and Sir Thomas Smith. During Philip and Mary's entry into London in July 1554 he noticed that one of the tableaux painted in celebration of the Tudor dynasty contained an image of Henry VIII holding a copy of the English Bible. Gardiner was apoplectic with rage and an artist was summoned to replace the Bible with a pair of gloves.[4]

Innovation and analysis

Fears that reactionaries such as Gardiner would be in charge of the land may account for what can be interpreted as signs that Salesbury rushed his dictionary through the last stages of production; for example, some of the English entries have been omitted, there are occasional errors in alphabetical order and two of the seven arts (Rhetoric and Logic) are missing.[5]

However, these minor blemishes may be partly explained by the hugely ambitious challenge that Salesbury had set himself. Apart from Palsgrave's *Lesclarcissement* and Thomas Elyot's *Latin Dictionary* of 1538, few works of this complexity would be attempted in Tudor or Jacobean England. Robert and Thomas Cowdray's *A Table Alphabeticall* (1604) had just 2,543 entries and Richard Mulcaster's list of words in *First Part of the Elementarie* (1582) had no definitions.

The book was printed in black letter by John Whaley,[6] with whom Salesbury had a seven-year licence, which was in effect a protection against pirated copies of any books they published.

Several academics[7] have commented on the title, *A Dictionary in Englyshe and Welshe*, not reflecting the order in which the words are presented: the Welsh words appear in the first and third columns of each page, with their English equivalents alongside them. It might not have occurred to Salesbury or his contemporaries that his description of the work should reflect the order in which the words occur. These were the pioneering days of a new linguistic phenomenon. The word 'dictionary' had appeared in print for the first time just nine years previously. Palsgrave had talked of 'vocabulysts' or 'vocabulers' and the word in common usage was 'calepin' after the word list in Latin and several other languages compiled by Ambrogio Calepino in 1502.

After the dedication to the King, the language changes to Welsh. There is an address to the reader, 'Wyllyam Salesburi wrth y darlleawdr' (William Salesbury to the reader), followed by a series of notes to help his countrymen acquire English, 'Athrawaeth i ddyscy darllen Saesnaec' (Doctrine for learning to read English).

As a champion of the Welsh language, why was Salesbury promoting the learning of English? It is important to remember that he was a lover of all languages and of learning. He would never have seen a cultural conflict between Welsh and English and later he would encourage the English, with some success, to learn Welsh. More importantly, the Bible was now available in English. Just like Tyndale, he wanted everyone to have access to it and at that time the easiest way for his countrymen to gain that access was by learning the language of their neighbours. Also, areas of learning which previously could have been studied only in Latin were now being opened up to dissemination through the medium of English, another reason to know the language.

Salesbury urges his readers to find English-speaking people 'for there is hardly a parish in Wales without some Englishmen in it' (tr.) to practise with and to listen to intently.

The notes on English and its pronunciation are excellent, with a depth of analysis that would have delighted Erasmus and Palsgrave. In fact they are so thorough that they have twice been reprinted for students of linguistics: in the nineteenth century in *On Early English Pronunciation* by Alexander John Ellis (with an English translation provided) and in the twentieth by the Scolar Press (in this case the complete dictionary).

Salesbury's analysis was also an important resource for E. J. Dobson's *English Pronunciation, 1500–1700.* His dictionary does not surpass the achievement of Palsgrave's *Lesclarcissement*, but in one narrow field, the pronunciation of English, Dobson comments that, 'An even more valuable description of English [than Palsgrave's] is in William Salesbury's *Dictionary in Englyshe and Welshe.*'

Before starting the notes, Salesbury explains the concept and use of alphabetical order, something novel to a nation with no prior knowledge of printed books and still a relatively new phenomenon in England: Palsgrave had been the first to use alphabetical ordering for the complete word, the previous practice had been for the first three letters only.

He then explains the English alphabet, with the values of letters in both languages compared, with all variations and combinations given, along with several examples of each. Letters absent in the Welsh alphabet, such as 'q' and 'x' are explained and he warns his readers that 'll', 'dd' and ch', which are separate letters in Welsh, are not to be treated as such in English.

He notes how in some parts of England 'l/ll' is pronounced as 'w', so that 'bold' becomes 'bowd', 'bull' 'boow' (which he writes in Welsh as 'bw').

Amongst other phenomena noted, invaluable to linguists such as Ellis and Dobson, are that words ending in '-old' and '-oll' are pronounced 'ow': 'cold' ('cowld'), 'toll' ('towl').

'Double o' words, such as 'good' and 'poor' are sounded with the long 'oo' as in 'zoo' and he warns that 'th' is sometimes sounded as a 't' as in 'Thomas', but also in 'throne'. (Interestingly, in *Hebrews, 12,* Tyndale uses 'trone'.)

The most vivid description of all is that of 'sh', which 'sometimes hisses like a snake, but to get the full feel of its pronunciation one should listen to the sound a shellfish makes when it is being boiled in water.' (tr.)

Copiousness and loan words

Apart from the acuteness of his observations what is most striking about Salesbury's prose is his style. The Renaissance influence is shown by the way his letter to Henry balances his praise for the King with the trope of modesty whenever he refers to himself. Also present, as can be seen in the extract quoted at the start of the chapter, is Erasmus's 'copiousness'.

It is there, too, in his address to the reader. Salesbury does not use one word when two will do. There is a multitude of phrases that consist of a pairing of synonyms, 'yngan a sonio', 'dangos a datclario', 'pa vudd a phwy broffit', 'order a threfyn'. They are reminiscent of Anglo-Saxon / Norman French pairings used in English legal phraseology, 'breaking and entering', 'aiding and abetting', and apart from the first example, he has to use or introduce loan words to formulate them.

Salesbury had come from a culture that was rich in poetry, but less fortunate in its reserves of prose. For a millennium the nation's creativity had been largely channelled into verse. There were the eleven surviving stories of the *Mabinogi*, but though the imagery can be striking (for example a woman made of flowers transformed into an owl), the language in which they are expressed tends to be simple and unadorned. Copies had survived of the chronicles of the princes and the lives of the saints and there were relatively recent examples of prose in the form of legal manuscripts that dated from after the Glyndŵr era. Salesbury would have been familiar with them, but to a disciple of Erasmus and Cicero, they would not have been seen as worthy examples of style to follow, but as a resource from which useful words and phrases could be extracted.

Salesbury's education had been through Latin, his conversation with Humanist intellectuals had taken place in Oxford and London and had been conducted either in Latin or English. The printed vernacular books that he read were overwhelmingly in English. He had no such wealth of native models to follow. If Salesbury's first foray into writing seems a little forced and clumsy and lacks the richness of vocabulary so evident in his dedication to the King, it is because it was the first time anyone had tried to forge a Welsh prose style worthy of the age of Humanism. His use of words derived directly from English was a necessity, but also a deliberate choice. He had seen how English had greatly expanded its lexicon by importing huge numbers of new terms from Latin and other languages. By doing the same in Welsh he could develop the language's 'copiousness'.

Palsgrave, an influence and a resource

The dictionary that follows is made up of 141 pages with approximately fifty to fifty-five Welsh words per page. Occasionally, as mentioned previously, the English entry or definition is missing. Nouns, adjectives and verbs are not distinguished. No doubt Salesbury assumed that his readers knew from the Welsh that, for example, 'Addfed' ('Rype') was the adjective and 'Addfedy' ('Rype') was the verb.

After such initial observations the question arises as to the method and reasoning behind the choice of entries. The answer was provided by W. Alun Mathias, the twentieth century's leading authority on Salesbury. In an essay[8] published in 1989 he reveals that Palsgrave was not just an influence and a role model but had been of great practical benefit. Salesbury had taken the 'vocabulysts' of *Lesclarcissement* as the basis of his own work, selecting from them the words he wanted in his dictionary.

(There are terms that originate with Salesbury rather than Palsgrave, including some that reflect a personal interest or concern, but approximately two thirds of the words, according to Mathias, are derived from *Lesclarcissement*.)

Salesbury did not acknowledge his debt to Palsgrave in print, but it was a very understandable and very necessary short-cut to ensure completing a project that demanded so many man-hours. There is no evidence and no reason to assume that he had any help during the two to three years needed to complete the work. (In contrast, Johnson's dictionary took nine years to complete, but with the help of six clerks and a wealth of printed material, books, newspapers and broadsheets, at his disposal.)[9]

Curiously, having saved a great deal of time and work through using Palsgrave, Salesbury then creates more work. Having found the Welsh equivalents of the English words, he set himself the mammoth task of placing all those Welsh words in their alphabetical order. He clearly thought it important that the Welsh word appeared first, possibly because he thought it the more effective way for the Welsh to seek out English vocabulary or it could have been a matter of linguistic pride.

How were those Welsh words chosen? Palsgrave had English and French books from which to collect his vocabulary, but whilst Salesbury was compiling the dictionary there was no printed material in Welsh.

A possible answer is provided by the nature of the words he used. The casual reader is soon struck by the number of words of English origin, such as, 'Battel', 'Ffridwm', 'Hair', 'Mockio' and 'Nasiwn', which are listed along with their (pure Welsh) synonyms, 'Kad' (battle), 'Ryddit' (liberty/freedom), 'Gwallt' (hair), 'Gwatwor' (to mock) and 'Gwlad' (land).

There are 'an astonishing number of borrowings'.[10] Commentators have attributed this to Salesbury's dependence on Palsgrave and this theory will be discussed later in the chapter. However, the fact that there was no printed material in Welsh at that time suggests another possibility. The one substantial source of manuscript material at Salesbury's disposal consisted largely of poetry, the sort of collection that a gentleman of his station would have accrued and inherited. These poems, especially those of the fourteenth and fifteenth centuries would have contained loan words. Could this be the reason for the high 'English' content in the dictionary?

At first this would seem a highly illogical suggestion and the idea that the bards used English words would seem counter-intuitive. They saw themselves as the custodians of the language and its literature, were deeply conservative and some, most notably Guto'r Glyn, were anti-English. It is as if the members of L'Académie française were pursuing a campaign of flooding their language with words such as 'le pub', 'le weekend' and 'les blue-jeans'.

Although individual poems from the fifteenth and early sixteenth century may contain no more than four or five loan words per poem, the quantity of poetry produced means that this soon builds to a large number.

Formal poetry was written in strict metre, *cynghanedd*. Its principles are simple,[11] the pattern of consonants of the first part of the line is repeated in the second. What makes it more complicated is the number of variations of patterns (some include rhyme) and the exceptions and special cases that are permitted.

Here is an English example, written by Gerard Manley Hopkins:[12]

'Warm-laid grave of a womb-life grey.'

The w–m–l of the first part is repeated in the second. Hopkins also repeats the g–r, but this would not be counted as the 'd' of 'laid' and the 'f' of 'life' have disrupted the pattern.

Here are examples from the bards:

'Llew ac amrel holl Gymru'
(ll–g*–m–r repeated) (* 'ac' is sounded as 'ag')

'Carliaid a wnaeth y curlaw'
(c–r–l repeated)

'Ar ddannedd y Nordd unwaith'
(r–dd–n repeated)

'Doed aliwns, nis didolir'
(d–d–l repeated)

In each of these lines the bards (Hywel Swrdwal and Guto'r Glyn, both fifteenth century)[13] have used an English loan word 'amrel' (admiral), 'carliaid' (carls), 'nordd' (north) and 'aliwns' (aliens) to achieve *cynghanedd*.[14]

All four words are in the dictionary.

Many of the fifteenth-century bards could not speak English or did so imperfectly, but the gentry they served could and, with the decline of the Welsh courts, were often making use of English for contracts, agreements and other official or semi-official documents. Despite the prohibitions put on the Welsh, a few individuals played major roles in the violent dynastic struggles of England, most notably William Herbert (ancestor of Catherine Parr's brother-in-law) who, until his execution[15] in 1469, was a key player in English politics. Many bards, amongst them Guto'r Glyn, Hywel Swrdwal and Lewis Glyn Cothi, enjoyed the hospitality of Raglan Castle, Herbert's stronghold, and would have heard the foreign terms of real-politik and government that were entering the language. Being able to use these new words would make their work easier and many seized the opportunity.

Is that the reason for the high English content of the dictionary? Possibly, but two other explanations present themselves, which may be more convincing. It would have pleased Salesbury that there were precedents amongst the bards' works for many of the English terms he used, but the chief reason for their appearance is likely to have been speed. The kingdom was in a state of great anxiety as to who would be the effective ruler or rulers after the King's death. It was vital that the dictionary was printed before the new regime, whatever its complexion, took power. If that had not been achieved, there was every chance it might never have appeared. In the rush to produce the work, in many instances Salesbury took the quickest and easiest option and reproduced the word used by Palsgrave in a slightly altered, Cymricised form.

However, even in a state of anxiety and under tremendous pressure, Salesbury was a lover and respecter of language. There was often another reason for using a borrowed term. A synonym might come close to the meaning of a particular word, but it would not be the exact equivalent or have the same layers of nuance. 'Gwlad', for example, means 'land', which is not the same as the concept of 'nation'. By introducing the word 'nasiwn' Salesbury was also introducing the concept into Welsh.

English has adopted and naturalised foreign words for so many centuries that they go un-noticed. Many English speakers would not recognise the Norman French origin of 'nation', but the word stands out in Welsh. This did not seem to concern Salesbury or, if it did, not sufficiently to change his course of action. One reason for this was that the practice was so established in English, a language whose energy, vibrancy and power he admired, that in all likelihood he wished to introduce it into Welsh. Another is that, as a disciple of Erasmus and his concept of *copia*, this was an easy and quick method of expanding the lexicon.

For example, an analysis of the entries under the letter 'A' reveals that the words that lack definitions tend to be 'pure' Welsh: Achub, Adec, Amlwc, Angerdd, Arlloes, Ascyrnyc. The only loan words under 'A' to go undefined are 'Acolit' (acolyte) and 'Arcolidaeth' (undefined, but easily recognised as the noun formed from 'Acolit'). In contrast, words such as 'Act', 'Aliwn', 'Ambyr', 'Argument', 'Arithmetik', 'Astronomi' and 'Awditor' are given their meaning in Welsh. This would seem to support the argument that it was dependence on Palsgrave (because of the urgency in getting the dictionary printed) that explains the phenomenon of so many loan words.

Another feature of the dictionary is that there are errors in the alphabetical order; not gross errors, such as a 'D' word appearing under 'G', but 'Edyn' ('A foule') following immediately after 'Edlaes' (not defined (it means slack)) and before 'Ednogyn' ('A gnatte'). This may be explained by the rushed nature of the printing or it may reflect Salesbury's inability to resist the temptation to add new words even as a page was being set up.

A word trove

Despite the minor blemishes brought about by the manner of its production and the sheer enormity of the task he had set himself, the dictionary is a word-lover's paradise. There is a multitude of examples of how both languages have subtly changed over the centuries as well as insights into the life and thinking of the sixteenth century.

'Nigh' is preferred to 'near', 'swift' to 'fast', 'spinner' to 'spider', 'osell' to 'blackbird'. In Welsh 'Klod' is given as 'fame', but most people today would think of it as 'praise', 'Klymy' as 'knit', but 'tie' is its more modern meaning.

Vowel shifts are also there 'Uchneidio' (to sigh) has become 'ochneidio' and the English word 'barn' is recorded as 'bern'. Every casual visit to the work is rewarded with an insight into language. It is one of the few books in which serendipity is guaranteed.

On a personal level the dictionary is the closest we can come to glimpsing something of Salesbury's character, interests and those who had shaped his thinking.

His interests were wide ranging, as is to be expected of an antiquary and man of letters. He includes the word 'Breuan' (quern)[16] and in 1632 John Davies included that term in his Latin/Welsh dictionary, recording that Salesbury had one on display in his house. There are astronomic terms, 'Satwrnws' (Saturn), 'Kaer Gwdion' (Milky Way)[17] and the Welsh forms of the names of classical writers such as Homer and Cato are given.

As already seen in his notes, he is a meticulous recorder of language. When there are similar versions of a word in use, 'Haern'/ 'Hayarn' (iron), 'Saimlud'/ 'Seimlud' (greasy), he records both rather than appoint himself as a linguistic arbiter. (There is, though, the suspicion that this might have been a way of promoting copiousness, that the hope was that two forms might develop into two distinct, though related, meanings.)

Salesbury has shown himself to be bold, in taking on the powerful vested interests of the Price clan, and innovative, in presenting the King with his proposals for a dictionary. The finished product, however, may show a more cautious side to his nature. Amongst the non-partisan religious words (Christmas, Easter) are those that are closely associated with Catholicism, the saints' days, 'Yscrin' (shrine) and 'Trental' (the mass said daily for thirty days). Was this the caution of someone aware of the dangers of showing religious allegiance at a time when the political situation could change overnight with deadly consequences or was it the policy of a dedicated lexicographer who would not let his beliefs interfere with his professional duty?

Enforced speed results in Salesbury not being as ordered as one would have expected under normal circumstances. There are no distinct groupings of related subjects, for example the planets, the seven arts, the humours. Where such groupings occur, as with the days of the week or the months of the year, it is fortuitous: their alphabetical order has thrown them together.

The interest that shines out most obviously from the dictionary is that of botany. There are over fifty entries for plants and while some are there as general items or foods (oak, rose, strawberry), the bulk are there for their medicinal properties. Most of the botanical entries, such as 'Llydan y ffordd' (plantain), 'Gwyddwydd' (honeysuckle) and 'Suran yr yd' (sorrel) appear in his herbal, the preoccupation of his final years.

Of course, before John Whaley the printer could start setting up the first block of type, he had to receive his instructions from Salesbury on which letters were to be used. The two men faced the same problems as those that Prise and Whitchurch had encountered. There is one key similarity. Salesbury might have wished to use 'k' throughout but, like Prise, was forced to introduce 'c'. (There are forty-one columns of 'k' words, just two starting with 'c'.)

There are several differences, however. 'Ll' and 'dd' are used rather than 'lh' and 'δ' and 'f' is used for 'v'. 'Ff' is used throughout the dictionary, but in the 'ff' section of the dictionary the initial letter is given as 'f'. Similarly, 'rh' appears within words ('Anrhec', present), but is reduced to 'r' at the beginning. No doubt Whaley had an insufficient supply of 'f's and 'h's. The slightly varying approaches used by the two authors may not be down to differences in philosophy but to causes as prosaic as their respective printers' stock of letters and flexibility.

Salesbury the Latinist

In orthography, however, there was a distinct difference in philosophy. Whilst Prise considered and then rejected the use of Greek letters, Salesbury did not hesitate to introduce Latin spelling into Welsh. He was much more a child of Humanism than his colleague. He was steeped in it and his love of language, all languages, was great. In his letter to the reader he had been full of his praise for English, 'a language that is today honoured by every kind of learning, a language full of talent and grandeur.' (tr.)

In a book of 1550 he again sang the praises of English, 'most expediente, and most worthiest to be learned, studied and enhaunced... even for the attaynement of knowledge in Gods word, and other liberall sciences whyche... be communely hadde and sette forth in the said English tongue.'[18]

He could see the English language gaining strength from other languages, adopting the sonnet form and blank verse from Italy,[19] increasing its lexicon by absorbing vocabulary from a host of languages but overwhelmingly from Latin, all of which meant that it could now be used for any field of enquiry.

Could he foresee the time when an aristocrat like Sidney whilst staying at Wilton, or grammar-school lads like Shakespeare and Marlowe, lodging in Southwark and Deptford, had an armoury of imported and manufactured words and learning that, coupled with native wit and liveliness, enabled the

English language to flourish as never before? Or was it looking at English from the perspective of Welsh that gave Salesbury his insight? There were no cosmopolitan influences on Welsh, no borrowing of forms from Italy, no great (contemporary) influx of words from Latin. At a time when native commentators felt that English was a plain, humble language unworthy of great works of literature and in need of even more adornment and expansion of its vocabulary, Salesbury could see just how vibrant it was and how great was its potential. With that evaluation of English it would have been inconsistent of him not to have wanted exactly the same developments for Welsh.

Great changes were taking place in English spelling, driven by the influence of many scholars, but most of all of Thomas Elyot, who had introduced words such as 'participate', 'persist' and 'maturity'. 'Dout' became 'doubt' to show its Latin root, 'dubito', 'dette' became 'debt' (debitum) and 'parffet' 'perfect' (perfectum).

'Habit', 'debit', 'study' and 'literal' have single letters, signifying their Latin origins, whereas 'rabbit', 'muddy', 'ballad' and 'litter' are English and double-lettered .

Latinisation waxed ever stronger: anchor, advance, advantage, adventure, advice, falcon, fault, island, receipt, scissors and vault all had their spellings changed by the addition of the letters underlined.

Nor was the Latin trend confined to spelling. Hundreds of 'new' words were being added to the vocabulary: 'dismiss', 'celebrate', 'commit', 'capacity', 'ingenious'.

These changes to English were resented and opposed by many. They dismissed the innovations as 'Inkhorn' terms and the leading opponent of the trend, John Cheke (a reforming voice in Greek), coined many 'English' terms to counter the modish new entries, 'hundreder' for 'centurion', 'mooned' for 'lunatic'.[20]

The debate raged for decades, but it was the 'Inkhorns' who had the tide of history on their side and who triumphed. Latin was still dominating the language of intellectual life two centuries later. When Dr Johnson gave Boswell his opinion on a play in plain English, 'It hath not wit enough to keep it sweet', he checked himself and revised his remark to, 'It has not vitality enough to preserve it from putrefaction.'[21]

The number of Latinised words that Salesbury introduced was very small, less than a dozen in all.[22] For example, colomen (dove) becomes 'Colomben' (Latin, columba), pobl (people) is 'Popol' (populus).

It is possible that a contemporary user of the dictionary who was not familiar with Latin might have thought that these words were misprints or a variant form from another part of the country (without a capital, university or royal family Welsh was a very atomised language). However, one Latinised word appeared frequently as a heading (roughly once in every three pages) and could not be dismissed as an error. That word was 'Kamberaec' (Welsh). The usual form, used by Prise, is 'Kymraeg'.[23] This, too, is used as a heading by Salesbury, as is 'Camraec'.

In the other examples of Latinisation Salesbury has taken words genuinely derived from Latin and modified them slightly to emphasise their roots. It would have been a matter of pride that whilst England was having to import Latin into its language, there was already a significant element in Welsh dating from the Roman occupation ('canu', 'ffenestr', 'mur', 'pont'), and augmented by further naturalisations from ecclesiastical Latin and, indirectly, from Norman French. The Humanists revered the three classical languages: to have one making up a significant part of your language's vocabulary gave it great kudos.

However, with 'Kamberaec' Salesbury is imposing a Latin root (Cambria) on a word that does not have one. He may also be referring to Geoffrey of Monmouth's Kamber, a son of Brutus the Trojan and the founder of Wales.

There are no surviving records of contemporary reaction to the dictionary. Salesbury's Latinised spellings would play a major role in criticism of his future work, but at this stage the instances of its use, apart from 'Kamberaec' are so few as to make them barely noticeable.

A personal note

The dictionary is a hugely valuable document for lovers of both languages and a great academic and practical achievement. Great use was made of it in John Davies's Welsh/Latin dictionary, *Dictionarium Duplex*, of 1632, which superseded Salesbury's as the dictionary for the educated classes and in later dictionaries including *Y Geiriadur Mawr* of 1958. It was reprinted in 1877 by the Honourable Society of Cymmrodorion. Fourteen copies[24] of *A Dictionary in Englyshe and Welshe* survive, housed in collections as diverse as the National Library of Wales, the British Library, the Bodleian and the Folger. The most famous copy is the one that was owned by Dr John Dee, which is in Trinity College, Dublin. Dee's annotations can be found in the margins.

Salesbury had provided a dictionary for a land without a university, printing press or bookshop and done so sixty-five years before Italy, home of the Renaissance, got its first vernacular dictionary and two centuries before Johnson's celebrated work was published.

Johnson, of course, is noted for his many colourful definitions:

Oats: 'A grain, which in England is generally given to horses, but in Scotland appears to support the people.'
Patron: 'Commonly a wretch who supports with insolence, and is paid with flattery.'

In contrast Salesbury's definitions are brief, factual and impersonal, with one famous exception,

'Wynwyn' (onion) carries the following entry:

'A vegetable that women put next to their eyes to induce crying when their husbands die.' (tr.)

This is not a casual verbal slip that betrays what is now perceived as the misogyny of the age. It is heartfelt, deeply personal and very pointed. The sentence could have been drafted at any time in the previous two years, but Salesbury had had over two months to edit it from the dictionary whilst it was being printed. Perhaps he had, temporarily, but its appearance here means that any reconciliation between husband and wife had been brief. The appeal by Elis and Cadwaladr Price for him to take Catrin back would be ignored.[25]

The arbitration settlement had not brought about peace and reconciliation. The bitter legal wrangles would continue and Price had a further blow to deliver, literally.

Chapter Ten

Proverbs, hope and further conflict

A new work

Shortly after the appearance of his dictionary Salesbury published his second book, *Oll Synnwyr pen Kembero ygyd* [All the Wisdom of a Welshman's Head], a collection of over nine hundred proverbs inspired by Erasmus's *Adagia*. (It is generally referred to as *Oll Synnwyr*.)

Salesbury was not the book's author, nor did he claim to be. The title page courteously acknowledges it as the work of his friend, Gruffudd Hiraethog:

Oll

Synnwyr

pen

Kembero

ygyd/

Wedy r gynnull, ei gynnwys ae

gyfansoddi mewn crynodab ddos-

parthus a threfn odidawc drwy

ddyval ystryw

Gruffyd Hi-

raethoc prydydd o wy-

nedd

Is Conwy.

[All the sense of a Welshman's head, collected and its contents established in an orderly compendium and excellent arrangement through the diligent stratagem of Gruffudd Hiraethog poet of Gwynedd Is Conwy.]

The book,[1] which uses Small Pica for the preface and 'English' for the proverbs, with occasional use of an italic-like type for headings and contrast, was 'imprynted at London in Saynt Iohns Strete, by Nycholas Hyll.'[2] Whaley's being replaced by Hill is unlikely to be significant. Printers were very supportive of one another and when overstretched, would farm out work to a colleague. The change of printer suggests that this was a work that was rushed into publication (and so Whaley was unavailable). Salesbury's preface, examined later in the chapter, supports this theory. Hill's later work for the campaigning Protestant printer, William Seres, may well indicate that Salesbury was already moving in radical circles.

As with *Yny lhyvyr hwnn*, there is one surviving copy. Neither author nor printer dated the book. It could have appeared at any time from 1547 to 1550, but an analysis of its contents and other documents points to the summer of 1547 as its most likely date of publication.[3]

Salesbury opens with an eleven-page address to the reader, which is followed by fifty-one pages of adages, with an average of nineteen per page.

This is Gruffudd Hiraethog's collection and Salesbury rightly praises him for the work he has done, but there is no doubt that without Salesbury it would never have appeared in print and the scholarship involved might well have been lost. Though Gruffudd was something of an exception in his openness to Humanism and other influences, the bards showed little interest in the printing press, which they are likely to have viewed with some hostility as a threat to their role as copyists.

Nicholas Hill's use of letters to convey the Welsh sounds is similar to Whaley's. Those proverbs that start with 'k' keep the letter, but elsewhere 'c' is brought in to augment the supply of 'k's. 'Rh' is replaced by 'R' when it is the initial letter of an adage: elsewhere 'rh' is used just nine times, outnumbered by 'r' and 'rr'. 'Ff' is replaced by 'F' at the start of a proverb, elsewhere it is 'ff', but often appears as 'f'.

(It is impossible to tell whether Salesbury used 'rr' and 'r' for 'rh' in response to a request from Hill, who might have been concerned that his stock of aitches was insufficient, or if the idea was his. There are examples of 'rr' for 'rh' being used in manuscripts and documents at this time.[4] In adapting Welsh to meet the demands of the press, Salesbury was facing problems similar to those encountered by Caxton and Pynson fifty or sixty years previously. Whatever the explanation, the practice was not repeated in later works.)

It is interesting that there is the same indifference to consistency of spelling as there is in English books of that time. 'Nid' (not) appears as 'nid', 'nit', 'nyd' and 'nyt', just as Tyndale spelt 'it' as 'it', 'hit', 'yt' and 'hyt' within the space of two pages. The responsibility for this is Salesbury's, not Gruffudd's.

The collection finishes with a couplet:

'Yspys y dengys y dyn,
O ba radd y bo i wreiddyn.'

[prose translation, 'A man reveals to all the
social level into which he was born.']

which comes from a poem by Tudur Aled.[5]

Whilst the lover of words is enthralled by the dictionary, the proverbs are more of a mild amusement. There are those still in use:

'I'r pant y red y dwfyr.'
[Water runs to the hollow: i.e. wealth/success always goes to the same people.]

'Iro blonhogen.'
[Greasing fat: i.e. wasting one's time/effort.]

Some that are incomprehensible or bizarre:

'Os gŵr mawr cawr, os gŵr bychan cor.'
[If a big man's a giant, a little man's a dwarf.]

And some that really do stand out for their wit or insight:

'Ymryson a fol ti a vyddy folach.'
[Argue with a fool and you'll be more foolish.]

But proverbs are rarely as entertaining or cutting as the aphorisms of Wilde or Voltaire. At least one had a classical origin:

'Am caro i, caret vycki.'
[Love me, love my dog.]

And there are two that come from the Bible:

'Nid prophwyt neb yn i wlat ehun.'
[No man is a prophet in his own land.]

'Pan dywyso'r dall dall arall, y ddau a ddygwydd i'r pwll.'
[When a blind man leads a blind man, they will both fall into the ditch (pit).]

There are those that are the same as or very similar to English proverbs:

'Allan o olwc, allan o veddwl.'
[Out of sight, out of mind.]

'Kau'r estabyl wedi dwyn y march.'
[Closing the stable after the horse has been taken.]

A year earlier, John Heywood, one of England's leading early playwrights, had produced the first book of English proverbs. Comparing the two collections is instructive. One of the great pleasures of reading through Heywood's is discovering adages that would be used or adapted by Shakespeare or other writers:

'All is well that endes well.'
'A proverb never stale in thrifty mind.'
(*The Merchant of Venice*, Act 3, Scene 5.)

'At six and seven.'
(*Richard II*, Act 2, Scene 2.)

'Two may keep coursed when the third's away.'
(*Titus Andronicus*, Act 4, Scene 2.)

To Salesbury's contemporaries *Oll Synnwyr* was no less interesting than Heywood's *Proverbes*. What makes the difference today and gives Heywood's adages their vibrancy, is the sheer number of novels and popular literature, good, bad, highbrow and lowbrow, produced in English compared with those in Welsh. Though there were a handful of popular novelists, such as Daniel Owen in the nineteenth century, secular works in prose tended to be looked on with suspicion until well into the twentieth century.

Oll Synnwyr, though not the product of his own pen, was a triumph for Salesbury and for Welsh Humanism, which now had its equivalent of Erasmus's *Adagia*, but a study of its accompanying letter reveals his motivation for publication and gives insights into his thoughts and hopes and a brief glimpse into his personal life.

A call to arms

Most people skim through or even ignore a book's introductory pages. *Oll Synnwyr* is one of those rare books where the interest lies in the introduction and the content is secondary. It is not the passage of time that has brought this about, it was Salesbury's intention. A unique opportunity had arisen and Salesbury needed a pretext to rush into print to take advantage of it.

The well-founded fear of a Catholic domination of the kingdom had failed to materialise, quite the opposite. The young king was determinedly Protestant; his uncle, Edward Seymour, had manoeuvred against the wishes of Henry's will and had had himself appointed Protector. Catholic bishops such as Gardiner (Winchester), Bonner (London) and Day (Chichester) were being removed from office and replaced by Protestants, and Cranmer was busy preparing a prayer book and a book of homilies that would mark a profound shift in the doctrine of the Church of England. Not only was a Protestant revolution under way but Seymour had removed many of the restrictions that had once so vigorously been applied to printing.

As the impossible happened all around him, Salesbury allowed himself to voice thoughts that just months previously would either have had him labelled as a lunatic or brought about his destruction. In 1544, the most that Salesbury could have hoped to achieve was his dictionary, a hugely ambitious project which would require royal approval and an about-turn on a key clause of the Act of Union. It would enable some of his countrymen to read the English Bible. In the summer of 1546, Salesbury's employer, Sir Richard Rich, was torturing the Protestant heroine, Anne Askew, in an attempt to link her to the Queen Consort and so bring about their downfall. It would have seemed to Salesbury that his well-concealed dream of a Welsh Bible would have to stay hidden forever.

Within months of Henry's death all that had changed. *Oll Synnwyr* is Salesbury's means of launching his campaign for the translation of the scriptures into Welsh. The urgency with which he speaks is evident not just in his tone but in the way that he forgets to use paragraphs.

Here is a précis of what he writes, accompanied by a commentary:[6]

Now in London, he recalls travelling there with Gruffudd three years before and how he 'stole' the proverbs from him and copied them. A thousand learned Welshmen will now benefit from that 'theft'.

He wishes other books could be 'stolen', so that it would be easier to understand preachers and so that preachers could more easily understand the word of God. A Welshman long exiled from his land would find it easier to translate a second language than Welsh. He appeals for God's sake, not his own, for those with Welsh books to bring them out for the good of the nation. Good books or bad bring them out, for they are of benefit.

Why let books go mouldy in a chest, especially the scriptures? The lack of the scriptures prevents the Welsh from discussing the important things of life; a language that is used just for buying and selling, eating and drinking is not suitable for translating the scriptures. Without the finer things in life we are no better than animals.

We need to know Christ's faith. Some Welsh people have no hope of learning English or another language. Without knowing God's word they will be no better than animals, so insist on the scriptures in your own language. The ancient Britons had the scriptures in Welsh, but they were then neglected and allowed to gather dust in corners.

Go barefoot on pilgrimage to the King and his council to petition for the scriptures in your own language as a substantial number of the Welsh will not be able to learn English.

Some from his country will not let him enjoy what should be his and have plundered from him. Because of this the best he can do is wish his country a good turn and pray that God sends his opponents a better spirit.

He returns to the proverbs, stating that all the credit should go to Gruffudd Hiraethog. Gruffudd is trying to perfect the language. Proverbs are the bones that hold the language together; as stars are to the sky so are proverbs to the language; they are as gems or sparks of God's wisdom.

They are the sum of a nation's language, the soul of a nation. If a proverb is difficult to understand, for whatever reason, ask the chief author [Gruffudd].

He reminds the reader how wise and educated the ancient Britons were, giving the examples of those who gathered the laws of Hywel Dda, the bards who sang englynion yr eira (the snow englyns) and Aneirin who sang englynion y misoedd (the englyns of the months).

He praises John Heywood for his collection of English proverbs, Polydore Vergil for his Latin collection and Erasmus for his Latin and Greek proverbs. (He realises that his countrymen will not like his praise for Polydore.)

Would such men have done these things if people did not benefit as a result? He mentions some of the old Welsh bards such as Merlyn Emrys, Taliesin and Merlyn[7] Wyllt and states that some of Gruffudd's verse is as good as theirs. If you agree why not thank God that there is in your lifetime someone so good at his craft to adorn the language?

Other bards cannot write as well as Gruffudd. He gives him further praise, stating that he had brought about the salvation of the language for generations to come.

Salesbury ends this page with two quotations from Cicero, 'Honos alit artes' and 'Virtus laudata crescit' (Honour sustains the arts and Virtue grows from praise).[8]

On the last page he hopes that good teaching and spiritual knowledge will grow amongst his readers. He asks that every Welshman loves his language and finishes with a (slightly adapted) couplet from Dafydd ap Gwilym:

'Cof am gariad taladwy
Ni ddyly hi y mi mwy.'[9]

[Memory of a love that's due
She has no further claim on me.]

his wish being that no educated man will say those words. (Dafydd is referring to his love for Morfudd, Salesbury's 'She' refers to the Welsh language.)

Salesbury understood the potential of the printing press at a time when no one else in Wales did. (Prise's one other venture into print would be posthumous and in Latin. A few exiles, such as Robert Recorde, would produce books, but they would be for an English audience.)

A manifesto

Salesbury, in glorious isolation, is using the power of the press to reach out to the people of a sparsely populated country whose geography made travel and communication difficult in order to influence their thinking and shape the course of events.

He is a political idealist, but he does not address those who already think as he does. He avoids the tendency of so many idealists of preaching turgidly and at length, limiting his message to eleven pages which are aimed at the hearts and minds of his audience, his fellow gentry. His words are as carefully crafted as those of a modern political strategist or advertising executive.

He uses flattery, but very discreetly. When he talks about people of education he is inviting the audience to identify themselves as such, a tactic used again with the quotation from Cicero which is accompanied by a translation, just in case the reader is not educated. Throughout the letter he is winding the reader in to a shared identity, a modern Welsh Humanism concerned for the souls of the common people.

His goal is noble – the translation of the scriptures into Welsh – but he is not above appealing to his audience's patriotism, to a shared love of their native language and he uses that powerful political weapon, nostalgia for a golden age and a desire for its return: he looks back to a time when the bards were great, when the laws of Hywel Dda were being codified and the Bible could be read in Welsh. (The last is pure myth, but one in which Salesbury had implicit faith.)

Besides a talent for propaganda and persuasion he shows political realism. He knows where power lies, with the King and his council, and that is where he directs those who take up his cause to focus their attention.

And Salesbury was practical. He understood language. For centuries the language of intellectual discourse had been Latin, which under Erasmus's influence had gained even greater powers of expression and eloquence. It was the language in which Salesbury had been educated and which had opened up the world to him.

Salesbury saw, too, the great strengthening of the English language as it absorbed new vocabulary from Latin and Greek that fitted it to ever greater artistic potential and intellectual enquiry. He could hear how Hebrew expressions from Tyndale's translation of the Old Testament ('the fat of the land', 'the apple of his eye') had entered the language so seamlessly that people would forget their origin.

He could see how, after more than two centuries when Welsh had not been a language of government nor a medium for administration, education, religious debate and many other official or creative endeavours other than poetry or the law (up until the Act of Union), it was unprepared for the challenge to come should his appeal be successful.

That is what lies behind the desperate appeal for manuscripts that are locked away mouldering in chests and corners. Adding to the meagre number of chronicles and saints' lives[10] that had survived would make translation so much easier and the resources unearthed would enrich the vocabulary and extend the language's range of expression into fields that had lain fallow for centuries.

Salesbury's use of language suggests that the first part of the letter was written at a different time from the second. Pages six to eleven show the enthusiastic Humanist adorning his words with all the trappings of copiousness and classical rhetoric, just as any European man of letters would, 'Erasmus… who collected not a hundred, not a thousand, not a legion, not a myriad, not a hundred thousand and not a million but a great storehouse of Greek and Latin adages.' (tr.)[11]

In contrast, pages one to five have a breathless quality, their language is simple and urgent and when a copious phrase does occur it is a modest two- or three-word variation, not something that would interfere with the pressing need to deliver his message as his pen raced to keep up with the thoughts issuing from his brain.

The contrast in styles suggests that he had prepared a letter with a vague intention of publication at some yet to be decided time and then, when the course of events was offering Wales an opportunity that might never be repeated, he dashed off a new opening section which he added to a slightly revised version of the original. It gives added weight to the argument that the book was rushed and opportunistic.

However it came about, it is a remarkable document and, though it is an anachronistic comparison, it does read very much like a modern-day political or artistic manifesto, which is exactly what Wales's greatest literary figure of the twentieth century, Saunders Lewis, called it, 'The manifesto of the Renaissance and Protestant Humanism in Wales.' (tr.)[12]

Another distinguishing feature of the letter and the book is its unselfishness. In an age of ruthless and vicious veniality, Salesbury was not trying to make money, acquire a huge estate or build a magnificent country house; he desired something which would show him no profit but which would save the souls of thousands upon thousands of his ordinary countrymen. Not only was this a selfless act, it was one that required great courage. The pioneer is lauded by later generations, but is often a subject of contempt or ridicule to his contemporaries.

How foolish was such an appeal in a rural, deeply conservative country where innovation was regarded with suspicion and hostility, where Protestantism had made few converts, which had no university, no press and no bookshop and was ruled by an amoral gentry that flouted the law with impunity?

Salesbury knew the answer to that question, yet with the moral certainty, or insanity, of a visionary, he ignored 'common sense', did as his conscience demanded and appealed for the translation of the scriptures into Welsh.

The Inkhorn controversy

Those who admire his courage, are sympathetic to his cause and impressed by the sophisticated way in which he tried to win over his countrymen may pick out from the letter and the proverbs a detail that could be seen as the one weak point of his campaign and which could be used by those hostile or indifferent to his cause as a means to discredit and mock him.

England had an education system (two universities, the Inns of Court and grammar schools in almost every town) that produced a well-educated section of society that was open to innovation, yet the introduction of Latinisms and Latin-inspired spellings had caused great controversy and division amongst those very people. The first, fledgling grammar schools in Wales date from the 1540s.[13] A growing number of the sons of the gentry were attending university, but many of them stayed in England to pursue their careers (the flow of gentry from Wales and its effect on Welsh cultural life greatly concerned Gruffudd Hiraethog). There did not exist in Wales an educated class, that is, a group of people at ease in Latin and familiar with the ideas of Humanism and the Renaissance, of any size. That being so, pursuing a policy of Latinising the vocabulary and spelling of Welsh might not have been a wise tactic.

Despite that, Salesbury increases the number of Latinised spellings he uses. The 'Kembero' (Welshman) in the title and used throughout this book appeared in the dictionary, as did 'popul' (people) ('popol' in the dictionary). Appearing for the first time are 'eccleis' / 'ecclwys' (church, Latin ecclesia) and 'discipl' (disciple, Latin discipulus). These do not stand out greatly: 'eglwys' and 'disgybl' are the forms used today; regional variations in Welsh meant that 'c' for 'g' would not have appeared unusual.

However, there were two words that could not have been taken as a variation or misprint. The word for 'God', 'Duw', which is how it appeared in the dictionary has now become 'Deo'. The Latin word is 'deus', but in the dative and ablative cases it becomes 'deo'. The other word to be adapted into a Latin form is 'Heddyw' (as it was in the dictionary, which means 'today'), which is now 'heddyo' / 'heddio' to appear like the Latin, 'hodie'.

On two occasions Salesbury forgets his new spellings and uses the everyday forms, 'heddyw' and 'heddy'. It is easy to overlook 'heddyo', but in a book of proverbs accompanied by a letter appealing for the word of God to be translated into Welsh, 'Deo' makes frequent appearances (thirteen and twenty-six respectively). It would have inflamed any Welshman of the anti-Inkhorn persuasion.

Another innovation is Salesbury's decision not to use nasal mutation,[14] which occurs when 'fy' (my) and 'yn' (in) are followed by a word starting with a particular letter and also in certain compound words.

So, yng ghred oll (in everybody's belief) becomes 'yn cred oll', amharod (unprepared) becomes 'amparat' and vy nghi (my dog) 'vycki'.

There are examples in medieval manuscripts of nasal mutation not being shown. Salesbury might well have been following this precedent and had coupled it with Erasmus's philosophy of *ad fontes*. In a book of 1567 he explains that he did not show the mutation, as he wanted to reveal the 'essence' of the words involved. (He expected the words to be sounded as they were spoken, not as they were written, a well-established practice in English, but not in Welsh.)

Could he not have resisted the temptation? He had tailored the contents of his letter so astutely to the thinking of its intended audience, did he not consider using an orthography that would not cause division?

Salesbury could not be anything other than the man he was, the man who had been shaped by Oxford, Thavies Inn, Erasmus, Cicero, Palsgrave, Tyndale and Thomas Elyot. The Protestant, Humanist scholar and linguist who had the audacity to produce a dictionary, a Welsh version of the *Adagia* and an appeal for the translation of the scriptures into the vernacular could not have cast aside so important a part of the cultural mix that had produced him, nor would it have occurred to him to do so.

The power of the press

Though his appeal for the scriptures was the overpowering motive for rushing into print so soon after his first book, there was another reason. Salesbury had realised the power of the press and that its uses could be personal as well as political. What had Salesbury meant by the reference to those who would not let him enjoy his profit, who plundered from him and whom he wished would show a better spirit?

His readers in Wales, certainly in north Wales, would have understood. A cautious lawyer, he names no names, but he does not miss an opportunity to make his countrymen aware of a matter in which he felt he had been treated badly.

In the National Archives is a case that he brought in the Court of Star Chamber[15] against Elis Price. It bears no date, but is from the reign of Edward VI (1547–1553). In it Salesbury describes how Price, aided by John Lloyd, Richard ab John, Cadwaladr ap John Wyn o'r Foelas and other unidentified assailants overtook him between Wrexham and Holt, as he was travelling to London, pulled him from his horse and took from him a box containing documents and a canvas wallet holding items worth more than twenty shillings.

It is reasonable to assume that the attack did not occur before November

1546, the date of the arbitration, as Salesbury would never have accepted Elis Price as an arbiter after such an action.

In *Oll Synnwyr* Salesbury refers to having travelled to London three years ago in May[16] with Gruffudd Hiraethog. If the conjecture that Gruffudd accompanied Salesbury to London in 1544 is correct, then a short while after May 1547, possibly July or August, would have been the date of publication. All of which points to the attack taking place in January 1547.

That is a timescale that accommodates Henry VIII signing the licence for the dictionary on 13 December 1546, Salesbury handing over the manuscript pages to Whaley for printing and then returning to Wales for Christmas. In the New Year he would have set off for London to see the dictionary through the last stages of production. He had not left his native county before Price took the opportunity to strike.

W. Alun Mathias,[17] the leading expert on Salesbury's printed work, puts forward the idea that he had been dissatisfied with aspects of the settlement and had collected documents in preparation for an appeal against the clauses to which he had taken exception.

Price already had a record of taking criminal action in pursuit of building up the family fortune. He must have been deeply irritated by Salesbury's stand against him. A further legal challenge would have been too much to bear.

In his Star Chamber statement Salesbury says of Price and John Lloyd that they are 'of great substance and so greatly Frynded on the cuntre there that thys ther offence should be clokyd and hyd'.

He knew that had he taken action against Price in Denbighshire then the magistrates who conducted the case would have been Price's placemen. (Price himself was M.P. for Merioneth in 1553 and Sheriff of the same county in 1556. In 1574 his position as a Justice of the Peace in Denbighshire did not prevent his involvement in rioting at Gresford: the leader of the other party involved was also a J.P.)[18]

The outcome of the case is unknown, but the appearance of those lines in *Oll Synnwyr* would have given Salesbury some satisfaction.

Chapter Eleven

Building bridges

London and the Lord Chancellor

In the three years after 1547 Salesbury published nothing. This period of literary inactivity ended abruptly in 1550 with four books[1] within the calendar year.

The nature of these volumes, two works of Protestant propaganda, a pronunciation guide for Welsh and the first science book[2] in the English language, all point to Salesbury spending the intervening years in London.[3]

One of those pieces of propaganda, *The baterie of the Popes Botereulx*, appears to have been commissioned by Nicholas Ridley, bishop of London, who was determined to introduce Protestant ideology and practices as quickly as possible. The assumed connection to Ridley, strong circumstantial evidence that indicates contact with men such as William Cecil, William Turner and John Hooper and firm evidence of links to John Bale and Robert Crowley[4] all add weight to the contention that Salesbury stayed in London and was moving in the circles of the governing classes.

The political nous that he displayed in getting his dictionary into print, complete with a privilege for seven years from the King, shows that Salesbury understood the intricacies of power. There is no evidence that his call for the scriptures in Welsh had gained any support amongst his countrymen, but he knew, as he had known with the dictionary, that the matter would be settled in London, not in Wales.

Salesbury was cultivating the powerful and influential in the church and the state to achieve his great ambition. This was the cool and calculating side of his nature, but after years of keeping his faith a secret, he must have found it exhilarating to be caught up in the religious revolution that was sweeping through the capital. Cranmer was producing the first Book of Common Prayer, the Catholic old guard were being removed from office, Ridley was about to let loose a wave of iconoclasm and new ideas were pouring from a re-invigorated press. Bliss was it in that dawn to be alive.

Was there anything to draw Salesbury back to Wales? Certainly not Elis Price and his confederates, nor his country's continuing attachment to the old religion. If he was still working as Rich's deputy, that would have necessitated his occasional return, which he could combine with seeing his children and checking that his mother and grandmother were coping with the running of the estate in his absence.[5] There was nothing else to draw him back and his campaign against Price would be more profitably waged in the courts of London than in Denbighshire.

Evidence for his presence in the city is strong.

Details of a court case held sometime between 1547 and 1551 show that he took an action in the Court of Chancery for recovery of the Crown debt of Richard Irlam.[6]

There is the case[7] that he brought against Elis Price and his other assailants. Again, the date is unknown, but probably 1547 or 1548. This was brought at the Court of Star Chamber which, meeting at the Palace of Westminster and consisting of Privy Councillors augmented by judges, allowed Salesbury to pursue his case without fear of intimidation, blacken Price's name in the presence of the most powerful people in the land and at the same time impress them with the sharpness of his legal mind.

The outcome of the case is not known, but in 1549 Salesbury achieved what would have been seen at the time as his victory over Price. In the National Archives, in the Calendar of Patent Rolls (Roll 809, C66, Membrane 21) and dated 18 February 1548 (1549 under present custom) is recorded:

> Grant to John Puleston, knight, of an annuity of £9.11s.8d. to be assigned by
> the Court of wards in the lands in Methebroyde called Pennant, Melogen [thirty
> parishes or villages are listed in Denbighshire, including 'Llansanan'] … and
> Cunlerverche, co. Caernarvon, late of Robert Salysbury of Llanroust, gentleman,
> deceased, in the king's hands by the minority of Gwen' and Ellen verch Roberte,
> daughters and co-heirs of the said Robert, who held of Henry VIII by knight's
> service; also the custody of the bodies and the marriage…[8]

Salesbury's tenacity had paid off. He had wrested his nieces from the clutches of Elis Price.

Sir John Puleston[9] belonged to a minor branch of the powerful Puleston dynasty of Bersham, Denbighshire. He had been Constable of Caernarfon Castle for many years and M.P. for Caernarfonshire since 1545. A dependable man, he also had experience of ward-ship, having gained that of his three granddaughters, whose widowed mother (his daughter) was locked in an inheritance dispute with her brother-in-law (the similarities with Salesbury's case are striking). Reassuringly, one of his closest friends and allies was Sir John Salusbury of Lleweni. Intriguingly, one of the executors of Puleston's will was William Paulet, who was the Master of the Wards throughout Edward's reign, having first been appointed in 1526.[10]

Salesbury's use of the courts in London to pursue his legal battle with Elis Price was critical to his success. The London courts empowered him. Whatever the rights and wrongs of his case, he could not have had a fair hearing back in Denbighshire. If he were ever to lose access to those courts, he would lose his one recourse to justice.

It is quite possible that the flair and effectiveness he showed in pursuing his case brought him to the attention of some very important people. That, his espousal and eloquent support of the Protestant cause and his keeping company with such people as John Bale, Robert Crowley and, quite probably, William Cecil[11] are likely to have marked him out as someone who could fill an essential role for the country's rulers.

Peter R. Roberts argues that Salesbury acted as Rich's deputy in Wales, but the fact that one of his 1550 books is dedicated to Rich, who was by then Lord Chancellor, suggests he also served him in that office. If that is so, why would the ardently Protestant Salesbury wish to serve the torturer and destroyer of Anne Askew? If he had not heard of Rich's behaviour during the summer of 1546 whilst he was in Wales, he would have done so on his arrival in London. John Bale's accounts of Askew's torture, *The First examinacyon* and *The lattre examinacyon* had been printed by November 1546 and January 1547, and though the printing was done overseas, they would soon have been on sale in England.

(At her execution by fire Anne's body was so broken that she was unable to stand or support herself and had to be strapped into a chair, but her spirit was so resolute that throughout the sermon preached before the kindling was lit, she disputed with the priest in as strong a voice as she could muster.)

When control of the kingdom fell so quickly into the hands of the Protestants after the death of Henry, Rich underwent a very unconvincing Pauline conversion to Protestantism. He betrayed his old ally, Wriothesley, who as Lord Chancellor, was the one obstacle blocking Edward Seymour's appointment as Lord Protector. Wriothesley's removal from office earned Rich the reward of being named as his successor.[12] Seymour was naïve in his political judgement, but even he would have known that Rich was someone who needed to be watched at all times.

Espionage and surveillance are not modern phenomena. Usually, spymasters of the Tudor era would use domestic servants as informers, but Rich was fluent in Latin and Law French. An inside man, fluent in those languages and experienced in law was needed. Salesbury fitted all those requirements; he had also worked as Rich's deputy for the better part of two decades.

In 1550, Salesbury showed his dependability and his usefulness to the regime by producing two works of Protestant propaganda, one of which came at a time when the pace of reform had run ahead of what many members of the public were willing to accept. It was in the second of the two works[13] that the following dedication occurs, 'To hys singular good Lord, Syr Richarde Rych, Lord Ryche, and Lord Chancelloure of Englande: his mooste fayethfull and humble servaunte Wyllyam Salesburye wysheth everlasting felicitie', a possible indication that he was serving Rich, the Lord Chancellor of England rather than Rich, the Attorney General of Wales.

There is another document that strongly suggests that Salesbury spent most of Edward's reign, at least up to 1552, in London. In the *Calendar of the Patent Rolls, Edward VI*, dated 23 April 1550, appears the following record:

> Also grant of the manor and borough of Southwerk, late parish of the possessions
> of the archbishopric of Canterbury; and the yearly rents (and service) of 3s 2
> 1/2d from lands formerly of John Burcetour, knight, and now in tenure of
> William Glascocke, esquire, 3s from the messuage called 'the Swanne' of Roger
> Mannell…

There then follows a very long list of properties, their tenants and the rents charged. The last on the list is, '2s from a messuage of William Salburye, all which premises are in Suthwerke.'[14]

Salesbury's name is distinctive. There was only one other recorded William Salesbury of that time (the M.P. for Barnstaple) with the resources to rent a 'messuage' in London, but the name that appears here is very close to the Welsh form, *Salbri*. In all probability this is Salesbury.

Is this where he spent his time in London? The evidence to the contrary is that in two[15] of his books of 1550 he gives his address as Thavies Inn, where former students often lodged. However, Edward VI did not release the land in Southwark until that year; perhaps two of the books were drafted in his old Inn of Chancery before he moved into his new accommodation.

Southwark was convenient in many ways, very reasonably priced and with the city just a brief walk away over London Bridge or a five-minute crossing of the Thames in a waterman's rowing boat, but there was a reason for its low rents. The area was notorious for prostitution, bear-baiting and cock-fighting as well as Clink Prison. The other books of that year do not give an address. As a respected lawyer, servant of the Crown and upholder of the virtues of Protestantism, Salesbury might not have wished it to be known that he lived in London's equivalent of Gomorrah.

(If Salesbury was serving Rich in his position of Lord Chancellor, there is always the possibility that he was lodged in his household, or at least his London residence.)

A final argument for Salesbury's presence in London is that four books in one year would not have been possible without extensive contact having been built up with those in the printing world and, as two of the books supported the ideology of Somerset's regime, high-ranking people within that regime.

Unfortunately for students of Salesbury's life, he never thought to note (or perhaps he was being very discreet) the details of his life, apart from occasional references, often ambiguous, in the herbal that he compiled in his final years. Contacts have to be inferred. The temptation is to read too much into too little.

Crowley, Foxe and other leading Protestants

The one person whom Salesbury indisputably knew in London was Robert Crowley, the radical, Protestant clergyman, scholar and printer, who produced three of the books of 1550 and his one, hugely important, work of 1551.

Crowley had been educated at Magdalen College, Oxford, with John Foxe, where they had been victimised for their Protestantism. After Magdalen he was tutor to the children of Sir Nicholas Poyntz[16] in Gloucestershire before moving in 1546 to London where he worked as a writer, chiefly as a composer of ballads which put forward the Commonweal cause, attacking social injustices and conspicuous displays of wealth. He also wrote books that supported Protestantism and took advantage of the freedom of the day to publish William Langland's *Pierce Plowman*, which contained many passages critical of church corruption.

Crowley worked with the radical Protestant printers John Day and William Seres who were based 'at the signe of the Resurrection a little above Holbourne Conduite'[17] before establishing his own press nearby at Ely Rents, close to Thavies Inn. Crowley was ordained[18] by Nicholas Ridley, bishop of London, in 1551 and is likely to have renewed his friendship with Foxe in London after the latter's arrival there in 1547.

Amongst the influential Protestants in Foxe's circle[19] at this time were John Rogers, William Turner, Thomas Lever, John Hooper, John Bale, William Cecil and Ridley, who ordained him in 1550. Foxe, whilst in exile, was introduced by Bale to Conrad Gesner of Basel, the great Protestant humanist encyclopaedist, and is likely to have known Edmund Grindal during Edward's reign. He certainly knew Grindal in 1555, when he received financial support from him. (That Bale knew Salesbury is shown by his acknowledgement of 'Guilhelmus Salesbury' in his *Index Britanniae Scriptorum* of 1548.)

Throughout the reign of Edward a key member of the Council was William Herbert, created earl of Pembroke in 1551, whose wealth and power increased immensely during these years. Herbert is thought to have been Salesbury's mentor at the time the dictionary was being approved by Henry VIII, but he could be vindictive and destructive of a man's life and career, notably those of Robert Recorde, who would die broken and impoverished in a Southwark gaol in 1558. That would have affected Salesbury's attitude towards Herbert, but he was not a man to cross. A pun[20] on Salesbury and Salisbury Plain, near to Herbert's estate at Wilton, in one of his books of 1550 suggests that the Herbert connection was still intact.

Herbert never initiated policy, but reacted to events like a wily fox, moving his support seamlessly from Somerset to Northumberland to Mary to Elizabeth. In 1552 John Dee, who is known to have met Salesbury later in the decade, entered Herbert's service.

Salesbury is almost certain to have known Nicholas Ridley, the driving force behind the Protestant revolution, in support of whom he wrote *The baterie of the Popes Botereulx*. It could be that he wrote the book independently as an individual fired up by religious fervour, but it is more likely that he was commissioned to do so by Ridley or the Council or, at the very least, that Ridley had editorial authority over the finished version.

Among Ridley's extensive circle were William Turner, whom he counted a friend, Edmund Grindal, one of his chaplains who, as bishop of London in 1567, came to the aid of Salesbury in an hour of need,[21] strongly suggestive of a friendship that might have started at this time, and John Hooper, who would soon become a bishop and was in correspondence with Conrad Gesner, to whom he sent a copy of Salesbury's dictionary.[22]

Another person with whom Salesbury is likely to have made contact, though there is no definitive proof, is William Cecil, who at this time was working for Somerset, the de facto ruler of England. He also served Sir Thomas Smith, who had entered Somerset's household and was his Secretary of State. Smith is widely regarded as the most academically gifted man in the kingdom at that time. Cecil had been his pupil at Cambridge.

Smith was a friend of John Cheke (Cheke's sister had been Cecil's first wife), with whom he reformed Greek pronunciation. He was a promoter of the ideals of the Commonweal and the author of *The Discourse of the Commonweal*, 'the most impressive piece of economic analysis produced in the sixteenth century'.[23] Smith also promoted a system of spelling reform so radical that Salesbury's limited introduction of Inkhorn ideology into Welsh pales into insignificance in comparison.[24]

William Seres, already mentioned as a colleague of Crowley and printer of Bale's work, was 'Cecil's servant by late 1548',[25] playing a surrogate role for him in business transactions.

During Mary's reign John Day, publisher of works by Hooper, Latimer, Ponet, Turner, Crowley and Foxe, would join Seres on Cecil's estate where they would establish a clandestine Protestant press. There is mention in one of the manuscripts in the Bangor[26] collection of Day printing a series of *englynion* (an *englyn* is a verse form unique to Wales). That suggests a Salesbury connection, but there is no trace of such a book and no other reference to it.

Cecil's Welsh background is often overlooked, but he was a cousin of Princess Elizabeth's most loyal servant, Blanche Parry,[27] with whom he was in regular contact, and was quite possibly related to Thomas Parry,[28] Elizabeth's trusted but light-fingered cofferer, who played a key role in keeping his mistress from harm during Mary's reign. All three were Welsh speakers[29] and Cecil maintained an interest in the culture of Wales, receiving, in 1564, from Salesbury's close colleague Bishop Richard Davies, a manuscript of Giraldus Cambrensis annotated by Salesbury.[30] A particular reference dates the annotation to 1554, which shows that it must have belonged to Salesbury at that time (Davies was living in impoverished exile).

There are subtle indications of Cecil[31] aiding Salesbury, for example when the 1563 Act for the translation of the Bible into Welsh was going through parliament and another, personal, favour soon after Elizabeth's accession. As with Grindal's help in 1567, what can be construed as a personal favour suggests recognition of a past service or friendship.

Most tantalising of all the possible connections, because he is referred to so often in Salesbury's herbal, is William Turner. Today Turner is remembered as one of the great scientific minds of sixteenth-century England. A lifelong friend and correspondent of Gesner, whom he met in Zurich in the 1540s, he wrote books on fish and birds, but is most especially known for his pioneering work on botany. However, during his lifetime he was equally famous for his trenchant Protestantism, which was the cause of his exile from England not just during Mary's reign, but from 1541 to 1547.

He was a friend of Ridley, who ordained him in 1552, and from late 1547 Turner was a chaplain to Somerset. He ministered not only to Somerset's spiritual needs, but also to his medicinal and horticultural ones. Here are some references to him from the herbal, 'The true acanthus grows in gardens. So says Master Turner in the garden of the duke of Somerset in Sion.' (tr.) 'Master Turner says that this wormwood does not grow in this island.' (tr.)[32]

When Salesbury writes 'says', is he reporting what he has read, what he knows to have happened or is he giving an account of something he had witnessed? A vain or self-aggrandising man who had known such eminent people would not have left the matter in doubt and would have made much of such a connection to puff up his reputation but Salesbury, though stubbornly convinced that he was correct in matters of religious belief and orthography, seems to have been in all other respects a modest man.

His admiration for Turner is obvious from the twenty-six references[33] to him in the herbal; only Fuchs, with thirty-one, surpasses him. The likelihood is that as campaigning Protestants their paths crossed. If not, then with his lifelong interest in botany and herbalism, it is quite possible that Salesbury called on Turner to express admiration for his work and accomplishments.

Even more intriguing than that possibility is that Salesbury knew Edward Seymour, the duke of Somerset and Lord Protector. There are two references to him in the herbal, the one above and another where, still discussing wormwood, he notes Turner planting a German species in Somerset's garden.

Salesbury's kinsman, Sir John Salusbury, M.P. for Denbighshire, enjoyed Somerset's patronage and was appointed by him to three different posts in north Wales. In September 1548, he bought Rhuthun College from Seymour. The go-between for this purchase was Sir John Thynne, whose family originated in the Marches. (A record of the sale is preserved in the Longleat archive.)[34] Thynne was a close ally of Cecil and Parry. In addition, the Thynne family was famous for its manuscript collection, which might have included the now-titled Ellesmere Manuscript of Chaucer's *Canterbury Tales*: manuscript collecting was a passion that united many of the Protestant pioneers of Edward's reign, including Crowley, Bale, Cecil, Salesbury and Dee.

Besides Turner, there were two other men in London whom Salesbury would have admired and with whom he shared interests, men he would have wished to speak to, were the opportunity to arise.

The first was John Rogers, whose printer, Edward Whitchurch, had produced Prise's *Yny lhyvyr hwnn*. Rogers had met Tyndale in Antwerp shortly before the latter's arrest and execution and had daringly rescued his texts from certain destruction by the Emperor's officials. Still in Antwerp, he then organised the printing of the first English Bible, under the name of Thomas Matthew (the names of two of the disciples), using Myles Coverdale's translations of the missing sections of the Old Testament. This was the Bible on which Henry VIII's Great Bible of 1539 was based, but with the Protestant elements, for example 'congregation' and 'love' ('church' and 'charity') carefully removed.

Tyndale had been an inspiration to Salesbury. If the chance occurred to meet someone who had known the great man and completed his work, it would not have been spurned and as Rogers was, from 1550, the vicar of the Church of the Holy Sepulchre, situated near Thavies Inn, Salesbury might very well have met him. One of those who pledged security for Rogers on his return to London in 1547 was the printer, Richard Grafton, who is believed by at least one academic to have printed for Salesbury.[35]

The lack of firm evidence is what can tempt those who are interested in Salesbury's career into seeking connections where none might have existed, but a good working relationship with Crowley is indisputable and it is not unreasonable to assume a similar relationship with Cecil, Grindal, Ridley and Bale. Other possible connections are not sufficiently documented to be claimed with any confidence, but there can be no doubt that by 1550 Salesbury was moving in the circles of those who wielded power and influence and was making a name for himself.

Chapter Twelve

1550; the year of four books

Iconoclasm

Over the Whitsun weekend of 1550 masonry dust hung in the air of London's churches like a cloud of incense. Zealous Protestants were destroying and removing all trace of the capital's stone altars. Only one altar was left in London, St Paul's, and in June that, too, was obliterated.

Nicholas Ridley, bishop of London, had ordered the destruction. This bold act of iconoclasm angered and alienated traditionalists. Ridley received a letter[1] from the Council requesting him to 'cause to be declared to the people by some discreet preachers' the reasons for the royal policy, 'to persuade the weak to embrace our proceedings in this part' and 'thus our pleasure [may be] the more quickly executed.'

Sometime during the second half of 1550 Robert Crowley, a close supporter of Ridley, printed Salesbury's *The baterie of the Popes Botereulx, commonlye called the high Altare*[2] ('battery' refers to the cannons (arguments) which will destroy the altars ('botereulx'/buttresses) of the Pope). The military metaphor is sustained throughout the book's ninety-eight pages, which follow the three-and-a-half page address to Rich and a letter of the same length to the reader.

In the letter, Salesbury praises Ridley, 'the victorious Metropolitane of Englande', who is a 'grand captaine'. In the main part of the text Cranmer is praised as the 'chiefe undermyner'. Whether the book was commissioned by the authorities or is the result of earnest enthusiasm is unknown, but it seems unlikely that it would have been issued without some kind of vetting by Ridley or those close to him.

The copy that is presently in the library of Lambeth Palace has the following entry on its last page:

> Thys ys Harry Morgan's boke.
> Wyttnes Frauncys Spinke.
> Wreten the tenth day of Januarii 1550 (which now equates to 1551).[3]

Though he no doubt thought of the work as one that could be read in its entirety, one section in the letter 'I have here made a rude, and a simple lytle boke, even for the rude and simple people' suggests that Salesbury intended it as a sort of resource bank from which preachers and other champions of Protestantism could read out passages or use them, suitably adapted, in their sermons. ('Rude' and 'simple' did not, at that time, have a pejorative meaning.)

The book follows the classic Humanist convention, established by Erasmus, of presenting both sides of the argument. (Paradoxically, some readers might think that the Catholic case is the more eloquently presented. It may be that Salesbury, not weighed down with the passionate intensity of his Protestantism, was able to present the opposing philosophy with a greater elegance.)

A pioneer of classical translation?

The basis of the Protestant objection to the altar (which had now been replaced in all of Ridley's churches with a plain wooden table that was removed after each service) was that it was associated with ritual sacrifice. This was its Hebrew, and therefore non-Christian, origin: the altar is 'founded on Moses not Christ'. To provoke greater distaste for the practice of sacrifice Salesbury quotes from Ovid's *Medea*:

> Whan Medea was come home without the dores she stode,
> Using no mannes companye, whyle she was in that mode,
> Twey alters than of soddes she made, and garnished with bowes
> And a black Ramme she sacrificed, to twey great Godases

and

Geve heads too Pluto the God infernal
And Saturne his father, the fire lustral.

Associating the altar with a mother who slaughters her children was an effective, though not honourable, tactic. In doing so Salesbury provides the reader with one of the first translations of classical verse into English. Before 1550 'the great poets and tragic writers were practically untranslated.'[4] It is only a brief extract[5] and there may be other books from the period that contain similar short extracts, but it is remarkable. It was Golding's version of Ovid's *Metamorphoses* in 1567 (printed by Seres) that initiated the tradition of English translations of the classics. The language and spelling ('Whan', for example, though it is a form often used by Salesbury) suggest a fifteenth- rather than a sixteenth-century translation.

Salesbury's language is very mixed, with rhetorical flourishes mingling with classical tropes, extended metaphor, reasoned argument and expressions of contempt. At times the language is fiery, as when he attacks 'the cankred malice and wicked pollecye of the Popes soldiours', reflecting the passion and controversy raised by the issue, but he never resorts to the personal abuse that many Protestants used in their polemics, most notably John Ponet with his references to 'Carnal Phoole' (Cardinal Pole) and the 'Archbutcher of London' (Bishop Bonner).[6]

The champion of the Catholic side of the argument was George Day, bishop of Chichester, who stirred up such discontent within his diocese that a preacher was sent by the Council to Sussex to try to counter his arguments.

When Salesbury speaks of 'one of the best lerned papistical doctors gave me occasion by defending his aultares, and that with toth and nayle and fumish fearceness' he might well be referring to Day. By November 1550 Day's activities had become too much for the authorities to tolerate and he was brought before the Council. The following month he was committed to the Fleet prison.

(The actions taken against Day underline the critical nature of the debate and how vulnerable the country's leaders felt on the issue, all of which points to Salesbury's book playing a significant part in the war of words.)

Crossing the Rubicon

Though, as can be seen, the issue roused great passion in 1550, today, unless one is a theological historian, the question of whether a fixed, stone altar or a temporary, wooden table should be used during a Christian service cannot hold the modern reader's attention indefinitely.[7] Amusing invective, sophisticated debating tactics and imaginative metaphor begin to pall after a while, but there are other details that catch the eye. One is Salesbury's declaration of his Protestantism. Until this moment his sympathies could reasonably have been assumed but, had troubles arisen, he could have defended himself by saying that he was no more than a follower of Erasmus who favoured the translation of the Bible into his mother tongue, as had Henry VIII.

Salesbury gives details of his former beliefs and his conversion:

> Whan I was a holye Papiste, at what tyme I was at thys poynte wyth god. That if I had hearde masse boeth Sondaye and holye day, had sayde our Lady Mattens, or our ladyespsalter, kissed and lycked devoutly saintes fete (for so called thei their images) and besprynkeled my selfe well favouredlye with conjured water
>
> …
>
> And as I was thus tangeled and abhominablye deceived, and trained, and brought up in tender age, in the Popes holilyke Religion before Christes seconde byrthe here in Englande …

There could be no turning back.

When Salesbury refers to 'Englande' he means the kingdom of that name, which, of course, included Wales, but England is the more likely land of his conversion, in all probability during his student days. The main argument for his stay at Oxford or Thavies Inn being the time of the conversion is his acquisition of Hebrew, a sure sign of Protestant allegiance and something that was much easier to achieve amongst sympathetic young friends in a cosmopolitan setting than in a small town with no bookshop and limited lively company.

The most intriguing part of *The baterie*, however, is the dedication to Sir Richard Rich. Only two explanations present themselves. One is naivety; the other is revenge. No true Protestant could have forgiven or forgotten the suffering of Anne Askew. A man who had to deal with the machinations and assaults of Elis Price and could persuade Henry VIII to grant a licence for a dictionary in an outlawed language is unlikely to have thought Rich's conversion to Protestantism sincere:

> Even as I can not refrain but disclose and openly publish it, so can I not worthily express or declare, howe joyouse a thing it is to our eares, how confortable to our herte, and howe pleasaunt to our eyes, to hear, understand, and se that your lordshyppe … Openly repugne, suppres and beate downe those vayne ceremonies, and supersticious observaunces founded by the Byshoppe of Rome, that heretofore ye have (to the most part of men) bene thought to favoure, upholde, and maintaine.

Is the naïve tone a construct to hide Salesbury's true feelings? Though he might have regretted not being able to voice his opinion of Rich, coupling his name forever to a Protestant declaration would have given him some degree of satisfaction. Similarly, from the opposite end of the religious spectrum, X-rays of portraits of prominent Protestant officers of Elizabeth, such as Walsingham and Sackville, reveal that they were painted on top of images that they would have denounced as 'Papist'.[8]

More propaganda

In November 1548 Parliament passed an act 'to take awaye all posityve Lawes against Marriage of Priestes'. The ensuing heat and controversy provoked John Ponet into a robust defence of the policy, *A Defence for Mariage of Priestes by Scripture and Aunciente Wryters*, which appeared the following year.[9]

Sometime in 1550 Salesbury added his voice to Ponet's, publishing the bilingual pamphlet, *Ban wedy i dynny air / A Certaine Case Extracte*. As the marriage controversy pre-dates that of the altar, it is likely to have been published before *The baterie of the Popes Botereulx*, so it is possible, if Salesbury was indeed commissioned by Ridley to write *The baterie*, that this was the work that instigated that commission.

The pamphlet was issued anonymously. The absence of a name may be an oversight, but its Welsh content, its printer ('Roberte Crowley') and its orthography ('Kymbry', 'Deo') leave no doubt that Salesbury is the author.

The pamphlet consists of a bilingual frontispiece[10] followed by five and a half pages of text, the Welsh appearing first. It is likely that Salesbury composed the work in Welsh:[11] the English is more an equivalent of the Welsh than a direct translation and is slightly longer as Salesbury feels obliged to explain some details of the original terms. For example, in line two below he adds that Hywel Dda was the king of Wales; the Welsh version assumes knowledge of that fact.

Despite Welsh being the language in which the pamphlet was initially composed, the work appears to have been intended predominantly for an English audience, in particular the influential, sophisticated readership of London. Why, then, produce the work bilingually? Salesbury might have wished to introduce his English readers to an unfamiliar language and thereby arouse their curiosity. A bilingual publication would show that his native tongue was now a language of the printing press and demonstrate that if a Welsh version of the pamphlet could be published, then so could versions of the scriptures and the Prayer Book. For the Welshmen who would read it, it was a rebuttal of the argument that Protestantism was 'ffydd y Saeson', the faith of the English. How could it be, when it was being championed in their own language?

Here is the (abridged) case:

Here is yet another text (worthy to be noted for the antiquitie) of the aunciente lawe of Hoel da [Hywel Dda], than kynge of Wales, by the which ye maie easely gather that priests at that time had married wyves, neither was it prohibited or forbidden by the lawe: whyche lawe was accepted, confirmed, & auctorized by the bishop of Rome

...

Thys is the boke of the law which★[12] Hoel da made at Tuy gwyn ar daf [Whitland]: who dyd abrogate, repeale and disanull all the laws that were made before hym, and stabled thys Lawe in all hys dominions.

...

at the parliament holden of the same hoel at the sayde place, there were, vi. of the most prudent and wisest men of the layetee of every Commote in wales. And of the cleargye to the number of an. Cxl ... And of all thys number. xii. of the best learned and moste prudent were selected and chosen, yt after consultation had they might make the law[13]

...

> And Bleguaret doctor of both the laws, & archdeacon of Llandaphe was appointed to be pregnotarie. And immediatlye after that the lawe was fullye made and perfeicted, Hoel than bringing with him a royal rewarde oute of Wales and beynge accompanied wyth Lamberte byshop of saynt Davies, Mordefe byshop of Bangor, and Chebure bishop of S. Assaph and Bleyguaret archdeaken of Landaph: toke hys iorney to Rome to have the said lawe perused and examined bi Anastasius than bishop there. Which thing advisedly done, and everye parte therof founde to be consonant and agreeable wyth gods law, was ratified, confirmed and published by the bishop, and called the law of Hoel da. And thys was done in the yere of our Lords. ixc.xiiii.[14]

There is no argument and no invective. It is a very different document from *The baterie*. Salesbury has given, so he believes, indisputable proof that the marriage of priests was the law and the custom in tenth-century Wales and that the practice was accepted by the Pope. What else needed to be said?

Its appeal to English Protestants is that it gave them an ancient legal precedent from the same part of the kingdom in which the ruling royal dynasty had its origins. It also supported the otherness of Britain, something that since the break with Rome was becoming an important motif in the country's sense of identity.

Wales and Tyndale

Indeed, many of the pamphlet's readers would have been familiar with a passage from William Tyndale's *An Answer to Sir Thomas More's Dialogue*, 1531, which asserted the same argument now being put forward by Salesbury and might well have been his inspiration:

> And we find that wheresoever the pope reigneth, he came in with deceiving of the country, and then with his sword compelled the rest. The pope came but now late into Wales to reign there over the bishops and priests, and that with the sword of the king of England.[15]

Is Salesbury subtly associating the cause of Welsh Protestantism and his campaign for the scriptures to be translated with the great hero and martyr of English Protestantism and, in so doing, strengthening the chances of success or was the existence of a similar text by Tyndale a coincidence?

Welsh reaction to the marriage of priests is unknown. Logically, it could be assumed that, even though the country was ultra-conservative in its religious beliefs, this particular reform would have been welcomed. Far from the gaze of Canterbury, Welsh priests had been taking wives for centuries. Salesbury had married the (illegitimate) daughter of a married priest who became chancellor of St Asaph and fathered many children and during the 1560s Salesbury would work closely with Bishop Richard Davies, another child of a married priest. It would seem bizarre to oppose the legal recognition of the barely disguised norm, but people do not always react logically and might well have preferred the old way of doing things.

The work is so brief that Crowley's stock of letters would easily have coped with the demands of Welsh and yet Salesbury uses 'c' as well as 'k' and 'v' as well as 'f'. The one change in his choice of letters is that 'rh' is in regular use and not substituted by 'r' or 'rr'.

The Latinised spellings of 'Kymbry', 'Deo' and 'eccleis' all make re-appearances and are joined by 'testiolaeth' (evidence) (Latin 'testatio', calling to witness), modern Welsh, 'tystiolaeth'. He continues his policy of not showing nasal mutations, but occasionally slips into old habits.

A weakened argument

Though Salesbury does not add any arguments to the historical fact of ancient Welsh law's acceptance of married priests, there is an addition to his succinctly presented essay, in which he gives three instances under the law of gavelkind when a man is excluded from inheriting with his brother:

1. When a father has two sons of the same wife, but the first was born before the marriage. This illegitimate son will not inherit.

2. When a married 'Clarke' has a son and then, after being ordained a priest, has another son. 'The sonne that is begotten after the orders ought not to part lands with his brother that was begotten before the orders.'

3. When a man has two sons, one of whom is 'mute or dombe', the mute son does not inherit.

Only the second example is relevant to the marriage of priests and a cynical reader might suspect that the addition is connected to Salesbury's dispute with Elis Price. By showing the times when a brother does not inherit, none of which applies to him, he is emphasising the legitimacy of his inheritance of Robert's estate.[16]

However, one noted commentator, Professor Christine James,[17] argues that Salesbury intended example two of this last section [until this point no citation from Hywel's laws had been given in evidence] to be the conclusive proof of his assertion in the preamble that 'Ye maie easily gather that priests at that time had married wyves, neither was it prohibited or forbidden by the lawe' and then points out what she sees as weaknesses in the case put forward by Salesbury. One is that, 'Unlike the law of England and of the Church, *cyfraith Hywel* drew no sharp divide between legitimate and illegitimate offspring: both bastard and legitimate sons were entitled to receive equal shares of patrimony.'[18]

More importantly, stating that the son born after his father's ordination does not have the right to a share in the estate, undermines the argument. The 'Clarke' might have been allowed to marry, but any sons of that marriage did not enjoy the right to inherit, hardly a ringing endorsement.

There is a further weakening of the case. Though there are several copies of the Welsh laws[19] in which the text is as Salesbury has printed it, there are others, a majority, where an extra clause follows example two, 'Kanys yn erbyn dedyf y kahet' (because he is begotten contrary to the law), which makes it totally unambiguous, if there was any ambiguity in the first place, that the son born to the married priest is not legitimate.

An error unnoticed

Had Salesbury been aware that other versions contained this extra, damaging, clause? If so, did he believe that his copy was the correct one and that any other version was aberrant? It is unlikely that he was practising deception. He would never knowingly have allowed such a hostage to fortune to appear in print. If discovered, it would have given his opponents ammunition to damage the cause in which he believed. His campaign for the scriptures in Welsh, a campaign in which he was the sole activist, would have been badly compromised.

In the event, the potentially damaging error of the missing clause seems to have gone unremarked until the last decade of the twentieth century. Salesbury's enemies were not scholarly, Welsh Catholics did not start producing counter propaganda until 1568[20] and the pamphlet's intended audience was English Protestants, who would have readily accepted its arguments and would not have had access to copies of the Welsh laws.

Why did Salesbury, with his twenty years of legal experience and whose third book of 1550 (see below) would show his capacity for meticulous analysis, make such an error?

It is possible that he interpreted the key clause above as conferring legitimacy on 'the sonne that is begotten after the orders' rather than on the 'brother that was begotten before the orders'. No one to whom I have read the sentence has come to that conclusion, but it is a grammatical possibility. However, if one's point of view has already been determined, as is often the case with those who are fervent in their beliefs, then it is possible that Salesbury took those words as proof positive of his argument and presumably those who read his work were similarly persuaded.

Another explanation is that this was yet another case of his rushing into print to promote his cause. *Oll Synnwyr* had been a pretext for launching the campaign for scriptural translations into Welsh. Here the motive was to bring that cause to the attention of the most powerful and influential Protestants in the land, to show that he was a willing volunteer in their ranks and thereby bring his project much closer to fruition.

He was fortunate that this work, which contains his one poorly drafted piece of writing, was, as a political pamphlet, ephemeral. For *A Certaine Case Extracte* to be successful all that Salesbury needed was for his name and his cause to be noted.

Were prominent English Protestants aware of the book? It seems certain that John Bale was. This friend of John Foxe and future bishop of Ossory acknowledges in his *Index Britanniae Scriptorum*[21] that it was through 'Guilhelmus Salesbury' that he learned of the existence of Bleyguaret (Blegywryd, (B) Languoridus in Latin).

Whatever acclaim greeted *A Certaine Case Extracte*, it was very much overshadowed by Ponet's book. However, after 1556 and the appearance of the 'blasphemous' *A Shorte Treatise of Politike Power*, in which he argued that a monarch should not be obeyed if his commands were contrary to what a good man would consider right and true,[22] few people would risk using Ponet to vindicate their standpoint and Salesbury's pamphlet grew in significance.

Although a convinced Protestant, Queen Elizabeth retained an affection for some of the old Catholic ways and never reconciled herself to the non-celibate priesthood that she had been forced to yield to politically.

This was particularly difficult for Matthew Parker, the first archbishop of Canterbury of her reign, and married. In 1561 Cecil wrote to him, 'Her Majesty continueth very evil affected to the state of matrimony in the clergy. And if [I] were not therein very stiff, her majesty would utterly and openly condemn and forbid it.'[23]

Amongst the three surviving copies[24] of the pamphlet is the one that Parker kept, bound with other documents, in his library. It is now in Corpus Christi College Library, Cambridge. The other documents include a Latin manuscript of the Laws of Hywel Dda, which 'in all probability came from Salesbury himself'.[25]

A book on the British tongue

The third book of that year was *A briefe and a playne introduction*, 'teachyng how to pronounce the letters in the British tong, (now comenly called Walsh) ...'

Though Crowley is named as the printer, some academics suspect that it was Richard Grafton who was responsible for its production.[26] Crowley was particularly busy that year with his three editions of *Pierce Plowman* and though he might have been happy to be the publisher of Salesbury's book he might not have wished to be distracted from his great project by anything other than social or religious polemics.

It opens with a three-page letter written at Thavies Inn 'to hys lovynge frende, maister Rycharde Colynborne', an Englishman, probably from Aylesbury, who learned Welsh and eventually settled in Llangollen,[27] Gruffudd Hiraethog's hometown. There is no evidence to link him to Oxford or Thavies Inn.

The letter is written in the copious style which Salesbury so obviously relishes:

> The naturall inclination, the gentle amitie, and the fervent love and favoure, whyche you mooste affectuouslye, entirely, and perticlye, do not onely owe, but have, beare, and prosecute towarde me, my contrye, and contrye language and againe the sodayne semblable vehemente affecions whych I moste comparable and ardent, mutuallye and dulye do beare towards you: hath caused me to abortiat, (if I might speake my contry langage, I neaded not to borowe the latine terme, neyther make anye further explanation thereof) and to bring forthe my late conceived child before hys natural and destinated tyme of byrthe.

Salesbury can never resist the temptation to use the tricolon ('have, beare, and prosecute'), but there are many other rhetorical techniques in use, such as the sustained metaphor of his book being a child who must make his way in the world, the trope of modesty, 'this feble enterprise', and classical allusions, 'the botomeles floud of Lethe'. Shakespeare might have poked fun at this way of speaking, particularly when it issued from the mouths of teachers or clergymen, but Erasmus had established a manner of speech that would still be in use two centuries later.

'Abortiat' does not appear in the dictionary. It must be assumed from the opening paragraph and the metaphor of the book being a child that Salesbury had had to rush through the publication. If that is the case, then there are no indications of it in the work, which is highly accomplished and very well presented.

At the bottom of the first page Salesbury makes the pun that may well indicate his connection with William Herbert, 'and to be as plaine as the playne of Salesburie', Salisbury Plain being close to Wilton House, Herbert's country residence. Might it also indicate that Colyngborne was employed by Herbert? (Interestingly, there are several villages in the area that bear the name 'Collingbourne' (Collingbourne Ducis, for example) and although Colyngborne's family was from Buckinghamshire, they might very well have had a connection to these villages.)

Erasmus and Horace

There are three interesting quotes in the letter. The first is from Erasmus, 'the head learned man of all our tyme' … 'for it is true that there is not written so yll a boke, but it is worthy the reading for some consideration.'

The others are both from Horace's *Epistles*, written around 10 B.C. The first is an eight–line translation:[28]

> Whan that thy restles penne, of fame hath ought contrivd:
> At Metius eare se that thou tune, the cord in work recuvd
> And let them iudge therin, whose heares [*sic*] be grisely growne:
> Let midle age, let unripe yeres, theron their iudgment sowne
> Than maist thou well at wil (nine yeres in trial spente)
> Set forth the work of wisdoms braine, that the in lot is lent
> The sound escaped once, can not be called backe:
> But shut up thoughts in hert mai be, amended wher they lack.

As with the Ovid in *The baterie*, there is no trace of a previously published translation of this work. In the lines above, Horace refers to Spurius Metius Tarpa, a Roman censor and critic. The wait of nine years would prevent poor work from being made public. Is this modesty on Salesbury's part or is he concerned that he has rushed into print a book which may contain faults?

The second quote from Horace comes from *Ars Poetica* and is given in the original Latin, 'lest by unapt traduction of the same, I should disgrace the divine poeticall majestie'. (Is this more modesty or does it suggest that the translations he has used elsewhere are not his own?) The lines can be roughly translated as, 'An everyday lawyer [Salesbury is referring to himself] may not have the virtue [or courage] of the eloquent Messalla or the knowledge of Cascelius Aulus, but he has some value.'

Salesbury the Inkhorn

The most revealing part of the letter comes at the end:

> I neades muste commit thys boke ... not only to be redde, corrected, and
> perfected, but also to be defended frome the cancred malitious checkes of all those,
> who at all times canne be at better laysure to rebuke other mens doings, than to do
> ought them selves.

This is the first record of there being a negative reaction to his work. It possibly refers to the response to his call for the scriptures to be translated into Welsh and, if its publication pre-dates *The baterie of the Popes Botereulx*, to dislike of the position he takes in *Ban wedy i dynny air*, but is much more likely to reflect hostility to and bewilderment at his Latinised spellings in the dictionary and *Oll Synnwyr*.

The content of both books is sound, and so would not have aroused a critical reaction, though there are always those who are instinctively critical. It is undoubtedly the orthography that is the cause of the problem and the hostility it aroused would blight his reputation throughout his life and beyond. The anti-Inkhorn movement had taken root in Wales. Instead of being celebrated for his achievement, Salesbury was being attacked.

In a rural and deeply conservative society like Tudor Wales, innovation, even the mildest of changes, could be met with suspicion and hostility, especially if it was seen as originating from outside that society. Salesbury had dared to be different and he had made a name for himself in distant places. Such behaviour could well make life difficult.

There follows a letter to the reader in which he gives his reasons for writing the book. The immediate one is that following the appearance of the dictionary he was approached by Englishmen living in the Marches who wished to learn Welsh for professional reasons or to help them trade with monoglot Welsh speakers.

The second group of people to approach him were the sons of Welshmen who had settled in England and wished to regain a cultural heritage which had been lost.

Lastly were the Englishmen (presumably in London), lovers of language and learning, whose interest had been aroused. (Remember that the Welsh background of the Tudors, the Geoffrey of Monmouth controversy, the break with Rome, its attendant kindling of interest in things British and Salesbury's own dictionary had created a curiosity about the culture and language of England's nearest neighbour.)

To satisfy their curiosity concerning the language he has produced this guide, persuaded that it would lead to 'mutual amitie and brotherly love, and continuall frendshyppe.'

A master of analysis

There follow twenty-five pages of full, lucidly explained and clearly presented notes on the pronunciation of Welsh. Though the dictionary required a Herculean effort to complete and was a triumph, this is even more impressive. He shows himself a worthy pupil of Palsgrave and just as Palsgrave's work tells its readers as much about the English language as it does the French, so does *A briefe and a playne introduction* provide the student of English with an incredibly detailed analysis and picture of its mid-sixteenth-century pronunciation. It was reprinted in the nineteenth and the twentieth centuries for that very purpose.

The first page gives the alphabet[29] ('rh' and 'ph' are omitted), the vowels, the diphthongs (which, as Salesbury says, echoing Prise, are 'pronounced after the very Greke pronunciation') and the consonants.

This is followed by notes on each of the letters of the combined Welsh and English alphabets, accompanied by snippets of linguistic history and comparisons to the sounds of other languages, most often the three classical ones, but also German,[30] Spanish, Scottish and French. Most entries are about a page long.

Two of the shorter entries will give a flavour of the whole work:

The sounde of ch.
Ch, doeth whollye agree wyth the pronunciation
of ch, also in the Germayne tonge, of the Greke Chy,
or the Hebrue Cheth. or of gh, in Englyshe:
And it hath no affinitie at al wyth ch, in Englyshe, ex-
cepte in these wordes, Mychael, Mychaelmas, and
a fewe suche other. Ch also whan it is the radical letter in anye Walshe worde, remayneth immutable in
every place.

(We learn the pronunciation of Michael in 1550 and how 'gh' was sounded at that time, which explains, for example, why the anglicised spelling of the river Llwchwr is 'Loughor'.)

Of the straunge sounde of double.ll.
[The first paragraph is omitted.]
For the Walsh l, is spoken the tonge bowed up a
lyttle to the roufe of the mouth, and wyth that some-

what extending it selfe betwexte the fore teathe, the
lyppes not all touchynge togyther (but leaving open
as it were for a wyndowe) the ryghte wyke of the
mouthe for to breathe oute wyth a thycke aspirated
spirite the same ll. But as I sayde before, and if ye
wyl have the verye walshe sounde of thys letter: geve
eare to a walshman whan he speaketh culltell [cyllell], which
betokeneth a knife in Englishe: or ellyll a goste:
The Walsh man or the Hispanyard compose their
mouthes muche after one fashion whan they pronounce
their ll, savynge that the walsheman uttereth it wyth
a more thicker and a more mightier spirite.

No light is cast on English pronunciation in that particular entry, of course, but the passage gives a taste of Salesbury's approach to his work and his fondness for language, all language.

To compensate for the lack of English interest in 'Ll', here is some valuable information taken from the entry for 'Th':

Neither yet do we use to
write th, in anye worde, and to read the same as t, or
d, as it is communely done in these englysh words:
Thomas, throne, threasure, Thavies inne: whych be
moste universallye spoken after thys sorte: Tomas,
trone, treasure, Davies inne.

One final extract from the work will clarify Salesbury's position on an issue which was to blight his reputation, how he intended the words that he wrote to be pronounced. Writing about 'P' he says:

And an other whyle our tonge geveth us to sound
it, as it were an h, as whan we saye: ymhle, ymhlwy,
ymhlas [mutated forms], for ymple, ymplwy, ymplas.

He no more intended the last three words to be spoken as they were written than an English Humanist would expect the 'b' to be sounded in 'debt', 'doubt' or 'subtle'.

There is 'A briefe rehearsall of all the rules before, with certaine other additions therto pertaynynge.' The latter includes, amongst other things, a page on the similarities between Greek and Welsh, accent, 'The signification of Y' and 'A generall rule for the readynge of Walsh.' (The similarities between Welsh and Greek were the source of great pride to Welsh Humanists.)

Salesbury then resumes his letter to Colyngborne and in it reveals his thoughts on several matters. He continues to wish that all Welshmen would learn English 'for the attaynement of knowledge in Gods word, and other liberall sciences which thorowe the benefite of the learned men of our dayes be communely hadde and sette forth in the said Englishe tongue.'

He recognises that Welsh has not had the opportunity to develop as English has done, yet it is not 'so rude, so grosse, nor so barbarous, as straungers … do adjudge.' He gives a brief history of the language since the time of the ancient Britons, when it was adorned with 'worshypfull sciences, and honorable knowledge' and recounts that when Wales was conquered its nobles and other great men were imprisoned in the Tower of London, where they requested and were granted their 'many volumes, and sondrye bokes of diverse sciences and straunge matters.'

A challenge to the bards

He then turns to the contemporary bards and says that the books that they possess are 'folysh uncertantie and phantasticall vanities' and that they (the bards) claim that those Welsh books that escaped destruction in the Tower were destroyed during the revolt of Owain Glyndŵr. I interpret his tone as one of disbelief, as a suspicion that the bards were withholding precious knowledge.[31]

Salesbury returns to the subject of pronunciation and, like a sixteenth-century Henry Higgins, encourages the practice of what we would call 'tongue-twisters' in order to acquire excellence in pronunciation. He gives examples in Greek, Latin, English ('Three beans in a bladder, rattle bladder rattle') and Welsh.

Welsh again wins his praises and he states how it shares some characteristics with 'the holy language' (Hebrew). Tyndale had said very much the same about his own language, how phrases that sounded clumsy or laboured when translated into Greek or Latin, could be accommodated easily and elegantly into the grammatical structures of English. (Is there a hint here that Salesbury had already started experimenting with Biblical translations?)

He mentions the 'wonderous graces of the Brytishe meters [poetry]' and expresses his regret that 'there remayneth now but walsh pamphlets for the goodly Brytish bokes, sometime so well furnished wyth all kynde of literature: and so fewe Brytyshe fragmentes of the booke of Christes owne religion remaine unwormeaten and defended from injurye of tyme.'

Realising, with self-deprecating humour, that he needs to stop, he quotes, in Latin, an amusing jest by Diogenes[32] concerning the gates of the city of Myndum, which he uses against himself to say he has spoken for too long and bids Colyngborne farewell.

Salesbury's lament at 'so fewe Brytyshe fragmentes' is plaintive. He must have felt great disappointment that his appeal of 1547 had had no success. Perhaps that was his reason for clinging so fervently to his belief that the scriptures had once existed in Welsh. (Salesbury's assertion cannot be disproved, of course, but few today would support it.) Creating or perpetuating a historical myth in such circumstances is understandable and, perhaps, forgivable.

If Salesbury was looking around for someone to blame it was, as hinted in the letter to Colyngborne, the bards. His relationship with them was an uneasy one, bordering on hostility. Salesbury made no secret of his belief that the work of the contemporary bards, with the exception of his friend Gruffudd Hiraethog, was poor. It is no surprise then, that despite his being the leading literary and intellectual figure of the age only one bard, Gruffudd Hiraethog, wrote him a poem of praise.

There were several reasons for the bards' wariness. They were ultra-traditional, he was a radical innovator. They saw English culture as a threat, he championed it. The bards were overwhelmingly Catholic, Siôn Brwynog vehemently so, Salesbury adhered to 'ffydd y Saeson', the faith of the English. Salesbury had introduced the Welsh language to the possibilities of the printing press, the bards feared that the press would take away their livelihoods, not just as bards, but most especially as copyists and genealogists. Finally, the bards had manuscript books that held the secrets of their craft. These they kept to themselves. Humanists, in contrast, believed that knowledge should be shared.

Perhaps it was the jealousy with which they guarded their professional secrets that aroused in him a suspicion that there were other manuscripts and documents being hidden from him and why he finishes off the book with a very loud counterblast. There, on the last page is a couplet:

Cu adardy coed irdec
Cwvert hardd mewn cyvair tec[33]

[A fresh wood's pleasant aviary,
Sweet shelter in a fair place]

The couplet itself is unremarkable; it would have been well known to those members of the gentry who exchanged manuscript copies of collections of poetry. What is remarkable is that Salesbury, in a bold type that is the equivalent of throwing down a gauntlet, gives the two types of metre used, *cynghanedd* '*croes cyfnewidoc*' (first line) and *cynghanedd* '*traws*' (second line).

The intricacies of *cynghanedd* were the most closely guarded of all the secrets of the bards' profession. Salesbury was declaring that there was nothing that could be kept hidden. Not satisfied with this challenge to their authority, there appears in the lower part of the page an *englyn* (his own) in which he expresses the desire that printing (shunned by the ultra-traditionalist bards), is established in Wales, just as it has in other countries:

Pop gwlat aeth [o rat un a thri][34] Debraint
I brintio mewn trevi
Nid anos mewn Daoni
Bot yr un gwaith in Iaith ni.

[Every land has claimed [from the grace of one and three] the right
To print in towns
It is not more difficult in goodness
That [we have] the same for our language.][35]

Classicist, Humanist, Scientist

Salesbury gives the genesis of his fourth book of the year in the opening letter, which is addressed 'To his verye lovynge Cosen, John Edwardes of Chyrke'.

He writes that 'you have written unto me, to provide you of some

Boke, treatynge in Englyshe of the descripcion of the Sphere of the Worlde' but tells of his failure to find one, despite walking 'rounde aboute all Poules Churchyearde, from shop to shop'. However, there were some in Latin and as 'you stamer some what both in the Laten tonge, and in this science also', he has decided to translate the best of those available, Thomas Linacre's translation of Proclus Diadochus' *De Sphaera*, into English. This had been published in 1499 by the great Venetian printer Aldus Manutius,[36] who pioneered editions of the works of classical authors such as Aristophanes, Aristotle, Herodotus and Sophocles, both in their original Greek and in Latin and Italian translations. Linacre's was the first complete translation of Proclus into Latin.

The letter reveals an interesting side to the cultural life of the Welsh gentry at that time, with those visiting London, Oxford or other towns that were well provided with bookshops acting as agents for friends and relatives back home, seeking out works required. (The network of published learning which connected Venice, Frankfurt, Oxbridge and the bookstalls crowded around St Paul's did not stretch beyond Offa's Dyke.) No doubt colleagues returned the favour for Salesbury whenever he was confined to Llanrwst or Llansannan for any time.

If Edwards was the 'Edwards sunne dwelling not far from Chirk Castel' mentioned by Leland in his *Itinerary*,[37] then he would appear to have been not just someone interested in scientific instruments, 'And where you are els excedyngely well sene in all Geometrycall Devyces where you excelle in all humayne fabricature, and where you farre passe all other men in Unyversall knowledge' but to have been born into a family with a tradition of learning and of collecting manuscripts, a hypothesis supported by his ownership of Chaucer's *A Tretyse on the Astrolabe*, which was in his possession by 1551[38] and is now in the National Library of Wales (NLW 3567B). It is assumed that it was acquired for him by Salesbury.

Friends and colleagues

It also shows that Salesbury was not an isolated figure. He had enemies, Elis Price, the Wynn family (not yet, but soon) and others in that camp, and opponents, the bards and those who objected to his orthography and his campaign for the scriptures, but he had many friends and colleagues.

Besides John Edwards and Gruffudd Hiraethog, there was Humphrey Llwyd, Richard Langford, Jenkyn Gwyn, Gruffydd Dwnn, Edward Games (fellow antiquaries), Richard Davies (bishop), Thomas Wiliems (cleric and lexicographer), Huw Dryhurst and Robert Huxley (neighbours), as well as the extensive Salusbury clan who shared his antipathy to the Price faction.[39]

It is easy to stereotype a principled campaigner and scholar as someone dour and joyless, but this letter shows a man bubbling with enthusiasm for a new project, sociable, light-hearted and full of curiosity and it is here that we learn that English was not his first language, 'Englyshe was his [Linacre's] native tonge. Greke and Laten as well knowen, where as Englysshe to me of late yeares, was wholy to lerne, the Latyn not tasted of, the Greke not once harde of.'

In the very brief letter to the reader, we can see just how badly shaken Salesbury had been by criticism of his work. He says he does not worry if there are some honest mistakes in this book as the 'professoures' of this science are 'so gentyll harted, and of such excellente humanytie', whereas 'some that professe other Scyences … gnarre, snuffe and snatche, at whomsoever shall utter ought of hys mynde (specyallye yf it swarve but a here bredth, besyde the lyne of theyr phantasye)'.

It is impossible to tell to what criticism he is reacting, but the hurt it had caused is obvious.

Proclus and Wyer

Linacre had translated Proclus's book into Latin at a time when very few educated people could read Greek. By doing so he brought the work to a larger audience. Now, by 'Englishing' the text, Salesbury was continuing the process.

De Sphaera's author, Proclus, was born in Constantinople in A.D. 411. He abandoned the study of law in Alexandria in favour of his great passion, mathematics, becoming greatly influenced by the work and ideals of Pythagoras. In Athens he studied at Plato's Academy under Syrianus, whom he succeeded as principal (Diadochus means 'successor').

Proclus wrote hymns in praise of the gods and commentaries on the work of famous thinkers such as Euclid, Hipparchus and Ptolemy. His commentaries helped to preserve knowledge that otherwise would have been lost. One of his most intriguing works is a description of how Heron's water clock could be used to measure the diameter of the sun.

Proclus was not an original thinker, his book is a summation of the 'knowledge' accrued by the scientists of Ancient Greece, but it is nevertheless a valuable document. It is strange to think of that world of classical learning clinging on in Byzantine Athens alongside the state religion of Christianity whose followers would not have approved of his pagan activities. Stranger still when one considers that he lived after such important early Christian figures as St John of Chrysostom (347–407) and St Ambrose (337–397), both of whom are mentioned in works by Salesbury.

It would appear that Salesbury initiated this project as a light-hearted distraction from the serious world in which he had been living. He appears to have translated from Linacre's Latin rather than to have gone back to Proclus's Greek, which might have been difficult to procure. The publisher he found was Robert Wyer, who had made a name for himself and a profitable living from printing popular books on medicine.

One twentieth-century academic, H. R. Plomer,[40] dismisses Wyer as someone whose 'chief business as a printer and publisher [was] to purvey cheap books for the uneducated', but any weakness in his books reflects the woeful nature of the sixteenth century's understanding of the world, not any fault of the publisher: he popularised the writings of Ptolemy, which included works on astrology as well as astronomy and it would not be until Harvey's discovery of the role played by the heart in the circulation of the blood that doctors would be disabused of Galen's theory that blood originated in the liver.

Another academic, H. B. Lathrop, calls Wyer's books 'dingy', but *The Descripcion of the Sphere* appears very well produced, the print is certainly clearer than Whaley's or Crowley's. It is the first of Salesbury's books to contain elaborate woodblock prints; the frontispiece is a picture of Ptolemy holding a sextant, with behind him the moon, a constellation of seven stars and the Milky Way and on the floor an armillary sphere.

The first science book

One academic, Francis R. Johnson,[41] has hailed it as the first scientific book in the English language. (There had been translations of medieval science books, but this was the first from a classical source. It was followed in 1552 by Anthony Ascham's *A Lytel treatyse of Astronomy* and in 1556 by Robert Recorde's *The Castle of Knowledge*.)

After the address to the reader, Salesbury lists the book's contents:

The Table
The Epystle
The Preface to the reader
Of the Axtre [axis] and the Poles
Of the Cyrcles of the Sphere
The reason why, that v[42] parallel cyrcles are onely in the Sphere
Of the appearance and none appearance of the v parallel cyrcles
Of the number of the parallelles
Of the ordre of the v parallel circles
Of the power of the v parallels
Of the space between the parallels
Of the Colures
Of the zodiacke
Of the horizon
Of the meridian Cyrcles
Of the Cyrcle Galaxias
Of the fyre zones
Of the Celestyall Sygnes

Though our understanding of the solar system is now heliocentric, our language continues to be pre-Copernican, 'sun-rise', 'sun-set'. Salesbury's world view was shared by Shakespeare, which explains Andrew Aguecheek saying, 'In sooth, thou wast in very gracious fooling last night when thou spokest of Pigromitus, of the Vapians passing the equinoctial of Queubus'.

The 'Equynoctiall' is one of the five parallels, immediately recognisable as the Equator. The 'Artik' and 'Antartike' are familiar, but the two tropics are referred to as 'Estyvall' (summer) and 'Brumall (winter). 'The Estival Tropike [is] in the first degree of Cancer, and the Brumall tropic in the first degree of Capricorne.'

We are told that these parallels do not exist but are 'supposed onely in our Imagynation' and that 'The Equynoctiall circle is the mooste greatest of all the v parallel circles, and is so parted of the horizon, that the one halfe circle is above the earth, the other halfe circle lyeth hyd under the horizon.'

The meridian is explained, 'a circle that goeth through the poles of the world and thorowe the poynte that is just over our hedes' and there is a guide to the major constellations and the 'Zodiake'.

It is not until one comes across a reference to a star that can be seen in 'Rodes', 'but in Alexandria, she is not sene at all' that one remembers that the book does not originate in Tudor times.

The last three pages owe nothing to Proclus, Linacre or Salesbury. Wyer, whose prime motive was profit, gives details of phlebotomy, the science of how and when, depending on humours and signs of the zodiac, to perform blood- letting. His thinking must have been that if readers worried that the original text was too dry or abstruse, this section would overcome any doubts and entice them to make the purchase.

Copernicus had published *De revolutionibus orbium coelestium* in 1543, but it made little impact on the world of thought until Galileo's championing of the heliocentric system in the following century.

Even so, Galileo's discoveries did not invalidate *The Descripcion of the Sphere* as a useful guide for navigation. (It was only with Harrison's invention of the chronometer and its attendant mastery of longitude that the book became truly redundant.)

The book was so popular that it went into a second print run within the year. There is one surviving copy of the first edition[43] (in the Hunterian Museum, Glasgow) and several copies of the second. One of them was bought by a senior civil servant whose career blossomed on his appointment in 1660 as Clerk of the Acts to the Navy Board. An avid book collector, he might have bought this volume sometime in middle age as an idle curiosity or it might have been that as a newly appointed twenty-seven year old with no experience of the sea, he felt the need to embark on a rapid course of familiarisation so as not to make a fool of himself in front of his peers.

The name of the civil servant was Samuel Pepys and the book still forms a part of his library.

Chapter Thirteen

A prayer book by any other name

Shifting sands

The four books of 1550 placed Salesbury in as strong a political position as he could have hoped for, establishing him as a trusted lieutenant with a proven record of service, the champion of the new religion in Wales and a respected author who could give a 'British' perspective to the Protestant cause.

Despite those achievements and the many useful connections he had made, his ability to influence the decision-makers was negligible. The political credit he had gained was being eroded by changes in England's power structure. His goal of the scriptures in Welsh was as far away as ever.

In October 1549 Somerset, along with Sir Thomas Smith and William Cecil, 'his only remaining friends in office',[1] had been arrested and sent to the Tower. Smith and Cecil were soon released, but Somerset was detained until February 1550.

John Dudley, the earl of Warwick, had staged a coup. Unlike his rival, he was highly accomplished in the art of holding on to power. The coup was effective, but protracted. Warwick controlled the Council, but Somerset still enjoyed the support of Parliament; Warwick ensured that Parliament was not called that year.

There was a bizarre break in the hostilities in June 1550, when Somerset's daughter, Anne, married Warwick's eldest son, John, but that did not deter the usurper from manoeuvring to gain total control of the kingdom. He worked assiduously on the King, gaining the boy's trust by skilfully granting him more of the trappings and the illusion of the power that his youth denied him, whilst imperceptibly increasing his personal control.

In October 1551, Warwick was created duke of Northumberland and his leading supporters were also ennobled, notably Sir William Herbert, who became the earl of Pembroke. Five days later Somerset was arrested. On 23 January 1552, he was executed.

Warwick's takeover of power had not halted the Protestant revolution, far from it, but any actions taken by him were either for his political benefit or for personal gain. (When the Catholic bishop of Durham, Cuthbert Tunstall, was deprived in 1551, almost all of the lands of the diocese were appropriated by the newly-created duke.)

Somerset had been an ineffective leader, but he was, by the standards of the age, something of an idealist. To gain official sanction for the scriptures in Welsh Salesbury needed to convince principled leaders of government of the spiritual needs of his countrymen. Unfortunately, such people were no longer in power.

It is possible that Salesbury had already made such an appeal. In 1547 he had called on the Welsh to petition the King and a reference he makes in a book of 1567, 'Behold how the clemencye of God hath now heard my long desired petition',[2] is evidence that he followed his own advice. A manuscript (NLW MS Gwysanau 27) of this petition survives, but only a fragment and it would appear to be a draft rather than a final version. The opening passage is missing, but Salesbury's use of 'your Good Lordships' (twice) and 'your good Lordship' (once; I think he has omitted the final 's') suggests that its intended recipients were either the bishops of Wales or the members of the Privy Council. It is impossible to date the document any more accurately than between 1547–1553 or 1558–1563. (The reign of Mary, 1553–1558, can safely be discounted.) That it was in 1567 that Salesbury wrote that his 'long desired'[3] petition (for the scriptures in Welsh) had come about makes the years of Edward's reign, but not 1552 or 1553, the most likely date.

What made the situation more urgent for Salesbury was Parliament's approval in 1548 of Cranmer's Prayer Book, which was introduced into every one of the kingdom's churches on Whit Sunday 1549. In the West Country it proved deeply unpopular and led to a rebellion that was brutally suppressed. The rest of the kingdom accepted the reform. The Welsh, like the rest of Edward's subjects, would no longer worship in Latin but in English, a language that for 90 per cent[4] of them or more was no more comprehensible than Latin.

Salesbury would have welcomed the Prayer Book, but not his people's exclusion from church services in their own language. The solution would be a Welsh version, but it was not one that was on offer, a state of affairs underlined by the appointment by Warwick (from 1548 to 1550 Lord President of the Council of the Marches), of John Oswen of Ipswich as the council's official printer. In January 1549 Oswen moved to Worcester[5] to take up his post, having received a seven-year privilege[6] from Edward VI to print service books and books of instruction for his subjects 'of the principality of Wales, and the marches thereunto belonging'. No one could doubt Oswen's Protestantism, but there was no hint of any concession to the Welsh language; for the whole of his five-year stay in Worcester his output was exclusively in English.

Unilateral action

This was the background to Salesbury's decision in 1551 to publish his own translation of all the readings that appeared in the Prayer Book. He would have been aware that he was risking severe punishment for printing such a book without the permission of either church or state. His dictionary had been sanctioned by the king, as had Prise's *Yny lhyvyr hwnn*. His two books of propaganda were either commissioned by or had won the acceptance of a senior churchman. Cranmer's Prayer Book was the most important publication of Edward's reign. The 1549 version had been approved by Parliament.[7] His revised edition of 1552 would be approved by Convocation and Parliament. It was the document on which the spiritual well-being of the kingdom depended in an age when religion dominated the lives of everybody. To bring out an unsolicited, unofficial version could have been interpreted as an act of rebellion, a challenge to authority.

Rebellion was not tolerated. The Western Rebellion, religious in nature, had been brutally put down, as had the Eastern (or Kett's) Rebellion, which had been caused by social and economic deprivation. Rebellion by an individual could be dealt with far more easily than one by thousands of men armed with scythes and sticks.

Warwick had been succeeded as Lord President of the Marches by

William Herbert, but the man who had appointed Oswen was now the de facto ruler of the country. He had played a leading part in the suppression of Kett's Rebellion. Though Warwick implemented Protestant policies, that did not mean that Protestants were safe: in 1550 the Anabaptist, Joan Bocher, who had been a friend of Anne Askew, was burnt at the stake for heresy, the following year her co-religionist, George Van Parris, suffered the same fate.

Legal niceties and a resolute friend

The fear of possible consequences may account for Salesbury not translating the Prayer Book in full; to have done so would have required very little extra effort. Providing the lessons meant that a competent, well-educated parish priest (a rare commodity in Tudor Wales) had only to complete the relatively simple task of making a Welsh paraphrase of the words that preceded the reading for the entire service to be conducted in a language understood by the whole congregation.

It was a subtle legal distinction, one that would have appealed to the legally trained mind and one reminiscent of scholastic philosophy, but a translation of only a part of the Prayer Book meant that it was not the Prayer Book that was being reproduced. Nor did the title that he gave the book, *Kynniver Llith a Ban* [A Multitude of Lessons and Verses],[8] display its origin and purpose.

That Salesbury was nervous at what he was doing is shown by his inclusion at the end of the book of 'A copy of the kynges moste gracious Privilege', granted by Henry VIII in 1546 for the printing of the dictionary, a privilege granted for a different work by a now dead king, but it was for the duration of seven years and so, it could be argued, was still valid. It also commanded and charged all subjects 'as well printers as bookesellers and other persons within our dominions, that they ne anye of them presume to print, or cause to be printed the sayde Dictionary or any part thereof, or anye other boke or bokes first translated and printed by the saide Wylliam'. Those words, 'first translated', might have given Salesbury a fragile sense of security.

Many printers would have been too fearful to have produced *Kynniver Llith a Ban*. Fortunately, Salesbury's colleague, Robert Crowley, was not of a fearful disposition. He was a man of great courage and daring who was never cowed by authority into tempering his criticism of the greed of the aristocrats who grew ever richer whilst the poor starved. Nor did he hesitate to criticise their seizure of church assets for private gain rather than public good:

> As I walked alone, and mused on things
> That have in my time been done by great Kings,
> I bethought me of Abbeys that sometimes I saw,
> Which are now suppressed all by a Law.
> O Lord (thought I then) what occasion was here
> To provide for learning and make poverty cheer!
> The land and the jewels that hereby were had
> Would have found godly preachers which might well had led
> The people aright that now go astray,
> And have fed the poor that famish every day.
>
> For a Lordely house was builte
> Where the hospital should be.

Crowley had even managed to write sympathetically about the demands of those involved in Kett's Rebellion.[9] He had done so and survived by balancing that sympathy with condemnation of the disloyalty shown to the King. Though he incurred the displeasure of those in authority, his closeness to Ridley might have played a part in his freedom from prosecution.

There was a further risk for Salesbury and that was the financial one. Several hundred copies of a substantial book, 176 pages long, twelve pages longer than the dictionary, would cost a considerable amount of money to produce. With no official approval there would be no guaranteed sales and no help with the logistical problem of distributing copies of the book to booksellers, individual buyers and parish churches. Salesbury had enjoyed commercial success with *The Descripcion of the Sphere*. Perhaps *A briefe and a playne introduction* had made a profit, too, but if he had not inherited his brother's estate and not fought off Elis Price's attempts to take it over, then he would not have had the time or money to produce such an ambitious work.

New territory

It was Salesbury's most intellectually challenging project to date. The dictionary had required a great deal of labour, but little original thought. Producing a diatribe against altars came as naturally as breathing to a lawyer of twenty years' experience. The descriptive analysis of pronunciation was challenging, but it was the analysis of something that already existed. No one had ever translated large tracts of the Bible into Welsh. The commandments and the Lord's Prayer had appeared in *Yny lhyvyr hwnn*, but apart from these and a few fragments, there were no precedents.[10]

The first translation of any text is always the most daunting. There is so much more than just the surface meaning of the words; there are the subtleties of tone, colour, rhythm and cadence. How do you translate idioms or references that are unknown in the culture of your countrymen, such as 'publican' (as in tax-collector) or 'synagogue'? How do you translate something expressed in a construction that is alien to your language? Doubt always creeps in; ambiguities appear, in the original or in the translation; there can be three or four ways of expressing the same thought, but none of them is exactly right.

Probably the most perplexing of problems when translating from the Bible is that of tone. Do you choose a dignified, courtly tone, perhaps with slightly archaic forms of grammar and vocabulary to give the work an air of gravitas? Or do you opt for clarity and simplicity, using the vocabulary of the marketplace and the patterns of everyday speech? The first option risks being seen as pompous or out of touch (remember that Tyndale wanted the scriptures as much for the plough boy as the king). The second could be seen as disrespectful, even blasphemous, and whichever choice you made, how far would you allow yourself to stray from the original in order to create the effect you desired?

None of these questions had troubled Cranmer as he compiled the Prayer Book. There is a general consensus amongst commentators that the archbishop, who had many weighty matters to deal with, chose overwhelmingly to use the words of the Great Bible, Myles Coverdale's 1539 version of the Bible that used Tyndale's translations and his own work for the unfinished sections.

Another question that Salesbury might have asked himself was whether he should continue to introduce Latinised spelling and vocabulary into Welsh and should he persist in his practice of not showing nasal mutation, both of which had met with a hostile reception. The latter, showing the 'essence' of the word, was his own innovation, based, presumably, on his interpretation of the teachings of Erasmus.[11] The former was the great phenomenon of sixteenth-century English, a language that Salesbury loved and admired. He saw the vibrancy of the English language as it developed to meet the needs of a modern nation state, swelling its lexicon with great imports of words from imperial Rome and from around the world, adopting grammatical structures from Hebrew, rhetorical tropes from the ancients and literary forms from Italy.

Salesbury saw a causal link between the Latinised approach to language and the growing power of English. Why then should he deny his mother tongue the same benefits? Similarly, why should he not introduce a linguistic reform that was derived from Erasmus, 'the most learned, eloquent and authoritative teacher in everybody's belief'?[12] The likelihood is that the question was never asked.

Taliesin and Holinshed

As the copies of *Kynniver Llith a Ban* started to mount up in the printer's workshop, a visitor would have been impressed by the dimensions and appearance of the book. It was a Colossus in comparison to his *Oll Synnwyr* or Prise's diminutive *Yny lhyvyr hwnn*.

The title page reads, 'Kynniver llith a ban or yscrythur lan ac a ddarlleir yr Eccleis pryd Commun / y Sulieu a'r Gwilieu trwy'r vlwyddyn : o Cambereiciat / W.S.' (A multitude of lessons and verses from the holy scripture which are to be read in church at Communion, Sundays and on Holy Days throughout the year: from W.S.'s Welsh translation.) and is followed by quotations from Paul's epistles to Titus (Chapter 2) and to the Romans (Chapter 1):

> For the grace of God, that bringeth health unto all men, hath appeared and teacheth us that we should deny ungodliness, and worldly lusts, and that we should live honestly, righteously, and godly in this present world, looking for that blessed hope, and glorious appearing of the mighty God, and of our saviour Jesus Christ, which gave himself for us, to rid us from all unrighteousness, and to purge us a peculiar people unto himself fervently given unto good works. (tr.)

> For I am not ashamed of the gospel of Christ, because it is the power of God unto salvation to all that believe. (tr.)[13]

These aptly Protestant verses are followed on the next page by another from an unexpected source, the sixth-century poet, Taliesin:

Woe be to that priest yborne
That will not cleanely weed his corn
And preach his charge among.
Woe be to that shepheard (I say)
That will not watch his fold alway.
Woe be to him that doth not keep
From ravening Romish wolves his sheep
With staff and weapon strong. (tr.)

The poem can be found in *Llyfr Coch Hergest* [The Red Book of Hergest], which was owned by John Prise. The translation above is the one that appeared in *Chronicles of England, Scotland, and Ireland* by Raphael Holinshed, published in 1587, a source book for many of Shakespeare's plays. It follows this passage concerning the monks of Bangor in 1146:

… having utterly forgotten the lesson which Ambrosius Telesinus [Taliesin] had taught them, (who writ in the year 540 when the right christian faith which Joseph of Arimethia [*sic*] taught the Isle of Avalon reigned in this land, before the proud and bloodthirsty monk Augustine inflicted it with the poison of Romish errors) in a certain ode, a poet whereof are these few verses ensuing.

Holinshed gives the poem in both languages. There are differences in the spellings of the two poems,[14] but the year of the poem is the same as that which appears in *Kynniver Llith a Ban*. Holinshed is using material that originally appeared in the work of Salesbury. It came to him by way of Salesbury's good friend, Humphrey Llwyd, who prepared *The Description of Cambria*, which was expanded by David Powel into *The History of Cambria, now called Wales* (1584).

This shows just how successful was that small band of Welsh Humanists, primarily Salesbury, Prise and Llwyd, in winning over the writers and historians of England to their 'British' version of history. For Salesbury and Llwyd, who gave the story a Protestant perspective, it would have been particularly gratifying.

The bishops' letter

There is one more diversion before the main body of the book is reached, a two-page letter in Latin to the bishops of St Davids, Llandaf, Bangor, St Asaph and Hereford, Robert Ferrar, Anthony Kitchen, Arthur Bulkeley, Robert Parfew and John Skip. It is most likely that Latin, rather than English, would have been his choice of language for the letter whatever the background to the circumstances under which the translation was produced, but it meant that the whole book contained no word of English until the very last pages, something that would help it to stay under the radar of any potential hostile forces.

(Salesbury's name is given in the letter as 'Guilelmus Salesburius'. The English version of his name does not appear until the end of the book, in the privilege and in the declaration, 'Imprinted at London: by Robert Crowley for William Salesbury dwellynge in Elye rentes in Holbourne, Anno Domini M.D.L.J.'[15])

He uses his explanation of why he has produced the book to castigate the bishops for not having done so themselves:

> For a long time I had been hoping, that either the people themselves for the love of God, which they profess, or those set over them, by reason of their office, or you their most watchful pastors, to whom above all others their charge has been committed, would have been stirred up as suppliants to pray, and on your knees to ask, and, in short, unceasingly importune the King's most excellent Majesty, Christ's Vicar on earth, that he would think out how he can entirely overthrow and destroy the worst tyranny of the Bishop of Rome, by banishing it from the subjects of his said Highness; I mean, those walls of foreign tongues, built with circumscribed limits, within which, as in fetters alas! the Word of God is confined … no hope had dawned on me, nor had there appeared the least probability that someday someone would undertake the task.[16]

So, there being no one else to undertake the task, he has done so, though he is 'but a young soldier' (a military metaphor that echoes that of *The baterie*) and is driven by 'the necessity of Diomedes', an expression taken from Erasmus's *Adagia* and which is applied to those who act under compulsion.

He asks the bishops, all but one of whom were English,[17] to appoint six men in each diocese to examine the book so that it can be granted their approval if found worthy, or rejected, if not. He will not be ashamed to be advised of any errors that are found. (Official sanction was obviously important to him.)

Salesbury explains that he has kept to the 'strict rule' of translation and not paraphrased and has kept closely to the Hebrew idiom in Matthew, 'because the Hebrew diction more nearly approaches ours'. (There is a widespread belief that the gospel of Matthew was originally written in Hebrew and in *A briefe and a playne introduction* Salesbury had expressed his delight at the similarities between Welsh and the 'holy language'.) Elsewhere he has 'given great heed to the Greek, preferring the fountain head ... to the river'. ('Fountain head' is his second reference to Erasmus, although the Latin term used is not actually *ad fontes*.)

As a north-Walian he apologises for any mistakes he has made when he has used the Demetian (south-west Wales) dialect,[18] revealing his desire that the translation appeal to people of every part of Wales. 'Let me say, once for all, that I have set before my critics' eyes these few cautions instead of more, lest they should pass a hasty judgement upon this my simple little work, which has been hurriedly produced without a Theseus (as the saying is).'

('Hasty judgement' suggests that he feared an adverse reaction to his work. 'Without a Theseus'[19] is his third Erasmian reference, another saying from the *Adagia*.)

Finally, Salesbury states that if the translation is to be condemned, he will suppress it and add his vote to the votes 'of those who will make good my shortcomings'.

The willingness to accept the findings of others scarcely hides the bitterness in his words. Cranmer has given his English flock the Prayer Book in their own language, yet the leaders of the church in Wales have done nothing for their people. He has had to provide the translation because no one else would. Critics have already reacted with hostility to his work and he assumes that they will do so again. Fine, let them put it right. It is not the most gracious of messages, even if the sentiments are couched in polite language, but it is an understandable response to all that had happened.

(The lack of grace might well have been caused by nervousness at official reaction to the work. Salesbury also had to combine translating the readings and seeing them through the press with his continuing work for Rich. Another cause of tension would have been the ongoing struggle behind the throne for political dominance and fears for the fate of Somerset, the man favoured by most of Salesbury's friends and colleagues, but there was news from Wales that would have further unsettled Salesbury. In January 1551, Sir John Puleston, his nieces' ward, had died. Unease at the possible repercussions of his death and the possibility that it would trigger a fresh assault on his estate by Elis Price must have haunted Salesbury throughout that year. He had access to London's courts, should anything happen, and powerful friends, but Price and his allies were also gaining positions and influence. Puleston's successor as M.P. for Caernarfonshire was none other than John Wyn ap Maredudd and Price was insinuating himself into Northumberland's camp, as he had done with Cromwell and as he would do again with the earl of Leicester, Northumberland's son.)

A hurried work

The first thing that strikes the reader of *Kynniver Llith a Ban*, despite its impressive appearance, is its rushed nature. When he spoke of the book being 'hurriedly produced', it was not a modest disclaimer, as with *A briefe and a playne introduction*, but the truth. The symbol ^ appears at least once on many of the pages, accompanied by the word or phrase that Crowley has omitted from the text. It is not just individual words; some 'passages have been omitted or overlooked in the text, for which the printer may have been to some extent responsible.'[20] Salesbury, like Tyndale, never enjoyed the luxury of a printer who understood his mother tongue.

Why is it hurried? The deadly game of politics was being played out throughout that year, with Warwick inexorably gaining the ascendency, but Edward's reign was not threatened, nor was the Protestant revolution. It would not be until early in the following year that the King's fatal illness would become apparent, so politics would not appear to be the reason for the rush.

It could have been another external factor. Perhaps the time that Crowley was able to devote to Salesbury's project was limited, a case of 'We must finish it by the end of next month or abandon it'. Or possibly it was a change in

Salesbury's circumstances. He appears to have moved back to Wales in 1552. Rich was removed from the office of Lord Chancellor, which might have precipitated the move, but his dismissal did not occur until the last day of 1551.

Whatever the cause of the rushed printing, it may account for Salesbury not always 'preferring the fountain head' (translating from the Greek) but often translating directly from the Great Bible or Prayer Book. Experts in Biblical studies can hear occasional echoes of the Vulgate, probably not a conscious decision by Salesbury, but the familiar words of his Catholic childhood re-emerging.

Of the handful of Welsh scriptural texts[21] that had survived, Salesbury made use of one, *Gwassanaeth Meir*, which was a late fourteenth-century translation of *Officium Parvum Beatae Mariae Virginis*. His renderings of Luke, 1, 26–38 (The Annunciation) and Luke, 1, 68–79 (Benedictus) show the influence of this work.[22]

For the seven readings[23] that originate in the Old Testament, Salesbury appears to have made great use of Sebastian Munster's Hebrew Bible (which came with a Latin translation) and occasional use of the Great Bible and the Vulgate.

Crowley's choice of typeface makes an immediate impact: black letter is used for page headings and the initial letter of each epistle or gospel, but for the text he uses a rather florid typeface which I have been unable to identify. Although the text looks deceptively clear and attractive, for the modern reader it is no more legible than the black letter books of old.

Copia and Latinisms

Omissions are not the only words to occur in the margins. Salesbury uses them to give explanations of the terms he has used and, as a disciple of Erasmus and the philosophy of copiousness, alternatives to the words chosen for his translation, for example, 'emmynny' (to hymn) is given for 'canmol Deo' (to praise God), 'y nos hon' (this night) for 'heno' (tonight). Sometimes he gives more than one synonym, as with 'tuylwyth' (family) and 'cereint' (relatives) for 'cenetl' (kindred).

Amongst the words that Salesbury invents or re-fashions for new or culturally alien terms are 'communfa' for 'congregation', 'athro' (teacher) for 'rabbi', 'tollwr' (one who collects tolls) for 'publican' and 'eccleis' (church) for 'synagogue'.[24]

His use of letters is the same as in previous books with, for example, 'f' and 'v', 'c' and 'k' continuing to co-exist. The one difference is that in the main body of the work he uses δ for 'dd'. (In the margins he reverts to 'dd'.)

Several of his Latin spellings recur, for example, 'Deo', 'popol' / 'popul', 'discipulon', 'eccleis', 'testiolaeth' and are joined by newly coined forms: 'Natalic' (modern Welsh 'Nadolig', Christmas, Latin, natalis, 'natal'), 'espryt' (ysbryd, spirit, Latin, spiritus), 'descen' (disgyn, descend, Latin, descendo), 'ymperawtr' (ymerawdwr, emperor, imperator), 'crus' (croes, cross, Latin, crux), 'sanct' (sant, saint, Latin sanctus), 'Iueddeon' ('Iddewon', Jews, Latin, Iudaei) and 'commun' (communion, cymun, Latin communionis).

There is even an instance of Hellenisation, with 'pump' (five) becoming 'pemp',[25] Greek 'pente', which leads to the hybridised Graeco-Roman 'pemp cent' (five hundred) for 'pump cant'.

The Latinised words, apart from 'Deo', are infrequent, but for a reader determined to react with hostility, their presence and that of non-mutated forms such as 'ympen' and 'ym Beth-lechem', would have provided a convenient justification.

Judgement

What would a modern reader willing to accept Salesbury's reformed spellings think of this work? As someone who has become familiar with his innovations (and familiarity and open-mindedness are crucial factors in this debate), my reaction is a positive one.

Sentences such as:

Yny dechre yδoeδ y gair ar gair oeδ a deo a deo oeδ y gair. (John i)
[In the beginning was the word and the word was with God and God was the word.]

Ieshu a δyvot wrth Petr: Canlyn vi : Petr a droses ac a welei y discipl yn canlyn yr hwn oeδ hoff gan yr Ieshu ar hwn hevyd a ogwyδaδ ar y δwyfron ef ar swper ac a δywawδ. Arglwyδ pwy ydyw hwnnw ath vradycha di? (John xxi)

[Jesus said to Peter: Follow me: Peter turned and saw that disciple following, who was loved by Jesus and who also had leaned upon his breast at supper and said, Lord who is he that will betray you?]

Gwedy geni Ieshu ym Beth-lechem dinas yn Iehuda yn dyδie Herod vrenhin: Nycha/dewinion a δaethant or dwyrein i Caersalem can δoeδyt: Ym pa le y may hwn a anet yn vrenhin ar yr Iuδeon? Cans nyny a welsam eu seren ef yn y dwyrein a ny a δaetham yw aδoly ef. (Matthew ii)

[After the birth of Jesus in Bethlehem, a city in Judea, in the days of King Herod: Lo/wise men came from the east to Jerusalem saying: Where is he who was born King of the Jews? For we have seen his star and we have come to worship him.][26]

convey their meaning simply and clearly, with an economy of style and with a grandeur that avoids pomposity.

The judgement of others should also be sought (the author has the disadvantage of speaking Welsh as a second language and so may lack the sensitivity to the subtlest of nuances that a first-language speaker has).

The Reverend Isaac Thomas, an expert in Biblical translations, says, 'But when we bear in mind that this was the first attempt at translating the Scriptures into Welsh from the original languages we cannot but marvel at Salesbury's understanding of the language of the New Testament and his sure grasp of Welsh idiom.'[27]

Glanmor Williams, professor of history, '... a most remarkable achievement ... Moreover, even at this early stage, it revealed Salesbury's mastery of the original languages of scripture and his accuracy and expertise as a translator. Large parts of it ... were excellent as pieces of Welsh prose.'

Finally, Professor Thomas Parry, author of *A History of Welsh Literature* and the editor of *The Oxford Book of Welsh Verse*, says of Salesbury's prose, generally, 'It is now agreed that in terms of style, substance and eloquence his translation was splendid ...'

Those are words that any author would be pleased to hear, but it was the reactions of his peers that Salesbury awaited and, judging from some of the comments that he made in his books of 1550, it was with a degree of nervousness.

Chapter Fourteen

A book in manuscript

Troubled times

It is reasonable to assume that Salesbury returned to Wales in 1552. Rich was no longer Lord Chancellor, though it is possible that Salesbury continued to work as his deputy in Wales. January saw the execution of Somerset and the appointment of Thomas Goodrich, bishop of Ely, as Lord Chancellor. There was no position for Salesbury, but the likelihood is that he wished to return to Wales. He would have reasoned that with the publication of *Kynniver Llith a Ban* he had achieved all that was possible under the current regime. It was from early in 1552 that the young king's health began to deteriorate. Fears for the future and the positioning and plotting behind the throne made this an age of anxiety. A quieter life in a rural backwater might suddenly have looked attractive.

There had been no hostile reaction from the authorities over the printing of his unofficial prayer book, but the possibility of a change of attitude on the Council's part, meant that distance from the seat of power would be a sensible precaution. Out of sight was out of mind. More practically, he needed to sell as many copies as he could. The cost of printing must have been substantial. There is no dedication in the book, so it must be assumed that Salesbury had met the costs himself. With the future uncertain he needed to recoup the money as quickly as possible. Great wealth had not saved Somerset, but money gives a certain security or at least a sense of security. Furthermore, there was little point in risking so much to produce a prayer book if it was not going to be used by the clergy. The response of those whom he approached is unknown but, with their generally poor level of education and suspicion of innovation, it is likely to have been a dispiriting one.

Another reason for his return was the nature of his next book, for which he would need access to his manuscript collection. Throughout Europe, Humanists were adopting and promoting the figures of speech that had adorned classical literature. Salesbury wished to familiarise his countrymen, but especially the bards, with the techniques of rhetoric and to do so he would need to give examples from Welsh poetry.

Such a project would provide a distraction from the growing unease he would have felt concerning his estate. In 1550, Salesbury's cousin, Jane verch Dafydd ap William of Cochwillan, had married Puleston's greatest enemy, Rhys Gruffydd, the man who claimed Puleston's granddaughters' inheritance; it would not have pleased the man who held the ward-ship of Gwen and Elen Salesbury. Puleston's death the following year made matters uncertain. Who held the ward-ship now? Had it gone into abeyance or been inherited or had it been sold? There is no mention of it or of Gwen and Elen in Puleston's will.[1] There is no further evidence of the dispute until 1554.[2] Equally worrying for Salesbury would have been that Puleston's widow, Jonet, was the sister of John Wyn ap Maredudd, who was infamous for his ruthless acquisition of land with no regard given to legal or moral considerations.

The balance of power had tipped back towards Price. Salesbury's political contacts had tended to be in Somerset's camp. Northumberland was now in control of the kingdom and Price and his allies were well placed locally and within the Northumberland sphere of influence.[3] While Salesbury still had access to London and the Court of Star Chamber, he had a means to defend himself, but he would have been aware of his weakened position.

A legal document from the 1590s[4] (a protracted and tedious land dispute in which the plaintiff was the widower of Elen Salusbury, Salesbury's niece) casts light on an event that took place forty years earlier, 'This do you know or [same ?] you remember that the said Ellyn Salusburye by virtue of the lande [----- ?] grant the said farm of Trefriw to her uncle Ellis Price Doctor at lawe who occupied the farme by his sister Katrin lloid for the span of x to xij years.'

Though it is not a contemporary document and 'x to xij years' is a little vague, it is the only record of the number of years that Catrin was 'put away' and illustrates the depth of ill-feeling caused by the dispute. It is not known how soon after Robert Salusbury's death in 1540 that the strain on the relationship led to the estrangement between Salesbury and Catrin. If it occurred within a short time and the 1590s' document is accurate, the date of reconciliation would have been sometime between 1550 and 1554. Salesbury's presence in London up to 1552 makes 1550 and 1551 improbable. It might well be that 1552 was the year that he decided to take Catrin back into the family home.

Perhaps a genuine reconciliation took place, but taking into account the practical, hard-headed nature of marriage during Tudor times, it is more likely that Salesbury realised that such a move on his part was inevitable. Should Edward die and be succeeded by the fervently Catholic Mary, the author of Protestant propaganda for Nicholas Ridley would no longer be in a position to seek justice in London. Taking Catrin back was the only card that he had to play. If he waited too long, it would lose its value. Hindsight suggests that it was the right move to make at that time, but Salesbury did not have the benefit of hindsight and might have delayed the reconciliation until it was not voluntary or tactical, but forced.

A book of rhetoric

Whatever his worries and whatever his domestic arrangements, after five books in two years, 1552 saw Salesbury's last work for more than a decade. Most people would have found it impossible to undertake a new literary project with so many concerns vying for supremacy, but Salesbury seems to have been capable of writing under the most difficult of circumstances.

He had been highly critical of the poetry produced by the bards, believing that Gruffudd Hiraethog was the only contemporary poet who cherished and gave succour to the language; he had said so in *Oll Synnwyr*.

Throughout Europe, Erasmus and the other Humanist teachers had inspired a fascination with the works of the classical poets and orators, which in turn had led to the study of the techniques used by writers such as Ovid, Virgil, Horace, Cicero and Cato. Books had started to appear on the subject, at first in Latin, most notably Petrus Mosellanus's *Tabulae de Schematibus et Tropis* (1516) and Joannes Susenbrotus's *Epitome Troporum ac Schematum* (1540), and then in vernacular languages, for example Leonard Cox's *The Arte or Crafte of Rhetoryke* (1530) and Richard Sherry's *A treatise of Schemes and Tropes* (1550).

Salesbury reasoned that a book on rhetoric, *Llyfr Rhetoreg*,[5] in which the bards could read about and see examples of the figures of speech that had adorned the finest works of Rome and Athens, was the solution to the problem. If something needed to be done and no one else was prepared to do it, then he would take action. When the Welsh were in need of a prayer book, he provided one, albeit in a discreet manner. The bards needed a book on rhetoric, so he would write one, though this book would not be printed but would circulate in manuscript form.

The immediate suspicion is that a lack of money determined this decision. Printing would be expensive and with a book aimed at so limited an audience there was no likelihood of recouping the costs and, in the absence of a Welsh press, printing would have required lengthy journeys to England.

But Salesbury understood the thinking of the bards. He knew that they were hostile towards the printed word, which represented an alien culture and was a threat to their livelihood, especially their work as copyists. The best way to reach out to them was to produce a handwritten text that could be freely circulated and copied, a strategy vindicated by its success. There are fifteen surviving manuscript copies of *Llyfr Rhetoreg* and no doubt there were many more. In fact, there are more surviving copies of this work than for all but a handful of his printed books.[6]

However, before he could start the process of circulating the work amongst the bards, he had to overcome the personal hostility they felt towards him, a state of affairs to which he had contributed. The blunt tone used in *Oll Synnwyr* had been repeated in *A briefe and a playne introduction* and been augmented with the publication, on the last page, of two of their traditional metres, a highly provocative act.

Fortunately, Gruffudd Hiraethog was there to act as a Trojan horse. As the leading bard of the day, he commanded respect and his example and recommendation would carry great weight. He was also a bardic teacher, whose pupils included Simwnt Fychan, Wiliam Llŷn, Owain Gwynedd, Wiliam Cynwal, Siôn Tudur, Siôn Philyp and Lewys ab Edward.[7]

One of the most famous copies is that made by Simwnt Fychan (MS J9), a very revealing document. Simwnt makes some changes to Salesbury's original version, but respects its integrity apart from any comment critical of the bards, which is suppressed. Salesbury added notes to Simwnt's copy (for example, giving the figures their Greek and Latin names, putting in some new Welsh examples and writing about hypozeugma and prozeugma), unaware of or unconcerned at the censorship that had taken place.

Simwnt's attitude seems typical of the response of the bards; their curiosity and commitment to their craft overcame any professional or personal hostility they felt towards Salesbury.

A unique survivor

Through good fortune, Salesbury's original manuscript and the letter[8] to Gruffudd Hiraethog that accompanied it have survived. Salesbury's other manuscript book, his herbal, is lost; it is known from copies made soon after Salesbury's death. No drafts survive of any of his printed books. There are manuscripts (most notably Peniarth 99 and Cwrtmawr 3) that contain his copies of Welsh poems, but this is the only extensive piece of his original prose in his own hand.

Plas Isa has been demolished and little remains of Cae Du. His grave is unmarked and there is no portrait. *Llyfr Rhetoreg* is the object that connects us most closely to William Salesbury.

It is, also, the only one of his works never to have been printed.

It is a small book, roughly octavo sized and is in a remarkably good condition. It is much easier to read than the Star Chamber document that records the attack on Salesbury by Elis Price and his accomplices. However, at some time in its history a bookbinder blessed with more enthusiasm than proficiency cropped the side and bottom edges of the pages, which means that some notes in the margin are lost or partly lost as, on occasion, is the word at the end of a line. Sometimes the end of the last sentence on the page is lost, as there is a tendency for Salesbury's writing to slope downwards from the line.

The hand is easy to read, bold but not over-big and leaning slightly to the right. From time to time Salesbury becomes so involved with what he is writing that he forgets the need for legibility, making deciphering more of a challenge. There are occasional crossings out. Halfway through the book he appears to be in a rush to finish: the writing gets smaller, then bigger and the crossings out more frequent. In the margins there is a comment accredited to Gruffudd Hiraethog and many notes in the hand of Simwnt Fychan.

The letter

The letter that accompanies the book is addressed to Gruffudd Hiraethog and 'eraill oei Gelfyddyd', others of his art.

Kynniver Llith a Ban is not mentioned by name, but in the opening paragraph, when he tells Gruffudd that he is considering abandoning writing altogether, we can infer the reception it was accorded, '... nid yn unic ar attal vy llaw rac escrivenny dim yn yr iaith yma, anid ar yscoi vyccolwc o ywrth pop llyfr y beddei dim o hanei escrivenedic ynto' (not only stopping my hand from writing anything in this language, but averting my gaze from every book in which there is any [Welsh] written.)

Salesbury had hinted in his books of 1550 that there had been adverse criticism of his work, but the rawness of this response clearly indicates a more recent setback. Compounding that feeling of despair and lack of recognition was the lack of any response from the five bishops; being ignored can be more humiliating than outright rejection.

What is surprising about Salesbury is not that he considered abandoning all attempts to write and help the people of his country, but that he persevered, somehow finding the will and energy to produce this, his last work before the long hiatus of his distinctly two-stage career.

Curiously, as he continues his letter he more often than not forgets to ignore nasal mutation, as if the disappointment had drained him of the energy to follow his own orthography, but soon his enthusiasm starts to reassert itself. He shows his penchant for puns, making an adjective meaning 'longing' (hiraeth) from Hiraethog, Gruffudd's bardic name. Gruffudd is referred to as Atlas, bearing the burden of maintaining the quality of Welsh poetry and Salesbury states that he must share the burden with him, hence the book. An allusion to Prometheus continues the classical theme.

Then there is one of those extended metaphors that he loved so much. He, himself, is not a carpenter (he describes the process of preparing the timber from the marking and felling of the oak trees to shaping the joints), his object is to turn an old monastery into a mansion, something that both John Prise and William Herbert had done.[9] In other words he wished, 'to move the pillars of the Latins to a building of Kamber's language [Welsh]' (tr.) 'ysmuto Cambyst y Llatinwyr i adeilad Kamber iaith.' (Note the Cambyst/Kamber pun.)

He continues the metaphor by calling the bards 'benseiri yr iaith' (the architects of the language), perhaps an attempt to divert their attention from his previous criticism. ('Saer' is carpenter, 'pensaer' is architect, but I think this is a coincidence rather than a pun.)

Salesbury speaks of his willingness to share the book with others, of Gruffudd's geniality and asks if Gruffudd would share his bardic information with him. (This is probably a disingenuous move on Salesbury's part to deflect suspicion from his friend, as Gruffudd is likely to have done so already.) He finishes the letter with Renaissance modesty, apologising for calling his work a book when it is no more than the 'germ' of a book, and hoping that Gruffudd will perfect it.

(If his letter did not win Gruffudd over to the cause of persuading the bards to use classical figures of speech in their work, there is a detail in the book itself that would have done so. Whilst discussing 'Aschematiston' he mentions an educated young Welshman he had met at St Paul's in London, who had been critical of Welsh poetry and its lack of adornment. The flow of Welshmen from Wales to England and the subsequent loss of their language and culture greatly concerned Gruffudd and he prepared a collection of texts, *Lloegr drigiant ddifyrrwch Bryttanaidd Gymro*,[10] in an attempt to maintain or rekindle their interest.)

Salesbury's work is an adaptation of Petrus Mosellanus's *Tabulae de Schematibus et Tropis*,[11] mentioned earlier. The words 'copyright' and 'plagiarism' might flash into the modern reader's mind, but the law of copyright did not exist, nor was there any real concept of such a thing. Similarly, originality was not regarded as the great virtue it later became. There was knowledge and it should be passed on, the figures of speech discussed no more belonged to Petrus Mosellanus than they did to Salesbury.

Structure

Llyfr Rhetoreg is divided into three sections: Figur (figure), Bai (fault) and Rinwedd (virtue).

Salesbury translated the book into Welsh from necessity; he knew that few of the bards could understand Latin and fewer still, if any, could speak Greek. Mosellanus gave transcription of the figures' Greek names as well as versions in Latin. Salesbury, who delighted in introducing Latinised spellings into Welsh, finds himself Cymricising Greek.

For most examples the process was not difficult; break down the Greek word into its elements, replace them with Welsh equivalents and unite them in a suitable form.[12]

So with 'metathesis', 'meta' (across) becomes 'traws', 'tithenai' (to place) becomes 'gosod' and the Welsh form is 'trawsodiat'. Similarly, 'prolepsis' is broken up into its elements of 'pro' (before) 'rhac' and 'lambanein' (to take) 'cymeryd' to produce 'rackymeriat'.

(Salesbury did not have to create new terms for parts of speech. Terms such as 'gender' (cenedl), 'noun' (enw) and 'mood' (modd) already existed and could be found in the bards' books of grammar, as they called their secret tomes. Salesbury uses these terms, an indication that he had had access to them.)

However, there is one term that did not meet with Gruffudd's approval. Salesbury abandons the process outlined above and translates 'hyperbole' as 'kelwydd' (a lie). Gruffudd (it is almost certainly his writing) urges him in the margin to give a fairer name to the figure, '… roi henw a vo tegach ar y fugur.'

Interestingly, in 1589 George Puttenham, nephew of Thomas Elyot, brought out *The Arte of English Poesie* and amongst the figures covered is, 'Hyperbole, or the Overreacher, otherwise called the Loud Liar.'[13]

The judgement found in the heading is repeated in the final sentence of the entry, 'I for his immoderate excess call him the Overreacher, right with his original, or Loud Liar, and methinks not amiss.'

Perhaps for the sixteenth-century reader this definition of hyperbole was too harsh, but today, when the shortened form of the word, 'hype', is a synonym for 'deception' and we are continually warned, 'Don't believe the hype', it has become a most appropriate translation and definition.

Salesbury's other innovation in *Llyfr Rhetoreg* is to give Welsh examples for the figures of speech. Again, this was an act of necessity, but one he would wholeheartedly have embraced, allowing him the pleasure of trawling through his collection of poetry manuscripts to find the most suitable line. Other books of rhetoric in vernacular languages tended to give classical or biblical examples.

There are occasions where he uses a Latin example only, as with 'Epanalepsis', either because Welsh did not lend itself to that particular figure or he had failed to find a good illustration. For some entries he gives a Latin and a Welsh example, as with 'Paroemion' (alliteration).

Amongst the bards whose lines appear as examples are: Tudur Aled, Dafydd ap Gwilym, Lewis Glyn Cothi, Siôn Cent, Iolo Goch, Guto'r Glyn, Dafydd ab Edmwnd, Lewys Môn and, not surprisingly, Gruffudd Hiraethog. (Sadly, the Gruffudd quotation, it illustrates 'Synchysis', comes from a poem that is now lost, *Marwnad Ihon Puleston* [Elegy for John Puleston],[14] which in the light of the sea of troubles about to sweep over Salesbury is hugely ironic.)

For the illustration of the figure 'Paroemion' (mentioned above) Salesbury uses the lines that appeared on the last page of *A briefe and a playne introduction*:

> Kû adardûy Koed irdec
> Kofert hardd mewn kyfair tec.
>
> [A fresh wood's pleasant aviary,
> Sweet shelter in a fair place.]

There are occasional moments of carelessness in the work, such as the omission of examples or definitions, though there is always the possibility that some of these were not oversights and that he intended to fill in the gaps at a later date.

He uses his Latinised vocabulary ('Kamberaec' and 'cymporth' (a 'p' added as in English words such as 'receipt')), but in a technical book of this sort such words are not particularly frequent. It does not seem to have deterred the bards from studying the work, as shown by the numbers of copies that were made and circulated. It helped develop a common ground between them, though none of the bards saw fit to honour Salesbury with a poem.

Influence

The manuscript passed from Gruffudd to Simwnt Fychan, who made his copy, which he added to his own work, *Pum Llyfr Cerddwriaeth* [Five Books of Minstrelsy]. Soon after that, the original went missing and did not reappear until its acquisition by William Maurice of Llansilin[15] in 1664. During these years Simwnt's copy became the 'master copy' from which others worked.[16] The greater co-operation that developed between Salesbury and the members of Gruffudd's circle can be seen by his additions to Simwnt's copy, in the notes Wiliam Cynwal made on figures of speech (in MS Cardiff 38) and in Salesbury's additions to the Geirfa (compendium of vocabulary) of Wiliam Llŷn (MS Hafod 26).

Just as the dictionary was incorporated into John Davies's *Dictionarium Duplex* of 1632,[17] so *Llyfr Rhetoreg* was the basis, but not the sole source book, for Henri Perri's *Egluryn Phraethineb* [An Explanation of Eloquence], printed in 1595 by John Danter, printer of the first quarto of *Romeo and Juliet*.

Perri's use of *Llyfr Rhetoreg* is typical of the interest shown by antiquaries in Salesbury's work in the years after his death and a counterbalance to the reaction shown by many during his lifetime. Another copy of the book, one made by Rhisiart ap Siôn (MS Peniarth 159) was bought by Robert Vaughan of Hengwrt (*c.*1592–1667), whose priceless collection of manuscripts became the core around which the National Library of Wales was formed in 1907.

In his history of the literature of Wales, *Hanes Llenyddiaith Cymru*, Professor Thomas Parry writes, 'Nothing could be more contrary to the traditional ideas of the bards than the attitude of these men [the Humanists].' (tr.)[18]

Yet, in at least one respect, Salesbury managed to bridge that divide, arousing the bards' interest in the figures of speech used in the classical world. That was an achievement and if the artistic success enjoyed by Wiliam Llŷn, Siôn Phylip and Siôn Tudur, all pupils of Gruffudd Hiraethog and all members of the next generation of bards, is a guide then he succeeded in his primary aim of raising the standard of Welsh poetry.

In a land on the periphery of Europe, with none of the educational or cultural advantages enjoyed by rich and powerful states such as England, France and Spain, he had produced four works that were cornerstones of Humanism, a dictionary, a collection of adages, a substantial body of scriptural translations and a book of rhetoric. In terms of Humanist learning Wales was punching well above its weight and the man responsible was William Salesbury.

No doubt there were plaudits and thanks from within his circle of friends, but from the nation as a whole there was nothing. It would have been natural to brood bitterly on such ingratitude and lack of recognition, but in the years that were to follow it was danger and strategies for survival that would dominate Salesbury's thoughts, not resentment.

Chapter Fifteen

A Catholic Queen

Northumberland's fall, Mary's accession

During the last months of Edward's reign, Northumberland worked furiously to secure his own survival after the king's death.

Salesbury might have returned to Wales, but he could not escape the effects of events that would unfold in London. Surviving the dangerous and anxious years that lay ahead could not be guaranteed and every aspect of his life would be affected.

On Whit Sunday (21 May) 1553 the Lord Protector's second son, Lord Guildford Dudley, was married to Lady Jane Grey, the sixteen-year-old,[1] Protestant granddaughter of Mary Tudor, Henry VIII's younger sister. That same day William Herbert's older son, Henry, married Jane's sister, Lady Catherine. Alliances were being consolidated.

Henry VIII's will had stated that Princess Mary was to succeed Edward, but Northumberland persuaded the dying King to name Lady Jane Grey as his successor[2] and on 10 July she was proclaimed Queen of England.

There was support in the regions, too. Elis Price is thought to have been the man behind the declaration[3] in Denbigh of Jane as Queen and Mary as traitor, but Northumberland soon lost his authority. The Privy Council abandoned him, William Herbert shamelessly declaring to his fellow councillors, 'Either this sword shall make Mary queen or I'll lose my life.' As wily as ever, he had ensured that his son's marriage had not been consummated and it was soon annulled. Within hours of Mary being denounced as a traitor in Denbigh the townsfolk were informed that she had been proclaimed Queen.

(Price disassociated himself from Northumberland and served as M.P. for

Merioneth in 1553 and as its sheriff in 1556. Though Mary never fully trusted Herbert, he continued to be a presence at court.)

If Mary had been timorous, Northumberland might have succeeded, but on Edward's death she had ridden to East Anglia to raise an army of supporters. This display of courage and resolve was a major factor in her securing the crown. Towards the end of her progress towards the capital Mary was lavishly entertained by none other than Richard Rich, who during the reign became 'infamous for his energetic persecution of heretics'.[4]

The Queen entered London in triumph on 3 August. Nineteen days later Northumberland was executed. How Salesbury must have regretted his 'lauding' of Rich's conversion to Protestantism in *The baterie of the Popes Botereulx*. Though he might have relinquished his post as Rich's deputy in Wales sometime earlier, if he had not, it is unimaginable that he held the position during Mary's reign.

The following year, William Paulet resigned as the Master of the Court of Wards and Liveries[5] and was replaced by Sir Francis Englefield.[6] This was, no doubt, a reward for Englefield's loyalty to Mary during the difficult years of Edward's reign. In August 1551, he and two colleagues (Waldegrave and Rochester) had been sent to the Tower for not enforcing the ban on the princess saying mass. The council dispatched Rich, as Lord Chancellor, to Mary's residence, Copt Hall, to try to enforce the prohibition. She was defiant, refusing the deputation entry and informing them angrily that her three servants in the Tower were 'the honester men'. There is a possibility that Salesbury had accompanied Rich. If so, he would have witnessed the strength of Mary's religious beliefs at first hand.

It was not until the announcement of her forthcoming marriage to Philip of Spain that she attracted any hostility from those of her subjects who were not committed Protestants, but it was the followers of the new religion who tried to stop the marriage. Mostly the threats of revolt petered out; the one serious challenge, the Wyatt Rebellion[7] of January 1554, was brutally put down (Herbert had been in command of the troops defending London). Lady Jane Grey and her husband, neither of whom had been involved in the revolt, were executed. By July of that year the marriage had taken place and the kingdom was ruled by Philip and Mary.

(Herbert, earl of Pembroke, had greeted Philip on his arrival at Southampton and charmed him with his rough-diamond bonhomie so that despite the Queen's suspicions, his continued membership of the Privy Council was assured.)

Mary sanctioned Reginald Pole's return from exile and he replaced Cranmer as archbishop of Canterbury. The clergy was cleansed of Protestants, though in the middle and lower orders those who quietly acquiesced managed to retain their positions. Hundreds of Englishmen, clergy and laity, including colleagues of Salesbury such as Crowley and Bale, went into exile with their families. Just one prominent Welshman, Richard Davies (he would serve as a bishop under Elizabeth), joined them.

Mary accepted that she would be unable to undo the dissolution of the monasteries, but in all other respects the kingdom was undergoing a full return to the Catholic fold under the direction of the Queen, Archbishop Pole, Stephen Gardiner (bishop of Winchester) and Edmund Bonner ('Bloody Bonner', bishop of London).

In 1554, though they might have prayed fervently against it, there was no reason for Protestants to suspect that the project would not be successful. The Queen, at thirty-eight, was still young enough to give birth to an heir, who would be brought up in her faith. Even if she did not have a child, she was as likely as anyone in that age who had survived infancy to reach her three score years and ten, ample time to return England to Rome. With Lady Jane executed, the one hope for Salesbury's co-religionists was the survival of Princess Elizabeth, but hardline voices were demanding that the illegitimately conceived offspring of the, in their language, Protestant whore, Anne Boleyn, who had seduced the King with witchcraft and betrayed him with licentious and incestuous adultery, should meet the same fate as her mother. Elizabeth submitted herself to all the rituals of the Catholic Church. No one believed that she had undergone a conversion, but the observance of conformity was a factor in her survival.

Defenceless

Salesbury must have despaired at the state of the kingdom and would have feared for his well-being. He had supported Ridley and Cranmer in print and put forward arguments for the marriage of priests. Cranmer was about to be tried for heresy; his prosecutor would be Thomas Martin, author of *A Traictise Declaryng and plainly Provyng, That the Pretensed Marriage of Priestes, and Professed Persones, is No Mariage*. Ridley would be burnt in October 1555, as would Cranmer in March of the following year. Amongst the martyrs whom Salesbury might well have met during his time in London were Ridley, Rogers and Hooper. In addition, somewhere in north Wales was a stockpile of copies of *Kynniver Llith a Ban*.[8] A royal proclamation of 1555 would declare, 'No one to print in Latin or in English the Common Prayer Book of Edward VI set forth by the authority of Parliament. Anyone who has them to give them up within fifteen days. Bishops, Sheriffs, etc., to inquire as to persons owning such books.'[9]

Salesbury was as vulnerable as a newborn lamb. He dared not travel to London. (Within a short distance of Thavies Inn were Smithfield, where over two hundred Protestants[10] were burnt, and the Church of the Holy Sepulchre, where the remains of John Rogers, first of the martyrs, were laid to rest. In Southwark, where he had leased a property, the Church of St Mary Overie was used by Stephen Gardiner, bishop of Winchester, as a consistory court and seven people were tried there, found guilty of heresy and condemned to death.) Though there were no burnings in north Wales, and just three in the south,[11] Chester, less than forty miles from Llanrwst, was the scene of the martyrdom of George Marsh in April 1555. The assizes at Denbigh or Caernarfon would have been the limit of any journey he could make with any expectation of a safe return. If he wished to contest the ward-ship of Gwen and Elen, the master of the court was a hardline Catholic and loyal supporter of Mary who had been present at the trial of Bishop Hooper, the man who had sent Gesner a copy of Salesbury's dictionary.

On 1 October 1554, Elis Price struck. MS Bangor (Mostyn) 1926[12] is the agreement between him:

> John Wyn ap Meredythe, esq., Gruffuth Wynne ap John, his son, David
> Owein, clerk, and Morice Kyffin, his natural son ... concerning the estate of
> Robert Salusburie, gent. of Llanroste, deceased, consisting of a house called the
> 'mancione place of llan Roste' with its demesnes and other lands appurtenant
> thereto in the hundreds of Vuchaled, Issaled, Istulas and Dyffryn Klyed, co.

Denbigh, part of which is held in copyhold, part by soccage in freehold and part of the Crown by knight service, R.S. died leaving two daughters Gwen and Elyne, both under 21 years of age, by reason whereof the Crown is entitled to their wardship.

But William Salusburie, R.S.'s brother has wrongfully intruded into the estate and disinherited the two daughters. John Wyn ap Meredyth and David Owein have bought the wardship from Sir John Puleston, to whom it was granted by Edward VI, and it has been agreed that Gruffith Wynne shall marry Gwen and Morice Kyffin Elyne.

The parties accordingly covenant as follows:

(i)   Elice Price is to have the moiety of the estate, which will be legally conveyed to him by Griffith and Gwen and Morice and Elyne when Gwen and Elyne come of age;

(ii) John Wyn and David Owein, and Gruffith Wyn and Morice Kyffin to permit John Price of Egloisege, esq., to occupy and enjoy, during the minority of Gwen and Elyne, the lands which were lately in the possession of William Salusburie and receive the rents and profits thereof to the yearly value of five marks of that part of the lands as shall be theirs after the division made between them and Elice Price, to the use of Katherine verch Robert, natural sister of the said Elice;

(iii) Gruffith Wyn and Gwen and Morice Kyffin and Elyne, when Gwen and Elyne come of age, to make a sufficient assurance of the said Katherine Lloyd for her life and to her heirs by William Salusburie.[13]

Salesbury had lost everything. Price had gained his revenge or, if Salesbury really had 'wrongfully intruded into the estate and disinherited the two daughters', he had put right an injustice.

The character and record of Price cloud the judgement of those aware of his many misdemeanours. Ap Maredudd belonged to a class for whom aggressive acquisition was a natural and unquestioned form of behaviour. Had Puleston really sold the ward-ship of the two girls? A dead man could not contest that claim and his widow was ap Maredudd's sister. Perhaps, under pressure or naively, he had done; his chief concern, after all, was ensuring the inheritance of his three granddaughters. The matter is academic; Salesbury could do nothing about it. The case for Salesbury is as follows:

That both Price and ap Maredudd had been members of the arbitration panel that in 1546 divided Robert Salusbury's estate between Gwen and

Elen and Salesbury and his grandmother, Gwenhwyfar. Yet here they are dismembering that agreement.

The two men who would marry Gwen and Elen would thereby gain their inheritance. So ap Maredudd and Owen had a vested interest in taking as much from Salesbury as possible. (In the event, Elen's marriage to Kyffin did not take place.)

There was no reason for the girls to marry whilst they were minors. If they had waited until they were adults they could have chosen their own husbands. They could have chosen to remain single and kept their inheritance for themselves.

What right did Elis Price have to a 'moiety' of the inheritance after Gwen and Elen reached adulthood?

What right did his brother, John, have to a share of the inheritance 'lately in the possession of William Salusburie'?

Price's concern for his sister's well-being is admirable, but what right did she have to any part of her nieces' estate?

These are valid objections, but ones that Salesbury could not raise. Price's dominance of the local power structure can be seen in his holding of the following offices: High Sheriff of Merioneth in 1552 and 1556, High Sheriff of Denbighshire in 1557 and High Sheriff of Caernarfonshire in 1558. In addition, Morus Wynn was High Sheriff of Caernarfonshire in 1554, a post held by his father, John Wyn ap Maredudd in 1556.

There was only one way that Salesbury could have tried to mount a defence of his estate, by sending his grandmother (if she were still alive) or his mother as surrogates to the Court of Chancery. However drastic the times, that was not a course of action that he could have inflicted on his grandmother, who would have been in her eighties. Annes might only have been in her early sixties, but travel was arduous and potentially dangerous. Salesbury's sons would have been approaching their twentieth birthday and could have accompanied her, but if they did, might he not be endangering their well-being, too?

No action was taken. Perhaps Salesbury feared that an act of defiance would trigger a life-threatening retaliation.

Gwen's marriage went ahead as planned. Elen, however, did not marry Maurice Kyffin but Ieuan Llwyd (Lloyd) of Rhiwgoch, Merioneth. They had one son, Robert Lloyd who, with delightful irony, went on to become M.P. for his county in 1586, breaking 'Price's hold on the shire seat'.[14] After Ieuan's death, Elen married Owain Wynn, one of Gruffudd's four brothers. They had four children, John, Gwen, Elen and Gruffudd.[15]

Gwen and her husband settled in Berthddu, once owned by her father. Among other bequests in his father's will, Gruffudd was left £10 'in redie moneys towards the building of his house'.[16] Elen and Owain made their home near Trefriw at Caemelwr, which had been another of Robert's properties.[17] Berthddu, Caemelwr and Plas Isa are all within a mile or so of one another; Gwydir, home of the Wynns, is just a mile across the river Conwy from Llanrwst. If there was friction between the families during the 1560s and 1570s, when matters might be assumed to have settled down, there would have been many awkward or uncomfortable moments.

The sisters married into a wealthy dynasty, lived in spacious houses, had families and enjoyed lives of material comfort. The dispute between their uncles had not affected their life chances. Might it have done if the agreement of 1546 had still been in force? Had Salesbury gone beyond ensuring what was rightfully his (and his grandmother's) and taken from the girls? Few would doubt Price's villainy nor the complicity of his brother, the Wynns and David Owen, but that should not distract us from the possibility that Salesbury might also have been avaricious. It was an age of avarice when those who did not defend their property aggressively, lost it.

A mystery

The agreement states that Maurice Kyffin's[18] father, David Owen had, with ap Maredudd, bought the ward-ship from Sir John Puleston. The two men had joint, equal control of Gwen and Elen; so why did Kyffin's marriage to Elen not take place? Might there have been an act of betrayal by Elis Price? The evidence does not support that theory.

Though Salesbury was not in a position to travel to London, Henry Johns, parson of Llanrwst was and sometime in 1554 or 1555 he brought a case (NA C 1/1325/16–19) against Price and David Owen. It centred on the 'occupation of complainant's parsonage under a lease from Robert Salusbury, his predecessor, whose occupancy was annulled by marriage'. Johns brought the case in London rather than locally because the defendants were known 'most ... affectionately unto their kynne and friends by reason wherof your said orator can in no wyse have any hope of any indifferent tryall therof of the common law of thys Realm', the same argument Salesbury had used in his action against Price in 1547.

Price's response to the charges has survived. He does not defend himself, but counterattacks aggressively, stating that Johns's case is 'unsound' and 'insufficient in the lawe to be answered' and as part of his rebuttal of the charges, the names of 'Moryss Kyffyn' and 'Robert Wynn' are presented to bolster his arguments.

There is no reason, therefore, to suspect Price of reneging on his promise of Elen's hand to Kyffin. No other explanation for the marriage failing to take place is apparent.

Plas Isa

Finally, what was the fate of Plas Isa, the 'mancione place of llan Rooste'? It was the pride of the Salesbury family, conferring status upon them and symbolising their membership of the gentry. It had been inherited by his grandmother and she had brought it into the Salesbury domain on her marriage to Robert Salusbury senior.

The 1546 arbitration document, to which ap Maredudd and Price put their signatures, unequivocally awards it to Gwenhwyfar and Salesbury. The 1554 agreement is not well drafted and is open to several interpretations, not least that the 'mancione place' actually refers to Plas Isa, but it is not unreasonable to assume that Salesbury's home was taken from him.

There are three reasons to assume that this was the case, the first being that there was nothing to prevent Price and ap Maredudd from doing so and it was not in the nature of either man to resist temptation. Plas Isa was, in modern parlance, a prime piece of real estate. A document of 1546 to which they had put their names would not have constrained them in 1554.

Second is the deep-seated local belief that Salesbury spent Mary's reign at Cae Du. Llansannan would have been no safer than Llanrwst, had Mary's lieutenants been despatched to find him. In fact, being slightly closer to Chester (scene of a burning) and to St Asaph (seat of a Catholic bishop) it was marginally less safe. Salesbury would not have chosen a cramped house in Llansannan (whether it was Cae Du or another) in preference to the spacious and well-appointed environs of Plas Isa unless the decision had been forced upon him. With Catrin now back in the family home and their brood of children growing bigger as a result, Salesbury would have sought refuge from his woes and worries in silent study; Plas Isa could amply have provided that, Cae Du much less so.

Further evidence comes from the will of John Wyn ap Maredudd,[19] who died shortly after Queen Elizabeth's accession, an event which enabled Salesbury to resume his campaign for restitution of what he regarded as his rightful estate, but above all, his family home. A passage in the will states that he is openly prepared to declare that if any man could prove that he had wrongfully taken any of his goods, his executors Elen (his widow), Morus and Gruffudd (his two eldest sons) were to compensate the complainant, which suggests in its hurt tone of bafflement that someone could think him capable of misdemeanours and its faux air of injured innocence that Salesbury had already unleashed his dogs of war and that the squire of Gwydir was greatly discomforted by them.

Life in internal exile

The reader knows that Salesbury had to survive for five years and that he would then be free, but he was not to know that the new Queen's reign would last no longer than that of her sickly half-brother. When, on 30 April 1555, the bells of London rang out in celebration of the birth of a royal heir, the Protestants of England and Wales would have abandoned all hope. Gradually the news spread of the bizarre and pitiable phenomenon of Mary's phantom pregnancy. There was hope, but no respite from danger and anxiety. Even as Mary's death was approaching, on 10 November 1558, one week before she breathed her last, five heretics were executed in Canterbury.

Until the announcement of Mary's death there had been only one moment of professional solace for Salesbury. In 1555, Conrad Gesner, the great encyclopaedist of Protestant Humanism, published *Mithridates de*

Linguarum Observationes & Primum in general in which he catalogued all the known languages of the world. Amongst them, with a respectable entry of two pages, was Welsh. For twenty-two of the more than one hundred languages listed there was an even greater honour. Each of these entries contained a vernacular translation of the Lord's Prayer, and one of those languages was Welsh.

The orthography and vocabulary used show that the translation is not Salesbury's,[20] but it was undoubtedly his four key Humanist texts, most of all the dictionary, which Hooper had sent to Gesner, that had led to this European recognition of the language; that and his friendship with leading English Humanists (Gesner dedicated the book to Bale).

Whilst some records of Marian Wales have survived and the difficulties experienced by Protestants in general can be understood, very little is known of his life during these five years.

In nineteenth-century Wales, a society in which many people regarded the Bible as a sacred object and believed that the overwhelming reason for literacy was to study the 'good book' and so save one's soul, Salesbury's role as the pioneer of scriptural translation made him a folk hero and the story of his spending Mary's reign hidden in the secret chamber of Cae Du labouring long hours by candlelight to provide his countrymen with the New Testament captured the public imagination.

Salesbury did own property in Llansannan, the parish in which he was born, but it is oral tradition alone that places him in Cae Du. The survey of 1910 supports the existence of a 'secret chamber', but 'architectural anomaly' is an equally valid description. There was no reason to translate the New Testament. It would have been too dangerous and only a few years earlier he had completed and published a substantial translation of scriptural texts. There would be no hope of further translations until Elizabeth ascended the throne, which in 1554 appeared unlikely.

For the period of 1553 to 1558 only two of Salesbury's actions are known. A reference in his annotations[21] to the Giraldus Cambrensis manuscript (NLW MS 3024) shows that this work was undertaken in 1554 and, in 1556, John Dee 'got a Bacon Manuscript [CM 44] from Sarrisbury', which is interpreted by the authors of *John Dee's Catalogue* as Salesbury. 'Sarrisbury'[22] was an alternative form of Salisbury and throughout his life and even today Salesbury is often referred to as Salisbury, the form used by Bennett in his *English Books and Readers, 1475 to 1557.*

Whether Salesbury worked locally as a lawyer is unknown. All surviving legal cases which carry his name or the names of those he is likely to have represented are from the courts of London. What can be said with confidence is that those 'lost' years were indeed spent in Llansannan and that Catrin was living with him.

Considering the worry, danger, anger and humiliation (at the loss of his estate) that haunted every day of this period, it would appear perverse to say that Salesbury was in many ways a fortunate man, but he was. He had what Napoleon sought in his generals, 'luck'.

He had a safe part of the realm to which he could retreat. Whilst he had hostile neighbours, he also had the powerful Salusbury clan and other allied families to protect him. Having lost his wealth, there was no incentive, other than malice, to denounce him to the authorities. He was a gentleman, albeit impoverished; apart from leading church figures, the Protestant martyrs were overwhelmingly from the artisan class. His brother-in-law had waited for over a decade to see the end of the family disgrace of his sister being 'put away'; he was unlikely to undermine that long-cherished state of respectability by betraying Salesbury. Besides, were Salesbury to become a martyr, Price would have to bear the costs of looking after Catrin and her children.[23] Salesbury's pamphlet in support of the marriage of priests, a factual, academic document, had been overshadowed by the much larger and more contentious *A Defence for Mariage of Priestes by Scripture and Aunciente Wryters* of John Ponet. (It was to Ponet, not to Salesbury, that Thomas Martin addressed his blistering response.) Finally, the book that was the most likely to get him into trouble, *Kynniver Llith a Ban*, was in a language that the capital's authorities did not understand, had a misleading title, bore its author's initials rather than his name on the frontispiece, had not been widely distributed and had not been sanctioned by Northumberland's regime.[24]

Salesbury had been very fortunate and though he was living in reduced circumstances, his colleagues who had fled abroad were, generally, living in direst poverty. To many people being largely confined to one's house with only limited opportunity to travel would have been akin to imprisonment but, so long as he had access to books, manuscripts, pen and paper, Salesbury would seem to have been the sort of man who had the inner resources to cope with such an ordeal.

Secret works?

Three manuscripts, two of them already mentioned, point to the possibility that Salesbury might have been involved in activities that were far more dangerous than translating the scriptures. The evidence is circumstantial, but the activity that can be inferred from it is one where participants avoid leaving traces of their involvement.

Salesbury annotated the Giraldus manuscript in 1554. In the mid-1560s it was presented to William Cecil by Richard Davies, bishop of St Davids, who became Salesbury's colleague in the campaign for a Welsh Bible. It was common for manuscripts to pass upward through the social strata, with the gift often rewarded by a personal or political favour.

During Mary's reign, apart from some minor diplomatic work, Cecil played no part in public life, retiring to the country and, to all appearances, busying himself with estate management and local duties. However, within hours of Mary's death, Elizabeth had been declared queen and all the instruments of government were under her control. There was no opposition, despite the existence of four legitimate claimants to the throne.[25] Had there been any resistance to the well planned takeover, Lord Thynne was standing by with a force of ten thousand men at his disposal. Cecil was appointed Secretary of State, a post he held for the rest of his long life, despite moments of friction and conflict when he told the Queen what she did not wish to hear.

The assumption of many is that far from spending these years in rural isolation, Cecil had been establishing an underground network of men who would defend Elizabeth's life should it be threatened and who were ready to safeguard her ascent to the throne should misfortune befall her half-sister.

Cecil was well placed for such a task. He had been part of Somerset's government and had learnt crucial lessons from the failures and weaknesses that had led to his master's downfall. He had a host of valuable contacts from that time and from his time at Cambridge (his generation of students were to dominate the positions of power of both state and church for the rest of the century). He also had two highly important contacts within Elizabeth's household. One was his cousin,[26] Blanche Parry, the Princess's longest serving and most faithful female attendant, who had been appointed Elizabeth's nurse in 1536. In 1565 she would become her Chief Gentlewoman.

The other was a fellow Welshman, Thomas Parry, possibly a 'distant cousin', noted for his corpulence and for his habit of dipping his fingers into Elizabeth's coffers (to which his employer turned a blind eye). Apart from his petty thieving Elizabeth's chief of staff was in all other respects a model employee, loyal, incredibly cunning and devious on his mistress's behalf and an organisational genius.

Parry and Elizabeth easily, almost contemptuously, outwitted Sir Henry Bedingfield, a mixture of Polonius and Malvolio, Mary's appointee as guard and watchman at the Palace of Woodstock, where the princess was under house arrest. So ineffective was the cordon that Bedingfield placed around Woodstock that Elizabeth and her cofferer, with the help of Parry's stepson, John Fortescue, were able to send out a constant stream of messages to supporters in the country and receive intelligence of all that was happening at court.

(It was due to Parry's 'organizing genius'[27] that contact had been made with Sir John Thynne at Longleat. (Thynne had served under Somerset. He was also a colleague of Sir John Salusbury[28] of Lleweni.) It was Parry who was in contact with the garrison at Berwick-upon-Tweed, in case reinforcements were needed.)

Parry's service was recognised immediately upon Elizabeth's accession. He was made a privy councillor and was regarded as the equal of Cecil; he would have figured prominently amongst her ministers had it not been for his early death in 1560.[29]

In 1565, Matthew Parker, archbishop of Canterbury, sent Salesbury an ancient and intriguing manuscript with a request that he examine it, decipher it if he could, and send him a report on his findings. The manuscript turned out to be an Armenian Psalter. Armenian was not a language known to Salesbury, but his detailed analysis (for example, the nature and direction of the script, the alphabet used, the occurrence of place names and personal names) impressed Parker, 'I praye youe thanke Mr. Salisbury [note the spelling] whose ful writing his conjectures I like wel, and as for deciphering my quayer, in such a strange charect: yt shalbe reseved to som other oportunitye to be considered.'[30]

Parker was his generation's most famous collector of manuscripts; his range was wide, but his speciality was the manuscripts of the Anglo-Saxons. His collection has survived intact and is housed in the library of Corpus Christi College, Cambridge.

It is known that during Elizabeth's reign, Parker had a copy of Salesbury's *A Certaine Case Extracte* to support his position as a married priest, Ponet by then being anathema to the establishment, but there is no record of the men ever meeting. (During Edward's reign Parker had prospered under Northumberland, not Somerset, so there would have been little overlap with Salesbury's time in London.) Who had recommended Salesbury to Parker as someone capable of deciphering a perplexing manuscript? The one possibility that springs to mind is Cecil. As head of Elizabeth's administration and head of her church the two men were in daily contact, usually by letter, sometimes face to face.

Cryptanalysts are usually either mathematicians (Turing or Thomas Phelippes, the breaker of Mary Stuart's code) or linguists (Champollion (hieroglyphics), Ventris (Linear B)), though until the Second World War it was the linguists who were usually the more favoured. Salesbury had studied mathematics at Oxford (arithmetic and geometry were two of the four subjects in the quadrivium), is likely to have known Robert Recorde, the leading mathematician of the day (Recorde worked for the earl of Pembroke) and was a colleague of Prise who had explained the use of Arabic numerals in *Yny lhyvyr hwnn*. He was also a linguist of prodigious accomplishment, fluent in at least ten languages.[31]

Cecil quite possibly met Salesbury during the latter's time in London (1547–1551), where they had moved in the same circles. They had several interests in common (the legal profession, Protestantism, antiquarianism, manuscript collecting) and each had a Welsh background, Salesbury as a native, Cecil as the son of a family in exile. Cecil might have heard of Salesbury's linguistic abilities, but a recommendation suggests first-hand knowledge. If

Salesbury did indeed keep Rich under surveillance, then Cecil might have known of it and marked him out for other duties.

Further evidence comes from Salesbury's meeting with Dee. There is a slight possibility that their paths overlapped in early 1552, when Dee entered Pembroke's service, but the likelihood is that Salesbury had by then returned to Wales. Like Salesbury he was an excellent linguist and, if he had continued to follow the path of true mathematics rather than more esoteric studies, would have succeeded Recorde as the finest mathematician of the day.

Dee was known in the early 1550s to have Protestant sympathies and in May 1555 was arrested and examined.[32] He was in deep trouble. However, in mysterious circumstances, Dee was released and no action was taken.

He was soon to be seen regularly in the company of Edmund Bonner, bishop of London who, like Mary, earned the soubriquet, 'Bloody'. He had none of the refinement or intelligence of Gardiner, who would come to see that the policy of burning heretics was counter-productive but died before he could make moves to persuade Mary and her chief advisors to end it. Bonner never doubted the policy. Not only is Dee recorded as being present at some of Bonner's interrogations, he is actually implicated in the executions of John Philpot and Bartlet Green.

Dee approached Queen Mary and asked to be appointed as her Royal Librarian,[33] a role he foresaw as being similar to that enjoyed by Leland under Henry VIII, travelling the country searching for and acquiring manuscripts that had survived the dissolution of the monasteries. There is no record of Mary agreeing to such an arrangement, but that did not prevent Dee from setting off on his self-appointed task. In so doing he was able to travel the kingdom without arousing suspicion. Many, if not most, of the manuscript collectors, men such as Bale, Crowley, Cecil, Parker and Salesbury, were Protestants. Dee had given himself carte blanche to travel where he liked meeting people, including those who had been active in church or state under Edward or friends or colleagues of such people. There is, for example a note about 'Robert Crowley sometime printer had Tully's translation of Cyropaedia.'[34] Crowley having fled to Frankfurt; this would, of course, entail meeting any number of his former associates in the search for the manuscript, all of whom would have been Protestant.

The whole arrangement was the perfect cover for a double agent, which is what Dee is assumed to have been. The most striking evidence for that statement is that no action was taken against him after the death of Mary.

Another piece of supporting evidence is the way he was treated in print by Foxe, who started detailing all of the martyrdoms as soon as it was safe to do so. Foxe's first account of Philpot's death came out in 1563 and includes Dee's role in the interrogation. However, by the time the account was included in the second edition of *Actes and Monumentes* (1576), his name has disappeared; he is referred to simply as 'a Doctor'. It might be surmised that someone in authority had had a discreet word with Foxe.

There is no record of Dee visiting Wales in 1556, but that may be because he chose not to make such a record. He did note, alongside the name of Robert Crowley, the names of 'Mr Edward ap Roger in Raubon 7 miles from Oswestree Northward and ... Edward Price at Mivod X miles from Oswestree, somewhat westwards.'[35] Alternatively, Salesbury might have risked a journey over the border. The manuscript that Dee bought was one by Roger Bacon, the greater part of which survives (Dee's library was vandalised in 1589) and can be found in the British Library in the volume Cotton Tiberius C.V., ff 2–151.

A study of some of the authors whose works were read by Salesbury may point to why Cecil put his name forward to Parker. Besides being one of the leading medieval scientists and mathematicians, Bacon was fascinated by codes and ciphers and was a pioneer of cryptography in the West.[36] One of his works was *Epistle on the Secret Works of Art and the Nullity of Magic*.

Chaucer, whose *Tretyse on the Astrolabe* was bought by Salesbury for John Edwards, was another author interested in codes. (He worked as a diplomat for Richard II, which might have given him a professional interest in the matter.) In fact, part of the *Tretyse on the Astrolabe*, *The Equatorie of the Planetis* contains several encrypted paragraphs.

As an accomplished Hebraist, as was Dee, Salesbury would have been aware that some of the words in the Old Testament were written in code (the Atbash cipher).

Finally, two of Salesbury's works[37] of 1567 contain the quotation 'Tra vo lleuad' (whilst the moon endureth), which comes from Psalm 72. Henry

Denham is credited as the printer of these books, but the printing was actually carried out by John Awdeley. In the second of these two books, *A playne and a familiar Introduction* the quotation is accompanied by a curious image that is, in fact, a cryptogram. It shows three intersecting crescent moons interspersed with Hebrew letters which have been interpreted as reading 'By John Awdeley'.[38]

These four pieces of evidence point to an interest in codes. Could they signify something more than an occasional pastime?

In November 1558 Mary died. Salesbury was free to travel to London and to resume friendships with old colleagues; he was no longer powerless. He had two objectives in life: to have the scriptures translated into Welsh with the full approval of Parliament and the Queen and to regain the family home of Plas Isa. To have supposed that a country lawyer from the middle of nowhere could have realised such unrealistically ambitious goals was verging on madness, but he did and of the two the latter was probably the greater challenge. There was a finality, an inevitability of Doomsday proportions, to the acquisition of property and land by the all-powerful local magnates. Once lost, a property was likely to be lost forever.

Yet Plas Isa was regained. Though the first reference to William Salesbury of Plas Isa does not occur until 1572, in Wiliam Cynwal's elegy to Catrin,[39] its re-acquisition is likely to have occurred long before that date. The family home was inherited by his son and heir, Siôn Wyn, whose widow, Elsbeth of 'Place Issa', bequeathed her estate to her two sons,[40] William and Reynald (Rheinallt), daughter, Lowri, and grandson, John.

There is no record of a court case in London. The conclusion could be drawn that Salesbury had called in a massive favour by someone who wielded enormous power. That might well be the reason for the bewilderment and defensiveness expressed in John Wyn ap Maredudd's will, the confusion of a man whose ascendency in his local domain had never been challenged suddenly meeting a force mightier than anything he could have imagined.

What exactly was William Salesbury doing in that 'secret chamber' in Cae Du between 1553 and 1558? Little is known of Cecil's years under Mary, but as Elizabeth's Secretary of State he developed a highly effective secret service, with Francis Walsingham at its head and Thomas Phelippes as the chief cryptographer.

On the same day that Mary died, her archbishop of Canterbury, Reginald Pole, breathed his last. Gardiner had died in 1555. Of the four people who instituted the policy of burning heretics, only Bonner survived. As bishop of London he stepped forward to greet the new Queen as she entered the city in triumph; he was ignored in as humiliating and contemptuous a manner as possible and imprisoned in the Marshalsea, where he ended his days.

Mysterious as ever, Dee was a frequent visitor to the disgraced and hated cleric.[41]

On 15 January 1559, Elizabeth was crowned Queen of England. The date had been carefully chosen as the most propitious for a long and successful reign. The method for determining the day was the casting of the Queen's horoscope. The man chosen for the task was Dr John Dee.[42]

Chapter Sixteen

Campaigning re-joined

Plas Isa

It is likely that regaining Plas Isa was Salesbury's prime concern in the months immediately after Mary's death, though it might have troubled his conscience that he was putting personal gain above his nation's spiritual salvation. He might also have worried that using the goodwill of the powerful for one objective might jeopardise his chances of achieving his other goal, parliamentary approval of the translation of the scriptures.

Perhaps he did not need the help of others to win back his home. He was, after all, an accomplished lawyer who had worked for the Lord Chancellor and he was a dogged and determined fighter. Though not exactly in his favour, the scales of justice were no longer tilted against him. John Wyn ap Maredudd might have preferred to settle out of court rather than have his name blackened in the Star Chamber.

If matters were still unresolved in July 1559, then the advantage would have shifted even more in Salesbury's favour. Ap Maredudd died and the greater part of his estate was inherited by his eldest son, Morus. In the will,[1] ap Maredudd names his widow, Elen, and his second son, Gruffudd, as joint executors with Morus, which may suggest a lack of confidence in his heir, a fear that he lacked the ruthlessness necessary for success in life and that he would need the resolve of others.

The gene for aggressive acquisition appears to have jumped a generation from ap Maredudd to his grandson, Sir John Wynn, who described his father, Morus, as being 'a man of a soft nature'.[2] It was not meant as a compliment.

Sir John did not allow kinship or friendship to come before profit. As shown in a previous chapter, he had made life for his uncle, Owain, difficult to the extent that the dispute between them 'grewe to great heate'.[3]

He was highly critical of the lack of iron in his father's dealings with his brother Robert (the third of the Wynn brothers) and Katheryn Salusbury of Llewenni.[4]

Morus seems to have been besotted with Katheryn,[5] a woman whose beauty was widely acclaimed and who was the granddaughter of Roland de Velville, reputed to be the illegitimate son of Henry VII. When Katherine's first husband, Sir John Salusbury, died in 1566, Morus Wynn attended the funeral intent on proposing to her, but he was already too late. When the man who had trumped him, Sir Richard Clough, died, Morus proposed again and was accepted. They had two children (Henry and Jane) before his death, after which Katheryn married for a fourth time.

If the infatuation had already developed by 1559, it would have been another weakness for Salesbury to exploit. Sir John Wynn would have put up a stubborn defence, his father does not seem to have been capable of doing so.

Finally, the last factor in Salesbury's favour is that his dispute was with Morus Wynn, not with Elis Price, who is likely to have welcomed seeing his sister as the mistress of one of the finest mansions in Denbighshire rather than a yeoman's farmhouse.

There is a bond of 1565 (in Latin)[6] in which Salesbury is referred to as 'Willielmum Salesbury de Llansannan', but this appears to be a reference to his birthplace rather than his current home. A 1567 will[7] that shows a relative living in Cae Du, the Llansannan house traditionally associated with Salesbury, adds weight to the belief that he was back in the family home several years before 1572, when a document records him as living there.[8]

The relationship with Price is intriguing. For two decades they had traded blows like heavyweights in a ring. Though both had come close to delivering knock-out punches, each saw his opponent standing, though somewhat punch drunk. Both were men of calculation and were likely to have realised that they had nothing to gain from continuing to fight except even more pain. Nothing is known of their relationship after 1554. The absence of any evidence strongly suggests that some sort of an accommodation was reached.

Salesbury is assumed to have had powerful contacts (he had, after all, gained access to Henry VIII who granted him a royal licence and he would gain the approval of the late king's daughter for the translation of the Bible, neither feat being possible without the aid of high-ranking intermediaries), but he had no ambition to build a great estate. His goals were the public-spirited ones of a Humanist. There was no danger that they would conflict with those of his brother-in-law.

Price had the low cunning to know that Salesbury was not a threat and that time spent sparring with him was unlikely to be profitable. There was easier prey to target, especially as he was soon to become immensely powerful in north Wales as 'a creature of the earl of Leicester',[9] that is the local agent and head enforcer of Robert Dudley, the son of the duke of Northumberland. Created baron of Denbigh by Elizabeth in 1563 and granted massive estates in the area, he is better known as the earl of Leicester, the title bestowed on him the following year.

Both had reason to be wary of the other. Leicester was one of the few people able to influence the Queen, and Elizabeth was known to be capricious, even petulant, and very unforgiving. One whispered word could undo years of campaigning. However, were that to happen, Salesbury would have nothing to lose in putting away Catrin for a second time. This could be the basis of the understanding, quite possibly never put into words, between them.

Price could never be accused of being a Humanist, but he had a deep love of Welsh poetry, was a patron to many bards and the main organiser of the great eisteddfod of 1567 and his son, Tomas,[10] would gain a reputation as an accomplished poet (he was also a rogue and a privateer). Price might not have understood his brother-in-law's desire to save the souls of his countrymen, but he would have had no reason to prevent him from doing so. Besides, with his connections in high places, Salesbury might one day be in a position to further Price's own plans.

A 'Welsh' Queen

With so much detail of Salesbury's life missing, conjecture is unavoidable. Whatever the history of his ownership of Plas Isa and his relationship with Price, the Wynns and other members of the local gentry, his campaign to obtain the scriptures in Welsh, which had begun in 1547 and was now being re-launched in earnest, is much less of a mystery.

Salesbury's status as a linguist and scholar has never been doubted. The quality of his translations has been a matter of debate, but he has champions as well as detractors. His praise as a political genius has never been sung, but is indisputable. His powers of observation and analysis, allied to an uncanny ability to see when an opportunity arose, made him unique in Tudor Wales. In addition, once an opportunity was identified, he had the organisational skills, the energy and the diplomacy to win over the people who could help him bring his project to fruition.

He had done so in the 1540s, when he and John Prise had gained royal permission for their books to be printed and within a few years he had produced four great Humanist works (the dictionary, the adages, a treatise on rhetoric (in manuscript form) and the (unsanctioned) translation of the scriptures), which brought his native culture to the attention of intellectuals across Europe.

After compiling the dictionary, he saw that it had become possible to make the call for a Welsh Bible. The move brought him scorn and won no support, but he had planted the idea in the minds of his compatriots. Now, after the despair of Mary's reign, he could see that all the positive factors that could make his grand desire a reality were moving into perfect alignment. The opportunity would never again arise.

The church in Wales was a completely different organisation (at the highest level, certainly) from the one whose bishops had ignored the letter addressed to them in *Kynniver Llith a Ban*: the friends and contacts he and his allies had in positions of power were not just vaguely sympathetic, but were prepared to listen and take action; there was renewed interest in 'British' culture; the fear of Catholic Wales being used as an invasion base (rooted deeply in a dynasty that had gained the throne by exactly the same strategy) made its conversion to Protestantism a priority and, perhaps most importantly of all, the ruling monarch, the last of the Tudors, would be more amenable to the idea of a Welsh Bible than any of her predecessors.

When Elizabeth's great, great grandfather, Owain ap Maredudd ap

Tudur, married Catherine of Valois, Henry V's widow, in 1429, there could have been no doubting his cultural and linguistic identity, but by the time his grandson, Henry Tudor, became king, the Welsh identity had vanished, though it had been usefully invoked to raise an army to fight Richard III. Mary and Edward would have given no thought to their Welsh inheritance, but their half-sister, by chance, had grown up with an awareness of and a familiarity with the language and culture of her ancestors.

The three people who had the greatest influence on the young Queen during her formative years had been Lady Kate Ashley, Blanche Parry[11] and Thomas Parry. (For much of her childhood Elizabeth saw little or nothing of her father.)

Lady Kate was the leading female figure in the young Elizabeth's household, which she joined a year after Blanche Parry. She was not Welsh, but her father, Sir Philip Champernowne, was a friend of Leland and a keen supporter of 'British-ness'. She was imprisoned for eight months in 1549, following the scandal of Thomas Seymour's improper behaviour towards the fourteen-year-old princess.[12] She was then allowed to return, but from May 1556 to Mary's death in November 1558, she was banned from seeing Elizabeth.

During those two periods Lady Kate's replacement as Chief Gentlewoman was Blanche Parry, who had been appointed a lady-in-waiting at around the time of Anne Boleyn's execution in 1536. Blanche succeeded Lady Kate as Chief Gentlewoman on the latter's death in 1565. She was also Keeper of the Queen's Jewels, but when her eyesight started to fail in the mid-1580s, the carer became the cared for. She died in 1589.

She was born in Bacton in Herefordshire, a Welsh-speaking area of the county. (William Herbert, who is reputed never to have been fully at ease in English, was also born in Herefordshire, at Ewyas Harold.) It is quite likely that the young Elizabeth was sung to sleep in Welsh as Blanche turned to the familiar lullabies of her childhood to soothe the infant princess and it would have been quite natural for the two Parrys to have spoken to each other in their mother tongue.

Elizabeth would have been familiar with the sounds and rhythms of the Welsh language. Bradford, Blanche Parry's biographer, writes, 'Since Princess

Elizabeth is said to have had a knowledge of Welsh, it is not unlikely that she owed this accomplishment to Blanche's teaching.'

As an excellent linguist, fluent in English, Latin, Greek, Italian, French and Spanish, Elizabeth could have developed her familiarity with the language through frequent exposure rather than from lessons.

It is not possible to determine exactly when Thomas Parry joined the Queen's household, but he was certainly there before the Seymour scandal. During his investigation into the affair Sir Robert Tyrwhitt realised that Parry had been pilfering from his employer. Nevertheless, Elizabeth took Parry back into service and her fondness and high regard for him can be seen by the knighthood bestowed on him when she became queen and in his being made a member of the Privy Council.

That which is familiar and associated with people whom you remember affectionately is unlikely to be seen as threatening. It is important not to exaggerate and portray the Queen as a champion of all things Welsh, but she had no animosity towards the language, nor was it seen as a threat in the way that Irish was seen as a barrier to English control of Ireland or as the Hanoverians would see the continuing existence of Gaelic as a threat to their dynasty.

The Church in Wales

Another factor now working in Salesbury's favour was the Church itself. Prior to the break with Rome the Church had a very relaxed attitude to the level of concern a bishop should show his diocese. George de Athequa,[13] Catherine of Aragon's confessor, a fellow Spaniard, was bishop of Llandaf from 1517 to 1536. I can find no record of his having visited the diocese. Similarly, opponents of Bishop Skevington of Bangor who, as abbot of Beaulieu, spent most of his time in Hampshire, alleged that he had been absent from the see from 1515 to 1529. The dioceses of Wales were seen as a brief first stepping stone for the ambitious, as places for absentees, or backwaters in which to lose the mediocre. Welshmen were rarely appointed.

There was no great improvement under Henry after 1533 or during Edward's reign, but Mary, in her zeal for re-establishing Catholicism, appointed well-educated bishops, all but one of them Welsh: William Glyn at Bangor,

Henry Morgan at St Davids and Thomas Goldwell at St Asaph. Glyn died in May 1558 and Morys Clynnog was named as his replacement, but Mary's death meant that he never took up the appointment.[14]

Elizabeth's need for a strong, effective church loyal to its Supreme Governor was immense. Wales was known to be strongly Catholic, the gentry in particular. The Pope (Pius V) would declare Elizabeth a heretic and excommunicate her. There would be the Northern Rebellion, the Babington Plot (in which a Salusbury was involved), the presence of Mary Stuart within her kingdom, the Spanish Armada and the constant arrival of clandestine Catholic priests and sowers of sedition like Edmund Campion.

Where Mary's appointment of able, Welsh bishops was a policy decision, for Elizabeth it was an absolute necessity. The church in Wales faced huge problems, many of which, because they were so intractable, were never overcome but, as far as the abilities, character and good intentions of the bishops are concerned, this was a golden age. Amongst the high quality appointees of Elizabeth's first years as queen were: Thomas Young (St Davids, then archbishop of York), Richard Davies (St Asaph, then St Davids), Rowland Meyrick (Bangor) and Thomas Davies (St Asaph). Amongst notable later appointments were Nicholas Robinson (Welsh, despite his English-sounding name) at Bangor, William Morgan at Llandaf, then St Asaph and Anthony Rudd, an Englishman appointed to St Davids in 1594. (A brilliant career was predicted for Rudd, but what had been intended as a light-hearted comment on the Queen's age was taken the wrong way and he spent the rest of his days in west Wales.)[15]

The irony is that whilst Elizabeth's bishops did all they could to strengthen the Church, many of the leading aristocrats, including favourites such as the earl of Leicester, were doing all they could to rob it of its assets.[16] Ever since the Dissolution, church lands and property had been seen as valid targets for acquisition and not even the threat of being overrun by the Spanish would change that attitude. It could be argued that the continuing impoverishment of the Church and the amount of time the bishops had to dedicate to fighting off the 'insatiable cormorants'[17] as Bishop Richard Davies called them, who were forever trying to wrest money from the dioceses, is the chief factor in the failure to achieve meaningful reform.

Finding allies

Bishop Richard Davies,[18] mentioned above, was Salesbury's great ally in the campaign for the Welsh Bible. Although he was born and raised no great distance from Llanrwst, there is no record of the two men meeting[19] until Davies returned from exile in Germany and was appointed bishop of St Asaph in 1559. Salesbury was the famous literary figure and Davies had lived in obscurity until his meteoric elevation to bishop, but the likelihood is that it was Salesbury who sought out Davies rather than the other way round. Salesbury was proactive and understood how politics worked (bishops had a seat in the House of Lords, could influence their peers and had access to the archbishop of Canterbury).

Davies was approximately the same age as Salesbury and had been born at Y Gyffin, about ten miles from Llanrwst, the son of a married priest, Dafydd ap Gronow. He was educated at New Inn Hall, Oxford, gaining his M.A. in 1530 and his B.D. in 1536. He then disappears from the record, no doubt because of his Protestant sympathies. There are possible 'sightings', but the ubiquity of his name makes them unreliable.

In 1549 he was appointed rector of Maids Moreton and the following year vicar of Burnham. Both parishes are in Buckinghamshire, a county noted for its Lollard sympathies. He married Dorothy Woodforde, daughter of a local landowner in 1549, the year in which the marriage of priests was legalised.

It is possible that on an occasion after April 1550, Davies preached a sermon in front of the King.[20] If so, he did not make a deep enough impression to win further recognition. Despite this presumed setback he built up a reputation as a preacher of eloquence and power. In 1576 the sentence, 'The girls of our parish think that the Welsh Sir Richard himself cannot make a better preach than I can' appeared in a book by George Pettie.[21] It is thought to refer to Davies.

Another claim to literary fame is the assumption by some academics that the character of Diggon Davie in Spenser's *Shepherd's Calendar* is based on Davies. (Spenser and Philip Sidney were friends and Davies was in frequent contact with Sir Henry Sidney (Philip's father) who was Lord President of the Council of the Marches. Davies's funeral speech for the first earl of

Essex, a possible source for Diggon Davie, was printed in London and widely distributed.)[22]

With the death of Edward, Davies found himself in grave danger. In September 1553 he was ordered to appear before the Privy Council. This was before the law allowing the marriage of priests was abolished, so it can be presumed that he was summoned either for holding 'heretical' views or, possibly, for having supported Lady Jane Grey.

In December 1553 he was replaced as vicar of Burnham. Fearing that much worse was to befall him he fled with his family to Frankfurt. Amongst his fellow exiles there were Robert Crowley and William Turner. An impromptu 'university' was established for and by the new English community and it is thought that it was here that Davies mastered Hebrew, which was taught by Robert Horne, who would later become bishop of Winchester.

There was a great schism amongst the English Protestants of Frankfurt between the 'moderates', who supported the Prayer Book of 1551, and those who thought it a weak, diluted form of Protestantism. The latter, followers of John Knox, decamped to Geneva. It was Davies's membership of the moderate camp that marked him as someone who could be trusted with high office in Elizabeth's cautiously Protestant church.

Whilst most Protestant exiles lived in extreme poverty (some were so poor that they chose to return to the possibility of death back in England), Davies somehow had enough money to buy a house, which he shared with John Matchett, a deprived priest from the Norwich diocese, and his family. Some exiles lived five families to a house, with predictable results for health and mortality.

Though less bleak than the conditions endured by others, Davies's time in Frankfurt would have been distressing. It was, however, a huge boost to his career. Fellow exiles, such as Robert Horne, whose time at St John's, Cambridge, overlapped with Cecil's, could vouch for his dependability and trustworthiness in matters of doctrine. When Grindal, bishop of London, spoke of the country's indebtedness to the cities that had harboured the exiles, he said, 'But above all else … Frankfurt.'[23]

Davies was appointed to St Asaph in December 1559 and consecrated in early 1560, but he stayed in London until March, helping Grindal to consecrate parish clergy. He is not likely to have taken up office in his diocese until the summer, making this the earliest time that he and Salesbury could have forged an alliance.

Another confederate

The other key ally was the Denbighshire-born Humphrey Llwyd,[24] some twenty years the junior of Salesbury and Davies. A kinsman of Salesbury, he was educated at Brasenose (M.A., 1551), then became librarian to the Arundel/Lumley family where, pursuing his antiquarian interests, he built up one of England's finest collection of books and manuscripts. The Arundel library was eventually acquired by James I for his son, Henry, Prince of Wales. Llwyd wrote several books, two of which, *An Almanacke and Kalender* and an English translation of Agostino Nifo's *De Auguriis*, have not survived. He wrote, in Latin, a history of Wales that so impressed Sir Henry Sidney that he had his chaplain, David Powel, translated it into English as *A Historie of Cambria, now Called Wales*. It was the unsurpassed history of pre-Conquest Wales for three centuries.

Llwyd married Barbara, sister of Lord Lumley, and served as M.P. for East Grinstead in 1559. He returned to Denbighshire and served as M.P. for Denbigh Boroughs from 1563 to 1567. From 1566 to 1567 he toured Europe, meeting the great cartographer, Ortelius, in Antwerp and it is as a pioneer of cartography that Llwyd is chiefly remembered today.

Tragically, within a year of his return he fell ill and died at just 41 years of age, his potential largely unrealised. Ortelius included Llwyd's *Cambriae typus* in a book of 1573, the same year in which he printed Llwyd's map of England and Wales.

His close association with the Arundel family has led to suspicions that he was a Catholic sympathiser, but his support for 'British-ness' was unequivocal, in fact, totally uncritical. He poured bile on all those writers who doubted Geoffrey of Monmouth, most notably Polydore Vergil, 'an infamous baggage-groom, ful fraught with envie and hatred'[25] and in support of the Welshman wrote *Commentarioli Britannicae descriptionis fragmentum*, better known as *The Breviary of Britain*, the title Thomas Twyne gave it in his English translation of 1573.

In January 1561 Thomas Young, bishop of St Davids, was transferred to York and Richard Davies was appointed as his replacement, taking up residence at the Bishop's Palace[26] in Carmarthen in September. There is no evidence of Llwyd's involvement in the campaign at this time, no evidence that he was back in Denbighshire. It was in 1563, when his position as an M.P. was an advantage to be exploited, that his role became critical.

(Was it purely fortuitous that Llwyd had moved from being M.P. for East Grinstead in 1559 to representing Denbigh Boroughs in 1563?[27] The Sussex seat was under the control of his employer and kinsman by marriage, the twelfth earl of Arundel. The Parliament of 1563 met at the beginning of the year, just before Robert Dudley was granted his estates in Wales. Amongst the prominent gentry who could have influenced the outcome of the Denbigh election were Elis Price (who was also M.P. for Merioneth) and Richard Myddelton, governor of Denbigh Castle.[28] The Myddeltons, some of whom lived in Llansannan, were allies of the Salusburys, to whom they were connected through marriage.)

The campaign

The seventeen months that Davies spent in St Asaph with Salesbury within easy reach at Llansannan, March 1560 to August 1561, provided the opportunity for close collaboration and planning. No doubt others were involved, Gruffudd Hiraethog, perhaps, and members of the Myddelton family, mentioned above, who were to build a reputation for support of native culture and scriptural publication. Salusbury clan members might also have given their support as might other allied gentry. Such support would not necessarily have been genuine, but might have been thought of as potentially advantageous in local power politics. It would have been welcomed, but what really counted was the support of those in power. Devices such as petitions, speeches and pamphlets were already in use, but success in politics depended upon patronage and connections, upon the intense lobbying of the mighty.

That, no doubt, was the tactic embraced by Salesbury and Davies. It does not tend to leave a paper trail. The one surviving document[29] of their campaign is an appeal, sometime in 1560 or early 1561, for Welsh and Cornish children to be instructed in the catechism in their mother tongue.

The appeal (B.L. Egerton MS 2350, 54) is universally attributed to Davies and Salesbury.

In May 1561 Davies travelled to Greenwich to take the oath of allegiance. This provided him with the opportunity to canvas his fellow bishops, most particularly Edmund Grindal (bishop of London, who in 1554 had been in Frankfurt) and Parker (archbishop of Canterbury) and any other figure of authority. Intense lobbying of this type was the action most likely to prove effective.

The two men would have learnt the lesson of *Kynniver Llith a Ban* that a translation without official authorisation carried little weight, would be difficult to distribute and could be easily boycotted. The translation that they sought would have to have the full authority of the Queen (the country's sovereign and the Supreme Governor of the Church of England) and of Parliament. The Queen and her parliament could be persuaded to sanction this, but it is unimaginable that they would have initiated such an action unprompted.

Davies departed for Carmarthen in September 1561. There is no record of the two men collaborating again until 1564/5, but it is reasonable to assume that they remained in contact during this time and continued to champion their cause if not jointly, then individually.

An interim solution

Salesbury appears to have focused immediately on Davies's successor as bishop of St Asaph, Thomas Davies, for in November 1561 he issued an order to his clergy that after 'the epistle and gospel in English the same should also be read in Welsh.' This, of course, entailed reading from Salesbury's *Kynniver Llith a Ban*, the only translation available. Not only was it starting to be used in churches, it was gaining semi-official recognition.

The following year, John Whaley, printer of Salesbury's dictionary, took out a licence (price 4d) to print the Litany in Welsh.[30] A pattern was emerging: the passages from the Prayer Book could be supplied by *Kynniver Llith a Ban*, parts of the Catechism were available in Prise's *Yny lhyvyr hwnn* and the missing element, the Litany, was about to be provided by Salesbury. Not only were Davies, Salesbury and colleagues zealous and purposeful in pursuit of their goal of obtaining the scriptures in Welsh and with official blessing, they showed an equal determination that until that goal was realised, the best temporary solution should be put in place and as quickly as possible. Such urgency, selflessness and sense of purpose had not been seen in Welsh political life since the time of Glyndŵr.

In 1547 only one man had dared to raise his voice to call for the scriptures in Welsh; his countrymen had ignored him. By the early 1560s he had won sufficient support to mount an effective campaign in pursuit of that goal.

There is a general consensus amongst historians that if the translation of the Bible had not occurred when it did, then the Welsh language would have slowly died, just as the Cornish and Manx languages did. Similarly, linguists point out that, in general, the European languages that have survived are those in which biblical translations appeared before 1600.

In early 1563 one of the draft bills placed before Parliament was 'An Act for the Translating of the Bible and the Divine Service into the WELSH Tongue.' Salesbury had triumphed.

Chapter Seventeen

The Act of 1563

Whereas the Queen's most Excellent Majesty... did in the First Year of her
Reign... set forth a Book of Common Prayer and Order of the Administration of
Sacraments in the vulgar English Tongue... the which tongue is not understanded
of the most and greatest Number of all her Majesty's most loving and obedient
Subjects inhabiting within her Highness Dominion and Country of WALES...
who therefore are utterly destituted of God's Holy Word, and do remain in
the like or rather more Darkness and Ignorance then they were, in the Time of
Papistry: Be it therefore enacted... that the whole Bible, containing the New
Testament and the Old, with the Book of Common Prayer and Administration
of the Sacraments... be truly and exactly translated into the British or WELSH
Tongue... before the First Day of March, Anno Dom. One thousand five hundred
sixty six. And that from that Day forth, the whole Divine Service shall be used
and said by the Curates and Ministers throughout all the said Dioceses where the
WELSH Tongue is commonly used.[1]

These words are the essence of the Bill laid before the Parliament of 1563.
They represent all that Salesbury had striven for over the last sixteen years.

On closer inspection

One of several notable points about the Bill above is that there was no call
on the Queen or her Parliament to finance the translation, printing and
distribution of the Bible and the Prayer Book. That was left for others to
arrange. Elizabeth was as parsimonious as her grandfather. She was not averse
to money being spent, just so long as it was not hers.

That was sure to have been a concession that the bill's supporters had
made to ensure its presence on the parliamentary timetable. The problem of
financing the project would be addressed at a later date, but for now the focus
would be on steering the act through Parliament.

Besides the financial arrangements, another aspect worthy of note is that the Book of Common Prayer was also to be translated. It had taken great daring to produce *Kynniver Llith a Ban*. Now it was to be replaced by a full, officially sanctioned version. Without the one, there would have been little likelihood of the other.

Salesbury could not have wished for more from the act. In fact, it matches so closely the practical framework and political formulae set out in the letter to the bishops at the start of *Kynniver Llith a Ban* that it is not unreasonable to suggest that he had written it. The five bishops (Bangor, Llandaf, St Asaph, St Davids and Hereford) now bore ultimate responsibility for the production and distribution of the two publications, 'the which Things if the said Bishops or their Successors neglect to do, then every one of them shall forfeit to the Queen's Majesty... the sum of Forty Pounds.'

What would also have delighted him and have been taken as a vindication of his lifetime's work is that the temporary arrangements to be put in place until the translations were completed are a copy of the programme recently introduced by Thomas Davies, bishop of St Asaph. Though Salesbury's name is not mentioned, the 'Epistle and Gospel of the Day in the Welsh tongue' and the Litany, which 'every minister and Curate' was now required to declare to his parishioners, were his translations. The other elements mentioned could be found in Prise's *Yny lhyvyr hwnn*.

Some have seen the last clause of the act, where churches are directed to make the Bible and Prayer Book available so that those who do not speak Welsh may 'sooner attain to the Knowledge of the English Tongue' as a concession to opponents of the bill, but Salesbury, a lover of both languages, would have had no problems with such a provision.

The only unsettling detail is the unrealistic deadline of 1566 for completion of the translations. Perhaps those who drafted it were too optimistic about the abilities of those who would undertake the task (it took forty-seven scholars seven years to complete the King James Bible and they had Tyndale's and Whittingham's work to consult). Those who could see the impracticality of what was suggested most likely thought that this was not the time to voice their doubts.

Seeing the Bill through its stages

How anxious would the three main supporters of the bill, Richard Davies, Humphrey Llwyd (one a member of the Lords, the other of the Commons) and Salesbury have been? The two big issues of that Parliament were the questions of Elizabeth's possible marriage and of the succession, the latter made more acute by the Queen having almost died from smallpox the previous year. Elizabeth, with her characteristic evasiveness, managed to avoid answering Parliament's petitions on these two matters.[2] The other dominant issue, bizarrely, was that of making Wednesday a fish-eating day, the idea being to support the financial well-being of fishermen, who would act as a sort of unofficial naval reserve. The Welsh bill would not have been seen as of great importance. That in itself might have caused worry; if an emergency arose (plague, an insurrection, an invasion, civil disturbance) and some bills had to be sacrificed, theirs would be an easy one to abandon. Would it ever be given parliamentary time again? Quite probably not.

Outright opposition was unlikely to have caused concern. The bill's existence meant that it had the support of the Queen and her Council. The strength of that support should not be exaggerated, but it meant that no one with social or political ambition was likely to oppose it. Nor was the bill controversial (it merely made available in Welsh what already existed in English), but its champions would have spent a nervous four months foreseeing the difficulties that could arise and fearing the unforeseeable.[3]

One worry was that English M.P.s might not have seen the bill as relevant to their concerns and so would be absent when voting took place. Fortunately, Llwyd had been the M.P. for East Grinstead in the previous parliament and had spent many years in the service of the Arundels. He had many contacts within Parliament and without. In addition, there was a fourth supporter of the bill, William Cecil, who would be willing to give his proactive support if there were any possibility of it being lost.

Paradoxically, if there was a danger of opposition, then it was more likely to come from Welsh M.P.s, amongst whose number were Elis Price (Merioneth) and Morus Wynn (Caernarfonshire).

No one was more associated with the bill than Salesbury, who can be regarded as its author, quite possibly literally. His books and his use of innovative 'Inkhorn' Welsh had met with scornful criticism. Most M.P.s were members of the gentry, who in Wales were predominantly traditional, if not downright reactionary. To such people Salesbury represented everything they disliked, metropolitan sophistication, an openness to new ideas, including those from Europe, and a concern for the moral condition of the ordinary people.

England's antiquaries, with their interest in 'British' culture would have welcomed the bill, and the political elite, centred around Cecil, would have seen it as essential to the defence of the realm, a measure to wean Wales from Catholicism and prevent it from becoming an invasion base for Spain. The backwoodsmen of Wales would have lacked such perspective.

In 1567 Salesbury refers to attempts to prevent the publication of the Prayer Book and the New Testament.[4] Those who took the action (he did not name them) were Welsh and one of the two causes cited was their opposition to his orthography. Two decades later, William Morgan, translator of the 1588 Bible, encountered similar opposition. Though in his case orthography did not play a part, the hostility of the gentry was as great as it had been in Salesbury's time, if not greater. Significant numbers of them had become thoroughly anglicised and had developed contempt for the language. They thought of it as fit only for peasants, for whom they had no moral or spiritual concern: a Welsh Bible was a waste of time.

Though some Welsh M.P.s might have had a very low opinion of Salesbury, either based on personal conflict (Elis Price and Morus Wynn) or because he represented a stereotype they resented, they were highly unlikely to oppose the Queen's will.

However, factionalism and the politics of the personal could work in the bill's favour. There were many gentlemen with a deep-seated hatred of and animosity towards the Prices and the Wynns. They would be only too happy to support someone who had long been a thorn in the side of such people. Even if Humphrey Llwyd (Denbigh Boroughs) had not been a friend, he would certainly have been in the Salusbury camp, as would Simon Thelwall (Denbighshire). (Katheryn Salusbury's fourth and final husband would be Edward Thelwall, a kinsman.)

Numbers

There were twenty-six parliamentary constituencies in Wales[5] and at least seven of them (those in Glamorgan, Monmouthshire and Montgomery) were in the control of the Herbert dynasty; three of the M.P.s from those counties bore the Herbert surname and Herbert's large estates in the West Country meant that he also controlled many English members. Salesbury's relationship with Herbert after the 1540s is unknown. No one from the world of Humanist learning would have approved of his appalling, and fatal, treatment of Robert Recorde, who died in gaol, financially ruined by his entanglement with the earl, but Salesbury would not have been openly critical. Herbert's opposition to the religious settlement of 1559 had displeased the Queen. He is unlikely to have risked her displeasure again.

The other great magnate in Wales was Robert Dudley. It would be later in the year, 9 June, that he would be granted his Welsh estates, but many of the gentry there, notably the Prices and the Wynns, had served with or been allies of his father, the duke of Northumberland. Though personally close to the Queen, Dudley was unlikely to have risked her ire by having his placemen oppose one of her acts of parliament, especially one in which he had little interest.

The bill had to pass through the Commons first. There were around 420 M.P.s in all, some of them Catholic. This was the last Parliament for three hundred years in which Catholics would be allowed to sit; their number is estimated to have been twenty-seven, one more than the entire Welsh contingent. If Humphrey Llwyd encountered any difficulties, they are not recorded. The *Journal of the House of Commons* gives a brief mention to the bill, but no evidence as to how members voted. This information might once have existed but, if so, would have been destroyed in the fire of 1834.

Apart from the bishops, there was no real Welsh representation in the House of Lords (those few aristocrats with Welsh connections had been long established in England, the earl of Pembroke is likely to have been the sole Welsh-speaking noble). The other Welsh bishops were Rowland Meyrick (Bangor), Thomas Davies (St Asaph) and Anthony Kitchin (Llandaf), who was Catholic in his sympathies, but had taken the oath of allegiance and accepted the settlement of 1559.[6]

A complication for Richard Davies was that the 1563 Convocation was held in York and clashed with the Parliamentary session. 'Richardus Menevensis' (Richard of Menevia (St Davids)) appears in the records of sixteen of the first twenty-three sessions of Convocation from 12 January to 5 March.[7] There were thirteen further sessions and in these Davies's name appears just once, on 19 March, which allowed him a comfortable, though not too comfortable, eight days to return to London to see the Bill complete its stages in the Commons on 27 March. It then entered the Lords and he is recorded as being in attendance at all three of its readings there.

In the 1559 Parliament many of the bishops had been Catholic, and therefore loyal to Mary and antagonistic to Elizabeth, but by now the old guard had been cleared away to be replaced by loyal Protestants such as Cox, Grindal, Horne, Jewel, Sandys and Scory (bishop of Hereford). All of them would have been friends or, at the very least, allies of Davies, but Convocation might seriously have depleted their ranks. However, Davies had nothing to fear as he was assured of the votes of the lords temporal, of whom it is written, 'For most of them a government Bill which was known to have the backing of the Sovereign was tantamount to a royal command.'[8]

Cecil's intervention

The bill completed its way through both houses. Had there been any problems on the floor of the Commons? The lack of any extant comment on the matter or of any rumour of trouble suggests not, but one surviving letter is evidence that William Cecil decided that he was taking no chances and would play his trump card.

Cecil was in frequent contact with Sir Thomas Smith, his old mentor, with whom he had been briefly imprisoned by Northumberland for supporting Somerset. The bill entered the Commons on 22 February. In a letter dated 27 February 1562 (that is, 1563), there are three paragraphs of particular interest, 'A law is passed for sharpening lawes agaynst Papists, wherein some difficultie hath bene, because they be made very penal; but such be the humours of the commons house, as they thynk nothing sharp ynough against Papists' and

> Yesterdaie wer condemned two Pooles, Fortescugh, one Spencer, and Byngham, servants to the Lord Hastings of Loughborow, and one Barwyk.

> Fortescugh confessed all, and so was atteynted, and is therby never to take hold of mercy. The treason wer intents to come with a power into Wales, and to proclayme the Scottish Quene. The traytors seke therein defence by saying that they ment it not before the Quene our Soveraign shuld die, which, as they wer persuaded by one Prestall, shuld be about this March. But I trust God hath more store of his mercyes for us, than so to cast us over to devouring lyons.[9]

The first paragraph demonstrates the overwhelming mood of the Commons. That same year the Pope's council had resolved that 'A pardon to be granted to any that would assault the Queen.' Any mention of a Catholic plot involving Wales was guaranteed to see the bill through its readings and that was what the second and third paragraphs provide.

This was a private letter and would have been read in France, where Smith had been despatched to aid the ambassador, Sir Nicholas Throckmorton, but what Cecil said in a private letter, he would not have hesitated to say in the Commons, where he sat as the member for Northamptonshire alongside such heavyweight political allies as Sir Anthony Cooke (his father-in-law, and M.P. for Essex), Francis Walsingham (M.P. for Lyme Regis), Sir Francis Knollys (M.P. for Oxfordshire) and Dr Thomas Wilson (M.P. for Mitchell).

Recent English commentators have written that there is no evidence to show that Llwyd was the bill's guide through the Commons,[10] but in Wales, Gruffudd Hiraethog wrote a poem of praise to him,[11] describing him as:

Perl mewn Tŷ Parlment yw hwn
Peibl, wyneb pob haelioni,
A wnaeth yn act o'n hiaith ni.

[A pearl in the House of Parliament is he
The face of all generosity, he made
The Bible in our language an act.]

Perhaps Gruffudd should have addressed his poem to Cecil.[12]

Had Salesbury been present in London during this time, either as a nervous bystander or a behind-the-scenes manipulator? It is difficult to imagine that he could have been absent from what was the culmination of a sixteen-year campaign. This was, after all, the greatest achievement of his career to date. If he had let go of the lease in Southwark, Thavies Inn was always available as a place to stay.

Llwyd, as a member of the Lumley/Arundel family, would have had access to a comfortable resting place somewhere in the capital. Perhaps Richard Davies invited his two colleagues to stay with him at the bishop of St Davids London residence, the 'inn' situated against the north side of the Bridewell.[13]

On 6 April, the act was passed, but there was one more hurdle to clear before it became law; it had to gain royal approval. All three would have waited anxiously, knowing there was nothing they could do to affect the outcome. The Queen was known to be capricious. A wrong word, an imagined slight, a comment misconstrued could have spelt disaster. At the end of the parliamentary session, 10 April, Maundy Thursday, Elizabeth vetoed six bills,[14] two of them private, but not the bill for which Salesbury, Davies and Llwyd had worked so hard.

The following day, as Christians observed the most sombre day in their calendar, the few true Protestants of Wales would have quietly celebrated the removal of the linguistic barrier that had barred their countrymen from religious salvation.

If the three campaigners had planned to linger awhile in London to bask in the glow of their achievement, they had swiftly to change their plans; there was an outbreak of the plague. Had the Queen died the previous year from the smallpox which left her unconscious and on the point of death for four days or had the first cases of plague been announced just days earlier, then all would have been lost. Napoleon would have wanted Salesbury as a general; no matter that there were setbacks in his personal life, when he chose to fight a battle he was 'lucky'.

Chapter Eighteen

The translation

Response and responsibility

Now that the battle had been won, work on the translation could begin as well as all the administrative arrangements, but who would undertake the work and who would oversee it?

Salesbury's political formula of responsibility being shared by the five bishops,[1] had been a shrewd construct to gain approval for the act, but when it came to the practicalities of administration there was clear potential for misunderstanding and inactivity.

It is unlikely that the bishop of Hereford would have been expected to take an active role apart from at the end of the process when he would be responsible for distributing the texts to the Welsh-speaking parishes in his diocese. The bishop, John Scory, was strongly Protestant; he had been deprived of the bishopric of Chichester by Mary and had spent the following five years in exile, but he had no knowledge of Wales or its language and had little to offer the other bishops apart from good will.

The four dioceses of Wales, St Asaph, St Davids, Bangor and Llandaf, did not form a recognised theological or political unit. They were constituent dioceses of the Church of England and indistinguishable from any other diocese, such as Durham or Exeter. The only time that the four bishops were scheduled to meet was at Convocation or when Parliament was in session. Travel at that time was difficult anywhere in the kingdom; the geography of Wales made meetings between the four even more problematic. Regardless of the size or wealth of their dioceses, the bishops were of equal status; no one bishop had seniority over the others. It is quite possible to imagine a scenario where each one of them did nothing whilst waiting for one of his colleagues to initiate proceedings.

It must also be remembered that the bishops had been given responsibility for overseeing the translation of the texts, the printing of them, costing the project and raising the finance, activities of which they had no experience. Those few people in Wales who strongly supported the scheme would be fearful for its completion.

What did the four bishops have to offer individually? Or rather what did the three bishops have to offer, for Anthony Kitchen, bishop of Llandaf, died in 1563 and was not replaced, because the Queen took no action on the matter, until 1566.

Thomas Davies of St Asaph does not have a record of meeting problems forcefully or taking the initiative in any of the business of his diocese. He is noted for issuing the order in November 1561 for the epistle and gospel, the Litany and the catechism to be read in Welsh as well as English, but that action is likely to have been influenced by Salesbury rather than originating with him.

Rowland Meyrick at Bangor was highly educated and a former Principal of New Inn Hall, Oxford. He is most famous for his ferocious dispute with Bishop Ferrar of St Davids, which led to Ferrar's imprisonment and consequent martyrdom under Mary. There is no evidence that he was a proactive administrator and his appointment of Elis Price as Chancellor suggests either weakness or corruption.

Which leaves Richard Davies at St Davids, the sole bishop to have shown dynamism and principle, rather than merely responding to events. Although, technically, not senior to the others, St Davids did enjoy an elevated status by virtue of its association with the patron saint. (When Giraldus Cambrensis campaigned for autonomy for the Welsh church, he had envisaged St Davids as being the seat of the archbishop.)

By common consent or by default the responsibility fell on Richard Davies. Did he welcome the development or dread it? Just as importantly, what was Salesbury's attitude at this time? Following the act, there is no evidence of contact between the men until Davies's letter to Matthew Parker of 19 March 1565 in which he states, 'I am in hand to perform your request, and will use as much diligence and speed as I can, having small help for that or for the Welsh Bible. Mr Salisbury only taketh pain with me.'[2]

Reluctant or willing allies?

Davies's relief at Salesbury's help and his appreciation of it is obvious, but what were the attitudes of the two men in 1563?

Salesbury had seen his great ambition, an act for the translation of the Bible and the Prayer Book, realised. Did he wish to take on the translation? It is not clear whether he had regained ownership of Plas Isa, his other great goal. If he had not, would he have wanted any distraction from achieving it? His fortune had been seriously depleted during Mary's reign and he would have wanted to make good those losses. Legal work in Wales or London would do that, translating the Bible would not.

He was a gentleman with antiquarian interests. He wrote poetry.[3] He might have had plans for other projects, a Welsh grammar, perhaps, to accompany the dictionary. He was in his mid-fifties and indisputably his nation's greatest man of letters. Why take on another task, one more demanding than anything he had done before? Tyndale had been thirty-two when he started translating the Bible into English and Luther's German New Testament appeared when he was thirty-nine. The task demanded a young man's energies. Besides, he had been hurt by criticism of his work, 'the cancred malitious checkes of all those, who at all times canne be at better laysure to rebuke other mens doings, than to do aught them selves.'[4]

He believed that his orthography was correct, that it was what the language needed to make it vibrant and modern, as had happened with English. He knew he was right and defended himself vigorously, but that did not make the criticism less hurtful. Why should he lay himself open to further hurt?

On the other hand, it might always have been his intention to translate the two works himself. Who else could be trusted to do it? The introductions to his books are full of modesty, a prerequisite for a Humanist writer, but underneath that mannered voice there was a will of iron. Did he expect the job to be his as a matter of course?

In the summer of 1563, was Salesbury sitting at home waiting for the call, fuming at the delay and brooding at the insult to his dignity and status?

And what was Davies thinking as he sat in the Bishop's Palace in Carmarthen? As the de facto senior cleric of his nation did he feel that the job of translating was rightfully his? Did he want the responsibility? Did he feel that it was a challenge he could meet? You can admire a man and become his political ally without feeling any warmth or personal bond towards him. Did he feel overawed by Salesbury's learning, jealous even? Was the forcefulness of Salesbury's personality something he shied away from? He could not help but be aware of the controversy that his orthography had caused; was he searching for someone who would avoid controversy and disquiet? Did he, in the light of the debt owed to Salesbury in getting the act onto the statute book, feel obliged, albeit reluctantly, to appoint him as translator?

There is only one, tantalising piece of evidence. In MS Gwysanau 27 there are translations of the New Testament in Davies's handwriting. They do not appear in the 1567 *Testament Newydd* and they do not show the influence of Salesbury's orthography. There are two theories; that they are later revisions, done for academic pleasure or with the idea of a new edition of the work, or that they are trial pieces to see if it was feasible for Davies to complete the work himself.[5]

The weakness of the first theory is that after completing the New Testament Davies and Salesbury threw themselves into working on the Old Testament. There would have been no time for revisions of work already completed. The second theory is the more likely, especially as the translations are from the English of the Great Bible, not from the original Greek. Even without his work as bishop, the Bible and Prayer Book represented a challenge of Herculean proportions. His episcopal and other duties made it impossible.

St Davids was a huge but sparsely populated diocese that stretched from the west coast of Wales to the border and beyond and from the south coast to the Dyfi estuary (in effect, the whole of south Wales apart from Glamorgan and Monmouthshire). Its one town of any size was Carmarthen which, with a population of 2,000, was the largest in Wales. Davies faced the same problems as the other Welsh bishops, the presence of many Catholic sympathisers, a traditionally minded flock averse to change, poorly educated priests, a lack of money (largely due to the machinations of the gentry), dilapidated churches, parishes with no priest and priests who held several livings. To run the diocese efficiently and to lead its people to Protestant enlightenment was work enough for any man.[6] In addition, Davies had been appointed to the Council of the Marches, which meant visits to Ludlow and further responsibilities.

Yet more work had been given him by Archbishop Parker. As one of the few Hebraists amongst the bishops, Davies had been asked to translate the books of Joshua, Judges, Ruth and Samuel I and II for what was to become the Bishops' Bible. (The Bible then most used was the Geneva Bible, which was too 'Protestant' for Parker and the Queen. The Bishops' Bible was an attempt to replace it with Anglican blandness. The attempt failed. England's greatest generation of writers (Shakespeare, Marlowe, Jonson, Donne and many others) grew up listening to the rhythms and vocabulary of William Whittingham's translation.)[7]

Lastly, there was the never-ending struggle against the earls of Leicester and Pembroke and their local agents, such as Sir John Perrott and Fabian Phillips, who were determined to strip the Church of as many of its assets as possible.

There was no alternative to seeking help. In fact, there was no alternative to handing over the greater part of the responsibility for the whole project to someone else. Could that someone else have been anyone but Salesbury?

Alternative solutions

A 'quick-fix', academically shallow solution would have been a translation direct from the English of the Coverdale Bible and the Prayer Book, avoiding the need for Greek and Hebrew scholarship, but Davies had too much integrity to accept such a solution and Salesbury, in *Kynniver Llith a Ban*, had set a precedent (for much of the work) that invalidated it. Even if the English option were accepted, it would require an individual or team of individuals able to produce high quality Welsh prose of considerable length. Only one man had experience of doing so. (Not everyone in Europe set the same high standard as Salesbury. The first French Bible (sixteenth century) was translated from Latin and Italian. The Icelandic Bible was based on Luther's German version[8] and for the Great Bible Coverdale had used Jerome's Vulgate, Erasmus's Latin version and Luther's German.)

If the translations were to have intellectual integrity they needed to be made by scholars who were masters of Greek and Hebrew. The probability is that Davies and Salesbury were the only Welshmen who could read and write Hebrew. If the project was trimmed down to the New Testament and Prayer Book (which is what happened), so that only Greek was required,[9] then a reasonable number of potential translators would have been available, but none with experience of writing quality Welsh prose.

Had there been a sufficient number of such people, there remained one last problem. They would have to be prepared for several years' work that would be far from lucrative and whose sole reward would be critical acclaim if the end result was well received, and critical hostility if it was not. In Tudor society, with its obsession with avarice, there were few willing to make such a sacrifice. Only two possible candidates come readily to mind, Nicholas Robinson and Humphrey Llwyd.

Robinson would become bishop of Bangor in 1566, a job in which he proved himself able and efficient. He had studied Greek at Cambridge, where he had written Latin plays. He also translated an ancient Welsh text into Latin[10] and had the character to persevere at a task and do it as well as he could, but he played no part in the great work.

Llwyd's commitment to Welsh culture could not have been stronger, but he had written nothing in Welsh, and his great intellectual passion was not translation but cartography.

The call

So it was that sometime between summer 1563[11] and March 1565 Davies invited Salesbury to join him at the Bishop's Palace at Abergwili, one mile from Carmarthen, to start work on translating the Prayer Book and the New Testament. Whether the invitation was issued reluctantly or enthusiastically, immediately or after a long delay is not known, but Salesbury accepted and Davies was grateful.

Whatever the circumstances of Salesbury's move to Carmarthen, it has the air of inevitability about it. He had two decades' experience of writing, researching, printing, publishing and raising the finance for his work. No other living Welshman had printed a Welsh-language book.[12] With Robert

Recorde and John Gwynedd dead, he was probably the only man from his nation to have had a book published. He was the nation's only translator, the only man to have devoted time and learning to fashion a Welsh prose that would meet the demands and standards of the Humanist age. Apart from the bards, he was Wales's sole man of letters. He was the only Welshman to have made a personal sacrifice, to have risked imprisonment to benefit, not himself, but his nation's culture.

His orthography had met with vociferous opposition, but so had the orthography and Latinisation of the Inkhorns who had influenced him:

> the translators of thys age … do marre and mysframe our Englysshe tounge thorugh theyr termes unnedefullye borrowed of other languages … wyth theyr newe borrowed ynkehorne termes, and the common people of England do not understand the wrytynges ne yet the speache of them, for theyr trycke termes, of theyr own brayn shaped.[13]

In England the Inkhorns would prove victorious, changing the appearance and the lexicon of the language forever. Salesbury was a man of strong conviction and he had the intellectual toughness to stand his ground and fight for what he believed. He also knew how to use the press to his advantage and in 1567 he would need all those qualities.

The bishop's trials and tribulations

The site of the Bishop's Palace at Carmarthen is open to the public,[14] but the building that stands there replaced the one with which Salesbury would have become so familiar.

Whatever the problems Davies faced in defending his diocese from the acquisitive attacks of the 'insatiable cormorants', he and his wife, Dorothy, are likely to have kept a good table. Salesbury's time there would have been very comfortable and he would have enjoyed the company. Davies saw it as his duty to extend his hospitality to promising young scholars. Under Davies, Abergwili was the nearest that Wales came to producing the equivalent of an Oxbridge college for well over two hundred years.[15]

The bishop's letter to Archbishop Parker in which he says:

> Pleaseth it your grace to be advertised that I received that piece of the Bible which
> your grace hath committed to me to be recognised, the fourth day of March last;
> and your grace's letters dated the sixth of December, I received eight days before I
> received the portion of the Bible. I am in hand to perform your request, and will
> use as much diligence and speed as I can, having small help for that or for the welsh
> Bible. Mr Salisbury only taketh pain with me.

demonstrates just how much he had come to depend on Salesbury. (It could even be interpreted as evidence that Salesbury had helped him with the translations for the Bishops' Bible.)

The correspondence between the two men reveals a great deal of the everyday business of the diocese, church politics and the many problems that Davies faced. 'The earls of Pembroke and Leicester have written to me four letters in the behalf of Mr Bowen,[16] and they themselves have presented him by avowson which assuredly is counterfeit and void of truth.'

Bowen was the man the earls wished to see appointed to the living of Llanddewi Brefi in 1566.[17] For a short time Davies thwarted their plans, but the earls escalated their efforts and George Cary, a groom of the Queen's chamber, was enlisted to wreak havoc on the diocese and on the bishop. Despite a legal victory for Davies in 1567, eventually the diocese lost control of many of its parishes in Cardiganshire, which halved its annual income. It was also asked to pay £3,420 in arrears of rent and tithes and Davies was judged to owe £2,000. When Davies died in 1581, Cary harassed his widow, Dorothy, for the money.

It is no wonder that Davies readily accepted the support of Walter Devereux, Viscount Hereford (and from 1572, earl of Essex). Devereux and Leicester were intensely hostile to each other, which may account for Devereux's support being so readily given. After Essex's death from dysentery in Ireland in 1576,[18] Davies was without a powerful ally.

It is impossible not to sympathise with Davies, but it must be noted that he was not without the taint of corruption himself. In 1563 he appointed his second son, Peregrine, still a child, as archdeacon of Cardigan. In 1577 he appointed his youngest son, Gerson, who was fifteen years old, to two livings and a prebendaryship worth, jointly, £110 per year. In 1564 he appointed the ten-year-old Philip Sidney as prebendary of Llangynllo.[19]

Sidney's appointment would have played well with his father, Sir Henry Sidney, Lord President of the Council of the Marches in Wales, a man Davies would have been anxious to please.

It is in a letter to Davies (CCVIII), on 28 March 1566 that Archbishop Parker refers to Salesbury's attempts to decipher his 'quire in such strange charect'. Not knowing the language (it turned out to be Armenian), Salesbury had had to confine himself to analysis of proper nouns, the script and its direction and writing out its 'Waterloo of an alphabet' as Byron called it in 1816.[20] Nevertheless, Parker declared himself pleased with his attempt, 'I pray you thank Mr Salisbury, whose full writing his conjectures I like well; and as for deciphering my quire in strange charect, it shall be reserved to some other opportunity to be considered.'[21]

(The gulf in the intellectual capabilities of the host and his guest is also revealed. At a time when Salesbury was absent, February 1567, Davies was asked by Parker for information regarding Sulien, who had been a noted bishop of St Davids in the eleventh century. The archbishop's interest had been aroused by his discovery that Sulien had been married (Parker felt very defensive of his status as a married priest). He asked Davies to give him as much information as possible on Sulien. Fortunately there was a great deal about him and his family in *Brut y Tywysogion* [Chronicle of the Princes] and Davies set about translating the relevant passages into Latin.

Glanmor Williams wrote an article on Davies's response to the archbishop[22] and notes that 'A curious feature is Davies's failure to include the full notices of Sulien's fame and learning...' Williams says in Davies's defence, 'Possibly this omission is best explained by his having had a mutilated or otherwise defective original', but in the footnote that accompanies that statement he notes an elementary error in Davies's translation. After another defence of the bishop, he states, 'Of course, it is possible that Davies himself was to blame for not having perused the original more closely.' This would seem to be the correct interpretation as Williams goes on to draw attention to a 'still worse-bungled account' and then states, 'The same is true of the various accounts given of another battle.')

It is in Davies's letter to Parker (CCIV), in which he mentions 'Mr Salisbury' and his help that we learn that Parker, one of the greatest of the sixteenth-century manuscript collectors, especially those of Anglo-Saxon origin, had asked him to give details of what might be found in the diocese. Davies has to disappoint him, informing the archbishop that, 'For all such old monuments as we had, Mr Secretary [Cecil] hath them two years ago ... He had of me *Giraldus Cambrensis*, a chronicle of England the author unknown, and *Galfridus Monumetensis.*'

The *Giraldus Cambrensis* had, of course, been Salesbury's, the manuscript he had carefully annotated in 1554.

Church politics

Finally, and fascinatingly, the correspondence throws light on the politics behind the appointment of a new bishop of Bangor. Rowland Meyrick had died in 1566. Elis Price, who was keenly supported by Leicester (his employer and protector) and Pembroke, seems to have been considered for the post, even though he had never been ordained.

Fortunately, someone must have informed Parker of the nature of the beast, for in letter CXCVIII, he writes to Cecil:

> ... rather than Doctor Ellis, having been aforetimes sheriff of the shire, neither
> being priest nor having any priestly disposition. I had rather for my party dissent
> from my lord of Pembroke's request, than to command a doubtful man to the
> Queen's Highness, on whom, as yet persuaded, I would be loth to lay my hands
> on.

Earlier in that letter Parker had expressed his support for 'Mr Hewett', Davies's precentor. No doubt the bishop had put forward Huet's name. Davies's championing of the precentor may explain his being given responsibility for the translation of Revelations in the New Testament (a means of furthering his chances). Less than a month later Parker had also been informed of Huet's character. (One third of all advowsons granted in the diocese of St Davids went to members of either the Davies or Huet family. Huet was also accused of keeping three chapter-house seals to issue leases to himself.)[23] Briefed of Huet's dishonesty, Parker was soon writing to Cecil that, 'I think, all things accounted, I shall allow your judgement for Bangor toward Mr. Robinson; whom the country doth much desire, and be much afeard either of Ellis or

Hewett; very stout men, so only commended, and praeterea quond mores episcopales nihil.'

Was Salesbury aware of the infighting and, if so, did he give an honest account of his brother-in-law? Or did he use Price's desire for ecclesiastical office to gain concessions from him regarding Plas Isa? Was Cecil already aware of Huet's record or did someone from within the diocese warn him?

Hard work and Humphrey Toy

During his stay with Davies, Salesbury must have worked phenomenally hard. He translated the whole of the Prayer Book, all of the Psalms and all of the New Testament, apart from Timothy I, Hebrews, James and Peter I and II (Davies) and Revelations (Huet).[24]

Nor did Salesbury take short cuts or easy options. This was not a bland recycling of *Kynniver Llith a Ban* with some added new pieces. There had been over a decade's Biblical scholarship since then and he was determined to use it. The most detailed analysis of the Biblical translations of the sixteenth century can be found in the work of Dr Isaac Thomas. His research leads him to believe that for his translations of 1567 Salesbury used: Theodorus Beza's Latin translation of the New Testament (1556), the Geneva New Testament and Bible (1557 and 1560), a Greek text of the New Testament (possibly Stephanus's 1550 edition), *Kynniver Llith a Ban* and, very importantly, Theodorus Beza's New Testament of 1565, in which his new Greek translation appeared alongside his Latin translation and the Vulgate.[25]

Did Salesbury delay starting work until 1565? That would have been asking a great deal of him, although before that date he would have been able to work on those parts of the Prayer Book whose original language was English as well as the few readings that were in Hebrew and on the Psalms. However, a recently discovered document may explain why it is quite possible that he did not start on the main body of the work until 1565.

In the 1560s, Humphrey Toy, a London stationer, brought a case[26] against Robert Leeke ('Leche'), chancellor of Chester cathedral. Leche had ordered a substantial number of copies of *The Second Tome of Homelyes with the boke of Articles* from Toy at a cost of £50 6s 8d. Toy had not received payment;

hence the case, which was brought in the Court of Chancery in 'the fifth year' of the Queen's reign, 1564.

Who represented Toy and did the court find in his favour? The reason why these questions have relevance is that the man who financed the publishing of the Prayer Book and the New Testament of 1567 was Humphrey Toy. Was it through this case that the two men met? They appear to have become firm friends, Salesbury staying at Toy's house, 'at the sign of The Helmet', St Paul's Churchyard, for much of 1567. A successful outcome to the case would have caused Toy to regard Salesbury with admiration and gratitude. It would have also provided him with the ready money to finance the great project.

Though born and brought up in London, Toy had family connections to Carmarthen, where a Humphrey Toy (presumed to be an uncle) had been mayor[27] in 1557. It had been assumed that the contact with Toy had coincided with Salesbury staying at the Bishop's Palace and becoming acquainted with the Toys of Carmarthen. The legal case, involving as it does direct contact and money, would appear the more likely explanation.

If that was the case, had Salesbury already started the translation and taken time off to present the case with an eye to capitalising on the outcome? Or was the whole project hopelessly beached until a fortuitous coincidence provided it with the funds to get off the ground? If the latter, it would explain the use of Beza; it became available shortly after or just as the work on the translation began.

Another piece of evidence for 1565 being the starting date is a reference in a letter of 1567 to being in Ludlow at Michaelmas (September) three years previously.[28] Whenever it was that he first sat down to translate, Salesbury's work-rate was prodigious and yet two possible periods of absence (in addition to defending Toy) are recorded.

The first was in 1565 when he is in Denbighshire and signs a bond. The document is dated 2 April and is preserved in MS Gwysanau 27. The bond is for £100, borrowed from Thomas ap Rhys Wyn of Ffynogion.[29] Writing in 1902, D.R. Thomas assumed that the bond was either an honorarium to cover Salesbury's costs whilst translating or to cover the costs of the printing, but it is now generally considered to be a routine business transaction. Amongst the guarantors is Hugh ap David ap John, whose 1567 will names Salesbury as his father-in-law.

In September 1565, Salesbury stayed with Gruffudd Dwnn of Cydweli. (It is possible that he made more than one visit.) Dwnn was a noted genealogist and collector of manuscripts. Amongst the manuscripts that Salesbury studied there were Saint Greal (MS Mostyn 184), Cyfreithiau Hywel Dda (MS Llansteffan 116) and the Hendregadredd manuscript, one of the five great texts of Welsh literature.[30] The impression he made on Dwnn can be judged by the following verse:

> Maystr Salsbri uchi wychaer
> (o genedl) o Gonwy i swydd Gaer
> ag urddasglod gwrdd ddisclaer
> a bar waew tan y bwrw taer.
>
> [Master Salesbury brave above all
> (Of a nation) from Conwy to Cheshire
> With clear, dignified distinction
> That will be a spear in battle.][31]

Salesbury wrote two *englynion* to Dwnn. The first is dated 22 September 1565. The second is less specific; a note underneath it gives Salesbury as the author and 1566 as the year of composition. (It may be that Salesbury sent it to Dwnn, recalling his first visit, but a second visit appears more likely.)[32]

> Da y ceri di bob dydd dy helynt
> a hwylio yr iawnfydd
> Da y creffi diwg Ruffydd
> Da ar y gwawd diwyr gwydd
>
> [(It's) good you love each day your (life's) journey
> and sailing the true faith
> (It's) good you listen intently, genial Gruffydd,
> And well to the fine poetry of praise]
>
> Yn iach 'rwy'n bruddach o'r braw a gefais
> wrth gofio'r ymadaw
> Yn iach angel diogelaw
> Yn iach y Dwn ni chai daw.

[Farewell, I'm sadder from the experience I had

Remembering the leaving

Farewell guardian angel

Farewell Dwn who did not get silence.]

(The Dwnns of Cydweli were related to John Donne. How is not clear, but the Dwnn coat of arms appears on his portrait of 1591.)[33]

The other surviving poem by Salesbury from this period is a tribute to Edward Games of Brecon, who died in 1564.[34] Salesbury visited Ludlow in September of that year and on his travels might also have called on Games shortly before his death.

Another death that occurred at this time was that of Gruffudd Hiraethog. It is known that he died in 1564, possibly at Whitsun time.[35] Their friendship is likely to have been the longest of all those enjoyed by Salesbury and survived the hostility of the bards and the enmity of Elis Price, who was one of Gruffudd's most prominent patrons. His death is known to have been a sudden one. So, if Salesbury had started work on the translation, the probability is that the news of his death would not have reached Carmarthen until after the funeral had taken place.

Gruffudd had praised Humphrey Llwyd for his work in steering the act for the translation of the Bible through Parliament. Sadly Gruffudd did not live long enough to see the translation in print.

Sometime after Christmas 1566, Salesbury is thought to have travelled to Humphrey Toy's house in London to begin work on seeing the translations through the printing process. It is possible, even at this late date, that there were still sections to be tackled. He and Davies had put aside hopes of completing the whole of the Bible, but the Prayer Book, the Psalms and the New Testament would soon be rolling off the printing press. The Old Testament was to follow at a later date. Amongst the many emotions likely to be experienced by Salesbury as he travelled eastwards, pride, anticipation and trepidation would certainly have figured prominently.

A Postscript

In 1958, in Hatfield House, Hertfordshire, an illustrated page from an unknown manuscript of Chaucer's *Troilus and Criseyde* was discovered. The calligraphy was that of Scribe B, Chaucer's preferred scribe, who also produced the Hengwrt and Ellesmere manuscripts of *The Canterbury Tales*. In 2006, Scribe B lost his six centuries of anonymity, when Professor Linne Mooney of York University identified him as Adam Pinkhurst.[36]

Troilus and Criseyde is not a lost work, but the quality of the illustration and of Pinkhurst's craftsmanship testifies that a beautiful, priceless object has been lost to the world.

Chaucer had little, if any, connection with Wales, yet the National Library of Wales has a surprisingly large number of his manuscripts, all the more remarkable for an institution that was established as recently as 1907 (the Bodleian, for example, was founded in 1602). The most famous of its manuscripts is the Hengwrt *Canterbury Tales*, which for most of the sixteenth century (and possibly earlier) and for the early part of the seventeenth century was owned by the Dutton/Banister/Egerton/Brereton/Starkey clan of Chester[37] (there was a phenomenal rate of inter-marrying between the families, as well as occasional marriages to members of the Salusbury clan).[38]

By 1658 the manuscript was owned by Robert Vaughan of Hengwrt, Wales's greatest collector of books and manuscripts, whose Peniarth Collection, became the core around which the National Library's collection was formed.[39]

Other Chaucer manuscripts in Aberystwyth are Boece's *The Consolation of Philosophy* (Pen MS 393D), scribed by Pinkhurst,[40] origins unknown but known to have been in Wales since at least 1737; *A Tretyse on the Astrolabe* (Pen MS 359), generally assumed to have been acquired by Salesbury for his cousin, John Edwards of Chirk,[41] and the Merthyr Fragment (NLW MS 21972D),[42] discovered in Merthyr Mawr, south Wales, in 1937, but with notes in the margin which suggest that in the early seventeenth century it was in Caernarfonshire.

It may also be significant that the first collected edition of Chaucer's works, which appeared in 1532, was edited by William Thynne. His nephew, John, has forever associated the family name with Longleat, Wiltshire, but William, 'accumulated many offices, some of which show that he retained links with his native Welsh border country.'[43] (John was a political ally of

Somerset and of William Cecil and Thomas Parry, two Welsh exiles. Sir John Salusbury of Lleweni was also associated with the Thynnes.)

Why does there appear to be a correlation between the Welsh Marches and so many of the Chaucer manuscripts?

Chaucer was one of Richard II's most loyal supporters. Besides being, in effect, his court poet as well as a trusted diplomat and high-ranking official, he wrote at least one work, unfortunately lost, *The Book of the Leoun*, which might possibly have been a political allegory in support of Richard (the lion/ 'leoun').[44] Chaucer was also highly critical of the corrupt nature of the Church, as can be seen in his portraits of the Summoner, Pardoner, Monk and Friar.

There were other critics of the Church, the Lollards, clerics and laymen who questioned its doctrines, its corrupt practices and its exclusive use of Latin, a language that few people understood. The most prominent of these campaigners was John Wyclif. Traditional and reactionary voices in the Church called for action against the Lollards, but Richard followed a policy of tolerance. One of their strongholds was the Welsh borders. Sir John Oldcastle, for example, was a Herefordshire man and after being found guilty of heresy in 1413 and then mounting a failed rebellion, it was to the borders that he fled before going into hiding in Wales.

Richard's name was blackened very effectively by his usurper, Henry IV, and his closest political ally, Thomas Arundel. So much so that it is almost impossible to gauge the support given to the rightful king, but the one area of the kingdom that was indisputably loyal to Richard was Cheshire. Richard was King of England and France, Lord of Ireland and Prince of Chester. He raised Chester to the status of a principality, a status taken from it on Henry IV's usurpation. Richard's bodyguard, a personal force of some 300 to 500 men, was the Cheshire Guard.

Arundel, who served as Henry's archbishop of Canterbury and his Lord Chancellor (in 1399 and then again between 1407 and 1410) was brutal and ruthless in his suppression of the Lollards, of Richard's supporters and of anyone who questioned or mocked the authority of the Church. Chaucer was guilty of at least two of those crimes. That he feared for his life is shown by the sanctuary that he sought in Westminster Abbey. Shortly afterwards, he mysteriously 'disappeared'.

In a kingdom that had been transformed from tolerance and enlightenment to repressive and murderous philistinism, owning a Chaucer manuscript was as dangerous as being its author.[45] (The danger eased slightly with the death of Henry in 1410; Arundel lived for another year, but now had little power.) Even the mightiest of noble families had to be extremely careful. Where could the surviving friends, colleagues and admirers of Chaucer hide the offending and deeply incriminating evidence? Far from the prying eyes of Canterbury, London and Oxford would be the obvious answer and the Welsh borderland, with its Lollard sympathisers, isolation and semi-autonomous Marcher lordships would have been ideal. That may be the reason why the Hengwrt manuscript of *The Canterbury Tales* was in the possession of a Chester family in the sixteenth century. It may also be the reason for the number of Chaucer manuscripts in the National Library of Wales.

(The Hengwrt manuscript has 'builth'[46] written on one of its pages. John Oldcastle was in charge of the defence of Builth Castle in 1404, when it was attacked by Glyndŵr's forces.)

Salesbury was amongst that first generation of manuscript collectors, along with Leland, Bale and Prise. (He was also related by marriage to the owners of the Hengwrt manuscript.) Amongst the manuscripts he is known to have collected are the Giraldus Cambrensis (passed on to Cecil), the Roger Bacon (bought by Dee) and *The Lyfe of St Theulothoc*, which Robert Vaughan of Hengwrt sought in vain to locate.[47] A *Tretyse on the Astrolabe*, owned by John Edwards of Chirk, was almost certainly acquired for him by Salesbury. Salesbury had a great love of the English language and Chaucer as a 'proto-Protestant' was a writer who would have appealed to him, just as Langland was held in high regard by his colleague, Robert Crowley. (Pinkhurst was the scribe of one of the *Pierce Plowman* manuscripts owned by Crowley.) Prior to Mary's reign, Salesbury travelled the Marches widely in his role as Deputy Attorney General for Wales. If he had come across a Chaucer manuscript, he would have fallen upon it like a wolf on the fold.

Whilst Salesbury was enjoying Richard Davies's hospitality at Carmarthen, the bishop was receiving the protection of Walter Devereux, Viscount Hereford and, from 1572, first earl of Essex, in his battles against the earls of Leicester and Pembroke. Devereux had extensive estates in west Wales.

Is it possible that in recognition of that protection Davies offered the use of the young scholars who lodged in his bishop's palace for secretarial and administrative purposes?

In the 1560s Essex sold some parcels of land to Cecil. It was Cecil's younger son, Robert, who commissioned the building of Hatfield House. In 1958 the long lost page of the *Troilus and Criseyde* manuscript was discovered, '... sewn in the cover of a sixteenth century rent book containing surveys of some of the property of the Earl of Essex.' It was '... a single page of vellum taken from an unknown manuscript of the poem, and much cut down.' 'Whoever cut the page ... cared nothing for the writing.'[48]

Salesbury would not have allowed such a thing to happen, but on at least one occasion, the visit to Gruffudd Dwnn, he had been absent from Abergwili and most of 1567 was spent with Humphrey Toy in London seeing the Prayer Book, the New Testament and two other books into print. It was his intention to return to Carmarthen to start work on the Old Testament and so he is likely to have left his books and other possessions in the bishop's 'safe' keeping.

History has many examples of priceless manuscripts destroyed through ignorance or carelessness, the most famous being that of Betsy Baker, John Warburton's cook,[49] who used more than fifty of his Elizabethan and Jacobean play manuscripts as pie dish liners and kindling. It would take just one 'scholar' who was not as scholarly as had been assumed to commit the act of vandalism. An intriguing possibility.

Chapter Nineteen

A Godly enterprise

What needed thys waste?

The year 1567 was the one in which Salesbury achieved his life's ambition. He was back in London, surrounded by bookshops, within easy reach of his old colleagues and enjoying Toy's hospitality. By the end of his stay, his people would no longer be denied access to the words of Christ and his apostles. They would be able not just to hear the lessons of the daily and Sunday services in their own language, but could be baptised, married and buried in their mother tongue. It would be his *annus mirabilis*.

It would also be his *annus horribilis*. There were those who fiercely opposed his plans and did all they could to stop them coming to fruition. Their actions soured what should have been the proudest moments of his life.

The evidence can be found in Salesbury's own words. The 1 March (St David's Day) deadline was missed, but when *Lliver Gweddi Gyffredin* [the Book of Common Prayer] appeared on 6 May it was accompanied a few days later by a counterblast to his opponents, in which it becomes clear that they had called frequently on Toy to try to persuade him not to go ahead with the publication:

> I knowe well M. Toy, that synce the tyme ye tooke in hand the doing of this our Countrey matter, there resorted unto you divers with sundrye reasons, whereby, unles ye had most firmly purposed to bring to passe this godly enterprise, ye might, and that not without cause have been deterred, and brought to relynquishe the same unperfected.[1]

His anger is unrestrained (elsewhere he likens his opponents to 'fylthie flies forsaking the sownde partes [who] feede only on the sores'),[2] but ever the cautious lawyer, even in his anger, he does not name them or even hint at their identity.

Salesbury's writing career did not run smoothly. His major works could only be undertaken after years of campaigning to win approval for them from those in authority and in the aftermath of their publication he had to endure ferocious criticism often indistinguishable from personal abuse. Only those works produced for an English audience, such as *The Descripcion of the Sphere* and *A briefe and a playne introduction* were free of such concerns.

The early months of 1567 must have been the most trying of his career as belligerent trespassers, unconstrained by the fear of retribution from the Queen or Cecil as they would have been in 1563, invaded Toy's house demanding that he abandon the project to which Salesbury had devoted his life and three years of solid labour. A lesser man would have been broken by it, but Salesbury stood firm and Toy stayed loyal to him.

The opponents put forward two objections, the first being Salesbury's orthography. That was a valid point to make, one that had been made forcibly and frequently in the debate that had raged in England between the Latinists and their opponents. '... some exclamed, & perhaps meaning well and simply, but saving correction, though otherwise learned, not having most perfect knowledge herein, and affirmed to you that I had perverted the whole Ortographie of the tounge. Wher in deede it is not so.'

The other objection was, 'Some saying wyth Iudas the Traitor, what needed thys waste? For when ye have all done, there is fewe or none that can read it.'[3]

'What needed thys waste?' were the same words used twenty years later to try to stop William Morgan from completing the translation of the whole of the Bible. As a contemporary of Morgan commented, 'Could the devil himself have put it better?' Fortunately, Morgan had a powerful ally, Archbishop Whitgift, to support him.

The reaction of a sizeable sector of the Welsh gentry reflects several developments: their growing anglicisation and the accompanying loss of cultural attachment to Wales; their total indifference to the lot, material or spiritual, of the peasantry and the monumental intellectual torpor and inertia of an ultra-conservative and locally powerful governing class that viewed change of any sort as anathema.

(Regarding the orthography issue, there is no 'right' or 'wrong' side of the debate, however much passion is aroused and however vehemently Salesbury has been criticised by twentieth-century academics. 'Correct' spelling is merely the convention that has been adopted; present-day English spelling bears striking similarities to the innovations Salesbury tried to introduce into Welsh.)

Cynics may suggest that Toy's faith in Salesbury remained unshaken because he was about to make a substantial profit from the forthcoming publications. A copy of each book was to be placed in every church. That was a very large number of sales and no risk was involved. So long as the bishops had 'rated' 'the Prices of [the] Books' at a reasonable level, Toy would make a healthy profit.[4] There were only two areas of Wales where, through immigration, English had established itself as the dominant language, southern Pembrokeshire and the south of the Gower Peninsula.[5] The loss of sales from any of the churches in those two areas would have been compensated by sales to the Welsh-speaking parishes of the diocese of Hereford.

It would have been fascinating to have heard Salesbury confronting Toy's visitors outside the front door of his premises, using the oratory of a lawyer and the eloquence of a polemicist to support his case and quash that of his opponents. No doubt he delved deep into his learning, quoting from Cicero and other classical writers, from Erasmus and the European Humanists and from Thomas Elyot and other champions of the Inkhorn cause, nor would he have hesitated to use the example of Tyndale, Coverdale, Rogers and Erasmus (again) in defence of scriptural translation into the vernacular.

Stating his case in print

Few Welsh historians have taken account of the Inkhorn influence when assessing Salesbury's writing. At any one time there were scores and scores of English authors using and introducing the new (and continually evolving) orthography and Latinate vocabulary into the language. They were widely criticised by their contemporaries, but there were so many of them that the criticism was diffused and weakened and so could not be taken personally. When you are the sole writer of printed prose in your language, the sole public representative of a new school of thought, it is all but impossible not to take the criticism personally.

It is surely significant that the only pages in English in *Lliver Gweddi Gyffredin* are the four which appear under the heading, 'An explanation of certaine words being quarrelled withal', in which he defends his spelling. Two pages list particular words and phrases, the others give explanations of the punctuation and layout and advice on how to read the text.

Amongst the words he lists are 'cent' for 'cant' (hundred), 'pemp' for 'pump' (five) and 'Dew' (not 'Deo') for 'Duw' or 'Dyw' (God). Besides showing his love of Latinate and Hellenic forms, the last example displays a concern for the sensibilities of the southern Welsh. 'Duw' is the north Wales form, 'Dyw' the south Wales. In using 'Dew' he is reflecting the Latin origin of the word and may be affecting a compromise between north and south. Elsewhere Salesbury lists 'monyth' and 'tuy' as southern words he has used in preference to the northern 'mynydd' and 'tŷ'. William Morgan would show no such concern for unifying the language when he translated the Bible; northern terms and grammar dominate the text, with southern forms appearing infrequently.

(In fact, an inspection of the Prayer Book shows that, despite the passage above, Salesbury overwhelmingly uses 'Duw' or 'Dduw' (its mutated form). His philosophy of language was always evolving and it would seem that he had come to realise that 'Deo' was just too artificial a form, unlike 'colomben' or 'popul', for example. Similarly, the other artificial form 'heddyo' (hodie) was also dropped.)

Salesbury notes that he does not mutate words starting with 'p' and gives particular examples of his non-use of nasal mutation along with his reasons. Thus, 'Vy-Dew for vynuw … for the more significative expressing of the grace of the word.' and 'Vy-popul for vymhobl, to save the word the les maimed.'[6]

Two of the changes he made were accepted by his successors and became permanent features of Welsh. The first was his use of 'ei' (his/her). Until then the forms used had been either 'i', which also means 'to', or 'y' (the).

The confusion avoided by the adoption of the Latin-influenced ('eius', his) and non-phonetic 'ei' undermines many of the arguments put forward by the adherents of rigid phoneticism.

The other great change was the abandonment for practical reasons, 'because the Printers have not so many as the Welsh requireth' of 'k'.[7] The effect on the appearance of the language was striking. Welsh no longer resembled its sister languages of Breton or Cornish, which kept the 'k', but looked similar to Anglo-Saxon, to which it is not related.

The language of the four pages is restrained; the vitriol was reserved for elsewhere. Nor does his name appear anywhere in the Prayer Book. Any betrayal of the principle of anonymity would have weakened its status as representing the word of the Church of England. He was the translator, not the author.

It must have distressed him to have had to defend himself and it was unnecessary. If one considers the following lines by John Donne:

> Since I am comming to that Holy roome,
> Where, with thy Quire of Saints for evermore,
> I shall be made thy Musique[8]

it is of no matter whether the words are spelt in Jacobean English, modern British English or contemporary American English, it is the quality of the language that is the prime concern. Salesbury's literary career and his twentieth-century reputation were dogged and marred by an issue that is, actually, irrelevant.

Lliver Gweddi Gyffredin / The Book of Common Prayer

The unnamed protestors had been unsuccessful and after the May publication of *Lliver Gweddi Gyffredin* and the counterblast against his critics a few days later, there is no further mention of dispute or protest. His opponents appear to have admitted defeat.

It is interesting that Salesbury made the Prayer Book his priority. The New Testament did not exist in Welsh, but a version of the Prayer Book, *Kynniver Llith a Ban*, did and since 1563 had been officially sanctioned for use in church until the new translation appeared. But key sections of the Prayer

Book were missing from *Kynniver Llith a Ban*, in particular the services for the burial of the dead, christenings and marriages, as well as the collects. In addition, as a translation of the readings of the 1549 Prayer Book, it was not strictly a legal document. The Prayer Book of 1559 replaced all other versions; its Edwardian predecessors now had no validity in law.

Salesbury might also have reasoned that attending church on Sunday was a legal requirement of every subject, whilst reading the New Testament was not, which made the Prayer Book the more significant text. Reading the Bible for personal salvation and enlightenment was a characteristic of devout Protestants and there were very few of those in Wales. Besides, the New Testament required under the 1563 Act was intended for Church use. A moderately sized and modestly priced Bible intended for use at home by ordinary people would not become available until 1630.

So it was that the Prayer Book appeared first. *Lliver Gweddi Gyffredin* is a handsomely produced folio, with each page attractively and clearly set out. It is modelled very closely on the Prayer Book that was printed in 1564 by Jugge and Cawood. Cawood might even have given some assistance in its production. (Jugge and Cawood had long been friends and associates of the Toy family.)[9] Toy and Salesbury took great pains to avoid their version being seen as a poor relation of that found in English churches. The print is never small, cramped or difficult to read. Each collect and each lesson has an attractive, woodcut initial letter. The volume is paginated using Roman numerals. It is an impressive volume that would grace a collector's shelf.

The title page, decorated with four symmetrically arranged Renaissance-style woodcuts of putti, candlesticks and foliage, announces in black and red ink:

Lliver gweddi Gyffredin a gwenidogaeth y Sacramentae, ac eraill gynneddfeu a Ceremoniae yn Eccles Loecr,

Vewed, perused and allowed by the Bishops, accordyng to the Act stablished for the translation of the Bibles and thys Booke into the Brytyshe tongue.

Imprinted at London by Henry Denham, at the Costes and charges of Humfrey Toy. Anno 1567 6 Maij. Cum Privilegio.

Denham and Awdeley; Grindal and the bishops

Henry Denham was one of London's leading printers, but the actual printer was John Awdeley. It was common practice for printers to delegate work to others (during 1567 Denham took out licences to print no fewer than twelve books, more than enough work for one person) and nothing should be read into this discrepancy other than that Denham's name was the one that appeared in the Stationers' Register. The Toy and Awdeley families were close to each other,[10] but there might have been a particular reason for Awdeley being the printer chosen to deputise for Denham.

Awdeley was well educated. His 1575 book, *A Fraternity of Vacabondes*, would be a source of material for Shakespeare; he wrote a book on mathematics and printed a translation from the French of a work on navigation; his company and conversation would have been welcomed by Salesbury. He was also in the same Protestant camp as Salesbury and Crowley whom, in many ways, he resembled: he wrote ballads and in 1575 printed one of Crowley's sermons.

(That Awdeley is the printer is shown by the appearance at the end of the Prayer Book and again at the end of the Psalms of the words 'Tra vo' followed by a representation of a crescent moon. 'Tra vo lleuad' (Whilst the moon endureth) comes from Psalm 72. The quotation refers to the motif of the crescent moon, three of which are entwined in the Hebrew cryptogram devised by Salesbury (possibly in collaboration with Awdeley, but there is no evidence that the printer had mastered Hebrew). The Hebrew characters within the cryptogram can be read as 'By John Awdeley'.[11] The cryptogram is not included; its presence might have been deemed inappropriate, but the presence of the three words from the psalm could be interpreted not only as an acknowledgment of Awdeley's involvement in the printing but also as a discreet, subversive message of support for Crowley and his fellow campaigners.)

Though it would later become standard practice, including the Psalms in the Prayer Book was an innovation.[12] No doubt, it was Salesbury's love of Hebrew and his admiration for this most poetic book of the Bible that led to its inclusion. There is a distinct gap between the two parts of the book and a separate title page for the Psalms so that those who wished could have the Psalms bound separately as a Psalter.

The main title page states that the book had been 'vewed, perused and allowed by the byshops, according to the Act', a reference to the Welsh bishops and the bishop of Hereford. However, the register at Stationers Hall states that it was 'authorised by my Lord of London', that is Edmund Grindal, the bishop of London. This contradiction has never been explained. None of the five bishops is recorded as having been in London in May 1567. However, as members of the House of Lords, they are likely to have attended the Parliament of 1566–1567, which closed on 2 January. Did they inspect the Prayer book when it was in manuscript form and give it their approval? To add to the confusion, the New Testament, which appeared in October, carries no reference to its having been 'perused' by either Grindal or the Welsh bishops. Was the May authorisation thought to be sufficient for both books?

After the title page, *Lliver Gweddi Gyffredin* consists of a table of contents, 'An explanation of certaine words being quarreled withall', a translation into Welsh of the Act for the 1559 Prayer Book, a foreword, a table and calendar showing the order of the Psalms and the readings, an almanac for establishing the date of Easter and a calendar showing the saints' days. (Salesbury inserts that of Grwst, after whom Llanrwst is named.) After these pages come the services.

Though Salesbury's name is absent, the orthography is unmistakeably his. Ever true to scholarship and the cause of *copia*, Salesbury uses the margins to give alternatives to the words he has used in the text. This could have made the pages look cluttered and inelegant, but each page is so well set out that this is avoided.

The Psalter is as handsomely produced as the Prayer Book. Bound as a separate volume it, too, would have graced the shelves of any library or closet.

A letter home

On the same day as *Lliver Gweddi Gyffredin* appeared, Salesbury wrote a letter[13] to 'Boneddicion yr eisteddwyr ac y gwyr wrth gerdd' (Gentleman [members] of the eisteddfod and men of poetry). The fulfilment of his life's ambition meant that he had to miss the most important literary event of the late sixteenth century, the last eisteddfod of the bardic era. The previous one had been held in 1523. Ironically and sadly, his great friend Gruffudd Hiraethog, missed both those eisteddfodau, being too young (a teenager) for the first and not living long enough for the latter. The event was held at Caerwys, not far from Llansannan, and the chief organiser was Elis Price. It was not a competitive eisteddfod in the manner of the modern reinvention of the institution. Its purpose was to license bards (preventing inferior poets from peddling their wares), to set the standards that the licensed bards should meet and to discuss, and reform if necessary, the rules of *cynghanedd*. It was also a chance to meet old friends, listen to lots of poetry, socialise and be merry.

With hindsight there is huge symbolic significance to the printing of the Prayer Book and New Testament coinciding with the last eisteddfod. (Another, planned for the 1590s, never materialised.) The path that Salesbury had chosen, that of the printing press, of Renaissance and Humanist learning, of opening up the language to the cultural influences that were at work in English, French and the other major languages of Europe, was the one that assured the survival of Welsh in the modern era. The bards' way, clinging desperately to past traditions, not adapting to the invention of the press (already over a century old), turning their backs on the learning and culture of Europe, would have led the language into a wasteland. The late sixteenth century would produce some fine bards, most notably Wiliam Llŷn, a pupil of Gruffudd Hiraethog, but the whole system was being undermined by the inexorable erosion of the gentry's allegiance to the language. As their patronage withered away, so the bardic system died.

However, in 1567 there was still sufficient cultural commitment amongst the gentry who had not sought their fortunes in England for the eisteddfod to be a success.

With his letter Salesbury sends a copy of the statute of Gruffudd ap Cynan[14] and invites those present to read and discuss it. The statute lays down the rules concerning those who were allowed to *clera* (travel the country as a minstrel or poet). It was widely believed to have been the work of the prince of Gwynedd (d. 1137) whose name it bears.

The letter is brief, just four hundred words or so. No doubt, Salesbury wanted to greet his many friends and to express his regrets for his absence.

Perhaps he also meant the letter to be seen as an act of defiance to those who had called on Master Toy to try to force the abandonment of the project. (A conservatively-minded gentleman would have no trouble in supporting the bardic tradition whilst simultaneously opposing the Welsh Prayer Book.)

A letter to Master Toy

Eleven days later Salesbury published a new edition of *A briefe and a playne introduction* retitled *A playne and a familiar Introduction*. Denham is again named as printer, but Salesbury's inclusion at the end of the book of the Hebrew cryptogram (it replaces the two examples of *cynghanedd*) shows that it is the work of Awdeley. Though he no doubt hoped that sales would cover his costs, the motive was not commercial.[15] Just as he had used *Oll Synnwyr* to launch an attack on Elis Price and make the world aware of his brutal assault, so *A playne and a familiar Introduction* would be the vehicle for his counterattack on those who had tried to stop Toy from publishing *Lliver Gweddi Gyffredin*.

By far the most conspicuous and pugnacious addition to this second edition is the letter 'To my loving Friende Maister Humfrey Toy'. (The passages quoted at the beginning of this chapter come from the letter.) It is dated 6 May. Perhaps Salesbury had originally intended to include it in the Prayer Book, but then realised that for several reasons that would not be appropriate. It is a decidedly secular document and whilst the language is not profane, it is strong, as is illustrated by the comment that appears in the margin, 'The ignorant and malignant & contemptuous caused this digression.'

Here is Salesbury's letter, slightly abridged:

> Seeing that heretofore standing nothing in the lyke possiblitie and good hope of profiting the simple and unlearned of my Countrey, as I doe at this present, and have yet than published thys litle treatise, now can I not iustly at your request, deare Friende, who doeth so good a turne for all my Countrey, denye you to peruse the same
> ...[16]
> But considering that other nations, as the Hebrews, the Grekes, and the Romaines, who ruled all the world, have sustained such alteracion of language, such translation of countries, such invasion by alientes, shall now we than the posteritie of the old Britons, being never but a handful, in comparison of the least of any of those forenamed people, be well content to suffer the lyke?
> ...[16]

I knowe well M. Toy, that synce the tyme ye tooke in hand the doing of this our
Countrey matter, there resorted unto you divers with sundrye reasons, whereby,
unles ye had most firmly purposed to bring to passe this godly enterprise, ye might,
and that not without cause have bene deterred, and brought to relanquishe the
same unperfected. Some saying wyth *Iudas* the Traitor, what needed thys waste?
For when ye have all done, there is fewe or none that can reade it. Other some
exclamed, & perhaps meaning well and simply, but saving correction, though
otherwyse learned, not having most perfect knowledge herein, and affirmed to
you that I had perverted the whole Ortographie of the tounge. Wher in deede
it is not so; but true it is that I altered it very litle, and that in very few words, as
shall manifestlye appeare hereafter in the latter end of this booke. No, I altered it
in no mo wordes, but in suche as I coulde not fynde in my hart to lende my hand,
or abuse my penne to wryte them, otherwise than I have done. For who in the
time of most barbarousnes, and greatest corruption, dyd ever wryte every words
as he sounded it? As for example, they than wrate, *Ego dico tibi*, and yet read the
same, *Egu deicu teibei* : they wrate *Agnus Dei qui tollis*, but pronounced, *Angnus Dei
quei towllys*. And to come to the English tung. What yong Scoler did ever write
Byr Lady, for *by our Lady?* or *nunkle* for *unkle?* or *mychgoditio*, for *much good do it
you?* or *sein* for *signe?* And thus for my good wil molested of such wranglers, shal I
condescend to confirme their unskylful custome, or else contrary to *S. Augustines*
most true saying, who affirmeth that *Dura est pugna contra consuetudinem*, It is hard
to impugne or fight against custome? Or shall I prove what playne Dame Truth,
appearing in hir owne lykenes can woorke against the wrynckled face neme
Custome? Well, for thys time I am thus determined [not] to give eare to my
countrymens requests, to favor my friendes reasoninges, but rather to incline to that
which in my poore knowledge is most consonant with the infallible Truth. And
in thys I appeale to the Bardes, who can most exquisitelye can [sic] pronounce and
give iudgement in such contention. And least I shoulde spende more tyme then
the matter is worth, I cease from farther wordes, committing to you the requested
Copie, to dispose it at your discretion. And thus I wish the Lord Almighty to guide
you and your doynges wyth hys most holy Spirite. Amen.

   Soiurning at your house in Paules Churchyarde, the 6, of Maij.1567.

   Your, assuredly, welwyller, W. Salesbury.

Put more succinctly, his argument is: Languages evolve, both naturally
and from external pressures. Why should Welsh be any different? English is
full of disparities between its written and spoken forms. Why [the question
is implied] should Welsh be different? It is only the 'wrynckled face neme

Custome' that opposes my philosophy. (It is a sound, rational philosophy, though his assertion that he altered the orthography 'very litle' is disingenuous. The weakness in Salesbury's case is that he is addressing a nation whose cultural background is very different from that of England. Generally speaking, it would not be until the Industrial Revolution that radicalism and innovation would be welcomed rather than shunned in Wales.)

There are a few minor changes to the other letter in the book, the one to Colyngborne[17], but several additions to the main body of the work, all added to support his orthography. Salesbury explains how 'x' in Latin becomes 's' in Welsh (crux (cross) becomes croes or crws; exemplum (example) becomes esampyl; extendo, estennaf); how 'Also g is added to the beginning of such words as be derived of the Latine, which begyn with v, As Gwilym, gwic, gwynt, Gwent, gwin, gosper.' There are examples of how Latin words lose their last syllable when adopted into Welsh: cist/cista (chest), Natalic/Natalicus (Christmas), Caisar/Caesare (Caesar).

Having used examples from Latin and English in his letter to Toy, Salesbury now uses references to the work of some of the most famous Humanist scholars, such as Johann Hausschein, Johannes Aventinus and Philipp Melanchthon, 'And as M. Melanchthon affirmeth that c. k. q. had one sound in times past wyth the Latines …'

Whatever one feels about the debate, the campaign to stop the translations appears to have evaporated. Whilst Toy and the bishops set about the work of distributing the texts to the parishes of Wales and Hereford, Salesbury, though wounded and angered by the opposition he had encountered, could allow himself a few moments of satisfaction at what had been achieved before starting on the task of seeing the New Testament through the printing process.

Chapter Twenty

The New Testament

Robert Crowley

With the Prayer Book and Psalter set down in print, his enemies dispersed and the spring days lengthening to those of summer, Salesbury might now have allowed himself a little time to meet some of his old London friends, in much the same way that he had put aside his translations to visit Gruffudd Dwnn. If this was the case, then the old friend who would most have appreciated his company was Robert Crowley.

Though Elizabeth was undoubtedly Protestant, she retained a fondness for some of the old Catholic practices, a fondness attributed by one writer to the influence throughout her childhood of Blanche Parry,[1] who appears, unobtrusively but stubbornly, never to have abandoned the old rituals. On certain issues, such as the marriage of priests, Elizabeth had given way, but on others, such as priests' vestments, she had won the day. This greatly vexed the more radical members of the clergy and laity.

One of those vexed priests was Crowley. On his return from exile in 1559, he had been appointed archdeacon of Hereford, in which position he was a member of the 1563 Convocation, but by 1566, as vicar of St Giles, Cripplegate, his reputation as a 'trouble-maker' (or man of principle) was a constant source of concern to Archbishop Parker:

> I am complained to that Crowley and his curate gave a great occasion of much trouble yesterday in his church, for expelling out of his church divers clerks which were in their surplices to bury a dead corse, as customably they use.
>
> In the examination of Crowley fell out many fond paradoxes that tended to anabaptistical opinions ... saying, as pastor, he would resist the wolf if he can, meaning the surplice man.

> I did even presently discharge him of his flock and parish.
>
> As for Crowley's imprisonment into his own house, I have signified unto your honour [Cecil] by my former letters, and my lord of London [Grindal] who was with me sitting can shew you of his behaviour, that I could do no less.[2]

On a personal level Salesbury would not have hesitated to see his old friend who had been such a help and support in 1550 and 1551, but what if he feared that contact with this turbulent priest might jeopardise the great project? It is to be hoped that Salesbury was as much a man of principle as Crowley.

News would have reached Salesbury that summer of the death of his son-in-law, Hugh ap Dafydd ap John.[3] He had married Gwen, one of the children born after the reconciliation with Catrin. Just two years earlier Hugh had been a guarantor of the bond for £100. In his will he refers to Salesbury as his father-in-law and bequeaths him 'a penwen cowe & iiij nobles in money.' The main beneficiaries are his son, Piers, and his widow. As with the death of Gruffudd Hiraethog, the length of time that it took for news to travel and the need to complete the task he had undertaken, make it unlikely that Salesbury attended the funeral.

Another death that summer was that of Sir Richard Rich, the former Attorney General for Wales and Lord Chancellor of England for whom Salesbury had worked and to whom he had dedicated his Protestant polemic, *The baterie of the Popes Botereulx*. The man who had betrayed Thomas More to further his own career, had personally tortured Anne Askew and burnt more Protestants than any other local office-holder died peacefully in his bed. Perhaps Salesbury gained some satisfaction from the fact that the persecutor of his co-religionists had lived long enough to see his erstwhile servant strike so huge a blow for Welsh Protestantism.

A blessing for Salesbury as he worked through the summer was that the plague had not broken out. His successor as scriptural translator, William Morgan, would not be so fortunate. In 1603 Morgan had completed the manuscript version of his revised edition of the New Testament. It had been delivered to the printer, Thomas Salisbury (a member of the clan), but in the chaos that erupted as the plague broke out and London was evacuated by all those with the means to leave, the manuscript was lost forever.

A dedication to the Queen

In contrast, Salesbury was able to commit himself, free of worry, to the task of preparing the New Testament. It appeared on 7 October and this time Henry Denham really was the printer.

Y Testament Newydd, an impressively produced quarto, has a handsome title page in red and black ink with a woodcut depicting light and darkness accompanied by a verse from John, Chapter III, 'Hon yw'r barnedigaeth, gan ddyvot golaunt [*sic*][4] ir byt, a charu o ddynion y tywyllwch yn vwy na'r golauni' ('this is the condempnacion: Light is come into the worlde, and the men have loved darcknes more then light'). There is also a verse from Matthew, XIII. There is an almanac for twenty-five years and then a four-page dedication 'To the most Vertuous and noble Prince Elizabeth, by the grace of God, of England, Fraunce and Ireland Queene, defender of the Faith.'

The dedication begins, not with the obligatory praise of the Queen, but an anti-Catholic diatribe ('corrupted Religion', 'makers of alabaster images'), which navigates its way from the bead-makers of Pater Noster, London, to Wales and praise of the sovereign:

> so com I before your maiesties feete, and there lying prostrate not onely for my self, but also for the delivery of many thousandes of my country folks from the spirituall blyndnes of ignoraunce, and fowl infection of olde Idolatrie and false superstition, most humbly, and dutifully to acknowledge your incomparable benefite bestowed upon us in graunting the sacred Scriptures the verye remedie and salve of our gostly blyndnes and leprosie, to be had in our best knowen tongue.

If 'So com I before your maiesties feete' is literal rather than metaphorical, Salesbury formally presented the Queen with a copy. The great irony is that if Elizabeth had known that the chief translator had made ample use of the scholarship of Beza and of the Geneva versions of the Bible, she would have reacted with fury.

Salesbury goes on to praise Henry VII and Henry VIII, who are compared to David and Solomon. Whilst her father and grandfather granted Wales material wealth, Elizabeth now grants it spiritual wealth. There is then a list of British heroines, Cambria the fayre,[5] Martia the Good, Bunduica the

Warrior, Claudia Rufina, Helena (mother of Constantine) and St Ursula of Cornwall. Elizabeth, of course, is greater than all these, 'Many daughters have don vertuosly: but thou surmountest them all.' (Proverbs 31:29)

Whilst Mary Magdalene anointed Christ's body, Elizabeth has anointed the spiritual body of the Church and so is greater.

Salesbury then states that he is 'unworthy' of the great task given him by the bishops and then returns to the graciousness of the Queen:

> a booke of the Newe Testament of our Lorde Iesus Christ, translated into the
> British language, which is our vulgare tongue, wyshyng and most humbly praying,
> if it shall so seme good to your wysedome, that it myght remayne in your M.
> Librarie for a perpetuall moment of your graciouse bounties shewed herein to our
> country and the Church of Christ there.

The letter is signed, 'Your Maties most humble and faithfull subiect William Salesbury.'

Salesbury's pride at the realisation of his lifetime's work is all pervading. Does that explain the lack of anonymity? The New Testament is no less holy than the Prayer Book; should not Salesbury have respected its sacred nature by remaining anonymous? He was also doing the bishops' work, but was it not his role as a servant to be invisible?

Salesbury and Davies

Perhaps Richard Davies had given his full blessing to Salesbury's letter. It is not known whether he was in London on 7 October. It is difficult to imagine his not being present if there was a ceremonial presentation of a copy to the Queen.

There is no explanation or defence of orthography, but there are further preliminary pages. Twenty-five of them are taken up with Richard Davies's 'Epistol at y Cembru' (letter to the Welsh people) in which, amongst other things, he outlines his belief that the scriptures had long ago been translated into Welsh but had not survived (a belief strongly shared by Salesbury).[6] He also states that the Old Testament will follow.

The copy of Y Testament Newydd in the library of Corpus Christi College, Cambridge (in the Parker Collection), has notes in the margin, possibly in

Davies's hand, stating, alongside the words 'Escop Myniw' (bishop of St Davids), 'Nid yr audur … Willm Salesbury i gydymaith wrth brintio y llyfr, a wnaeth y dech[r]euad yma …' (Not the author … William Salesbury his colleague on printing did (wrote) this beginning …)

It goes on to note that Salesbury had added almost the whole of the first page to what was Davies's original letter. There is a brief note in the copy in the Cardiff Library that says the same in Latin.[7]

Later copies of the 1567 New Testament contain 'Apologi neu Atep am y Beiau y mae'r ei yn cael yn Epistol Episcop Menew' (An apology or answer for the faults that are to be found in the letter of the bishop of St Davids) where Salesbury justifies (the original meaning of apology) the mistakes that occurred.

Were the notes in the margin merely clarifying the authorship? There is no record of discord between them following the publication of the New Testament and no hint of acrimony in the notes in the margin. It could well be that Davies was so overwhelmed by his many duties that he was content for Salesbury to have full control of the whole project. Whatever the truth, Salesbury returned to Abergwili to start work on the Old Testament.

(An examination of Davies's sections of the New Testament also testifies to a good working relationship between the two men. Davies shows nasal mutation when it occurs; Salesbury did not try to impose that particular idea upon him or, if he did, he was not insistent. Davies does, however, tend to use the older forms of spelling, for example, the '-awl' ending for '-ol'. He might have favoured this policy anyway or it might be that he was finding common ground with his colleague. It seems that both men were capable of compromise.)

Following the bishop's letter there is a one-page letter by Salesbury that echoes the content of its predecessor, a short section given over to St John of Chrysostom in Latin and Welsh, then a list of the books in the Bible and, finally, 'Yr Argument', two pages which give the background to the gospels and their authors.

The New Testament follows, with each chapter preceded by a précis of its contents. The chapters are not divided into verses.[8] Each chapter begins with a monochrome, woodcut initial letter. The whole book is paginated and Salesbury provides plentiful alternative words or notes in the margins, including for those sections translated by Davies and Huet. One typographical change is that in the Prayer Book words or phrases that have been added for clarification but do not appear in the original text are denoted by square brackets; in the New Testament Salesbury uses a different typeface for those words. The consensus is that the use of brackets was less intrusive.

Proverbs and triads

There was one more work for which Salesbury was responsible that year. A letter[9] that appears to have coincided with the publication of the book has been preserved in a copied form and can be dated to between March and October 1567. As Salesbury would not have given the book priority over the New Testament, it is reasonable to assume that it appeared shortly after.

It is not known whether Toy financed this last publication. There is no reason to suppose that he did and as no one took out a licence at the Company of Stationers, neither printer nor publisher can be traced. The fact that the print run appears to have been very small (within a decade of it being published it was difficult to find printed copies) suggests that Salesbury covered the costs; though he had had free board and lodging for at least three years, he had had no income from legal work, which may explain why so few copies were printed.

Denham or Awdeley might have been involved, but it is impossible to tell as just two fragments of the book survive. They are to be found in the British Library. The first fragment consists of a list of adages from 'Abyli pop pethau boddlono' to 'Anhael pop cypydd'[10], the second resumes the list with 'Dewys or ddwy vachddu hwch' and continues through the alphabet to 'Yspys y dengys pop dyn / O ba 'radd i vo i wreiddyn' and is followed by twelve pages of triads. A triad is a literary form peculiar to Wales, where three phenomena are grouped together under a definition of their common factor:

Tri hael Ynys Brytain
Nudd hael ap Senylt
Nordaf hael ap Sernan
Rydderch hael ap Tudwal Tudclyd

[The three generous (men) of Britain
Generous Nudd[11] son of Senylt
Generous Nordaf son of Sernan
Generous Rhydderch son of Tudwal Tudclyd]

The proverbs are instantly recognisable as those that appeared in *Oll Synnwyr*, though there are some additions to the list. There is a collection of triads in Salesbury's handwriting (MS Cwrtmawr 3), but it bears no resemblance to the triads in the fragment.

Fortunately, W. Alun Mathias, the great Salesbury scholar, discovered a 1577 manuscript copy (MS NLW 6434) of Salesbury's printed book.[12] It was commissioned by Thomas Wynn,[13] the copyist being Ieuan Llwyd ab Edwart ap Wiliam. It is this need to resort to copying so soon after publication allied to the survival of just one imperfect copy that leads to the assumption that few copies were printed.

Ieuan Llwyd might have been a professional copyist, but he was not a good one; he leaves out at least thirty proverbs, does not correct misprints and at one stage turns over two pages by mistake, does not notice that he has done so and continues copying, even though the resulting triad is gibberish. The title of the book, assuming there is no error, is *Crynodab or Diarebion sathredig: Trioedd ynys prydain a thalm or philosophi neur hen athronddysg camberaig* [A compendium of common proverbs: the Triads of the Isle of Britain and a portion of the philosophy or old learning of the Welsh language].

The book consisted of seven parts: the proverbs (derived from Gruffudd Hiraethog), the triads (source unknown, but possibly *Llyfr Coch Hergest*), *Geirie Gwir Taliesin* [Taliesin's Words of Truth], *Llyma xxiiij Gwell* [Behold, Twenty-four Better (Things)], *Llyma Gas Bethau Owain Kyveiliog* [Behold the Hated Things of Owain Cyfeiliog], *Traethawt o Athronddysg Gamberaig* [An Essay on Welsh Learning] and *Traethawt o Gymmendawt cambereig* [An Essay on Welsh Eloquence].

Items three to six are taken from works written or compiled by Gruffudd Hiraethog, but Salesbury has made extensive revisions to them. The final piece appears to be Salesbury's own, a list of sayings that all start with 'Nid' (not), followed by ten quotations from the works of Marcus Aurelius translated into Welsh.

Salesbury would certainly have acknowledged his debt to Gruffudd in the foreword, just as he did with *Oll Synnwyr*. It might even be that Salesbury intended the book as a tribute to his recently departed friend. Gruffudd was a perceptive observer of cultural trends. As mentioned in an earlier chapter, one of his great worries was the flow of young Welshmen to England; they quickly lost contact with and commitment to their native culture. His solution had been *Lloegr drigiant ddifyrrwch Bryttanaidd Gymro* [British Entertainment for a Welshman living in England],[14] a work similar to Salesbury's in content. The hope was that it would inspire young exiles to retain an interest in their native literature.

Gruffudd, of course, never had his work printed; he still held to the bardic tradition of manuscripts being circulated and copied. Salesbury understood the power of the printed word. He might also have realised that it was even more important that the gentry who remained in Wales be persuaded to retain their cultural identity. Gradually they were becoming English gentlemen domiciled in Wales. Gruffudd's pupils would be the last generation of bards with sufficient numbers of patrons to provide them with a living.

It is unfortunate that so few copies of Salesbury's last book were printed. Only four 'sightings' are recorded. Thomas Wynn must have had a copy or the loan of a copy in 1577. William Camden used the section on the triads for his 1586 work, *Britannia*.[15] Dr John Davies made copies of the essays on Welsh eloquence and learning, but his source is unknown, and Robert Vaughan of Hengwrt knew of the book's existence. In a letter to Archbishop Ussher dated 1 November 1623, he writes:

> I have not as yet had any tyme to looke to the Triades, but after this moneth is ended I will (if it please God) make the best survey I cann of yt. I am tould (and I thinke it is true) that it hath beene printed long since together with some Welshe proverbs, but I cannot learne where any printed copy is to be found.

Had Vaughan succeeded, the resulting copy would now most likely be lodged on the shelves of Trinity College Library, Dublin, alongside its copy of Salesbury's dictionary.

How the fragments arrived at the British Library is unknown.[16] Examining its remaining pages is more akin to studying a manuscript. A printed book, even one many centuries old, is still a mass-made object, but these pages are unique. The marks and marginalia give tantalising hints as to who might have owned and studied the book, but no concrete evidence.

In the same manuscript in which Ieuan Llwyd copied Salesbury's book is the letter (mentioned briefly above) that Salesbury wrote to three friends, Humphrey Llwyd, Richard Langford and Jenkyn Gwyn. (Langford was a noted collector of manuscripts, Gwyn a respected antiquary and correspondent of Dr Dee.)[17] The inclusion of the letter in the manuscript that contains Ieuan Llwyd's copy (together with its tone and contents) points to its having been part of the book. Salesbury obviously shared Gruffudd's concern at the ebbing of interest in matters Welsh amongst the gentry. This is both a tribute to his friend and a continuation of his cultural campaign.

The letter starts:

> Ar [sic] y Brytanaidd Voneddigion master Richard longford [sic] o Drefalyn master humfre Lloyd o Ddynbych a master Iankyn Gwyn o lan Idlos: William Salesbury yn anvon anerch.
>
> [To the British Gentlemen, Master Richard Langford of Trefalun, Master Humphrey Llwyd of Denbigh and Master Jenkin Gwyn of Llanidloes: William Salesbury sends a greeting.]

Ever the sophisticated political operator, Salesbury associates his book and the cause it espouses with the three most famous Welsh antiquaries of the day (Humphrey Llwyd's reputation extended far beyond Wales to England and to Europe).

In a pun-ridden opening section Salesbury mentions and praises Edward Games, Gruffudd ap Ieuan ap Llewelyn Vachan, and Master [Tomas] Talai (all deceased). Gruffudd ap Ieuan was Richard Davies's uncle and a bard of some note. If there had been discord over Salesbury's additions to Davies's *Epistol at y Cembru*, Gruffudd's inclusion could be interpreted as a peace-offering or bridge-building exercise.

Salesbury speaks of the need to adorn the language, an obvious reference to Erasmian copiousness and his own orthography. He compares Welsh favourably to Cornish and Breton, which had not been adorned as Welsh had.

He praises Langford, Llwyd and Gwyn for their achievements and the collections of proverbs they had made, which he hopes they will share with him. Llwyd had recently returned from travelling in Italy with Lord Arundel and Salesbury hopes that he will introduce some of the Italian proverbs into Welsh.

Salesbury refers to Gwyn having borrowed *Llyfr Coch Hergest* from Sir Henry Sidney, Lord President of the Council of the Marches, and mentions that he too had seen it in Ludlow three years earlier. In so doing he associates an interest in Welsh learning with one of England's leading aristocrats, who just happened to be the most powerful man in Wales.

He states that his hope is that young scholars will not only know 'the phrases of the language' (tr.) but that they, too, will go on to adorn their native tongue.

Salesbury's name does not appear, not in the copied version at least, but the orthography and content leaves no doubt as to who had written the letter. It finishes with, 'Or vonwent yn y Gaer' (from the cemetery (churchyard) in the fortress [London]).

The date is given as 21 November 1572, another error or misunderstanding by the copyist, as Humphrey Llwyd, very much alive and in Wales at the time the letter was written, died in August 1568.[18] He had returned from Italy in March 1567. References to Sir Harry Sidney serving as deputy Lord President of Ireland mean that the letter must have been written before 13 October 1567 (or a little later, if news of his return had not yet reached London). The overwhelming likelihood is that the letter was written sometime between the publication of *Y Testament Newydd* and 13 October and was an integral part of *Crynodab or Diarebion sathredig.*

The book was an accomplished example of Welsh Humanist learning. Two factors might have prevented it from achieving its aim: the small number of copies printed and the sheer force of cultural trends, which seem to have a power all of their own.

Salesbury was not to know, but this would be the last of his books to be published in his lifetime.

An assessment

After the disastrous start to the year, with opponents putting pressure on Toy
to abandon his support for the publications, Salesbury would have returned
to Wales exhausted after nine months of hard, tedious work but exhilarated at
what had been achieved. There is certainly nothing in the letter that suggests
otherwise. Was that satisfaction warranted? How good are the translations and
how were they received?

There is no record of a negative response. The only valid evidence is
that of Bishop Nicholas Robinson who in 1576 reported to Grindal, now
archbishop of Canterbury, that 'in the church all things are done in Welsh'.[19]

Academics and critics who have studied Salesbury's prose speak highly of
the Prayer Book and the Psalter. Many regard them as his masterpieces.

'His Prayer Book is surely one of the major triumphs of humanist prose
in Welsh.' Professor R. Geraint Gruffydd;[20]

'Indeed, the more the Psalter of 1567 is read the more the reader
appreciates the charm of its sound and sense. Truly, Salesbury's excellence as
a translator of the scriptures is at its shining best in this exceptional version.'
(tr.) Isaac Thomas;[21]

'Perhaps Salesbury's masterpiece as a translator and it is the basis of
William Morgan's version of the Psalms in the 1588 Bible.' (tr.) From the
General Foreword to Y *Beibl Cymraeg Newydd* (1988).

Here is an example of the elegance of Salesbury's translation:

Pan glybu Ioan ac ef yn-carchar oywrth weithredoedd Christ, e ddanvones ddau
oei ddiscipulon, ac a ddyvot wrthaw: Ae ti yw hwn a ddaw, ai dysgwyl a wnawn
am arall. Iesu a atebawdd ac a ddyvot wrthynt, Ewch, a manegwch i Ioan y
pethae a glywsoch ac a welsoch. Y mae'r daillion yn cahel ei golwc a'r cloffion yn
rhodiaw: a'r cleifion gohanol wedy ei glanhau, a r byddar yn clywet, a'r meirw y
gyfodir, a'r tlodion yn derbyn yr Evangel.[22]

[When Jhon beinge in preson herde the works of Christ, he sent two of his
disciples and sayde unto him. Arte thou he that shall come: or shall we loke for
another. Jesus answered and sayde unto them. Go and shewe Jhon what ye have
herde and sene. The blind se, the halt goo, the lyppers ar clensed: The deef heare,
the ded are reysed up ageine, and the gospel is preachede to the povre.] Matthew
11

The Prayer Book was not replaced until 1599, which means that for thirty–two years[23] the Welsh people listened to Salesbury's prose every Sunday of the year and were christened, married and buried to a pattern of words that had been weighed, considered and balanced into a harmony inspired by the philosophy and craftsmanship of Erasmus, Tyndale, Cicero, Beza and Luther and poets such as Dafydd ap Gwilym and Taliesin. It could be argued that no other person has had a greater influence on the language than Salesbury.

For the whole of his literary career Salesbury's orthography had been controversial, but after the early months of 1567, when his opponents had besieged the home of Humphrey Toy, there is no record of further criticism during his lifetime. Indeed, it is easy to overlook the fact that there were many who supported his linguistic philosophy. The lexicographer, Sir Thomas Wiliems, writing in 1574 stated his appreciation of Salesbury's prose style, '… [It] will become used in every place … accent-less, pure language, wholly clear, yes in my opinion, and proved to everyone who wishes, such that none in all Wales could improve it.' (tr.)[24]

Salesbury and his successors

The quality of *Lliver Gweddi Gyffredin* can be gauged by studying the text that eventually replaced it, Bishop William Morgan's Prayer Book of 1599. The first thing to consider is that Morgan made translating the Bible his priority. That is understandable, the Old Testament had yet to appear in print and the Book of Revelations, translated by Huet, is not generally well regarded, but the Prayer Book was the text that was critical for everyday religious observance. If Morgan had had concerns about its quality, he would have felt obliged to make it his priority. He did not. In fact, there was a gap of eleven years between the appearance of Morgan's Bible and his Prayer Book, hardly an indication of a sense of urgency, especially when the relative brevity of the latter is taken into account.

(That Salesbury's *Lliver Gweddi Gyffredin* was fulfilling its purpose effectively is evidenced by the reprint of 1586. Salesbury is believed to have died by this date.[25] The reprint was a purely commercial venture by Thomas Chard, the London printer who now held the rights to the translation. He is unlikely to have speculated money on a volume that was not well regarded.)

Lastly, there is Morgan's translation itself. When he translated the New Testament section of the Bible, he greatly revised Salesbury's orthography but was more judicious with the text, sometimes abandoning his forerunner's formulation, at other times making minor changes or sticking to the original quite faithfully. (Morgan's changes are discussed in a later chapter.) However, when the bishop translated *Lliver Gweddi Gyffredin*, though he once again rejected Salesbury's orthography, he strayed from the original words on far, far fewer occasions.

One reason was that after thirty-two years of use the words would have become so familiar, so much a part of one's consciousness, that changing them would have become almost impossible. (Morgan, during his time as a parish priest would have made hundreds upon hundreds of readings from it.) The other reason was that they were so good that they needed very little alteration.

In fact, not only did Morgan respect Salesbury's prose, so did John Davies, who was responsible for the new edition of the Welsh Prayer Book of 1620. There were further printings of Davies's Prayer Book in 1630, 1634 and 1664. Compare the following versions of the same passage (the second collect from the Morning Prayer), the first from 1567 and the second from 1664.

'Duw, yr hwn wyt Awdur tangneddyf, a charwr cyntundeb, yrhwn oth iawn adnabot y mae yn buchedd tragwydd yn sevyll arnaw, ath wasanaeth yw gwir vraint: amddeffen nyni dy ostyngedic weision …'

'Duw, yr hwn wyt Awdur tangneddyf, a charwr cyttundeb, yr hwn o'th iawn adnabod, y mae ein buchedd dragwydd yn sefyll arnaw, a'th wasanaeth yw gwir fraint: Amddeffyn nyni dy ostyngedic weision …'

Few authors or translators would object to their work being read and used daily, barely changed, for close to a century.

A last judgement

What of Salesbury's translation of the New Testament? Unlike the Prayer Book and the Psalter, he was not the sole author. He did not have sole editorial control, though he was the dominant figure out of the trio of translators. Perhaps that is the reason why no one has called the New Testament a masterpiece. Mathias regards it as uneven ('anwastad')[26] in its quality, which is not to say that there are not passages as accomplished as anything he wrote that year.

Knowing that the work would not be entirely his could well have made a psychological difference, so could weariness and the fact that the Prayer Book and the Psalms were very much his priorities. Another factor that might have played a part is that the Prayer Book, to a great extent, was his second version of *Kynniver Llith a Ban*. He was already intimately aware of the passages and the problems their translation posed. He had had over a decade to reflect on errors and on sections where the words did not flow well.

(The reason for the consistently high quality of the language of the Psalter may be that this was his first opportunity to work from Hebrew, a language he loved, and that the Book of Psalms is, arguably, the most beautiful of all the books of the Bible. Salesbury, a master of prose, was provided with all the necessary poetic requirements (powerful imagery and faultless use of metre, metaphor and personification) to produce his greatest work.)

If he had been given a second chance to translate the New Testament, then perhaps the outcome would have been different, but his great task now was to complete the Bible.

The greatest achievement and most significant legacy of Salesbury's translations of 1567 and the keenest riposte to his critics is the rich vocabulary he bequeathed to his compatriots. This is best illustrated by an exercise carried out in 1988. D. Simon Evans[27] took the University of Wales dictionary and studied the entries that appear under the letter A. He listed all the common and familiar words that were fashioned for or were first used in the Prayer Book or New Testament:

> adfent, afiethus, aflendid, aflesol, agen, angenfilaidd, anghaffael, anghenus, anghofio, anghofus, anghrediniaeth, anghymeradwy, anghymarus, anghytuno, ailenedigaeth, ailgyfodiad, amherffeithrwydd, amheus, amhosibl, amhroffidiol, amlygiad, anadlu, anedifeiriol, anenwog, anerchiad, anewyllysgar, anfarwoldeb, anfri, anfuddiol, anffortunus, anhynod, annllythrennog, annheilyngdod, annuwioldeb, anwaraidd, anwiredd, anwybodaeth, arddodiad, areithiwr, arfogi, arglwyddiaethu, argraff, argraffu, argyhoeddi, ariangar, arogli, arswydus, aruthrol, arweiniwr, ategu, atgof, atgyfodi, atolwg.

Salesbury's legacy

In the same year that Salesbury produced his last four books, Gruffydd Robert, a Catholic exile, secretary to Cardinal Borromeo of Milan, published *Dosparth Byrr ar y rhan gyntaf i ramadeg cymraeg* [A short rationale on the first part of a Welsh grammar]. His interest in language had been kindled by reading Salesbury's account of the Latin influence on Welsh in *A briefe and a playne introduction*.[28] (It was not a grammar in the Palsgrave sense of the word, but a manual to instruct Welshmen in the techniques, discipline and strategies necessary to produce prose of the highest standard.)

For two decades Salesbury had been the sole author of Welsh-language books. The year 1567 was of huge significance in the history of Wales. It saw the last eisteddfod, which marked the beginnings of the demise of the bardic system on which the country's cultural identity had depended. At the same time the Welsh tongue took its place alongside English, German and other north European vernacular languages as a medium for Protestant worship and the country's intellectuals, on both sides of the religious divide, celebrated the arrival of the first of the Welsh authors who would follow Salesbury into print. Other books were to follow, not a flood, no more than a trickle, but enough to ensure the survival of the language and its culture.

The debt owed to those pioneers, men such as John Prise, William Salesbury, Gruffydd Robert, William Morgan and John Davies, is immense, but the biggest debt by far is owed to Salesbury.

Chapter Twenty-One

Salesbury's last book

An unreliable witness

There can be no doubting that Salesbury and Davies intended to complete the Old Testament. Davies had stated in his *Epistol at y Cembru*, 'Here is the one part ready, that which is called the New Testament, whilst you wait (God grant that it will not be long) the other part that is called the Old Testament.' (tr.)[1]

Following the printing of *Crynodab or Diarebion sathredig* or *Y Diarebion Camberaec* as it is usually known, Salesbury is likely to have returned to Denbighshire for a time to see his family and oversee the management of his estate before heading south to rejoin forces with Davies. Certainly, by the New Year (he might have spent Christmas at Plas Isa) he would have been busily at work in the Bishop's Palace.

There is evidence to support this assumption, though written fifty years after the event:

> He [Davies] call'd to him Wm Salusbury Esqr of Plas Issa near Llanrwst in ye County of Denbigh, & divers others, Welshmen, profound schollars & skillfull linguists. And Translated The New Testament, The Psalms, & Book of Com'on prayer into ye Welch tongue, & was very far onward with ye Old Testament ...[2]

The words, taken from *The History of the Gwydir Family*, are those of Sir John Wynn of Gwydir, grandson of John Wyn ap Maredudd who took advantage of Salesbury's weakened position during Queen Mary's reign to acquire Plas Isa. The estate that Sir John had inherited covered vast swathes of north Wales, but the security and position that his inherited wealth had given him had done nothing to moderate the aggressive avarice of the Wynns. He used his book to pour scorn on Salesbury's successor as scriptural translator, William Morgan. At the time of his death in 1604, Morgan was bishop of St Asaph. He took his duties seriously and though he was far from wealthy, he used his own money to repair the cathedral's roof. When Wynn sought to lease the tithe of Llanrwst parish, Morgan stood up to him. The bishop was in poor health and did not have long to live, but Wynn's persecution of him was relentless and the death of the unfortunate cleric did nothing to moderate Wynn's anger, leading him, when he came to write his book, to suggest that Morgan had plagiarised the work of Davies and Salesbury, 'He translated ye old Testamt into ye Welch Tongue before he was Bishop wherein he had ye benefit & help of Bish' Davies & Wm Salusbury's works, who had done a great part thereof, yet he carried ye name of yt all.'[3]

Salesbury was more fortunate; his standing up to the Wynns was sufficiently distant to be overlooked and he was related to Wynn through his nieces, Gwen and Elen, Sir John's aunts. Indeed, Wynn is quite complimentary towards him, '[He] gave over writing (more was ye pity) for he was a rare schollar, & especially an Hebrician, whereof there was not many in those days'.[4]

As can be seen by his attitude towards Morgan, the author of *The History of the Gwydir Family* was not an impartial historian. Nor did he take care with his 'facts'. Richard Davies, of whom he speaks well, is recorded as having been in exile in Geneva.[5] Had this been the case, it is unlikely that Elizabeth or Parker would have agreed to his being made a bishop. Similarly, Thomas Skevington, bishop of Bangor from 1509 to 1533, is referred to as abbot of Bermondsey,[6] when he was, in fact, abbot of Beaulieu.

His 'history' is a mixture of malice, gossip, genealogy, biographical details of local alumni, the puffing up of his family's importance and miscellaneous snippets of information. He was not a reliable witness. He liked to pass on a good story; it is unlikely that he went to any great length to establish if it was true or not, which is why the following account must be treated with some scepticism:

> [Bishop Davies] was very far onward with ye Old Testament & had gone through
> with it, if Variance had not happened between him & Wm Salusbury (who
> had liven almost Two years with him in that business) for ye general sense &
> Etymology of one word, wch ye Bish' wd have to be one way & Wm Salusbury

another, to the great loss of the Old British and Mother tongue, for, being together they drew Homilies, Books & divers other Tracts in ye Brittish Tongue & had done far more, if yt unlucky division had not happen'd.[7]

During the nineteenth century, when Salesbury was a celebrated figure, this incident ranked alongside the image of the imperilled translator working away in secret in his hidden chamber in Cae Du, placing him firmly in the national psyche.

The story may be true, but Wynn offers no evidence to corroborate it and there are no documents from the 1570s that specifically record the fate of the Old Testament. Had there been such a high-profile falling out, would not Thomas Wiliems, Salesbury's supporter and admirer, have recorded it?

After 1567, the evidence for the events of Salesbury's life becomes infrequent and what survives is often one step removed from the man, so that a degree of informed speculation becomes necessary.

Salesbury and Morgan

Questioning Wynn's reliability throws up another problem. His is the only evidence that Salesbury returned to Carmarthen to set about the translation of the Old Testament. If the critical reader is minded to reject the story of the quarrel, should he not also reject the return to the Bishop's Palace?

Charging Morgan with plagiarism shows Wynn's limitations as an objective and informed commentator. Wynn was not 'a rare scholar'. He had no understanding of the art and science of translation. Salesbury made use of the works of others when translating. It is a great boon to have other people's versions and attempts at transposing the meaning (often multi-layered), the weight, balance, rhythms, idioms and idiosyncracies of what is expressed in one language into another. Before translating a sentence one must be sure that one's interpretation of it is correct and what may seem an insignificant detail can make even the most proficient of linguists doubt himself.

If translations by Salesbury and Davies[8] were available, Morgan would most certainly have used them (he would have been foolish not to have done) and there is orthographical evidence in a small number of sections of the Old Testament of his 1588 Bible to indicate that he had had access to translations prepared by Salesbury. (This will be discussed in a later chapter.)

Are there explanations other than a heated argument for the abandonment of the Old Testament? Most certainly, the first being the Herculean size of the labour they had set themselves. The Old Testament, even without the Psalms, is three times the length of the New. When Salesbury began work on the New, he had had the experience of compiling *Kynniver Llith a Ban* and there were a small number of medieval translations that had survived. The Old Testament was a blank canvas, a journey into uncharted territory and the two men undertaking it were now in their sixties. Not only that, there was no one on whom they could call for assistance; they appear to have been the only Welshmen of their generation to have mastered Hebrew.

This introduces the question of William Morgan and the possibility of some sort of understanding between the older men and their successor. Morgan graduated B.A. at St John's, Cambridge, in 1568, was ordained the same year by the bishop of Ely, gained his M.A. in 1571 and then began seven years of Biblical studies (which presumably included the study of Hebrew) leading to his B.D. in 1578 and his D.D. in 1583. However, his first clerical post was at Llanbadarn Fawr in 1572. This is in the St Davids diocese, so Richard Davies would have been aware of him. If he and Salesbury were floundering in their work, who better to ask for help? Did they make an approach at this early stage or was Morgan's knowledge of Hebrew not yet considered strong enough to meet the challenge? Did the two men feel so proprietorial about the Old Testament that they were unable to let go of it? Were they too proud to do so? Morgan did eventually take on the role that had been Salesbury's, but the record of how that happened is lost.

The other great problem that faced the two men is the huge workload that Davies's various positions of authority imposed. There would have been little time left over for helping Salesbury. Progress would have been slow and this would have been demoralising. In addition, there was the constant anxiety caused by Leicester's campaign against the diocese, which would have drained Davies of his energy and his will to carry on. The final blow for Davies might have been an argument over a single word, but it was more likely to have been the death in Ireland in September 1576 of his great protector, the earl of Essex.

Walter Devereux had been Davies's last hope of salvation from Leicester's unceasing incursions. There seems little likelihood that he would have had the energy or time to have continued with the Old Testament thereafter. Perhaps Salesbury soldiered on for a while, vainly hoping to complete his life's work before he, too, admitted defeat. He was by then approaching his seventieth birthday.

The 'lost' years

It is reasonable to assume that Salesbury returned to Carmarthen in 1568 and that he spent extended periods there until 1571 (or quite possibly later) working on the translation of the Old Testament.[9]

At some time in 1572 or 1573, Salesbury's wife, Catrin, died and an elegy was commissioned to honour her memory.[10] The assumption must be that he had returned to Llanrwst, either for an extended stay or permanently, but on closer examination of the evidence, the elegy itself, that assumption appears doubtful.

The first cause for suspicion is the person chosen to write the elegy, Wiliam Cynwal. He was a local bard who had been a pupil of Gruffudd Hiraethog, but he was very much a journeyman. The most accomplished of Gruffudd's pupils was Wiliam Llŷn, who would have been the first choice of any discerning gentleman for such a work.[11] Not far behind Wiliam in poetic renown was Simwnt Fychan. Both men had been influenced by Humanist learning and are likely to have had contact with Salesbury.[12] Simwnt published a Welsh translation of an extract from Martial's *Epigram on the Happy Life*[13] and made a copy of Salesbury's book on rhetoric,[14] to which Salesbury added further entries.

In contrast, Wiliam Cynwal showed no interest in Salesbury's work or in Humanism.[15] He was very much a bard of the traditionalist persuasion and his antagonism towards Humanism can be seen clearly in his *ymryson* (bardic contest)[16] with the poet Edmwnd Prys.[17]

Taking the abilities of the three bards into consideration as well as their attitudes towards the Humanist ideals that Salesbury held dear, it is clear that Wiliam Cynwal would not have been his first or second choice for the commission.

The mystery deepens when the poem is examined in detail. The elegy is eighty-two lines long. It follows all the conventions of the traditional elegy to a beloved wife and all the elements, for example her hospitality, her virtues, the nobility of her family, are present. It is not a bad poem in any way; it is well crafted, but in the lines which record the grief of her son Siôn Wyn is a section which sits uneasily in a poem supposedly commissioned by Salesbury:

> Elis Prys, hwylus parhau,
> Eithr gwir, ei ewythr gorau.
> Doctor aeth dectir i'w ôl,
> Duw a'i croeso'n deg grasol.
> Oer oedd i hwn, mae'n bruddhad,
> Farw ei chwaer fawr ei chariad.
>
> [Elis Price, happily remains,
> In all truth, his best uncle.
> [The] Doctor went [in] fairness back to him,
> God and his fair, gracious welcome.
> It was cold for him, it's a sadness,
> The death of his sister, great her love.]

Salesbury, the grieving husband, is the subject of lines fifty-five to sixty; his son and heir Siôn Wyn (John Wyn) is the focus of lines sixty-one to sixty-eight; Elis Prys (Price), uncle to John and brother to Catrin has as many lines, sixty-nine to seventy-six, dedicated to him as her son and two more than her husband.

Catrin's family, her father, Robert, and her grandfather, Rhys, are mentioned in the early part of the poem. If any of her many siblings were to be listed, that would have been the appropriate place. Any bard, but especially a local bard, would have known of the unhappy history between Salesbury and Price. Even if the two men had reached some kind of understanding, any elegist who risked including Price in the poem would have had enough diplomacy not to have given him a greater role than the widowed husband and not to place him in the same section of the work, just as it was reaching its climax. More startling still, given the nature of the conflict between the men, is the revelation that Price is now acting as a 'help' to John Wyn. John was at least twenty-seven years old by then.

There is no record of an illness or disability that would have necessitated some form of protection and, if there had been, no reason why Salesbury himself would not have met that responsibility. If guardianship by another had been necessary, a lawyer of Salesbury's experience and knowledge would have made such a provision for his son within the framework of the law, not through a word-of-mouth agreement with an untrustworthy man with a history of assault and theft.

The evidence points to Elis Price rather than Salesbury being the instigator of the poem. Price was not an honourable man, but he had a sense of honour where his family were concerned, and that honour had been tarnished by Salesbury's 'putting away' of Catrin. An elegy to his sister would erase that dishonour, especially if the assumption was made that it had been requested by her husband. If this theory is correct, it would indicate that Salesbury was absent from Llanrwst for long periods around the time of Catrin's death and that Price was able to capitalise on those periods of absence, all of which points to Salesbury still working on the translation around the time of his wife's death, that is, around 1572.

A year or more later there was a second death in the family. Salesbury's youngest son, Elisau,[18] died in December 1573. (The date given on the will is 13 December; it was proved in the January following). One sentence in the will is highly significant:

> The residue of all my goodes and catells, moveable and unmoveable, that was devided to me in parte from my mother Kathrin Lloide, deceased, I geve and bequeathe to my father William Salusbry whome I ordaine and constitute my sole executor to order the same at his pleasure beinge good to my brother [in law] Robert Harrie and my suster Marcelie …

It is proof that Catrin has died and it shows that Salesbury was as concerned as ever that Elis Price would not get his hands on any part of the family inheritance; he almost certainly drafted the will. (The other bequests are to his aunt and to the poor of the parish of Llansannan, where Elisau was living at the time of his death.)

The deaths of his wife and youngest son within the space of two years might have drained Salesbury of the will to carry on with the Old Testament.

After the funeral of Elisau could he bear to return to Carmarthen or was such a distraction from his grief to be welcomed?

Salesbury and the London press

A possible sighting of Salesbury in the years following his return to the Bishop's Palace after the publications of 1567 is in 1571. It is known that he left the work of translating the Prayer Book and New Testament to visit Gruffudd Dwnn for a short time. He might have allowed himself a similar break from his work on the Old Testament. The evidence can be found in the broadsheet of Martial's poetry translated by Simwnt Fychan, mentioned earlier in the chapter.

The title of the work is, 'Martial to himself treating of worldly blessedness, in Latin, English and Walsch.' It consists of thirteen lines from *M valer Martialis ad seipsum Libro, 10*, 'The Same in English' (three verses of seven lines) and 'The Same in the Britishe tong, which the people at this day in the English Saxons speech, call Walsche' (eight introductory lines followed by seventeen couplets). The printer was John Awdeley. The Welsh version carries these words, 'wrth arch ac esponiat M. S. Th.' (at the request and explanation of M. S. Th.)

M. S. Th. is Simon Thelwall,[19] Simwnt's patron, a Denbighshire lawyer, fluent in almost as many languages as Salesbury and related to him through his first marriage to Alis Salusbury of Rug. ('Explanation' shows that Simwnt needed help with the Latin.) Thelwall had been M.P. for Denbighshire in the Parliament of 1563 and so might have played a part in seeing the bill for the translating of the Bible into Welsh through the Commons.

The use and spelling of certain words, 'ei', 'esponiat', 'Britishe' and 'Walsche', point to Salesbury's influence, but what jumps out from the broadsheet is the inclusion of the 'Tra vo lleuad' cryptogram devised by him.

Thelwall had been trained as a lawyer in the Inner Temple. He had been an M.P. on several occasions. He was as familiar with London as Salesbury, but he knew nothing about printing. Salesbury did. The choice of printer looks significant, as does the use of the cryptogram. Could it be that Awdeley is acknowledging Salesbury's involvement in the project by using the very device that had been used to signal his participation in the printing of the Prayer Book? Salesbury would have enjoyed another visit to London to see old friends and stock up on reading matter, but his involvement, if he was involved, might have extended no further than words of advice to Thelwall and a letter of introduction to Awdeley.

There is another foray into printing, though again any involvement of Salesbury is a matter of inference, that may provide the crucial evidence as to when the plans for the Old Testament were abandoned.

In 1573, eighteen years after the death of Sir John Prise, *Historiae Brytannicae Defensio* finally appeared in print. Prise had left instructions in his will[20] for his defence of Geoffrey of Monmouth to be published, but his family had taken no action to do so. The man who provided the finance for the project was Humphrey Toy. The printer was Henry Bynneman, a colleague of Henry Denham (Denham acted as his executor). The book was dedicated to Lord Burghley (William Cecil).

There are several indications of Salesbury's possible involvement. The first is the title. Prise had written *Historiae Britannicae Defensio*. The changing of the 'i' to a 'y' is a Salesburian trademark; it is assumed that Bale had made the same change in spelling under his influence ('Britanniae' in his book of 1548 becomes 'Brytanniae' in that of 1558).[21]

The second is the inclusion in the volume of Humphrey Llwyd's essay on Anglesey, *De Mona Druidium insula epistola H. Lhuyd*. Prise had been Salesbury's colleague in the 1540s. He would have wished to remember and celebrate his co-pioneer of Welsh printing through this work, but his feelings for his friend and fellow campaigner for the Welsh Bible would have been stronger still. Hence the likelihood that Salesbury played a prominent part in this publication and that he persuaded the others involved to include Llwyd.

(It was not just Salesbury who thought highly of Llwyd. So did Sir Henry Sidney and it should be noted that Bynneman, the printer, was closely associated with the Sidney family.)

However, the most persuasive argument for Salesbury playing a role in the printing of Prise's work is that Toy was the publisher. Toy was a friend and an admirer of Salesbury. He had financed the Prayer Book and the New Testament and was set to do the same for the Old Testament. That would have provided him with an assured profit as every church in Wales was required to purchase a copy. There was no such assurance with *Defensio*, so why take the risk?

The most convincing scenario is that this marks the time when Davies and Salesbury had concluded that the Old Testament was not going to appear. Toy had money set aside for that publication. Rather than let this money go to waste the two translators, or possibly just Salesbury, thought that it should go to a project that would boost 'British' culture almost as much as the missing scriptural translation and Toy was persuaded to channel his investment elsewhere. Salesbury's disappointment at the abandonment of his dream would be assuaged by a fitting tribute to two colleagues.

The other publication that could be seen to signify the demise of the Old Testament is that of Davies's funeral sermon for the earl of Essex in early 1577.[22] As stated earlier, the death was a huge blow to Davies and to the diocese of St Davids. The sermon can be seen as both a tribute to Devereux and as a desperate last attempt to fend off Leicester. (William Herbert, earl of Pembroke had died in 1570.)

The sermon is twenty-eight pages long and is accompanied by a letter to Robert, Devereux's son, eleven pages of genealogy, a poem in the three classical languages and ten more poems in Latin. Sermons were popular reading matter in Elizabethan and Jacobean England, easily outselling reading matter such as plays. (Towards the end of his life John Donne's sermons were routinely pirated by printers seeking a quick, easy profit.[23]) Davies's sermon was well received in London, but it did nothing to alleviate his difficulties.

Davies's printer was Henry Denham. Davies had almost certainly met him at some time in late 1566 or in 1567 when Denham was involved with the printing of the Prayer Book and New Testament. It would have been natural to have turned to him, the one printer he knew, but Davies had no first-hand experience of seeing a text through the printing process, whereas his old colleague, Salesbury, did. Did Salesbury give practical advice and assistance? If it could be shown that he did, it would disprove Wynn's story of the argument over a single word.

Of the two events, the publication of *Defensio* and that of the funeral sermon, the one more likely to be connected to the loss of the Old Testament is the first. What tips the balance in its favour is the involvement of Toy. Further support comes from the fact that by this time (1573) Salesbury might have been involved in other projects. There are the notes, some quite extensive, to Simwnt Fychan's copy of his book on rhetoric, almost certainly made with Simwnt's knowledge,[24] quite possibly at his request. There are a few, minimal additions to Wiliam Cynwal's *Ffugrau* that two academics[25] believe are in Salesbury's handwriting, but no suggestion of any collaboration between the two men.

There is no way of dating these additions. However, the Hafod 26 manuscript contains a copy made by Thomas Wiliems of Wiliam Llŷn's *Geirlyfr*, which he states was completed on 17 February 1574. Both he and Salesbury made additions, he sometime later, but Salesbury, it is assumed, soon after. If the assumption is correct, this places Salesbury in Denbighshire, either at Plas Isa or nearby at Wiliems' house in Trefriw, during or after February 1574.[26] Unfortunately, the work required to make the additions would not have taken up a substantial amount of his time, which means it is possible that he was still based in Carmarthen and was allowing himself some time off from the translating.

What is needed is a reference to a work of some length which would not have allowed time for other literary activities. There was such a work and Wiliems might be referring to it when he writes (in MS Hafod 26):

> physicwr godicoc, ac wedy cymerud cyfryw lavur yn ymchwelud y Testament newydd hayach ir Vrythonaec, y Psalmae a llawer gyd a hynny, oni ddylai Cymru vyth ei goffau, ac or Duw'n y blaen e geir eto (os gwyl Duw vod yn iawn gael ono einioes) lawer o bethau arbenic oi waith.

> [an excellent physician, and [he] has taken such pains ('labour') to translate the New Testament into British (Welsh), the Psalms and much else with that, so that Wales should ever commemorate him, and with God to the fore may there be again (if God sees it right to give him life) many special pieces of his work.]

The herbal

Wiliems' words are open to many interpretations. Does the first reference to God suggest an expectation of seeing the Old Testament soon in print? Why is he not more specific about the works he hopes will appear? Note the use of the plural. Only one more work was forthcoming. Have the others been lost or were there plans that did not come to fruition? The one word that, with hindsight, gives the reader an indication of what to expect is 'physicwr' (physician), which informs us of Salesbury's interest in medicine. It appears that he had been studying medical botany for several decades. He writes of his transplanting radishes[27] taken from Aberconwy Abbey, presumably at the time of the dissolution. It is likely that for many years he had been making his own observations, noting down snippets of information and reading the works of Fuchs and other leaders in the field. Sometime in the 1570s he started compiling his *Llysieulyfr Meddygol* (Medical Herbal) in earnest, producing his last known book.

The main printed sources for the herbal are Fuchs's *De Historiae Stirpium* (first published in Basel in 1542) and William Turner's *Libellus de re Herbaria Novus* (1538), *The Names of Herbes* (1548) and *A New Herball* (in three parts, 1551, 1562 and 1568). There are references to Rembert Dodoens, a Dutchman whose *A new herbal or historie of plants* appeared in English in 1578. This has led one expert on the herbal to state that Salesbury must have started work on it in that year or shortly after. Such a reliable date would be welcome.

However, a French translation of Dodoens's book had been published in 1557[28] and Salesbury was fluent in that language and through his connections in the book trade was able to acquire books printed abroad within a very short time, as he did with the Beza of 1565. He might not have started work on the herbal until 1578 or later, but there is no way of knowing. Mathias believes the herbal was completed between 1568 and 1574; Edgar, the expert mentioned in the previous paragraph, citing the Dodoens evidence, suggests a date after 1578.[29] If Salesbury had a copy of the French edition of the Dodoens, then the most likely dates would appear to be from 1574 to around 1578. (Intriguingly, Edgar believes that Salesbury used a French-printed edition of Fuchs for the herbal.)

Rather than spending time regretting the lack of specific dates we should celebrate the survival of this last book, which shows the breadth of Salesbury's learning. Like Conrad Gesner, William Turner and other Protestant Humanists his interests ranged far. The original manuscript is lost, but the work survives in the form of several copied versions, of which the best and earliest (1597) is NLW MS 4581. The copyist, Roger Morris, was a craftsman of the first order who had borrowed the original from Thomas Wiliems.

Salesbury's herbal eventually appeared in print in 1916, edited by E. Stanton Roberts, but the version that Roberts worked from was NLW MS 686, a copy (not of the best quality) of Roger Morris's work, which had been missing for some considerable time. Roberts must have felt truly wretched when six years later Morris's original was discovered in the possession of two elderly sisters from the Vale of Glamorgan, Miss Edmondes and Mrs Laurence Williams, who donated it to the National Library of Wales. This superior version was eventually published in 1997, exactly four centuries after it was made, under the editorship of Iwan Rhys Edgar.

Morris[30] kept to Salesbury's orthography. There are 148[31] entries and then the words, 'Hyd yma o lyfr o law W. Salsburie a gawsid ei venthic gan Syr Tomas ap Wiliam. 1597. Deo gratias.' (Up to here from the book in the hand of W. Salesbury, which was borrowed from Sir Thomas Wiliems. 1597. Thanks be to God.)

Morris had become so interested in the subject that he carries on Salesbury's work, compiling entries of his own (just twelve; sadly he died soon after completing the original section).[32]

The format that Salesbury uses is based on Fuchs's *De Historia Stirpium*, where each plant is given its Nomina, Forma, Locus, Tempus and Temperamentum. Salesbury translates these terms as 'yr enwae', 'y phurf', 'y lle', 'yr amser' and 'yr artemper'. Finally he gives 'y rhinweddae', which is nearer to Turner's 'virtues' than the 'Vires' (strengths) of Fuchs. Occasionally he adds a new category, 'y rhywiae' (the types). (Note the Latin plural ending, 'ae', that Salesbury gives the words above; the colloquial Welsh ending would have been 'e'.)

The name of each plant is given in Welsh, English (showing his high regard for that language), Latin and Greek. Sometimes he gives the French or German name. Where the plant is not native to Wales he invents a name based on the Latin, Greek or English elements, for example, 'Phicuspren' (fig-tree, Latin *Ficus*) and 'Phenicul' (fennel, Latin *Feniculum*). ('Yr artemper' for 'Temperamentum' is also an invention.)

Many of Salesbury's inventions were accepted into 'educated' Welsh through their inclusion in Thomas Wiliems's unpublished dictionary, which was in turn incorporated into John Davies's highly influential *Dictionarum Duplex* of 1632, but only a handful worked their way into the oral tradition: 'ysgaw Mair', elder; 'tagaradr', rest harrow and 'cancwlwm', knot grass.

Salesbury could easily have compiled the herbal in Latin, but he was following the Humanist innovation of democratising knowledge. Just as the Bible was now available to everyone, including the plough boy cited by Tyndale, so science and medicine would no longer be the preserve of those fortunate enough to have been granted a mastery of Latin. Turner had followed the same path. His first book on botany had been in Latin, those that followed were in English.

A critical reader

The work is mostly based on the information he has gathered from Turner and Fuchs, but there is also a reference to Dodoens and many more to classical scientists such as Discorides, Pliny and Galen. Sixteenth-century attitudes to knowledge differed from our own. There was no concept of copyright. Salesbury makes no secret of where he gained his knowledge, but he does not slavishly or unquestioningly accept what he read in the works of others, no matter how renowned they were.

He is not afraid to give his own observations and voice disagreement. For example, he gives species of wheat not listed by Fuchs, differs from him on the length of devil's bit scabious and when Fuchs, influenced by classical sources, states that mistletoe grows commonly on oak trees, Salesbury questions this, saying that he had never seen such a thing. He also disagrees with Fuchs on when the flowers of the mouse-ear hawkweed start to wither.

Whilst Salesbury's mind is as acute as ever, the book leaves the reader with the impression that it was written at a leisurely pace, that there was no deadline to be met. From time to time Salesbury breaks off his main discourse to recall an incident or story from earlier years and from these memories valuable information can be gleaned about the man.

It is in these pages[33] that we learn that he was born in Llansannan ('sef yn y plwy y ganwyt vi'), that he spent some of his childhood in Lancashire, that he transplanted radishes from a nearby abbey and that the summer of 1555 was particularly dismal and the harvest notably late.

Thirteen people are mentioned in connection with estates or gardens where particular plants can be found and it is reasonable to assume that these are some of his many friends amongst the local gentry, people such as Robert Huxley, Sir John Salusbury, Huw Dryhurst, John Edwards (his cousin), Elisa ap Wiliam and Grono ap Meredydd.

There are also the references to the duke of Somerset, Lord Protector during the first part of Edward VI's reign, and to William Turner. Is a pun he makes based on their sharing of the same forename evidence of a friendship with Turner?[34]

Many exotic locations are mentioned (Syria, Italy, Macedonia, Spain and others), but this is information gained from other writers. Paris is the one overseas city named that Salesbury may well have visited. The most frequent places names are those of north Wales and the northern Marches as far south as Ludlow. There is just one mention of south Wales ('Y Deheubarth'), when the southern name, 'yr ystyllenlys', for plantain is given.

The herbal is not a controversial work, but there is a moment when the author of *The baterie of the Popes Botereulx* reveals his thoughts on religion. Having recorded the practice of decorating the eaves of the house with *Artemisia* on St John's Eve, he then dismisses it as 'rhyw hen goec ddefot' (some old vain [that is, Catholic] custom).

Reading those words would not have pleased Thomas Wiliems. His attachment to the Catholic faith grew ever stronger, but his admiration for the substance of Salesbury's work never dimmed. He had wished in 1574 for 'many [more] special pieces of work' (tr.). The herbal was all that was forthcoming and it owes its survival to Wiliems allowing it to be copied. The details of its compilation are obscure, but it is a wonderful work to mark the end of a literary career. The greatest regret is not the absence of further books by Salesbury but that other gentlemen did not come forward in any great number to grace their native culture with works of Humanist learning.

Salesbury's successors

The 1586 Prayer Book

After the herbal nothing more is heard of Salesbury. The last date on which it can be stated with certainty that he was alive is 10 July 1580, when he witnessed the will of Ifan ap Siôn Pigod (Evan ap John Pigott). Ifan bequeathed 'twentie shillinges' to Salesbury and forty shillings to 'John Wynne Salusburie', his son.[1]

Sir John Wynn states that Salesbury lived for twenty-four years[2] after the alleged dispute with Richard Davies, which would give a date of 1594 or a little later, but those who have studied his life and work believe that he was dead by 1586. There are two pieces of circumstantial evidence that strongly support this theory. The first is that this was the year in which his grandson, Piers ap Huw ap Dafydd, died and there is no mention of Salesbury in the will.[3] An examination of the second edition of his Prayer Book,[4] printed that same year by 'John Windet at the costs and charges of Thomas Chard' supports that assumption. Awdeley had died in 1575, Toy in 1577 and control of his business had passed to Chard, his former apprentice.

Unlike Toy, Chard had no Welsh connections, no knowledge of the country and no cultural attachment to it. It is likely that his sole motivation for printing was profit; somehow he must have discovered that new copies were needed and in sufficient numbers to minimise the risk of a loss. Though Morgan's Bible was just two years away, his version of the Prayer Book would not appear for another thirteen years. The reprint is proof of the widespread use of Salesbury's translation and is testimony to Chard's total ignorance of Welsh.

The original Prayer Book contained two secret references to its printer,

John Awdeley, in the form of the phrase 'Tra vo lleuad' (whilst there be a moon) (the cryptogram was omitted). The word 'lleuad' was not printed but shown by a representation of a crescent moon. Chard must have lacked such a representation, but nevertheless prints 'Tra vo', which is now meaningless.

Even more farcical is his one addition to the new edition. He decided to add a calendar of verses to the Prayer Book. There are twelve wood block prints each depicting a month and accompanied by an appropriate verse. This is a charming and thoughtful gesture. Indeed, it is another first in the history of printing in Welsh, as the verses are not written in *cynghanedd*, but in free metre. There was a rich tradition of free metre poetry, written either by 'lesser' bards or by high-ranking bards who produced the work for informal occasions or purely for fun. Regrettably, there is a much smaller quantity of surviving free metre verse from before the middle of the sixteenth century than there is of its more formal counterpart.

Unfortunately, Chard was unable to vet the quality of what he was printing. The verses are so weak that they are reminiscent of those of McGonagall. Worse still are the typographical errors and other mistakes. The verse for October is a repeat of that for September, though they are not identical because of the misprints. Only a few of the illustrations show the activities described in the verses. One academic thinks that ten of the verses are based on advice contained in a best-selling agricultural book of the time. The remaining two appear to be based on advice given in Prise's *Yny lhyvyr hwnn*. (Thankfully, the main body of the Prayer Book is reproduced accurately.)

This clumsiness leads commentators to believe that Salesbury must have died by then. There were times when he had to work to a very tight deadline, which left errors in the printing, but nothing that remotely approaches what Chard produced. Nor is there a foreword to the new edition. Salesbury would not have missed the opportunity to make his views known to the public, either to taunt his critics with the triumph (wreathed about with tropes of modesty) of a second edition or to prepare the ground for the imminent arrival of the complete Welsh Bible.

However, there is a document that suggests that Salesbury's death occurred even earlier. The date of the assassination of William, Prince of Orange, was 10 July 1584, an event which inspired a savagely anti-protestant poem, *Cowydd Marwnad yn Llawn Cabledd i'r Prins Orens* [An Elegy Full of Blasphemy to the Prince of Orange],[5] in which prominent reformers such as Ridley and Jewel are imagined in hell. Alongside them is Salesbury:

> lle mae Salbri'n sorri'n siŵr
> ar trwyn slwt, y translatiwr
>
> [Where Salesbury is surely sorry
> With the slut's nose, the translator]

Salesbury is in hell and will regret for eternity his sin of translating the scriptures from the language of the one true church. There is a change of tense and Protestants who were very much alive, such as John Foxe and Gabriel Goodman, dean of Westminster, are included. The first of these to die was Foxe ('lle ra r llwynog' (where the fox will go)) in 1587. The topicality of the poem makes 1584 the most likely date of composition.

Morgan and Whitgift

Two years after Chard's reprint of the Prayer Book, Morgan's Bible appeared. It had been a long struggle made worse by constant trouble from his parishioners, mainly in the form of Ifan Maredudd, a local gentleman, and his allies. There was threatening behaviour, or so it was alleged, claim and counter claim and court cases brought at Ludlow and then at the Star Chamber in London.[6] At times Morgan had come close, like Salesbury and Davies, to abandoning the project, at one stage considering limiting his work to the Pentateuch.

Significantly, he had encountered opposition,[7] just as Salesbury had done. Whilst many of those who badgered Toy to withdraw his support for the publications of 1567 cited the issue of orthography, there were others who asked 'what needed thys waste? For when ye have all done, there is few or none that can read it.'[8] Their numbers do not seem to have lessened, in fact quite the opposite.[9] The speed with which so many members of the gentry switched their cultural allegiance is startling, especially as it was accompanied not by indifference to their native culture and language but vehement opposition and hostility.

Morgan was doubly fortunate. Not only could he argue that the Bible was needed to bring salvation to the ordinary people and to turn them away from Rome[10] onto the path of Protestantism, he could state that Parliament had legislated for a Welsh Bible and until such time as it appeared the five bishops were in breach of the law. Not only did he have a legal precedent to fall back on, he had the support, practical and moral, of some very influential people. Gabriel Goodman, dean of Westminster (a native of Rhuthun), provided him with board and lodging in London far from his fractious parishioners so that he could oversee the printing, but his most important ally was John Whitgift, archbishop of Canterbury.

Whilst Whitgift was serving as bishop of Worcester (from 1577), Sir Henry Sidney, Lord President of the Marches of Wales, was sent to Ireland (1575–9). For some of that time Whitgift acted as his deputy and was appalled at the laxness Sidney had shown to Catholic recusancy. Two Welshmen (Hugh Owen and Thomas Morgan) had been involved in the Ridolfi Plot, priests moved from house to house, Catholic rituals were practised, clergy who barely concealed their true allegiance remained unchallenged in their posts and there was regular contact with the many exiles abroad, with a noticeably large proportion of students at the English College (a Catholic seminary in Douai) being Welsh.[11]

After Whitgift's term of office at Ludlow was over, a clandestine printing press would be established at the Great Orme and, most shocking of all for the Salusbury clan would be the involvement of Thomas Salusbury of Lleweni in the Babington Plot of 1586, for which he was executed along with his compatriot, Edward Jones, and others. Salesbury's 'cousin', John Edwards[12] of Chirk, was a noted Catholic supporter until the capture and execution of Richard White, the Catholic martyr, brought about a public recantation of his beliefs.

Whitgift's time in Wales persuaded him of the urgent need for a Welsh Bible as a means of converting the Welsh to Protestantism, thus protecting them from Catholic influence. When he became archbishop of Canterbury, he was in a position to give effective and practical support rather than mere encouragement.

Whitgift and Penry

Ironically, the other great spur to his desire to see a Welsh Bible came from the opposite end of the religious spectrum. Puritanism had few adherents in Wales at this time, but what Welsh Puritanism lacked in terms of numbers was more than compensated for by the energy and courage of John Penry. In three publications that appeared between 1587 and 1588[13] he set out in uncompromising language the faults and weaknesses of the Church in Wales: the ignorance, non-residence and pluralism of the clergy; the immorality of those clergy who were present; the absence of licensed preachers and the non-existence of the Old Testament. What was galling for Whitgift, who abhorred Puritanism, was that he recognised the truth of much of what Penry said.

In 1588, the following words appeared in Penry's *An Exhortation*:

> A few psalmes, a few praiers, with one chapter of the newe Testament in Welch (for the olde never spake Welch in our daies, though, to my comfort, I understand it is all readie to be printed) most pitifully evill read of the reader, and not understoode of among tenne of the hearers.

Some have chosen to interpret that sentence as a criticism of Salesbury's orthography, but Penry was not one to repress his thoughts. If he had been critical of the New Testament's spelling, he would have said so. He did not. There is no mention of Salesbury in his polemics, though there is evidence of his influence (his use of 'Cymbrûbrittons' and his belief that the pre-Augustine Church had been proto-Protestant). In the few places where Penry uses Welsh ('Nû waeth genûf dhim am y tad y gwr craûlon hinnû onûd cydymaith da ûwr mab'),[14] his spelling is as 'eccentric' as Salesbury's and in no way resembles the system that would be adopted by Morgan.

Elsewhere he writes that the bishops have appointed as clergy, 'dumbe and greedy dogs that delight in sleeping', 'unlearned dolts', 'rogues, and vacabounds', 'spendthrifts and serving men', 'knowen adulterers, knowen drunkardes, theeves, roisters [roisterers], most abhominable swearers.'[15]

A Star Chamber case of the period[16] supports Penry's assertions. Richard Kyffin and Richard ap Howell, their wives, sons, sons-in-law and daughters are accused of excessive indulgence in drink, of cheating at cards and dice, of 'taking no order' in their churches and being at evensong too drunk even to walk.

Little wonder then, that the psalms, prayers and New Testament were 'most pitifully evill read of the reader.'

(Penry's criticism of the Church, its clergy and, above all, its bishops, so angered the authorities that in 1590 he fled to Scotland in fear of his life. On his return in 1593 he was arrested and tried. Whitgift's name heads the list of those who signed his death warrant. Penry was twenty-nine years old.)

Morgan's Bible

So it was that a series of fortuitous events (Whitgift's appointment to Worcester, then to Ludlow, the stinging attacks of Penry and the fact that there was a talented Welsh cleric with a mastery of Hebrew available) led to the publication of the Welsh Bible in 1588, as momentous a year for Wales as it was for England. The conventional wisdom amongst historians and linguists, a wisdom that none has sought to challenge, is that those European languages into which the Bible was translated prior to 1600 are the ones that have survived.

The printing is credited to Christopher Barker, the Queen's printer. How it was financed is unknown. It is assumed by many that Whitgift paid for it, perhaps with a contribution from Morgan. It is impressive in size, even a little forbidding, and was sold at a price of twenty shillings. It is prefaced with the usual dedications and letters and, in his letter to the Queen, Morgan has generous words of praise for Salesbury. Richard Davies, as etiquette demanded, receives the recognition for the New Testament of 1567, but these words follow immediately, 'auxilante Gulielmo Salesburio, de nostra ecclesia viro optime merito' (with the help of William Salesbury, a man who gave the very best (of his ability) to our church.) The next sentence begins, 'It is not easy to express how great a benefit came to our fellow countrymen through this work ...' (tr.)

Morgan did not have to say these words. He could easily have ignored his predecessor. He recognised the huge debt owed to Salesbury (and to a lesser extent to Davies). When faced with opposition to the very idea of a Welsh Bible, he and Whitgift, besides other arguments, were able to point to the legislation that Salesbury through the agency of Davies and Llwyd, had steered through Parliament.

Morgan knew that his historic achievement would not have been possible had not a Denbighshire lawyer forty years previously called for the translation of the scriptures into Welsh and battled through years of contempt, indifference and danger to make it a reality.

That Morgan chose to include the same verse on the title page of his Bible (Romans 1, 16) as Salesbury had used on the title page of *Kynniver Llith a Ban* may be the greatest acknowledgement of the debt he owed his predecessor.

Humanist prose

However, it was not just for his campaign that Morgan would have felt indebted to Salesbury. As someone who had spent long years of toil at the very same work, he would have known the huge physical and mental reserves Salesbury had needed to complete his three pioneering volumes[17] and though he differed from him in orthography and in some aspects of vocabulary and phrasing, he recognised his achievement in forging a prose style that was fit for the Humanist age and capable of conveying what every European of the sixteenth century considered the most important words ever written.

Welsh had been exiled from the world of government and, to a great extent, the law. There was no great mass of high-quality prose when Salesbury took up the call for the scriptures in his own language. There were historical chronicles and lives of the saints along with a number of legal documents and the few, eleven, surviving stories from *Y Mabinogi*. In contrast, England had had a century of mass-produced books and broadsheets which catered for all tastes, of central and local government whose language was English and of a legal system which had largely thrown off the use of 'Law-French' and generated huge volumes of documents whose importance demanded a meticulous and carefully crafted use of grammar and vocabulary. With a literature centred overwhelmingly on poetry and in the absence of a single printing press, the concept of a prose style was less developed in Wales than in other cultures.

The scale of the problem that faced Salesbury can be judged by the following assessment of the quality of the prose found in the most famous of medieval Welsh writing, 'The prose of the *Mabinogion* was primitive in every sense [of the word] … similar, simple, single sentences sufficient to tell a story but totally insufficient to express opinion on abstract subjects or debate an argument'. (tr.)

The words were those of W.J. Gruffydd,[18] one of Wales's greatest academics and critics. Salesbury had responded with flexibility, inventing words, borrowing from Classical and European sources, resurrecting archaic terms, adapting and adopting whatever examples came his way and all the while introducing the rhetorical skills of Rome and Athens. He was Wales's great improviser. English writers had already followed the same path and would continue to do so. Here is what one academic has said of the work of Edmund Spenser, 'When Spenser began to write he was faced with the problem of remaking the English language for the purposes of poetry.'[19]

Orthography …

Morgan was at liberty to select whichever elements appealed to him from the Humanist prose style that had been set before him, but the fare from which he made his selection and to which he was free to add had been prepared by Salesbury. The most obvious difference between the two men was their orthography. With a few exceptions, Morgan returned to the spellings standard in contemporary literary Welsh. He kept 'c' for 'k', but that was a necessity imposed by printing. The possessive pronoun 'ei' (his/her) was kept, along with Salesbury's other inventions, 'ein' (our), 'eich' (your) and 'mai' (the emphatic form of 'that'). Salesbury's Latinate spellings were rejected, apart from 'sanctaidd' (holy), as was his Latinised plural ending, '-ae'.[20]

Salesbury, imbued with the spirit of the Renaissance and the belief in the superior achievements of the past, had based his orthography on that of Middle Welsh. In particular, he used the endings '-awdd', '-awd', '-awl' for the modern '-odd', '-od', '-ol' and tended to end his words with 'p', 't' and 'c' rather than 'b', 'd' and 'g'.[21] Morgan used the modern forms. He also rejected the idea of not showing nasal mutation.

Gone, too, were the archaic words and those from the south, with just a few exceptions, such as 'gyda' (with). Morgan imposed regularity of spelling, in contrast to Salesbury's habit of haphazard variations of the same word.[22]

In typography, Morgan decided to drop Salesbury's practice of giving synonyms and explanations in the margins. Those who approve state that the pages no longer look 'cluttered', others might comment that one man's clutter is another man's treasure house.

... and style

After clearing away all these Salesburian motifs, what remains?

A great deal; Morgan's approach was pragmatic. He had sufficient confidence in his judgement and ability to stick with Salesbury's translations when his interpretation of the words and his aesthetic feel for the rhythm, cadence and weighting of the sentence aligned with those of Salesbury.

Here are two passages for comparison, Salesbury's first, then Morgan's:

Matthew, ii, 10

'A' phan welsant y seren, llawenhay a wnethau a llawenydd mawr dros pen.'

'A phan welsant y seren, llawenhau a wnaethant a llawenydd mawr dros benn.'

[When they saw the star, they rejoiced with exceeding great joy.]

Luke, vii, 9

'Pan glybu'r Iesu y pethe hyn, rhyveddu a oruc wrthaw, a' throi, a dewedyt wrth y bobl ...'

'Pan glybu'r Iesu y pethau hyn, rhyfeddu a wnaeth o'i blegit ef, a throi, a dywedyd wrth y bobl ...'

[When Jesus heard these things, he marvelled at him, and turned him about, and said unto the people ...]

Of course, it is possible to choose passages which show a greater variance than this, but it is reasonable to estimate that about seventy-five per cent of Salesbury's New Testament survives in that of Morgan. To the cynical or the maliciously minded (such as Sir John Wynn), that might arouse suspicion, but it should not. Many would argue that it should be seen as a positive comment on Salesbury's abilities as a translator and shaper of prose. (Academics estimate that approximately eighty per cent[23] of the King James New Testament is Tyndale's and roughly seventy-five per cent of the books of the Old Testament that Tyndale completed can be found in the corresponding books of the King James Bible.)

Salesbury's Old Testament

What of Sir John Wynn's comments that 'He [Morgan] translated ye old Testamt into ye Welch Tongue before he was Bishop wherein he had ye benefit & help of Bish' Davies & Wm Salusbury's works, who had done a great part thereof, yet he carried ye name of yt all.'[24] Wynn is speaking with malicious intent, but if Salesbury's translations of the Old Testament had been available to him, it would have been perverse of Morgan not to have made use of them. Nothing now survives of the earlier, unpublished work. It is impossible to know what proportion of the Old Testament the two men, or possibly just Salesbury, completed, but there are clear signs that Morgan made use of their work.

Here are the titles given to two of the books of the Old Testament and one of the Apocrypha:

'Y llyfr cyntaf o'r Cronicl, yr hwn a elwir yn yr Ebre-aec Difre Haiamim, ac yn Gamber-aec Hanesion yr Amseroedd,'[25]

'Llyfr Caniadau Solomon, yr hwn yn Hebrae-aec a elwir Shir Hashirim, ac yn lladin Canticum Canticorum.'

'Darn o lyfr Esther heb fod yn yr Hebrae-aec, nac yn y Calde-aec ac yn y Groec yn dechreu yn y ddecfed bennod.'

Salesbury's orthography is unmistakable, yet it appears in a volume from which all traces of his spellings had been, so it is assumed, surgically removed. The only explanation is that amongst the hundreds upon hundreds of manuscript papers handed over to the printer, these words had been left unrevised. The typesetter did not speak Welsh and with a whole Bible to proofread it is not surprising that Morgan missed three brief passages.

(If Morgan did have access to Salesbury's Old Testament translations and had not received them directly from him or from Richard Davies, the most likely source would be Edmwnd Prys. A native of Llanrwst, accomplished poet, senior clergyman and master of the three classical languages, Prys was not just a Protestant Humanist but a relative who shared Salesbury's goals and ideals. He would have been in his mid-thirties when Salesbury died.

In his foreword to the Bible, Morgan acknowledges the help of Prys (and others). None of Salesbury's sons appears to have been academically or linguistically gifted. If there was a person in whom Salesbury had sufficient confidence to entrust his translations, it would have been Prys.)

It would appear that Morgan's debt to Salesbury was huge. He knew it, recognised it and publicly acknowledged it, though for most of the twentieth century many critics and academics chose to laud Morgan uncritically and either vilify or ignore Salesbury.

Morgan and John Davies

From 1547, when he made his call for the scriptures to be translated into Welsh, until the 1570s, when he abandoned work on the Old Testament, Salesbury had just one able colleague, Bishop Richard Davies, to support him. In contrast, in the letter that prefaces the 1588 Bible, Morgan acknowledged the help of six people.[26] After expressing his gratitude for the moral and practical support given by Archbishop Whitgift (and his influence with the Privy Council), he names the following clergymen: The bishops of Bangor and St Asaph, for their loan of books and their approval of the work; Gabriel Goodman, dean of Westminster, for reviewing the work with him and advising him, granting approval of the work and allowing him to lodge at his house whilst he saw the work into print; David Powel, Sir Henry Sidney's chaplain; Edmwnd Prys, archdeacon of Merioneth, and Richard Vaughan, provost of St. John's College, Lutterworth, the nature of whose help is not specified, though Prys is noted for his (later) verse translations of the Psalms.

The one person whom Morgan does not name is John Davies,[27] who never rose higher than rector of Mallwyd, yet was, in his quiet and unassuming way, the greatest of all the Welsh Humanists and scriptural translators. 'The young John Davies almost certainly gave William Morgan some assistance with the work, probably as an amanuensis.'[28]

In the foreword to his *Gramadeg* of 1621, Davies writes that he had twice assisted in the translation of the Holy Scriptures and there are several similar statements in poems of the time, for example:

> Help a roes hael, pur ei waith,
> Oedd dda i droi'r Beibl ddwywaith.[29]
>
> [He gave help generously, pure his work,
> [It] was good to translate the Bible twice.]

Davies entered Jesus College, Oxford, in 1589, graduated in 1594 and is believed to have worked with Morgan on the new edition of the Prayer Book, printed in 1599, which was prepared at the Bishop's Palace at Mathern, Monmouthshire.[30] When Morgan was appointed bishop of St Asaph in 1601, Davies accompanied him back to the north.

Postscript, the abnormal sentence

Though Morgan certainly removed the traces of Salesbury's Inkhorn-influenced spellings, there was one practice that, contrary to expectation, he not only retained, but augmented.

The normal word order in Welsh is verb, subject, object. The only occasion on which the order can be changed is in the emphatic sentence, when the part of the sentence you wish to emphasise is put at the front. In any other circumstance a sentence that does not follow the correct order is 'abnormal'. However, in Middle Welsh, the 'abnormal sentence' was not shunned but was used quite extensively and Salesbury, taking the past as his template, sometimes used it in his New Testament. Morgan rarely revised Salesbury's use of this structure. In fact, in the two examples given above to show how closely Morgan would often keep to Salesbury's original the second clause of each sentence is abnormal.

As if Morgan's acceptance of this practice were not strange enough, when he translated the Old Testament the frequency of his use of the abnormal sentence was greater than that of Salesbury in the New. This makes his prose sound strange to the Welsh ear. It is as if an English speaker were listening to a literal, not modified, translation from the German.

Morgan's Bible is, therefore, not without its 'quirks' and yet criticism of it is rarely heard and despite the widespread belief to the contrary, it is not the definitive, standard Welsh Bible. It was superseded in 1620 by the version that was largely the work of his faithful helper, John Davies, and that, too, was the fate of Morgan's Prayer Book.[31]

In those publications Davies was as generous as Morgan in his tributes to the pioneering work of Salesbury. It is only now, with the benefit of the research of W. Alun Mathias and others that a clearer and fairer picture is emerging of the evolution of the Welsh Bible.

Chapter Twenty-Three

Post mortem

Kyffin's revenge

With the 1588 Bible replacing Salesbury's New Testament, it might be expected, notwithstanding Morgan's acknowledgement of his predecessor's importance and achievement, that Salesbury's name would soon be forgotten and his influence fade.

However, his Prayer Book would continue to be the medium of church services in Wales for another eleven years and his pioneering of a Welsh-language press meant that another generation of authors and translators was following him into print.

The year 1595 saw the publication of three significant books: Henri Perri's *Egluryn Phraethineb* [An Explanation of Eloquence]; Huw Lewys's *Perl mewn adfyd* [A Pearl in Adversity] and Maurice Kyffin's *Deffyniad Ffydd Eglwys Lloegr* [A Defence of the Faith of the Church of England]. The first was a book on rhetoric inspired and influenced by Salesbury's *Llyfr Rhetoreg*; the second was a translation from Coverdale's English version, *A spirituall and moste precious pearle*, of a work in German by Otto Werdmüller and the third was a translation of Jewel's *Apologia Ecclesiae Anglicanae*.

Perri was a Flintshire gentleman, Lewys a north Wales cleric and Kyffin was the Maurice Kyffin who in 1554 had been set to marry Elen Salusbury, Salesbury's niece.

Kyffin's grandmother had been Annes, half-sister of Gwenhwyfar, the grandmother of Robert and William Salesbury. When Rhys ap Einion, Gwenhwyfar's father, died, she inherited his substantial estate. Annes, his illegitimate daughter, received 'nothing comparable'.[1] The marriage to Elen (brokered by Kyffin's father) would have seen a substantial part of Rhys's estate return to that side of the family. But the marriage did not take place; the reason is unknown. It is possible that Salesbury used his influence to prevent it, but with his power, finances and personal security at their lowest ebb, it is difficult to imagine how he could have done so. Kyffin, however, seems not to have doubted that he was the person responsible. Forty years later, he chose to use his foreword to *Deffyniad Ffydd* to criticise a man who had been dead for more than a decade.

After praising Morgan's Bible, he gives his opinion of the work it had replaced, Salesbury's New Testament, 'There was such a broad "accent" and so much that was strange in the printed version that the ear of a true Welshman could not bear to listen to it.' (tr.)[2]

There seems to be no rational motive for attacking a work that had been printed thirty years previously, was no longer in circulation or use and whose author was no longer alive. (Note that Lewys, also published that year, made no mention of Salesbury.) Salesbury's Prayer Book, however, was in use. If a true Welshman could not bear to listen to it, Kyffin had a duty to make that known to the authorities. Attacking the 1567 New Testament was risk-free, criticising the current Prayer Book could be construed as a criticism of the Church, a 'crime' that had led to John Penry's execution. This was Kyffin's first and only book for a Welsh audience,[3] his one opportunity to right what he saw as an injustice. His assault on Salesbury was an icily-served revenge for the hurt of long ago.

There is a studied malevolence in Kyffin's attack. Salesbury is not mentioned directly, but his colleague, Richard Davies is named and praised for the quality of his *Epistol at y Cembru*, 'The bishop wrote this letter in clear, proficient, eloquent Welsh, which doubtless was of great benefit to every Welshman who read it.'[4]

Kyffin's translation, though an accomplished work, would not become widely read until it was reprinted in 1671 and it should be noted that, apart from that reprint, no further critical reference to Salesbury would appear for three centuries.

Salesbury in the new century

It is only a slight exaggeration to describe Morgan's Prayer Book as Salesbury's with the orthography revised and the same is true of the Psalms. Nor did John

Davies make any great changes in his 1620 edition of the Prayer Book. In fact, there are occasions in his translation of the Bible when Davies rejects Morgan's formulations and reverts to those Salesbury had used in his New Testament, either in the main body of the text or in the margin.

For example, Salesbury devised the word 'goruchystavell' (upper room). Morgan rejected this and used 'stafell fawr' (large room) and 'lloft' (loft), but Davies preferred Salesbury's word, though he changed the spelling to 'goruwchystafell'.[5]

Where Salesbury wrote, 'Vy-pen ac oleo nid iraist', Morgan had, 'Nid iraist fy mhenn ag olew', but Davies reverts to Salesbury's word order, 'Fy mhen ag olew nid iraist.'[6] (Luke 7, 46: 'Myne heed with oyle thou didst nott anoynte' (Tyndale's version).)

Many of the words that Salesbury created found their way not just into the works of 1588 and 1620, but into everyday use and into the dictionary, words such as 'bara croyw'[7] (unleavened bread), 'diafol' (devil, a Latin-derived term that became an alternative to 'diawl') and 'anfri' (disrespect, disgrace).

Just as Morgan had praised Salesbury, so did Davies, writing of him, 'In quorum omnium gratiam Wilielmus Salesburius, de Ecclesia linguaque Brit. vir plurimum meritus, Dictionariolum Anglo-Brit. Regi Henrico approbatum & dedicatum, annoque salutis humanae 1547 impressum, edidit.' (*Dictionarium Duplex*, 1632)

One feature of Davies's dictionary, noted in Ceri Davies's[8] study of his work, *John Davies o Fallwyd*, is the number of words that he includes from the New Testament of 1567, both from the text and the margins. Many of them had been overlooked by Morgan and Davies in their translations, but Davies nevertheless valued them highly.

This regard for Salesbury and his achievement is evident in his grammar, *Antiquae Linguae Britannicae*, 1621, where he gives due mention to Salesbury's book on rhetoric and includes 'W. Salesburius' in the list of authors of note, alongside Pliny, Seneca, Xenophon, Camden, Tremellius and many others.

The Bards and Edmwnd Prys

Salesbury's secular books continued to be read and studied, particularly his book on rhetoric. It had so impressed Henri Perri that he produced his own, printed, version, but the survival of fourteen[9] manuscript copies of Salesbury's original ranging in date from 1575 to the second half of the eighteenth century shows whose work was preferred.

Whilst the respect given to Salesbury by the bards was grudging, Edmwnd Prys, who represented the new phenomenon of the intellectual poet rather than the craftsman bard, did not hesitate to praise his Humanist kinsman in his *ymryson* with Wiliam Cynwal:

Am William a ganmolir,[10]
Salbri gynt ar ddwyslwybr gwir

[It is William who is to be praised,
Salbri of old on truth's solemn path]

After castigating the bards for their failure to praise him and to appreciate his learning, he continues:

Eithr i ni athrawon art,
Lliaws iaith oll o seithart;
A'fod o barch i'w nodi,
Ymhell yn well na nyni.
Am bedair iaith eurwaith âr,
A deall wybr a daear,
A ffrwyth eu gyd byd eb au
Yr hyn oedd eu rhinweddau;
Drwg yw na wyddyd ragawr,
A dull mydr lle doe wall mawr.

[But to us men of art [he gave]
A host of language from the seven disciplines;
And out of respect [we] celebrate him,
[As] far and away superior to us.
Four languages he made a golden field
[For] understanding heaven and earth
And the fruit of all their worlds
Were their virtues;
It's bad he did not know better
Poetry where yesterday was [your] silence.]

(Prys, born *c.*1544, would have been in his late thirties when Salesbury died and as a relative and a fellow man of letters is certain to have known him personally. Cynwal died in 1588 and the lines above must date from shortly before his death, which brought the *ymryson* to an end.)

Ussher, Dee and Davies

Interest in 'British' culture remained strong in Elizabethan England. Camden, author of *Britannia* and highly influential amongst writers and antiquaries, was a fluent Welsh speaker who kept a Welsh manservant to help him maintain his mastery of the language. There is no evidence of his having used the dictionary or the guide to pronunciation, but he made use of the section on triads in *Y Diarebion Camberaec* for his most famous work and Archbishop Ussher in the 1650s would have studied the same source had Robert Vaughan of Hengwrt been able to find a copy for him.

In *General and Rare Memorials Pertaining to the Perfect Art of Navigation* and *Brytanici Imperii Limites* Dr John Dee promoted British-ness to bolster English claims to North America, with tales (whose truth he faithfully accepted) of an Arthurian empire in the Atlantic and the revived story of Prince Madog discovering the new continent in the twelfth century. (Salesbury cannot be blamed for Dee's fantasies.) Amongst Dee's many interests was language. He was an excellent Hebraist and believed uncritically in the existence of the Adamic language. He started to learn Welsh towards the end of his life to which end he used Salesbury's dictionary, making copious notes in the margin.[11] The dictionary was later acquired by Archbishop Ussher and is now in Trinity College Library, Dublin.

The dictionary, like his book on rhetoric, was not so much replaced but subsumed into a larger work, John Davies's *Dictionarium Duplex* of 1632. As part of the entry for 'breuan' (quern, Latin molendinuum) Davies writes that 'Gan WS yr oedd un i'w gweled anno 1574' (WS had one that could be seen in the year 1574). The most likely source for this information is either Thomas Wiliems, whose own Latin/Welsh dictionary was incorporated into *Dictionarium,* or Edmwnd Prys. Such a detail, included in a work of great scholarship, shows that Salesbury was still a subject of interest to writers and antiquaries a half century after his death.

At the end of the dictionary Davies gives a list of 'Authorum Britannicorum', in which 'Wilielmus Salesburius', is included.

Included in *Dictionarium Duplex* are many of the plant names from the herbal.[12] These names had been included in Thomas Wiliems's unpublished dictionary, which had been incorporated into Davies's.

Manuscript collectors

Another reason for the continuing interest in Salesbury amongst seventeenth-century intellectuals was his manuscript collection. There were his two books in manuscript, the herbal and his work on rhetoric, and the collections of Welsh poetry that he had made or to which he had contributed copies, most notably MS Cwrtmawr 3 (Siôn Cent and others), MS Peniarth 99 (Dafydd ap Gwilym, Iolo Goch, Siôn Cent, Dafydd Nanmor, Dafydd ab Edmwnd, Tudur Aled and others), MS Gwysanau 4B (Guto'r Glyn, Tudur Aled) and MS Gwyneddon 3.

Even more enticing for bibliophiles and collectors was the possibility that he had owned thirteenth- or fourteenth-century manuscripts. It is known that Vaughan sought out the life of Saint Teulacus,[13] which he knew to have once been in Salesbury's possession.

Dee had acquired the Bacon manuscript from Salesbury and there is the possibility that he might have acquired others, as his passion for antiquities never abated and he did not die until 1608, though, by his old age, poverty had forced him to sell many of his most valued works. Jenkin Gwyn was a friend of both men and a possible conduit for the transfer of manuscripts from Salesbury to Dee.

Sir Robert Cotton acquired the Bacon manuscript and there are other Welsh or British manuscripts of his that might have originated with Salesbury. Archbishop Ussher, too, was interested in Dee's collection (and Bale's), which explains why Dee's copy of Salesbury's dictionary is in Trinity College.

Another great collector was Sir Thomas Egerton, who acquired the Ellesmere Canterbury Tales.[14] Amongst the Egerton collection in the British Library is the appeal written by Salesbury and Davies in 1560 or 1561 (Egerton MS 2350, 54), which argued that Welsh and Cornish children should receive instruction in the catechism in their own language. What else might Egerton have acquired from sources at one or two removes from Salesbury?

It is frustrating that so little information has survived about what Salesbury owned and where it went. His son, Siôn Wyn, does not appear to have made any great effort to have kept the collection intact. Perhaps he did not appreciate the value, either antiquarian or financial, of the dusty volumes that sat on the shelves of Plas Isa. One person who would have done was Jasper Gryffyth[15] (1560?–1614), a clergyman who amassed a substantial collection of manuscripts (including *Llyfr Du Caerfyrddin* and *Llyfr Gwyn Rhydderch*) and who was in contact with Cotton and with Salesbury's old friend, Richard Langford. For a time he was warden of Rhuthun hospital, which placed him in easy reach of Llanrwst. All that can be said is that Salesbury's library was likely to have been of sufficient quality to attract his attention.

Competing orthographies

By the time Vaughan, Ussher and others were seeking out the remains of Salesbury's manuscript collection it might be assumed that the success of Morgan's Bible and Prayer Book and Davies's revised editions of 1620 had removed all traces of Salesbury's orthography.

However, the reality is more complex than a Morgan vs Salesbury orthographical confrontation with a definitive date (1588 or 1599) for when orthodoxy triumphed. There were three systems of spelling besides Morgan's[16] that were in use at the end of the sixteenth century: Salesbury's, Gruffydd Robert's[17] and Siôn Dafydd Rhys's.

The chief feature of Robert's system was the use of dots to indicate the 'double' letters 'w' (u.), 'll' (l.) and 'dd' (d.). He did not adopt Salesbury's invention of 'ei', 'ein', 'eich' as Morgan had done, but like Salesbury he used the Middle Welsh word endings '-awl', '-awdd' and '-awd' rather than the more contemporary '-ol', '-odd' and '-od'.

In *Cambrobrytannicae Cymraecaeve Linguae institutions et rudimenta* (1592) Rhys had used devices such as 'γ' for 'w', 'bh' for 'f', 'lh' for 'll' and 'dh' for 'dd'.[18]

Many, such as Kyffin, adopted Morgan's orthography throughout their writing, though even in his work there are occasional lapses, such as 'Cymraec' for 'Cymraeg'. Others chose elements from all four systems, with fashion, religious sympathy, cultural attachment and whim all playing a part in the process.

In *Egluryn Phraethineb*, Henri Perri used elements of Rhys's orthography ('γ' and 'bh') alongside a mixture of Salesbury's and Morgan's ('Cymro' and 'Cymbro', 'dysciedic' and 'dysgiedig') and showed a clear preference for '-awl' over '-ol'.

Huw Lewys also included Salesburian spellings ('Cymbru', 'sainct Mathew', 'ysbrydawl', 'llygredic', '-awl' for '-ol', and 'c', 'p' and 't' endings), although he mostly favoured Morgan's.

Roger Morris the copyist, a Catholic, used Robert's system, as did the exiled Morris Clynnog in his 1567 letter to William Cecil. When Morris copied Salesbury's herbal, he respected the author's orthography and combined it with Robert's. When he compiled his own, original entries, he remained faithful to both orthographies.

Rhosier Smyth, a Catholic exile, published *Gorsedd y byd*, his translation of Pierre Boaistuau's *Theater du Mond* [*sic*] in 1615 in Paris. Whilst he mostly uses Morgan's spelling (but not 'ei'), there are many words that show the influence of Salesbury: 'henwae', 'emeroder', 'rhagorawl', 'discaediaeth' and the frequent use of 'ph' for 'ff'.

There are further examples of people using Salesburian spellings long after his death. One anonymous student[19] made the following comment in the margin of a manuscript which contained a fifteenth-century English poem written in Welsh metre:

> Llyma owdyl arall i dduw ag i fair a wnaeth Kymbro yn Rhydychen wrth ddysgu
> achos dwedyd o un or Saeson na oedd na mesur na chynganedd ynghymbraeg.
> Yntau ai atebodd i gwnai ef gerdd o Saesneg ar fesur a chynghanedd Kymraeg
> fal na fedreur Sais nag yr un oi gyfeillion wneythur moi math yn i hiaith i
> hunein ac i canodd ef val i canlyn ond am fy mod in scrivennu r llyfr hwn oll ag
> orthographie Kymbraeg e gaiff hyn o saesneg ganlyn yn llwybr ni: darllenwch ef
> val Kymbraec.

> [Here follows another awdl (ode) to God and (the Virgin) Mary composed by a
> Welshman in Oxford, when he was studying because an Englishman had stated
> that there was neither metre nor cynghanedd in Welsh. Then he replied by saying

that he would compose an English song in Welsh metre and cynghanedd, the like
of which neither the Englishman nor any of his friends could compose in their
own language and he sang as follows. But as I am writing this book throughout in
Welsh orthography, this much English must follow our path: read it as if it were in
Welsh.]

It is impossible to date that piece of writing with any accuracy, but
another scholar compiled a list of 'ysgrifenwyr Kamberaeg' and made the
following note, 'Doctor John Davies o fallwyd a wnaeth y dicsionari ag a droes
y Resolution yn Gamberaeg' (Doctor John Davies of Mallwyd who made
the dictionary and turned (translated) the Resolution into Welsh),[20] which
allows us to date the list after 1632, the year in which both books appeared.
More than fifty years after Salesbury's death, here is a mid-seventeenth
century Welshman continuing to use one of the earliest of his inventions,
'Kamberaeg/Gamberaeg', which had attracted so much opposition during his
lifetime. Words that Salesbury had constructed on the basis of the story of
Camber and the founding of Wales, so redolent of Trojan power and glory,
continued to appeal greatly to the antiquarian mind.

(It was not just in marginalia that Camberaeg/Camber-aec appeared.
There are six instances of its use in print in the frontispieces of translations of
religious works from English to Welsh, 'Gyfieithwyd i'r Gamberaeg', the last
of which is dated 1700.)[21]

Looking outwards, looking inwards

It is not just orthography that makes up a literary philosophy. Faced with the
problem of creating words and terms as a language adapts to new challenges,
the author or translator must decide on where to look for practical models.
In England, some intellectuals, such as John Cheke, looked to their own
language. The Inkhorns looked to the classical languages, Latin particularly,
and to French and Italian. Salesbury followed this course, adding English to
his list of possible sources. He was open to influences from the ancient world
and from across Europe.

By Morgan's time, though the Inkhorns had flooded the vocabulary of
English with their Latinised words and Italian and French poetic forms such as
the sonnet and the alexandrine had been naturalised, it was no longer fitting

for a scriptural translator to be so outward looking. Spain, France and Italy were dangerously Catholic and to Anglicans such as Whitgift and the Queen the ideas and literature of Germany, Geneva and Basel were dangerously Protestant. Morgan was more conservative, more Cheke-like, in his attitude to outside influence.

The great irony is that the Catholic exile, Gruffydd Robert, was much, much closer to Salesbury's philosophy than the Protestant William Morgan. It is difficult to be inward-looking when you are in exile and surrounded by languages, customs and ways of thinking that are not those of your homeland. Robert was firmly of the opinion that you should adopt and adapt from other languages. He listed his preferences in order: the classical languages, Italian, French, English. (Italian and French presumably owe their favoured position to their roots in Latin and their closer association with the Renaissance.) '[We] must borrow first from the Latin if it can be made Welsh without difficulty: but if there is a difficulty we must borrow from the Italians, French, Spanish, and if there are English words honoured in Wales it would not serve to refuse them.' (tr.)[22]

Robert also set out an ambitious plan for translating many of the great classical writers into Welsh. (His belief was that the priority for Welsh was translations of the classics rather than original work.) Sadly, his ambitions were not realised. Only five books by Catholic exiles were printed. Two were original works, Robert's *Gramadeg* (in three parts) and Robert Gwyn's *Y Drych Cristanagawl* (1587).[23] The other three were translations, none of them classical: Morys Clynnog's *Athrawaeth Gristnogawl* (1568) from a now lost work by Polanco, *De doctrina Christiana*; Smyth's 1609/11 translation of Canisius's *Catechism* (*Crynnodeb a addysc Cristnogawl*) and his 1618 *Theater du Mond*. The one piece of classical literature to be translated was the first part of Cicero's *De Senectute* (*Of Old Age*), which appeared at the end of the third and final part of Robert's *Gramadeg*.

Salesbury would have wholeheartedly approved of the secular part of Robert's programme. His work had been given over to the production of the Bible. If that had not been his life's goal, he is likely to have worked on translating writers such as Cicero or Ovid into his native tongue. On a very small scale he did translate some maxims of Marcus Aurelius for *Y*

Diarebion Camberaec and, possibly, assisted in Simwnt Fychan's translation of Martial. (It should also be remembered that much of the herbal originated in Fuchs's works, all in Latin, and in Turner's books, the first of which was in Latin.)

It was the conservative, safe philosophy of translation that was dominant in Wales after 1588, with Anglican books and tracts such as translations of Jewel (Kyffin), Coverdale (Lewys), Bayly's *The Practice of Piety* (Rowland Vaughan)[24] and Dent's *The Plain Man's Pathway to Heaven* (Robert Llwyd) appearing in Welsh, rather than classical or European works. However, when it came to formulating new words, the ordinary people (just like Salesbury, though not guided by him) thought nothing of taking the English word, often with minimal adaptation, and using it. The more academic have followed the example that Salesbury set when he compiled his book on rhetoric, using the structure of the Graeco-Roman derived word but replacing its elements with Welsh ones, so that 'computer' is not 'compiwtar' but 'cyfrifiadur', a device for counting.

Leading literary figures in Wales, such as John Davies and Robert Vaughan, corresponded with English antiquaries, most notably Sir Symonds D'Ewes (Davies) and Archbishop Ussher (Vaughan) so that, although interest in 'British' culture faded in London and Oxbridge, Salesbury's name was still known, which may account for his inclusion in Anthony Wood's *Athenae Oxonienses* of 1691 where he is described as:

> a most exact critic in British antiquities, was born of an ancient and genteel family in Denbighshire, spent several years in academical learning either in St Alban's or Broadgate's Hall or both. Thence he went to an inn of chancery ... Afterwards he applied his muse to the searching of histories, especially those belonging to his own country, wherein he became so curious and critical that he wrote and published ... From the said dictionary, and Treatise, Dr John Davies obtained many materials when he was making his Dictionarium Britannico-Latinum.

It must also be remembered that Samuel Pepys in the 1660s found his *Descripcion of the Sphere* a very useful handbook.[25]

The eighteenth century

The world of eighteenth-century Welsh letters was dominated by the Morris brothers (Lewis, Richard and William[26]) and their circle, which included Goronwy Owen, Evan Evans (Ieuan Fardd) and William Wynn (all poets, as was Lewis Morris).

Wales, which for so long had clung stubbornly to its Catholic faith, was now a Protestant country, but the Church hierarchy had developed an animosity towards the Welsh language. The four dioceses perpetually had English (or Scottish) bishops; the Church refused to print Welsh-language Bibles or prayer books and on at least one occasion a non-Welsh-speaking clergyman was appointed to a parish where few parishioners could speak English.

Within the Church there were individuals such as Griffith Jones and Madam Bevan who did all they could to support and promote worship through the medium of Welsh, but the unsympathetic attitude of the bishops was a major factor in the growth of Methodism and other non-conformist sects. It also meant that the Morris circle, who were all Anglican (Owen, Evans and Wynn were clergymen) looked back on Salesbury's time as a golden age. Bishop Richard Davies, Bishop William Morgan, Archdeacon Edmwnd Prys and Dr John Davies had all helped to produce fine scriptural translations and other Humanist works and in their midst had been William Salesbury.

Richard Morris brought out new editions of the Bible and the Prayer Book financed, not by the Church, but the S.P.C.K. The orthography he used was that of Morgan and Davies, but in their correspondence to one another the brothers and their friends regularly used Salesburian spellings. In the spirit of the sixteenth century, they experimented with orthography, regularly using the Greek letter chi for 'ch'. Evans and Wynn went further and, taking medieval Welsh as their example, insisted on writing 'y' as 'i' whenever it formed a part of the verb to be.

As admirers of the Elizabethan and Jacobean Humanists, the *Morysiaid*, as they were called in Welsh, collected and studied their books. Several of the British Library's copies of these early texts have the name of Richard Morris written on their inside cover, including a copy of the 1567 New Testament.[27]

When he wrote to his brother William (in November 1761) to inform him of this acquisition, along with two other sixteenth-century books, the response could not have been more enthusiastic, 'You are so fortunate to be able to own books by the greatest [literary figures], W Salbri etc.' (tr.)

Evan Evans was the member of the circle who achieved the greatest fame outside Wales. His *Some Specimens of the Poetry of the Antient Welsh Bards* (1764) was admired by Thomas Gray, Thomas Percy, Dr Johnson and other literati and was used as a source book by Gray and Chatterton. The work includes the account of the destruction of Welsh books which occurs in *A playne and a familiar Introduction* (1567). Evans owned two copies of Salesbury's New Testament[28] and recognised him as Morgan's equal:

> O may those days in future annals shine,
> That made a Salesbury and a Morgan thine.[29]

Evans must have crossed Salesbury's path many times in his hunting down of ancient manuscripts, most notably when he came across a transcript of the Hendregadredd Manuscript. Salesbury had studied the original whilst the guest of Gruffudd Dwnn at Cydweli.

The nineteenth century

It was the nineteenth century that saw the great revival in interest in Salesbury. In England he was discovered by academics who were amazed at and delighted by the precision with which he had described the pronunciation of English in his works of 1547, 1550 and 1567. Extended passages from the dictionary and *A playne and a familiar Introduction* were included in A. J. Ellis's *On Early English Pronunciation* of 1871 and, as a foot soldier who contributed to the Protestant revolution in England, his name appears in the small print of the monumental historical works of Strype (1643–1737),[30] many of which were reprinted in the first part of the century. Archbishop Parker's letter to Bishop Davies which praised Salesbury's attempts at decoding the Armenian Psalter appeared in the *Correspondence of Matthew Parker* of 1853.

In Wales, Salesbury became a hero. The Society of Friends in the seventeenth century and, to a much greater extent, the Methodists in the eighteenth, attracted Welsh men and women to a religious belief that was far more deep-seated and fervent than the pallid Anglicanism of England. It is wrong to stereotype or exaggerate. Significant numbers stayed loyal to the Church of England and many, many more devoted their lives to drinking, gambling, fornication and other deadly sins, but a substantial section of the nation lived a life built on the teachings of the Bible.

When Salesbury first made his call for the scriptures to be available in Welsh, no one rallied to his side. Two centuries later the desire to read the Bible was so great that literacy levels in Wales were amongst the highest in Europe. The circulating schools of Griffith Jones (mentioned above) sent teachers around the country. They stayed in a particular area and did not move on until the interested adults there were literate enough to read the Bible. This was not literacy for literacy's sake but for the salvation of the soul. The most celebrated literary figures were not poets but hymn writers such as William Williams and Ann Griffiths. Salesbury, too, was celebrated for having done so much to provide his land with the Bible.

Interest in his work grew. Part of his New Testament was reprinted in 1819[31] and a full version appeared in 1850. In 1877 the Society of Cymmrodorion reprinted his dictionary. Salesbury's life and work were matters of interest to all those who valued the culture of Wales.

The gentry who had dismissed Welsh as the language of the peasant had been proved right, but the peasants had nurtured the language and now it was more vibrant than it had been at any time since the Act of Union. The Industrial Revolution had been a great boon, providing sizeable urban populations avid for books and journals. In the industrial valleys of Monmouthshire and Glamorgan, local eisteddfodau enjoyed huge popularity amongst the working people. The legends of Salesbury translating the New Testament in his secret chamber and falling out with Richard Davies over the meaning of a single word entered the national psyche. It was a culture more restricted in its range than those of other European nations and at times it lacked intellectual rigour, with too ready an acceptance of sentimentality and arguments put forward without evidence, but it was a truly amazing phenomenon.

In 1888, the tercentenary of Morgan's Bible was marked with full recognition of Salesbury's role in its appearance. In the grounds of St Asaph cathedral a monument was erected that contains representations of Richard

Davies, Thomas Huet, William Morgan, Gabriel Goodman,[32] Edmund Prys, Richard Parry, John Davies and Salesbury. In 1899 a bronze statue[33] was erected in Llansannan to honour the leading literary figures of the area: Salesbury, Tudur Aled, Gwilym Hiraethog, Henry Rees and Iorwerth Glan Clwyd. In 1902 Salesbury and Davies were the subjects of a joint biography[34] and that same year new editions of *Oll Synnwyr* and *Ban wedy i dynny air/A Certaine Case Extracte* were produced.

Salesbury's place in history as the man who had achieved for his country what Dr Johnson, William Tyndale and William Caxton had done for England seemed assured, but the twentieth century would see his reputation under assault and his achievements devalued.

Decline and fall

Nineteenth-century Welsh culture

The development of Welsh culture in the late eighteenth and throughout the nineteenth century (especially the nineteenth century), sprang from two sources, religious fervour and the literary enthusiasm of the working classes, both urban and rural.

The religious side of Welsh cultural life produced beautiful hymns, powerful in word and melody, and occasional pieces of fine poetry. (Islwyn, for example, whose work was often stolid, could also compose the breathtakingly wonderful *Atgof* [Memory].)[1] However, Wales's greatest physical bequest to posterity was the many miles of library shelves stacked with religious commentaries, debates and sermons that now go unread. Preachers who could attract outdoor congregations of thousands are now forgotten.

Those whose efforts were channelled into secular works left a livelier, more entertaining legacy but it was not always one that was based on truth or respect for historical fact. Colourful characters such as Iolo Morganwg[2] (Edward Williams), a stonemason, battled against their limited, or even non-existent, education to produce poetry, histories, essays and other works, but there was no tradition of academic rigour to keep inventiveness within check. Williams circulated a 'long-lost' Druidic alphabet that he had 'discovered', included many 'long-lost' poems of Dafydd ap Gwilym in new collections of his work and organised (on Primrose Hill in London) the first eisteddfod of modern times complete with druidic rituals, costumes and insignia that had been 'long-lost' but which had recently 'come to light'. His amazing discoveries were never seriously challenged during his lifetime.

This was an age of literary invention. Europe fell in love with the 'Ossianic' poems 'translated' by James Macpherson. Then in 1770, the eighteen-year-old Thomas Chatterton took his own life. Under the name of Thomas Rowley, a fifteenth-century monk, he had produced verses which would win the admiration of Shelley, Wordsworth, Coleridge, Keats and many others. In the 1790s Samuel and William Henry Ireland (father and son) announced the discovery of a cache of Shakespearian documents, including two previously unknown plays. Boswell was enthusiastic in his welcome of the discovery and Sheridan announced his intention to stage the first of the plays, *Vortigern and Rowena*, but the forgeries were soon exposed.[3]

Forgeries are not necessarily without literary merit; Chatterton was an accomplished poet, but Scotland and England had academics and well-educated and sceptical critics such as Edmond Malone, whose forensic investigation of the Ireland manuscripts revealed their error-strewn falseness. Wales did not and without such intellectual rigour works of a critical or historical nature could never be of the first order.

Among the prominent Welsh authors and essayists of the nineteenth century were men such as Thomas Rowland, Daniel Silvan Evans and William Owen Pughe.[4] All came from non-advantaged backgrounds (Rowland's father was an estate worker) but they somehow managed to 'better' themselves by joining the clergy or, in Pughe's case, becoming a teacher. However, they were not classically trained nor were they great linguists.

It is easy to criticise their output, but they contributed to their native culture to the best of their ability and their intentions were good. Had they, and others like them, not compiled their grammars, dictionaries and studies of literature, nineteenth-century Welsh scholarship, flawed as it was, would have been less vibrant and greatly diminished in the range of topics covered. Their work aroused tremendous interest in the language and its literature. They were not responsible for the lack of opportunity afforded them. Nor was it their fault that the gentry or those few who had been to university contributed little or nothing to their native culture.

Orthography

Another consequence of a lack of a university (the first university college in Wales did not open until 1872) and of a tradition of critical peer review and of a centralised, dominant cultural authority was that a standard orthography had never been established. The Morgan/Davies orthography was followed in the Bible and the Prayer Book and the influence of these two books was considerable, but in secular works many variations in spelling could be found. Nineteenth-century writers favoured particular spellings for quite arbitrary reasons: whim, fashion, a beauty perceived to be present in one formulation but absent in another, a belief that this spelling conferred on the user extra authority or gravitas.

There is a certain anarchic charm about the lack of a standardised spelling, as if the lords of misrule had been sent to tear up the straitjacket of the dictionary, but to those who believe that rules should be strictly adhered to, it was a case of pandemonium.

Some of Salesbury's works had been reprinted in the nineteenth century and were in circulation. He was a hero to the religious literati (for his role in providing scriptural translations) and to more secular writers who would have admired his dictionary and other non-religious works. Both groups would have enjoyed and accepted the stories of the secret chamber and the quarrel with Davies.

The republication of his dictionary and New Testament meant that Salesbury's orthography was now added to the extensive buffet of spellings from which writers could pick and choose, mix and match.

'Gamber-aeg', invented by Salesbury, was briefly readopted in a publication of 1840. 'Tuy' for 'tŷ' (house) was widely used at this time. Whether it was Salesbury's influence or another's is uncertain, but 'Iuddewon' for 'Iddewon' (Jews, Latin Iudaei) also reappeared. It occurs, for example in the titles of two books (1852 and 1860) by John Mills.[5] To a non-conformist minister preparing a work for publication it was an excellent choice, impressive in look and sound, imbued with learning and with overtones of the Holy Land's Roman dominance. Why use 'Iddewon', when you could use 'Iuddewon'?

John Morris-Jones

There was, inevitably, a reaction against what some saw as lexicographical laxness and orthographical licence and the reaction came from Oxford. In the 1880s a group of Welsh undergraduates with a shared love of literature and language established *Cymdeithas Dafydd ap Gwilym* (the Dafydd ap Gwilym Society) to discuss, study and promote their native culture. The most prominent members were O. M. Edwards, J. Lleufer Thomas and John (Morris-) Jones.[6]

Jones was the son of shopkeepers in Anglesey. His parents had enough money to send him to Friars School, Bangor, where his prodigious talent at maths brought him to the attention of Daniel Lewis Lloyd. When Lloyd became headmaster of Christ College, Brecon, he took several Friars pupils with him including Jones, whom he started preparing for a maths scholarship at Oxford, but the death of his father meant that he had to return to Anglesey to work in the family shop. During this time Jones chanced upon some books of Welsh poetry, a discovery that changed his life. Every second of his spare time was spent in studying the subject. After a year of exile from formal education, Jones was able to return to Brecon and from there went on to his scholarship at Oxford, but language had replaced maths as his great passion. He graduated with a third but, critically, had come to the attention of Sir John Rhys, professor of Celtic at the university, and was able to continue post-graduate research under his aegis.

The name that he made for himself as an authority on manuscripts led to his appointment in 1889 as a lecturer at the recently established University College, Bangor. In 1895 he was elevated to the professorship. Shortly after taking the chair at Bangor he published a paper showing that the ancient rituals of the National Eisteddfod had been invented by Iolo Morganwg.

As a creative writer Jones possessed the inventiveness, imagination, flexibility and open-ness necessary for success. He published just one volume of poetry in his lifetime, *Caniadau* [Songs] in 1906; it was (and continues to be) well regarded. His own poetry was written in strict metre, but not his translations. He translated Heine into Welsh and produced an accomplished reworking of verses from Omar Kayyam (*Penillion Omar Kayyâm wedi eu cyfieithu o'r Berseg i'r Gymraeg*), not from Fitzgerald's English translation but, as the title points out, from the original Persian.

An ordered mind

However, when it came to academic matters, orthography in particular, Jones showed no such flexibility. He was not so much rigorous as rigid. It is important to bear in mind his early mathematical training and the scientific doctrines that dominated his formative years. The last decades of the nineteenth century were the high-point of scientific certainty. The universe ran with Newtonian, clockwork efficiency. Everything was black or white, right or wrong, logical or illogical. Relativity had yet to appear as a scientific concept; the very word undermines the foundations of certainty. Quantum Mechanics, the Uncertainty Principle and Fuzzy Logic were yet to make their appearance. Chomsky would undermine Jones's mechanistic view of language and grammar as rigid structures independent of humans whose rules had to be obeyed, just as a photon of light had to 'obey' nature and be a wave or a particle, but could not be both.

Welsh orthography was messy and anarchic and Jones saw it as his duty, his mission, to impose order and structure upon it. This was around the time that the *Oxford English Dictionary* was being published, in sections,[7] for the first time. On completion, in 1928, it would become the ultimate arbiter of a standardised English orthography throughout the Anglophone world apart from North America. Few would contest the need for a standardised Welsh orthography, but Jones pursued his goal with a messianic fervour that went beyond the call of duty.

Whilst he was at Oxford *Cymdeithas Dafydd ap Gwilym* commissioned a report on the subject (Jones is believed to have been the chief instigator of this move). The report was overwhelmingly his work. It was not universally welcomed; many complained of an elite group of scholars trying to force 'Oxford Welsh' onto the ordinary people, but Jones was determined to win this and every other battle he waged. He used his position at Bangor to do so. As a master of metrical poetry he adjudicated at eisteddfodau, large and small; this and the advice he gave to the governing bodies of these organisations further strengthened his ability to impose his vision of what was correct upon the nation.

His three works on grammar and orthography were: *A Welsh Grammar* (1913), *An Elementary Welsh Grammar* (1921), and *Orgraff yr iaith Gymraeg* (1928).

Whole sections of these works are excellently researched and show great scholarship, but there are other parts which are dominated by rigidity, prejudice and arbitrary judgements asserted as incontestable fact.

One example (from *A Welsh Grammar*) is the section on 'dynes',[8] a north Wales word for woman. The word has a logic of its own: 'dyn' means man and '-es' is a feminine ending, for example, 'llew(es)', lion(ess). The word emerged haphazardly, as words do, bubbling up from everyday discourse. That is how language evolves; language, after all, belongs to the people who speak it, but Jones rages against it and dismisses it as a 'vulgarism', a term that he uses frequently. Another term that occurs is 'debased dialect'.

A whole undercurrent of prejudice and snobbery can be detected in his attitude and his choice of vocabulary. Would Jones have objected to Jerome's *Vulgate* because it was intended for the people or to Luther's German Bible for his use of the language of the street and the market place to make his translation accessible to all? Or were their works acceptable because they themselves were not 'vulgar'?

In Jones's defence it must be said that this was the prevailing linguistic philosophy of the time. The same rigidity and certainty is present in his English contemporary, H. W. Fowler. Those who were taught or brought up to say 'different from' may still wince at the use of 'different to', but recognise that the supposed superiority of one form over another is based on nothing but one man's prejudice and supreme self-confidence.

Not only did Jones feel that people had no right to shape their own language, he also felt it his duty to launch personal attacks on those who, in his opinion, had perverted Welsh orthography. His immediate targets were William Owen Pughe (1759–1835), his bête-noir, and Daniel Silvan Evans (1818–1903). He felt no obligation to take into account the times or conditions in which the men worked. Nor did he feel the need to make allowances for their limited education. They were guilty of crimes against orthography and there were no extenuating circumstances.

Pughe's work is described as 'a fiction', his etymology as 'mad'; Evans is treated a little less harshly, his reasoning being dismissed merely as 'spurious'.[9] 'Even scholars have been deceived by the fictitious forms found in dictionaries; thus "dagr" given by Silvan Evans, after Pughe, as the sg. of "dagrau", is quoted as a genuine form even by Strachan, Intr. 23.' ('Dagrau' means 'tears'; the standard singular form is 'deigryn', though 'deigr' is recognised as an alternative.)

No attempt is made to differentiate the man from his work. Pointing out an 'error' and leaving the reader to draw his own conclusion of the worth of the man who made it is never an option.

Jones and Salesbury

Salesbury's role as the pioneer of Humanist prose means that he makes many appearances in this 1913 work. There is a passage near the start of the book in which veiled criticism lurks just below the surface:

> At the introduction of printing William Salesbury attempted in his works, including the New Testament (1567) to form a new literary dialect, in which the orthography should indicate the etymology rather than the sound. His practice was to write Latin loan words as if no change had taken place in them except the loss of the ending, thus eccles for eglwys 'church', descend for disgyn 'to descend'; any native word with a superficial resemblance to a Latin synonym was similarly treated, thus i (his/her) was written ei because the Latin is eius (perhaps eu 'their' suggested this). But Dr Morgan in his Bible (1588) adopted the standard literary language as it continued to be written by the bards, though he retained some of Salesbury's innovations (e.g. ei for i 'his').

The criticism, however, is not yet overt. Salesbury's contribution to the development of Welsh prose ensures that his name occurs frequently, but each time Jones describes one of his words, spellings or constructions, he does so objectively. On pages 172–3, as if justifying a Salesburian practice, he even notes that in late medieval Welsh nasal mutation is often unwritten.

However, by 1921 Jones can no longer tolerate Salesbury; precedents, whether from medieval Welsh or Humanist learning, are overlooked. Salesbury is subjected to the same treatment as Pughe and Evans. *An Elementary Welsh Grammar* contains Kyffin's 1595 condemnation of Salesbury and includes the following statement:

> Wm. Salesbury had translated the New Testament into a language of his own invention in which the words were written according to his idea of their

etymology; it was a travesty of Welsh, which Maurice Kyffin stated in 1595 to be 'intolerable to a good Welshman's ear'.[10]

That one sentence was to cast a blight on Salesbury's reputation for much of the twentieth century.

Previous academics and writers had noted Salesbury's orthography, but had not let it cloud their assessment of his achievements. J. Gwenogvryn Evans had in his monumental *Report on Manuscripts in the Welsh Language* of 1898–1903, but that did not prevent his recognition of Salesbury's importance, which led to his editorship of the 1902 reprint of *Oll Synnwyr*. In his introduction, Evans notes 'Certain peculiarities in Salesbury's orthography', but nevertheless concludes that he was 'tall enough to be seen of later generations'.

Similarly, D. R. Thomas had not seen Salesbury's orthography as a reason not to speak highly of him in *The Life and Work of Davies and Salesbury* (also 1902), 'his field was pre-eminently that of Welsh literature of which we may fairly call him the pioneer and champion.'[11]

However, Jones's influence was so all-pervading that from the moment his dismissive sentence appeared most Welsh academics felt obliged to accompany any mention of Salesbury in their work with a derogatory comment. His successor as professor of Welsh at Bangor, Sir Ifor Williams (1881–1965), continued the disparagement.

Just a few independent thinkers, such as Saunders Lewis and W. J. Gruffydd, were not drawn into the Jones mind-set. Jones's assessment of Salesbury's prose and orthography did not set it in the context of the learning and philosophy of his age and did not take Kyffin's personal animosity into account. Nor did he consider the problems Salesbury faced in developing a prose style in a language with no legal or administrative status any more than his need to create new terms. Lastly, he made no comparison with contemporary translators, Tyndale for example. No academic should have accepted an unsupported judgement but a majority of those in Wales did.

Even those who had the acuity to see that Salesbury was a product of his age and that his orthography should be seen in the context of Erasmus, Elyot and the influence of the English Inkhorns felt obliged to say so in an apologetic tone.

John Fisher edited the 1931 reprint of *Kynniver Llith a Ban* and wrote:

> But those who condemn him for taking such liberties with the language are
> probably not aware that he was really a victim of the Classicism of his age, which
> seems to have obsessed him from his Oxford days. Every country in Europe that
> became affected by the Renaissance produced a crop of spurious learning. Its effects
> may be noticed in England and France,[12]

as if the Renaissance was some sort of plague and Salesbury was a 'victim'
to be pitied.

Motivation

Evans and Pughe could be dismissed as men whose contribution to literature was
insubstantial and whose scholarship was weak, but why did Jones feel obliged
to dismiss Salesbury so forcefully? Both men were accomplished scholars and
linguists and both were pioneers of new thinking about language at times
when their nation was entering a challenging age that was very different from
its predecessor. Was there a jealousy behind the attack on Salesbury? Some
may see a parallel with Tolstoy's criticism of Shakespeare.

It appears odd today that one academic could have so long-lasting
an influence on undergraduate and postgraduate students, lecturers and
professors, but it is not unprecedented. W. W. Greg had a similar effect on
English bibliography. At the beginning of the twentieth century he set out
his case for the 'scientific' study of English manuscripts and playbooks of the
Elizabethan and Jacobean periods and championed the close investigation of
the 'suspect' texts of Shakespeare's plays. It was only after many generations
of students had been subjected, or had subjected themselves, to the criteria
and constraints established by Greg and his colleagues that it was realised
that his 'scientific' method was based on whatever he had deemed to be
'scientific' and that the branding of some texts as 'suspect' appeared to be
arbitrary: there were many valid reasons for the anomalies contained within
them.[13]

Jones made a few mildly critical remarks concerning Morgan, for
example on his use of 'fyng-halon' for 'fy nghalon' (my heart),[14] and the
third of the great scriptural translators, John Davies, was spared any assault
on his reputation. Their warm words of praise for Salesbury and their use of
his pioneering scholarship go unremarked. In fact, matters were made worse

for Salesbury by the apportioning of blame to him by other academics of 'Salesburian' inventions that were the responsibility of others.

It was not Salesbury who established 'minneu' and 'titheu' as the accepted forms of 'minne' and 'tithe'[15] but John Davies, who was also responsible for '-ai' rather than '-e' being used as the third person singular ending of the imperfect and pluperfect.

Redemption

Salesbury had been exiled from academic and critical respectability, but he had a champion, a postgraduate student whose choice of M.A. thesis must have raised eyebrows in the Welsh department of University College, Cardiff.

W. Alun Mathias's 'Astudiaeth o Weithgarwch Llenyddol William Salesbury' [A Study of the Literary Activities of William Salesbury],[16] which was presented in 1949, was the first step in Salesbury's rehabilitation. Mathias did not court controversy. He issued no challenges to authority. His approach was quiet and methodical, his case built on detailed, original scholarship which required hundreds and hundreds of hours of laborious searching through documents and manuscripts, often fruitlessly.

Mathias did not accept uncritically the opinions of others. He did not recycle other people's research. Salesbury's writings were examined as if they were being read for the first time and investigated forensically so that they could be put in their historical and literary context. Influences such as those of Erasmus and Palsgrave were traced and noted. No article published by Mathias was without significance. Armed only with scholarship and reason, his work changed academic perceptions of Salesbury, revealing his very real achievements. Two works in particular stand out, his discovery of Salesbury's method of compiling his dictionary and the debt to Palsgrave and the discovery of the manuscript from which he could reconstruct the contents of Salesbury's lost book, *Y Diarebion Camberaec*.[17]

Mathias did not write a biography of Salesbury. He showed no interest in the events of his life apart from when they affected his work. His case was that, though Salesbury's orthography looked odd to the modern eye and sounded odd if read phonetically rather than as he had intended, it was a product of its time. Taken in the context of Elyot and the Inkhorn controversy and the influence that Erasmus, Cicero and the Renaissance had in persuading writers to look to the glories of the past, it was not at all unusual. Above all, he taught people to look beyond the orthography and to read (and hear) Salesbury's prose as he had intended it to be read. Mathias's audience began to realise that, far from being a travesty, the translations were highly accomplished and often beautiful; that without Salesbury's establishment of Welsh as a printed language, his work in bringing about the Act of 1563 and his scriptural versions of 1567, Morgan's Bible would never have materialised. Salesbury's significance as the architect of Welsh prose writing was appreciated by a growing number of historians and writers.

There were setbacks. Mathias was overlooked for the task of writing the foreword and preface of the University of Wales Press's 1965 facsimile edition of the 1567 Prayer Book. The book itself was handsomely produced, but the foreword and preface that accompanied it must rank as one of the most error-strewn works produced by two reputable academics in the twentieth century.[18]

Mathias's response was to write a review which detailed all the mistakes, correcting them with pinpoint accuracy and referencing all the sources. His objective approach was a greater chastisement to those responsible than any subjective reaction.

In 1969 Mathias gave two lectures in the Jesus College (Oxford) Easter School on the history of Welsh prose. The lectures took their place in *Y Traddodiad Rhyddiaith* [The Prose Tradition],[19] a volume which outlines the history of Welsh prose down to the end of the nineteenth century. These lectures would seem to be the event which marked Salesbury's readmission into the world of academic respectability. Further articles by Mathias were complemented by books and papers by Isaac Thomas on the history of the Bible in Wales which gave additional evidence of the breadth of Salesbury's scholarship, linguistic awareness and of the beauty of his translations. Another academic who challenged preconceptions of Salesbury was Professor R. Geraint Gruffydd.

An academic barometer

The effectiveness of Mathias's research and essays can be seen in the writing of Professor Glanmor Williams. At the start of his career he accepted unquestioningly the judgement of John Morris-Jones. His attitude is exemplified in an early work, *Bywyd ac Amserau'r Esgob Richard Davies* [The Life and Times of Bishop Richard Davies] (1953). Williams talks of 'gwirciau ysmala Salesbury' (Salesbury's humorous quirks) (page 94) and states, 'Nid oes yr un o'i weithiau cydnabyddedig yn dwyn ôl ei gwirciau personol yn fwy na'r Sallwyr' (There is no other of his acknowledged works that bears the trace of his personal quirks more than the Psalter) (page 97).

On the same page he talks of Salesbury's 'fympwyon' (whims), then makes the case for Davies having an editorial role in the Prayer Book.[20] In fact, the Prayer Book is Salesbury's work alone, as Mathias had revealed in his thesis of 1949, but this is something that Williams was unable to accept. Nor could he accept Mathias's suggestion that Salesbury had died by 1586.[21]

There was a gradual shifting of position on Williams's part until, in his last major work, *Wales and the Reformation* (1997), he acknowledged the problems that Salesbury had faced as a translator, his role as a pioneer of printing and as a key protagonist in the 1563 Act, his scholarship and his achievements. He still considered Morgan to have played the most important part in the production of the Welsh Bible, but was able to write of the translator he had once dismissed as a man of 'quirks' and 'whims', 'Only William Salesbury comes anywhere near him [Morgan] in deserving a share of the credit for what has aptly been described as "the most important book in the Welsh language".'[22]

Further recognition

The rediscovery of Salesbury by English academics also helped burnish his reputation. Salesbury had figured prominently in E. J. Dobson's *English Pronunciation, 1500–1700* (1957). Dobson says of him:

> Salesbury is one of the more important sixteenth century sources because of the amount of his evidence ... his explanations and comments ... enable us to determine the meaning of the transcription with more exactitude than would otherwise be possible.

His contribution to the study of English linguistics was further recognised by the Scolar Press's 1969 reprint of his dictionary and of *A briefe and a playne introduction*.

By the time of the four hundredth anniversary of Morgan's Bible, Salesbury was sufficiently rehabilitated to be one of the four pioneers commemorated philatelically.[23] The four worthies depicted were Morgan, Salesbury, Bishop Parry and Bishop Richard Davies.

Further recognition came in 1997 with the publication of his herbal, this time from the superior copy made by Roger Morris, which had not been available in 1916. It was edited by Iwan Rhys Edgar,[24] who had completed a study of it for his Ph.D. Academic research on Salesbury was no longer regarded with suspicion.

His is no longer a household name, as it was in Victorian times, but in a highly secular age Tyndale, too, has experienced a similar eclipse in the English national consciousness. Salesbury could be seen not only as Wales's Johnson but also as its Caxton (another man of achievement no longer as widely celebrated as he once was), but his role in Welsh culture was far greater and more crucial than the important literary contributions Tyndale, Caxton and Johnson made to their nation. Without Salesbury's pioneering work and tireless campaigning it is highly unlikely that a Welsh-language Bible would have been produced. The consequence of that could well have been the eventual disappearance of the language and its culture.

In an age when greed was regarded as good, he was willing to risk public humiliation and put in jeopardy his life, health and personal fortune not for his own benefit, but for the spiritual well-being of his fellow countrymen.

A re-trial

Convention and conventional thinking

Salesbury's reputation as an able translator, stylist and pioneer of modern Welsh prose has been restored. Alun Mathias, Isaac Thomas and others did what should not have been necessary. It is as if English academics had been forced to salvage the good name of Tyndale or Spenser.

However, on one issue Salesbury remains a condemned man. Mathias's defence was that the orthography was irrelevant, that readers and critics should look beyond and through the spelling and appreciate the beauty, scholarship and achievement that was present in his work. Mathias's case is that of the lawyer who argues that the minor misdemeanour of an otherwise virtuous and upstanding citizen should be overlooked in recognition of his good work.

Mathias is justified in one respect. W. B. Yeats and John Lennon are reputed to have been poor spellers, but that does not diminish either man's accomplishment as a poet or lyricist, though there is a distinct difference between a writer who spells badly and one who fashions his own orthography. George Bernard Shaw was such a writer; his plays are printed in the phonetic manner that he championed, but no one has called his work a 'travesty'. Nor do English and American critics condemn the novels of those whose works are published on the 'wrong' side of the Atlantic.

But saying that Salesbury's orthography is irrelevant in assessing his achievement is implicitly saying that it was wrong. It was neither right nor wrong, just as 'center', 'honor' and 'thru' are neither right nor wrong. They are regarded as being right in America because they are the spellings that have become standard; all appeared in Noah Webster's dictionary of 1806.[1] Equally valid as phonic representations of spoken words are 'masheen', 'giv', 'reezon', 'thum', 'korus' and 'dawter', all of which appeared in the same volume but have not been adopted.

Standard orthography is simply a matter of convention. The reason that Salesbury's spellings look strange (his detractors would say 'quirky' or 'whimsical') is that they are unfamiliar. After a short period of study they lose their strangeness. Those elements of Salesbury's orthography that Morgan incorporated into his work, such as 'ei', 'ein', 'eich', 'mai' and 'sanctaidd', must once have appeared as strange as those other forms to which conservative forces reacted. Now they go un-remarked.

Every example of 'eccentricity' to which Jones and others took exception was or continues to be a feature accepted in the orthography of at least one European language. Every reform of spelling that Salesbury made had been championed by a major figure of sixteenth-century Humanism. He was not an originator of these reforms, but someone who adapted them to his native language.

Judged by some of the ideas that were current in Europe at the time, his thinking was conservative and staid. It should not be forgotten that Sir John Prise seriously considered using the Greek alphabet for *Yny lhyvyr hwnn*,[2] that in 1568 in *De recta et emendate linguae angliae scriptione* Sir Thomas Smith proposed a new 34 letter alphabet for English. John Hart[3] was another advocate of reforming the alphabet. One academic has said of him that his proposal 'was avant garde, but in continental terms it was déjà vu.' Both Gruffydd Robert and Siôn Dafydd Rhys introduced new letter forms into Welsh and in Venice Giangiorgio da Trissino (born 1470) advocated three new letters for the Italian alphabet and that 'j' be distinguished from 'i' and 'v' from 'u'.[4]

Salesbury does not need character witnesses to plead for a lenient judgement. He is innocent on all charges. Here is the case for the defence.

Archaic vocabulary and archaic spelling

The Renaissance valued ancient learning. To be contemporary one had to be ancient. Cicero was the writer to emulate. (The unquestioning adoration that the Roman orator attracted prompted Erasmus to write *Ciceronianus*.) The figures of rhetoric that appeared in the works of classical authors were studied and scholars were encouraged to use them when writing in their vernacular tongue as well as in Latin.

The grammar of sixteenth-century English was changing rapidly and Shakespeare's work gives evidence of that change. Yet in the King James Bible, which appeared in the same year as the playwright's last great drama, *The Tempest*, there is no such evidence. The committee of translators wanted dignity, gravitas and majesty for the word of God.

In Act 1, Scene II, Caliban says to Prospero:

'Thou didst prevent me; I had peopled else
This isle with Caliban.'

Prospero speaks, then Caliban replies:

'You taught me language; and my profit on't
Is, I know how to curse.'

Shakespeare moves from the centuries-old use of 'thou', 'thee', 'ye' and 'you' to the newly evolving universal second person form, 'you'. He does so frequently, though it is the traditional form that is the more used. However, the King James Bible favours the old form, which is used universally throughout the work. Similarly, third person (singular) verbs in the Bible end in '-th', whereas Shakespeare used both '-s' and '-th'.

The King James Bible receives almost universal veneration and part of its appeal is the archaic nature of its language, whereas Salesbury's scriptural translations have been criticised by commentators for exactly the same 'fault'.

The other argument in favour of Salesbury's use of the archaic is that it was an essential part of preparing the Welsh language to meet the challenges of the Humanist age, in particular that of scriptural translation.

In this regard he can be compared to Spenser:

'Full iolly knight he seemd, and faire did sitt.
As one for knightly guists and fierce encounters fit.'[5]

In the above extract (and it is not atypical) Spenser sounds more like

Chaucer, his predecessor by two hundred years, than a poet whose life overlapped with that of Shakespeare. Spenser was never sentenced to decades of academic criticism for his use of archaic language. Salesbury was.

Latinised Spellings

Salesbury Latinised Welsh spellings. He was greatly influenced by what was happening in England (this was the time of the Inkhorn controversy) and could see how the introduction of hundreds of new, Latin inspired words, such as 'dexterity', 'fraternity', 'feline', 'incantation' and 'puerile', was expanding the lexicon.

Part of that process was the Latinising of existing words. Here are just a few of the many new forms introduced by the Inkhorns: anchor, advantage, advance, debt, doubt, fault, island, perfect, receipt, scissors and verdict.

Tyndale's New Testament of 1526 provides evidence of the changeover with forms such as 'dette' and 'debt', 'faut' and 'fault' appearing within the same volume. Tyndale is regarded by many as the greatest of the Protestant heroes and martyrs. This was the time when Salesbury was a student, when he was converting to the new religion and when he was at his most impressionable. It is little wonder that he followed the example of his peers.

Another reason for Latinising was that Welsh already contained a significant number of words of Latin origin (from the Roman occupation, Church Latin and via loan words from Norman French). By changing their spelling to show their Latin origin, Salesbury was not just embellishing his mother tongue and emulating the practice then current in England, he was giving it the reflected glory of one of the three classical languages. What is more he was doing so at a time when Polydore Vergil had removed from Wales the fame once granted it by Geoffrey of Monmouth's *Historia Regum Britanniae*. Salesbury was attempting to regain it.

The Inkhorn controversy waged for decades, with much vituperative language, especially from the antis, but the Inkhorns won and the orthography of English was changed forever. No critic has ever chastised H. E. Bates for making the character of Pop Larkin synonymous with the word 'perfik' rather than 'parfait'. The English debate involved so many that it was a debate of ideas, not of personalities. In Wales, the only protagonist of Latin spelling was Salesbury. He became the subject of personal abuse merely for trying to give to his own language the benefits being enjoyed by its mightier neighbour.

The Invention of Words

Sixteenth-century English was enriched by the invention and adoption of many hundreds of Latin words, as shown above. Hundreds more (such as 'abstergify', arreption', 'deruncinate', 'fatigate' and 'nidulate') did not find a permanent home. Nor was Latin the only language from which new English words were coined or borrowed. 'battallion' (battaglione), 'charlatan' (ciarlatano) and 'frigate' (fregato) all came from Italian via French.

With great foresight and as a disciple of copiousness Salesbury could see how beneficial this was to the language, providing its writers with a mighty armoury which could give their work both greater force and greater subtlety.

Shakespeare would mock pedantic scholars and priests such as Holofernes and Sir Hugh Evans who clung to the Erasmian and Inkhorn ways that by his time had gone out of fashion, but he was the greatest of all the beneficiaries of that legacy. In addition he is celebrated for the 1,500 or so new words that made their first appearance in his works and are attributed to him, in complete contrast to the treatment received by Salesbury, despite his motives being wholly honourable: to expand the Welsh lexicon and imbue it with the classical ethos of the age.

Invention was also a necessity; he had to devise new terms for scriptural vocabulary that had never been found in Welsh (for example, 'bara croyw' (unleavened bread) and 'tollwr' (publican)) and for rhetorical and botanical terms, where his use of calques ('rhag-gymeriad', prolepsis, 'phicuspren', fig tree) was a first for the language and set an excellent precedent. He was a wordsmith, as was Shakespeare.

It is an accolade to invent or be responsible for a word that enters the language as Sheridan (malapropism), Milton (pandemonium) and Aristophanes (cloud cuckoo land) did. Salesbury is the only writer to be derided for it.

Inconsistent spelling

From his very first book, the dictionary, Salesbury was inconsistent in his spelling. Many commentators, including Mathias,[6] attribute this to a desire to promote copiousness. It is true that words with the same root can enter a language and evolve different meanings (for example, 'hostel', hospital' and 'hotel') or keep the same meaning but have different forms ('bord' and 'bwrdd' (table) from the English, board), but this seems altogether too sophisticated a hypothesis.

The most likely reason is that he was following the example set by Tyndale and other writers in English. He admired the English language, had many English colleagues and friends and it was in England that he had been converted to Protestantism. Tyndale's New Testament is a treasure-trove of words with multiple variations of spelling (for example, it, itt, yt, ytt, hit, hitt, hyt, hytt),[7] sometimes with different forms appearing within the same sentence.

French writers, too, spurned consistency in spelling. One of the motives for Robert Estienne's dictionary, *Les Mots francais selon l'ordre des lettres ainsi que les fault escrire & tourner en latin* (1544) was to promote the consistency that was absent: he was a printer.[8]

Salesbury is guilty as charged, but so are the great writers who influenced him.

Use of dialect words

Salesbury wished to make his translations accessible to all and to do so he made a point of including words or variations of words from other areas of Wales, for example 'Monyth for mynydd: so they pronounce it at Sanct Davids'.[9]

The literary language of some countries was built on one particular dialect, either because of its political power or because the first great writers of that country originated there, as with the Florentines Dante, Boccaccio and Petrarch in Italy.

A dominant literary dialect, such as that of Florence or the English used by the powerful elite at court, though it excludes the majority, has the advantage of being an authentic language, spoken naturally by at least some of the nation.

Synthesising a literary dialect by using vocabulary and constructions from all parts of the land is fair, inclusive and democratic, but is, inevitably, artificial.

There are valid arguments for both practices; it is not a hanging offence.

Not showing the presence of nasal mutation

The non-representation of nasal mutations (for example, 'vy-pen' for 'vy mhen') is probably the Salesburian practice that most annoys his critics, even though he went to great lengths to emphasise that he expected the mutation to be sounded. ('For who in the time of most barbarousnes, and greatest corruption, dyd ever wryte every worde as he sounded it?')[10]

In late medieval manuscripts mutations were sometimes not written. The Renaissance looked on the past as a golden age and wished to emulate its practices. As a child of the Renaissance it was natural and logical for Salesbury to follow this path.

Mutations occur in many languages ('loaf', 'loaves', 'subscribe', 'subscription' in English and Latinised English). They are present in Slovak. At the age of sixteen students in Slovakia take their first important public examinations. Success enables the student to pursue an academic career. One of the elements that needs to be mastered to pass the language paper is when to spell certain constructions differently from how they are sounded, for example, that the phrase spoken as 'G getom' (with the 'g's elided) is written 'K detom'.

There is no evidence to suggest that Slovak pupils and students underperform compared to their European neighbours or are disadvantaged by this 'quirk' or 'whim' of their language's orthography.

The untrodden path

Some elements of Salesbury's orthography were incorporated into Welsh and have become an integral part of the language. There is no reason why his orthography as a whole could not have been adopted. It is easy to regard what is familiar as something inevitable or pre-ordained and yet so often it is chance that has been the arbiter.

Could chance have dictated that Salesbury's system prevailed? Had he been able to persuade his ageing body and mind to summon up the energy for one last, almighty effort and completed the Old Testament, then yes, he might have been the standard setter. Morgan's Bible would not have been necessary. In all probability there would have been a revised edition around 1620 by Davies and Parry or somebody else, but after fifty years of use it is likely that much more of the orthography of Salesbury's Bible would have been accepted.

However, there are several reasons why, even if he had completed the Bible, the scenario outlined above would not have come about. The first is that Salesbury was just too radical for a rural, deeply conservative society. He was too associated with everything that people of a reactionary nature find discomfiting. He was a Protestant in a Catholic country and represented new thinking and an open-ness to new ideas, especially those originating in foreign lands. He enjoyed cosmopolitanism and was feted in London. He forced his countrymen to accept the innovation of printing. He did things for reasons other than profit. Everything about him was suspect.

The times were against him. Whilst there were exceptions, the Welsh gentry generally were abandoning their culture and language. They enjoyed the praise of bards, but otherwise saw no role for the language, certainly not as a vehicle for the salvation of the Welsh-speaking peasantry. That Welsh became a language of the Bible, of the Church and of the press is due to the strength of character of a handful of men who, against the tide of opinion, introduced the lessons and benefits of the Humanist age to their native tongue. Though there are many who deserve an honourable mention, the three great benefactors were Salesbury, Morgan and John Davies.

The nature of the beast

Languages are not biological, yet each one has its distinct DNA. The chief characteristic of Welsh is its conservatism. It evolves slowly and is resistant to change. This may well be the prime reason why Salesbury's orthography was not accepted. The following words are from the sixth-century poem *Y Gododdin* by Aneirin:

Gwŷr a aeth Gatraeth oedd ffraeth eu llu;[11]
Glasfedd eu hancwyn, a gwenwyn fu.

[Men went to Catraeth, keen was their war-band;
Fresh mead for their feast, and bitter (poison) it was.]

The lines have been selected carefully. Much of the poem is inaccessible to an ordinary reader, but one and a half millennia later, the couplet is readily intelligible to most Welsh speakers. In contrast, few Englishmen or women could understand these lines of the seventh to tenth century *Beowulf*:

Hwaet wē Gār-Dena in geārdagum,[12]
ēodcyninga Þrym gefrūnon,
hū đā æÞelingas ellen fremedon.

[So. The Spear-Danes in days gone by
and the kings who ruled them had courage and greatness.
We have heard of those princes' heroic campaigns.]

It is all the more surprising, then, that any of Salesbury's radical reforms were accepted.

Phoneticism

Lastly, there is the phonetic nature of Welsh. Those whose first language is English, who learnt to read boatswain, gunwale, diaphragm, indict, lieutenant, pneumonia, psychology, rite, write and wright, Gloucester, Bicester, laughter and slaughter, bow and bough, Cholmondeley and Featherstonehaugh, habit and rabbit, litter and literal and thousands more eccentric and contradictory spellings before encountering the somewhat conventional 'quirkiness' of Salesbury, may fail to see what objections there can be.

However, Welsh has traditionally been spelt phonetically (not exclusively, but overwhelmingly). Many Welsh people take a pride in this aspect of the language and it is long established. Not everyone is so in awe of phonetic regularity and the Chinese have managed perfectly well without an alphabet, but Salesbury's reforms sailed against the tide of Welsh sentiment.

Though his ideas on orthography were rational and as mainstream as anything current in the sixteenth century, they were, almost inevitably, doomed to be rejected. Spelling can arouse great passion. In the early years of this century, plans to reform the orthography of German unravelled irretrievably after individuals and influential newspapers revolted, and the nascent revival of Cornish is being stymied by arguments over which of three rival spelling systems should be adopted.

It is fortunate that on the most important issue of all, the publication of a Welsh Bible, Salesbury triumphed. His pioneering of printing, his creation of a Welsh prose style worthy of the Humanist Age, his overseeing of the 1563 Act of Parliament through both houses and his translations of 1551 and 1567 prepared the way for the 1588 Bible. Had he not lived or had he chosen an easier path through life, we would not be able to celebrate and share in the glories of a language and literature that stretches from the sixth century to the present day and, hopefully, far into the future.

Endnotes

Chapter One: *Ad fontes*, his family and background

1. See Iwan Rhys Edgar (ed.), *Llysieulyfr*, p. 7.

2. 'Will of Robert ap Rice, Clerk', NA PROB 11/25/283, dated (probate) 25 January 1535.

3. NA C 4/1/54, a case brought by John Bosvel against the abbot of Beaulieu and 'his commoners', one of whom was 'William Salesbury'. The abbot was Thomas Skevington, bishop of Bangor until his death in 1533.

4. NLW MS Hafod 26 (p. 204), in which Sir Thomas Wiliems uses the phrase '… oi vebyd yd ei hen[ain]t …' (from his boyhood to his old age).

5. '*c*.1520' is the estimated year of Salesbury's birth that appears most frequently in reference books.

6. The privilege was signed by Henry VIII on 13 December 1546. It was not printed in the dictionary, but appeared in *KLlB* (1551).

7. The document is the will of Marged ferch Siôn Pigod, 1569. (See note 11.)

8. See *Hanes hen furddynod plwyf Llansannan*, pp. 24–5. The translation of the Welsh description appears on page 130 of Iorwerth Peate's *The Welsh House*. The description continues as follows: 'The overall length of the building was about 72ft and its breadth from wall to wall about 14ft. The first room was about 9ft long, but it had no fireplace and stood deep in the earth. The next, the central room, was the principal room, and measured 16ft: in it was the hearth and chimney. The two rooms were separated by a stone partition reaching to the roof. There was no loft above the first room, but there was one above the other two, and a small room formed in the chimney between the mantel (or the partition wall above the mantel) to the end wall of the room, and above the hearth. The loft above the kitchen was therefore smaller than the kitchen by the width of the chimney. There was no door from the principal bedroom into this small room, and no one could imagine that the room existed: the only entrance into it was by climbing up through the chimney. And this is the kind of place … the secret or sacred chamber as it can well be called … where was performed the holy work which gave the house such fame.'

9. The earliest printed reference that links Salesbury to Cae Du that I have found is in Thomas Richards, *Antiquae linguae britannicae thesauras* (1815). There is a handwritten reference to 'Wiliam Salsburi o'r Cau dû yn Llansannan'. It is unlikely to be later than 1759. (See Hugh Owen (ed.), *ALMA (1735–1786)*, Volume II, p. 404.) It refers to a copy of Salesbury's letter to Gruffudd Hiraethog (see Chapter Fourteen) (BL Add MS 14929). There may be earlier references that I have not found.

10. Raffe's will (1548), SA/1548/R2/185v, gives Llansannan as his parish.

11. In a bond of 1565 (NLW MS Gwysanau 27) Salesbury is described as 'de Llansannan'. An arbitration document of 1546 (in the NLW Panton Papers, no. 27) shows that Salesbury owned property in Llansannan and the will of his youngest son, Elisau, is headed 'T. Elizei Salusbry de Llansannan' and asks that he be buried in the parish church. A document that records the burial of Salesbury's father in Llansannan is MS Bangor 5943. It was compiled *c.*1570, but by a reliable source. (See note 23.) I have not discovered the identity of Marged ferch Siôn Pigod's husband, though the names of her sons show that he was a Salusbury. Her will is NLW S/A 3650003.

12. There are several contemporary references to Salesbury living at Plas Isa, most notably the poem 'Moliant William Salesbury o'r Plas Isaf' by Gruffudd Hiraethog (d. 1565). See D. J. Bowen (ed.), *GGH* (1990), pp. 83–5. Another Plas Isaf reference to Salesbury is in the elegy written to his wife in the 1570s by Wiliam Cynwal.

13. These positions only existed in Wales after the Acts of Union of 1536, 1543.

14. Elizabeth (Elsbeth) Salusbury, widow, of 'Place Issa' left a will dated 1625. Thomas Salusbury, gentleman, of 'Plas Issa', left a will dated 1667. These are both held in the NLW. The *Western Mail* describes Plas Isa as dilapidated, but in the 1901 census Sarah Roberts, widow, 38, and her five children are recorded as living there.

15. The report appeared in *Baner ac Amserau Cymru*, 18 September 1872.

16. The house is usually referred to as 'Plas Isa', but sometimes the form 'Plas Isaf' is used.

17. For Annes being Salebury's mother, see E. D. Jones, 'William Salesbury a'i Deulu', *BBCS*, vii (1934), p. 141. See also J. E. Griffiths, *PACF* (1914), a less reliable source. The house in which Annes grew up, Cochwillan, survives.

18. See Eilert Ekwall, *Place-names of Lancashire* (1922), pp. 70, 226, where he notes the 'quite remarkable' number of people bearing that surname (21 in 1334) in Denbighshire. (There are several instances of north Wales families having their roots in Lancashire or Cheshire, for example the Rossendales (who took the name Llwyd), the Knowsleys and the Bulkeleys.)

19. See Adrian Bristow, *Doctor Johnson and Mrs Thrale's tour in North Wales* (1995). On 2 August 1774, Johnson says of Bach-y-Graig church, 'A mean fabric; Mr Salusbury [Hester's father] was buried in it.' William's and Hester's shared ancestor was Thomas Salusbury, who is reputed to have been killed at the battle of Barnet, 1471. Salesbury was his great-grandson. (DWB notes that Gutun Owain, the bard, stated that Salusbury survived the battle and lived until 1490. See E. Bachellery's *L'oeuvre Poétique de Gutun Owain*, pp. 293–7.) Literary interest in the Salusbury dynasty no longer ends with Mrs Thrale. Her daughter, 'Queenie', is the subject of Beryl Bainbridge's, *According to Queenie*. (Among literary Salesburys not mentioned in the chapter are: Thomas Salisbury, printer (d. 1620); Henry Salusbury, whose *Grammatica Britannica* was published in 1593, and Thomas Salusbury (known to have died by 1666), the first biographer of Galileo (d. 1642).)

20. Foulk Salesbury, dean of St Asaph, appears, to have ignored his vow of celibacy. A document in the National Archive (C 1/1472/2-6) refers to 'Doarathye ... lat wife of ffoulk Salysbury

and executor and [?] of the last will and testament of the said Ffoulke Salysbury'. One cannot be certain, as Foulk(e) was a common name amongst the Salusburys, but as the case was against the bishop of St Asaph (where he had been the dean), it is likely. I have not been able to find his will, nor have I discovered if he had any children. Dorothy's second husband was another Salesbury, Robert. (There are many, many Robert Salesburys.)

21. Gwenhwyfar's inheritance and her marriage to Robert senior are noted in *HGF*, p. 17, written in the first quarter of the seventeenth century. 'Rice ap Eign' vaughan of llanrust … haveinge no yssue male … the greatest p'te of the poss'ions of that house wch weare nowe worthe a thousand markes a yeare came to the Salusburye for Robert Salsburye the elder, fowrthe sonne of thomas Salusburye of llewenny … maryed Gwenhoyvar the daughter of Rice ap Eign' … Lleyki [her sister] [received] nothing comparable.' However, Gruffydd Aled Williams in *Ymryson Edmwnd Prys and Wiliam Cynwal*, p. 347, produces a family tree, which gives Annes, not Lleucu, as the name of Gwenhwyfar's illegitimate half-sister.

22. Marged is named as the daughter of Robert Salusbury senior by D. J. Bowen in 'Cywyddau Gruffudd Hiraethog', *TCS*, p. 115. She married Pirs (Piers) ap Huw ap Ieuan Llwyd.

23. The date occurs in MS Bangor 5943, p. 356, possibly compiled by Wiliam Cynwal. It contains the pedigree of David Salusbury of Llanrhaeadr, near Denbigh. In 'Cywydd Gofyn Gruffudd Hiraethog i Ddeuddeg o Wŷr Llansannan', *GGH*, p. 315, Pirs Salbri (Piers Salusbury), Salusbury's cousin, is included. His father's patronymic name, Raffe ap Robert ap Tomas Hen Salbri, would appear to confirm the fact. The description of Foulk Salesbury (Robert and William's father) as 'son and heir' strongly suggests that the family had adapted the English practice of inheritance (primogeniture). The laws and practices of inheritance would be hugely important to Salesbury later in his life. Raffe's will (NLW SA/1548/R2/185v) shows that he died in 1548. It clearly names one son, Thomas. Piers may be mentioned in the will as an executor, but the relevant passage is particularly difficult to decipher.

24. NA, CI 781/40-1 (1533-8).

25. There was no effective attempt to improve conditions at the Fleet prior to the first half of the eighteenth century.

26. A mundane legal document (a land transfer from Salesbury to Lloyd ap Dafydd ap Meredydd) of 1546 was witnessed by Dryhurst. He is also mentioned in Salesbury's herbal (*Llysieulyfr*, p. 94).

27. See NLW Panton Papers, no 27.

28. No record of his attendance at Oxford has survived, but he is listed in Wood's *Athenae Oxonienses* (1691). Gruffudd Hiraethog also refers to his attendance at Oxford, 'Rhydychen' (line 54), in his poem to him.

29. In *The Descripcion of the Sphere or the Frame of the World*.

30. See *OBWV*, p. 130 or *Gwaith Guto'r Glyn*, edited Ifor Williams (1939).

31. See *WR*, p. 86.

32. Morgan is said to have been educated at Gwydir Castle through the generosity of Morus Wynn. He then studied at St John's College, Cambridge.

33. See *Llysieulyfr*, p. 141.

34. My thanks to Mr John S. Read, honorary archivist, QEGS.

35. For lawlessness in Wales, see Hugh Thomas, *A History of Wales, 1485–1600*, pp. 34–7.

36. In his preface to the 1902 edition of *Oll Synnwyr*, J. Gwenogvryn Evans wrote (p. xxi), 'and if Robert Salysburie, who supplicated for the B.A. degree at Oxford in May 1534 and determined in the Lent of 1535, was the elder brother of William ...' This particular Robert Salysburie is most likely to have been either: 'Robert Salysburie, Priest and one of the Prebendarys [*sic*] of the Cathedral Church of Rochester' (died March 1544, PROB 11/30/64) or Robert Salusbury, vicar of Llanrwst in 1540, who is mentioned in Robert's will and, in passing, in a court case of 1553–55 (C 1/1325/16-19). (I suspect that the Salysburie at Oxford in 1535 was the abbot of Valle Crucis, who was sent there by the local and Cistercian authorities (the abbey was already in crisis). 'Alas! Whilst at Oxford Robert Salusbury became the leader of a band of robbers, keeping the booty (£140) for himself. In May 1535, he was informed upon by one of his accomplices who had been caught, and fled.' The passage above comes from *The Welsh Cistercians*, p. 68, and is fully referenced. Salusbury was imprisoned in the Tower.

Chapter Two: Erasmus; a life-long influence

Amongst the books and articles used for this chapter were the excellent notes in Roger Clarke's translation of *Praise of Folly*, the entry in the *DNB*, 2004 and McConica, 'The Recusant Reputation of Thomas More', *CCHA, Report 30* (1963), pp. 47–61.

1. Another image of Erasmus is the engraving by Dürer.

2. In 1512 Erasmus published *De ratione studii*, based on the curriculum of St Paul's. It had a longlasting influence on pre-university education.

3. Erasmus wrote *Praise of Folly* in 1509 whilst living with More and his family. The title, *Moriae Encomium*, is a pun on More's name.

4. The works mentioned in this chapter are those that directly influenced Salesbury. They do not give a complete account of Erasmus's output.

5. These quotations of the sort of questions debated by the Scholastics are taken from *Praise of Folly* (pages 71–2 of the Clarke edition), so may be a little unfair.

6. The quotation comes from *Paracelsis (Exhortation to the reader)*.

7. A substantial section of *De copia* is devoted to the art of rhetoric.

8. See Stephen Greenblatt, *Will in the World*, p. 24.

9. Another influence on Shakespeare, or perhaps a trait shared by both men, was a fondness for puns.

10. The section in quotation marks is taken from *The Sonnets and A Lover's Complaint*, edited by John Kerrigan (Penguin Books, 1995), p. 174. Of the 154 sonnets, Number 145, dates from his youth in Stratford.

11. Salesbury's description comes from *Oll Synnwyr pen Kembero ygyd*.

Chapter Three: Oxford

1. See Anthony Wood, *Athenae Oxonienses* (1813 edition), p. 358.

2. See *GGH*, p. 84, lines 51–4. (Note that 'soffistri' is used in a positive sense.)

3. See Anthony Wood, *The History and Antiquities of the colleges and halls in the University of Oxford* (1786), p. 615.

4. For information on Oxford University I have made extensive use of James McConica's *The History of the University of Oxford*. The statistics regarding the number of halls comes from page 32.

5. See McConica, p. 522.

6. See *The baterie of the Popes Botereulx, commonlye called the high Altare*, printed in 1550.

7. For the social and political history of Tudor England at that time I have chiefly relied upon S. T. Bindoff, *Tudor England (The Pelican History of England)* and G. M. Trevelyan, *English Social History*.

8. 'Sturdy beggars' appears in quotation marks, because that is how the phrase appears in Trevelyan. See pages 110–13, 119 and 171.

9. During the protectorate of the duke of Somerset (the first half of Edward VI's reign) Thomas Smith was Somerset's (Seymour's) secretary (1547), and clerk to the Privy Council (1547–8), Thomas Beccon was Somerset's chaplain and John Hales, an M.P., was appointed as one of the commissioners to redress the problem of enclosure, but failed in his attempts to get any relevant legislation through parliament. Somerset is seen as sympathetic to the Commonweal supporters, but was as aggrandising and acquisitive as his fellow nobles.

10. Grammar schools were founded in Brecon (1541), Abergavenny (1543), Carmarthen (1543, then again, successfully, in the 1570s), Bangor (1561), Presteigne (1565), and Rhuthun (1574).

11. Salesbury is likely to have known Chester from his boyhood journey to and from Lancashire. He probably passed through at least one, possibly all three, of the other towns mentioned en route to Oxford.

12. See McConica, p. 646.

13. Ibid.

14. See Cogan, *Haven of Health*, p. 187.

15. See McConica, p. 648. He is quoting from R. L. Strong, *The Foundation and the Medieval College, 1379–1530*.

16. See McConica, p. 649.

17. See G. Lloyd Jones, *The Discovery of Hebrew in Tudor England: a third language*, p. 213.

18. See *HGF*, p. 64.

19. See McConica, pp. 166–7, 467.

20. See H. S. Bennett, *English Books and Readers 1475 to 1557*, pp. 22, 231–2, 234 and McConica, p. 467.

21. Luther was not excommunicated until 3 January 1521.

22. See Bennett, p. 73; originally from Foxe, *Actes and Monumentes*, volume VI (1887 edition), p. 804.

Chapter Four: London; Thavies Inn, Germans and Hebrew

For this chapter I have made extensive use of Brian Moynahan's *William Tyndale: If God Spare My Life* and Glanmor Williams's *WR*.

1. Foulk Salusbury's letter is in *LPFDH*, volume 8, p. 401: 'The bishop of St Asaph is dead. I have a benefice, called the deanery of St Asaph, worth one hundred marks a year, which I should be glad to put at your disposal, so that you do help me to the bishopric of St Asaph, which is not worth more than two hundred marks and a half yearly. Thus the King will get the first fruits of all the benefices I have. I have been chaplain to the King's father and himself thirty-two years. Give credence to the bearer. Whatever he promises, I will ratify.' The deceased bishop, Standish, was succeeded by William Barlow.

2. See *WR*, p. 67.

3. See *English Social History*, p. 77.

4. See Glanmor Williams, 'Wales and the Reign of Queen Mary', *Welsh History Review*, X, p. 355, and *WR*, p. 168.

5. See *WR*, p. 83.

6. See Hughson's *History of London*. For details of the Holborn area I have used *The London Encyclopaedia*, editors Ben Weinreb and Christopher Hibbert.

7. In *The Descripcion of the Sphere or Frame of the Worlde*, 1550. It also appears in *A briefe and a playne introduction*, which came out the same year.

8. See David Knowles, *The Religious Orders in England*, Vol. 3, p. 5.

9. See William Holdsworth, *A History of English Law*, Volume 2, p. 494.

10. See Moynahan, p. 48.

11. Act III, Scene IV.

12. Salesbury also mastered Spanish. There are references to these languages in several of his books.

13. See Moynahan, p. 118.

Chapter Five: *Lesclarcissement de la langue francoyse*

Details of Palsgrave's life can be found in the DNB. The entry is by Gabriele Stein, who wrote *John Palsgrave as Renaissance Linguist: A Pioneer in Vernacular Description* (Oxford, 1997), which examines *Lesclarcissement* in great detail. I have made use of her meticulous and absorbing analysis. I have studied *Lesclarcissement* (the 1969 reprint), and have added my own comments.

1. From *John Palsgrave as Renaissance Linguist*.

2. Fullonius (1493–1568) was a Dutch writer of Latin plays for schools. He became a Protestant, but was not sufficiently Lutheran for the Lutherans. Even so, Palsgrave had to tone down the Reformist content in *Acolastus*.

3. From the Scolar Press (Menston) introduction.

4. From Stein.

5. The book was Salesbury's *A Dictionary in Englyshe and Welshe*.

6.   *A briefe and a playne introduction, teaching how to pronounce the letters in the British tong* (1550), printer Robert Crowley.

Chapter Six: Early career, marriage and literary interests

1.   The book was *The baterie of the Popes Botereulx, commenlye called the high Altare.* Salesbury writes, 'To hys singular good Lord, Syr Richarde Rych, Lord Ryche, and Lord Chauncellore of Englande: his mooste fayethfull and humble servaunte Wyllyam Salesburye wysheth everlasting felicitie'.

2.   See Peter R. Roberts, 'The Welsh Language, English Law and Tudor Legislation', *TCS* (1989), pp. 19–75. Dr Roberts argues that Salesbury worked for Rich as his deputy in Wales, but was not part of his office during his time as Lord Chancellor. In a later chapter I will argue that not only was Salesbury Rich's deputy in Wales, but that he also worked for him as part of the Lord Chancellor's office during Edward's reign. Rich 'had held the office of attorney general of the marches since 1532. Rich must have held this office, which he did not relinquish until 1558, by deputy and it is perhaps more likely that Salesbury served under him in this capacity, at Ludlow and on circuit with the Council in the Marches, than in the Chancery in London.' (page 38)

3.   Siôn y bodiau (John of the thumbs) had been born with an extra thumb on each hand. The Salusburys, especially the Lleweni Salusburys, used the name 'John' more than any other, which can make differentiation difficult but I suspect that Siôn y Bodiau was the uncle of the Sir John Salusbury who had inherited Lleweni in 1530 and brother of William Salesbury's grandfather, Robert, and great-uncle, Foulk. He was, therefore, another great-uncle of Salesbury. It should be noted that Sir John Salusbury of Llewenni was an ally of Cromwell in 1533 (see note 23 below) as was Rich, who would play a part in Cromwell's downfall in 1540. The Salusburys were loyal servants of the Tudors. The DWB records that Thomas Salusbury of Lleweni fought for Henry VII at the Battle of Blackheath (1497). In *Gwaith Tudur Aled*, p. 667, the editor refers to BL MS 14866, where it is noted that Robert Salusbury (Salesbury's grandfather) had been a captain at the same battle.

4.   See Eric Ives's *The Life and Death of Anne Boleyn*, 2004 revised edition, p. 347.

5.   See *The Welsh Cistercians*, p. 67, where David H. Williams writes, 'At Valle Crucis, the problems remained, and a concerned William Brereton (Chamberlain of Chester and Steward of Holt Castle) and an anxious Lewis ap Thomas, Abbot of Cymer, tried to right affairs --- but both had a certain measure of self-interest: Lewis ap Thomas had already (May 1534) sought the abbacy for himself: Brereton wanted and obtained (in return for a loan of £1,000 to Salusbury [the abbot] and his kinsman, Fuke [*sic*], Dean of St. Asaph) the stewardship of the abbey with the tithes of Ruabon as his fee. ★The loan was to help the abbey, and perhaps the Salusburys personally, out of financial difficulties.' ★Williams gives the NA document E 326/10140 as the source of this information.

6.   See *The Life and Death of Anne Boleyn*, p. 347. A marriage settlement from 1542 (CR 72/ Appendix A/84) between Owen Brereton and Elizabeth Salusbury survives. This post-dates

Salesbury's appointment but is evidence of close ties between the families. The Brereton family was closely linked to the Duttons, to whom the Salusbury family were connected by marriage. For the dynastic and political alliances that linked the Breretons and Salusburys, see Louis A. Knafla, *Law and politics in Jacobean England: The Trials of Lord Egerton* (1977), p. 25.

7. The quote is from Roberts (above), p. 22.

8. Whitgift is quoted in Roberts (above), p. 36.

9. See *Victoria County History*, Volume 2, pp. 116–22.

10. See Arthur Ivor Pryce *The Diocese of Bangor in the Sixteenth Century*, p. xv. In *WR*, Glanmor Williams refers to William Glyn, 'vicar general', as Skevington's deputy (p. 43).

11. The quote is from Skevington's DNB entry. Although it is probable that the case dates from the last years of Skevington's life, it could date from any time between 1509 and 1533.

12. NA C 1/358/29 refers to Sydley as an auditor of the exchequer. There are other references to him as such under the name of 'Sedley', some from as early as 1493–4 (E 210/838). The reference to Bow Lane occurs in NA C 1/460/10. The reference to Elizabeth Gynkes (Jenks) being his first wife was found on a genealogical website and so may not be reliable, though he does refer to his first wife as 'Elizabeth' in his will, NA PROB 11/24/270, in which he calls himself 'John Sedley'. It is the documents that date as early as 1493–4 that show him to be older than Rich and Salesbury. There is a letter (no. 1935 in the volume of *LPFDH* that covers 1516) which records 'Great jousting at Greenwich on Monday and Tuesday last. The King, the Lords of Suffolk and Essex, Sir George Carewe, were challengers; Sir Will Kingston, Sir Giles Capell, [John] Sedley and others, defenders.'

13. Details of Rich's life are taken from his DNB entry. Drawings by Holbein of Elizabeth Rich and her husband survive. It was Roper, More's son-in-law who recorded his comments on Rich's character. The reference to his being the 'Autumn Reader' at the Middle Temple can be found in his entry in *HP*.

14. Glyn's will, NA PROB 11/25/341, refers to the church as 'Church of [illegible] Sepulcre, Newgate'. It reveals that he was married (to Margery) and had children. Skevington's will (PROB 11/25/59) has few details of interest apart from the fact that his body was to be buried at Beaulieu and his heart in Bangor. Sydley's will (PROB 11/24/270) reveals him to have been Catholic, with several bequests to religious bodies and a request for a 'trentall'.

15. The references to Rich being born in Basingstoke and being a kinsman of the Philpot family occur in his entry in *HP*, though this contradicts other sources, which state that he was born in the parish of St Lawrence Jewry, London.

16. There is still a property of that name in Llansannan.

17. *Oll Synnwyr pen Kembero ygyd*. The friend was Gruffudd Hiraethog.

18. 'Will of Robert ap Rice, Clerk', NA PROB 11/25/283, dated (probate) 25 January 1535.

19. The arbitration document is NLW MS Panton 27.

20. For details of Robert ap Rhys I have used *WR* and the DWB. The quotation concerning ap Rhys and his family is from *WR*, p. 44.

21. Details of Elis Price are taken from Williams and the DWB. The fellow commissioner who complained of Elis's 'riding about openly with his concubine' was Adam Becansaw (Burkinshaw). See *WR*, p. 67. Price's name is sometimes written as 'Prys'. He is also referred to as 'Y Doctor Coch' [The Red Doctor] on account of the red cloak he wore.

22. See *LPFDH*, Volume 9. Becansaw's letter (607) is dated 14 October 1535 and sent from Gresford. It was accompanied by a letter from Vaughan (608), which was as equally damning of Price. Lee's letter (841) and Price's (843) are dated 18 November 1535 and sent from Ludlow, where Lee was Lord President of the Council in the Marches. (It was Vaughan and Becansaw who had had Robert Salusbury, abbot of Valle Crucis, sent to the Tower for highway robbery (September 1535).)

23. The January letter (to Cromwell) (62) appears in the 1533 volume of *LPFDH*, as does the June letter (630), which is addressed to Henry Norris. The letters are sent from Denbigh.

24. If so, it was despite the great rivalry between the two men. NA STAC 2/31/108 is a case brought by ap Rhys against Foulk (and Thomas and Robert 'Salisburye'), which cites 'Vexatious suits' and 'seizure of properties'. Ap Rhys was not without taint. For example, in NA STAC 2/2 folio 39 he is charged with having 'falsely issued [a] copy of excommunication'. (It is assumed that Robert, the older of the Salesbury brothers, was the first to marry, but there is no evidence to support the assumption.)

25. Henry Standish was an absentee bishop who vehemently opposed Erasmus's Humanism (Erasmus called him an 'egregious numskull') and was involved in the trials for heresy of Robert Barnes (1526), Richard Foster, Thomas Bilney and Thomas Arthur (1527) and John Tewkesbury (1531). Salesbury's great-uncle, Foulk, was unsuccessful in his attempt to succeed Standish (d. 1535) as bishop. Standish's successors as bishop, William Barlow (1536) and Robert Wharton (1536–55) posed no threat to Salesbury. The executors of Richard Standish (Standish's nephew, whom he had appointed to a post in the diocese) brought a case against Salesbury and three others for debt in 1554. (CP 40 no 1157, O'Quinn Law Library, University of Houston.)

26. In MS Bangor Mostyn 1926, Catrin is referred to as 'Katherine verch Robert, natural sister of the said Elice'.

27. This Sir John Salusbury (of Lleweni) was the younger brother of Thomas, executed for treason in 1587. Both are mentioned in Chapter One. Ursula was the daughter of Henry Stanley, 4th earl of Derby, and thus half-sister to Ferdinando Stanley, a legitimate claimant of the throne had he survived Elizabeth.

28. Catrin's brother, Elis, went to great pains to protect her honour and status.

29. Lines 49–50 of 'Moliant William Salesbury o'r Plas Isaf' [In Praise of William Salesbury of Plas Isaf] in *GGH*, pp. 83–5.

30. In *English Books and Readers, 1475–1557*, p. 24, H. S. Bennett talks of Inge Ibert the Hereford bookseller and of a book-fair at Ludlow. In 1549 John Oswen, an Ipswich printer and bookseller, moved his business to Worcester.

31. Gruffudd Hiraethog is in the DNB and DWB. The fullest account of his life and work is in

GGH. The poem 'I ofyn Gwenyn Gan Ddeuddeg o Wŷr o Lansannan dros Lowri Ferch Robert' [To ask (for a gift of) Bees from Twelve men of Llansannan on behalf of Lowri daughter of Robert] is on pages 315–17 of that book and is discussed in an article by D. J. Bowen and Cledwyn Fychan in *TDHS*, no 24.

32.   Pirs (Piers/Pierce) Salbri (Salusbury) was the son of Foulk Salusbury's brother, Raffe (see Chapter One). Ifan's will is in the NLW; a copy of it can be read in 'William Salesbury a Llansannan', *TDHS*, 27. Maredudd ap Gronw is mentioned in *Llysieulyfr*, p.7 .

33.   For example, in J. Gwynfor Jones's 'The Wynn Estate of Gwydir: Aspects of its Growth and Development', *NLWJ*, XXII, 1981.

34.   See T. Gwynn Jones, *Gwaith Tudur Aled*, p. 95, for example, Robert and Gwenhwyfar (grandparents) and page 92, Foulk (great-uncle).

35.   MS Cwrtmawr 3, MS Gwysanau 4B and MS Peniarth 99 are mostly in Salesbury's handwriting. (See Mathias's M.A. thesis.) The fourth manuscript is MS Gwyneddon 3. The poets listed are the ones who occur most frequently.

36.   The words are John Bale's from his preface to *The laborious journey & serche of Johan Leylande for Englandes antiquitees* (ed. W. A. Copinger, 1895), pp. 18–19.

37.   Other notable collectors were Robert Talbot and John Bale.

38.   Details of Prise's life can be found in the DNB and DWB. Neil R. Ker's 'Sir John Prise' in *The Library*, 1955, details his role as a collector of manuscripts.

39.   Instead of 'lover of antiquities' another interpretation could be 'lover of the ancients'. Presumably it is these antiquities (or ancients) of whom Prise is a diligent illustrator. 'Rhesius' refers to Prise's father's name; it is the missing 'ap' which converts it to Prise (ap Rhys).

40.   See the relevant pages of the NLW website. Prise also acquired *Llyfr Coch Hergest* [The Red Book of Hergest], which by the 1560s was in the possession of Sir Henry Sidney, Lord President of the Council of the Marches.

41.   Bale's words. Leland lost his sanity in February 1547 and died in April 1552.

42.   See Toulmin Smith's *Leland's Itinerary in England and Wales*, volume 4 (1964 reprint), p. 84. The description of Llansannan is on page 98 of volume 3. The reference to 'Edwards sonne dwelling not far from Chirk Castel' is on page 72. Leland gives the 'British' name of the towns he visits, e.g. 'The castelle was named of the Britons Cair Bladun', (Malmesbury), Hereford 'in Welche is caulyd Heneford'; vol. 2, p. 65.

43.   From Salesbury's letter to Archbishop Matthew Parker (Parker's collection of manuscripts, Corpus Christi College Library, CXIV, art. 174, folio 491).

Chapter Seven: Death and discord

1.   See *The Life and Work of Davies and Salusbury*, p. 63. 'Sir' denotes a priest.

2.   MS Bangor (Mostyn) 1926.

3.   See letter 607 in *LPFDH* (vol. 5, 1535). Price was not married in 1540; his legitimate heir, Thomas, was born around 1564. In his will (1596) (NA PROB 11/87/399) Price requests Thomas 'to place my base sons in some service and not to suffer them to go beging.'

4. Salesbury had still to declare himself a Protestant. Price's actions were far more upsetting to Catholics. Back in Cromwell's employment, at his master's command he removed as many of the relics and statues of St Asaph diocese as possible, most notably the carving of Derfel Gadarn, burnt at Smithfield.

5. Aberconwy Abbey was originally at Conwy, but was moved to Maenan in Llanrwst in the thirteenth century, hence the two names Aberconwy/Conwy. In 1536 David Owen had been the candidate of the Bulkeleys for the abbotship of Aberconwy. They offered Cromwell a bribe of £100 to secure the position (*WR*, p. 67), but the Prices outbid them. In the family tree drawn up by Gruffydd Aled Williams (see Chapter One, note 21) David Owen, son of Owain ap Gruffudd and Annes, Gwenhwyfar's half-sister, was a half-cousin to Robert Salesbury's father, Foulk (Ffwg).

6. MS Bangor (Mostyn) 1926 records their joint agreement to the action.

7. See David Knowles, *The Religious Orders in England*, Vol. III, p. 197.

8. See Trevelyan, *English Social History*, p. 77.

9. See letter 1527, edited by Muriel St Clare Byrne in *The Lisle Letters*, volume v, pp. 635–6. It can also be found in volume 14, part 2 of *LPFDH*, p. 27. Viscount Lisle, Arthur Plantagenet, was the illegitimate son of Edward IV. Byrne thinks it likely that 'Lord Wyllyam' is Lord William Howard. (Note 4, p. 635.)

10. William Salesbury (Salusbury) M.P. for Barnstaple (1554, 1558) can be found in *HP*. On page 239 of *LPFDH* for 1535 (26 April), 'Wm Salesbury of Chester, alias of Suthwarke, Surrey, serving-man, &c, Pardon for having with others … entered the mansion-house of Thomas Gawyn … and stolen gold rings and seals &c.' On 22 October 1539, Edmund Atkynson sent a letter (no 373, p. 130, *LPFDH*) to 'Sir Wm Sayllysbery'. The letter is of no consequence. In the index, 'Sayllysbery' is listed as 'Sir William Salisbury, knight of St John'. For Nicholas Salysbery, see C 1/1090/5-6.

11. The document is NA C 1/1023/50. Foulke and his wife, Mary, are bringing a case against Robert Fletcher ('Fleccher') of Denbigh. Foulke became M.P. for Denbigh Boroughs in 1554 and in his entry (under the name 'Fulk Lloyd') in *HP* it is stated that his mother was Marged, daughter of Robert Salusbury of Llanrwst.

12. Elis Gruffydd was born in St Asaph. He wrote, in Welsh, an unpublished history of the world (MSS NLW 5276, Mostyn 158) that was largely a translation of English and French texts. He was the servant of Sir Robert Wingfield 'Alderman of Calais', who was his mentor. From 1524 to 1529, the most likely years of Salesbury's student days at Thavies Inn, he was keeper of Wingfield's house in London. Throughout the 1530s and probably to the end of his life (*c*.1553?) he served in Calais.

13. The herb is listed (*Llysieulyfr*, p. 28) under the name 'Ammi', which I take to be *ammi visnaga*. Under the heading *Y lle* (location), he writes, 'Yn garddae dinas Paris yn Phrainc y mae e yn llawn'. ('Kalais/Cales' and 'Paris/Pares' appear in Salesbury's dictionary (1547). Terms included tend to reflect his personal interests and experiences.)

14. There are up to twenty variations on the spelling of Bekynsaw. In the DNB and *HP*, his

entries are with the spelling 'Bekinsau'. He is recorded as being born in Wiltshire and is closely associated with Hampshire, but is thought to have connections with the Bekynsaws of Lancashire/Cheshire and, in all probability those of Denbighshire. (It was Adam Becensaw of Cheshire who complained to Cromwell of Elis Price's immoral behaviour during his 1535 inspection of the monasteries.) A John Birkenshaw had been abbot of Chester from 1493 to 1524. Maurice Birchinsaw was appointed rector of Denbigh in 1543 and William Birchinsaw (*fl.* 1584–1617) was a noted Denbighshire (Welsh language) poet.

15. Details of Bekynsaw's religious sympathies and actions or suspected actions are taken from his entry in *HP*. There is a letter to Cromwell in *LPFDH*, 22 October 1539, written after his return to Paris: 'Excuses himself for not returning as soon as he was expected. Was sore sick at Calais and Boulogne and had to travel in a cart. Did not arrive at Paris till Oct. 20. Hopes to be back in three weeks. The bearer, Mr Buclere, is he whom I commended to you, riding to your place of Murlac (Mortlake).'

16. In the 1539 volume of *LPFDH* under the heading 'Cromwell's accounts' and dated 1 October, p. 343, appears 'Bekensaw, a scholar of Parrys, 10 l.' At the bottom of the page is 'By my Lord's command.'

17. See 'The Welsh Language, English Law and Tudor Legislation', pp. 28–30. For the information concerning the Welsh law of inheritance that appears in the next paragraph. I am indebted to Dr Llinos Beverley-Smith of Aberystwyth University.

18. NLW MS Panton 27. Names are spelt as they appear in the document.

19. This will be discussed and referenced in a future chapter.

Chapter Eight: Literary beginnings

1. 'Moliant Syr Siôn Prys o Frycheiniog a Henffordd', *GGH*, pp. 71–3. Prise (knighted 1547) owned *Llyfr Du Caerfyrddin* and *Llyfr Coch Hergest* [The Red Book of Hergest], two of the five great manuscripts of Welsh poetry.

2. Vergil, born in Urbino, published his *Liber Proverborium* (a collection of adages) a year before Erasmus's *Adagia*. He began work on *Anglica Historia* in 1505 and finished it in 1533. I have used The Penguin Classic edition of Geoffrey's history, translated by Lewis Thorne.

3. The quotation is from Kendrick's foreword to the 1964 reprint of L. T. Smith's *Leland's Itinerary in England and Wales*.

4. Kendrick in *British Antiquity*, p. 87, refers to Prise's 'calm, well-ordered pages'.

5. The manuscript was dedicated to Sir Brian Tuke, one of Henry's courtiers.

6. The quotation is from *A Chronycle with a Genealogie* (1547). Kelton also wrote *A Commendacion of Welshmen* (1546).

7. Herbert (knighted in 1544) is in the DNB and DWB. Aubrey includes the story of the brawl in his account of 'Black Will Herbert'. His enjoyable gossip must be treated with a degree of scepticism. The details printed here are fact not gossip. Herbert's first wife was Anne Parr. She died in 1552.

8. The case is C 1/1385/9. The defendants were 'David Llwyd ap Nicholas' and 'Richard ap

John ap Elys'.'Salysburye' was not Salesbury's older son, Siôn (John), and Robert Salusbury (deceased father of the plaintiff) could not have been Salesbury's brother. In *The Register of Admissions to Gray's Inn, 1521–1889* (ed. John Foster, 1899), in folio 476 the name 'John Salisbury' appears under the date 1550.

9.　'I ofyn aelod ych o'r Nen Gan Dudur ap Robert o Ferain Dros Ddafydd Ifans, Porthor Iarll Penfro', *GGH*, pp. 318–20. Herbert is referred to as earl of Pembroke (title and line 26), which dates it to after 1551. Bowen thinks it likely that line 23 refers to Wilton.

10.　Details given in the chapters that deal with *Oll Synnwyr pen Kembero ygyd* and *A briefe and a playne introduction.*

11.　See *GGH*, pp. xxxii–xxxiii, and BL MS Egerton 2586, 270.

12.　See *The Coming of the Book* (Febvre and Martin, 1976), pp. 289–95.

13.　The privilege was signed by the King on 13 December 1546.

14.　The book is the 1567 edition of *Y Testament Newydd* [The New Testament] in which Bishop Davies in his letter 'Epistol at y Cembru', mentions Prise as the author. (Whitchurch worked closely with Richard Grafton, well known for his Protestant sympathies.

15.　For further information on *The King's Book* see J.J. Scarisbrick's *Henry VIII*, pp. 390–419.

16.　The date appears on the first page. A modern re-print (edited by John H. Davies) appeared in 1902.

17.　See Neil R. Ker's 'Sir John Prise', *The Library*, 1955.

18.　Whitchurch omits 'Thou shalt not steal', but includes it in the errata.

19.　For *Gwassanaeth Meir* and other manuscript sources used see R. Geraint Gruffydd's 'Yn Y Lhyver Hwnn (1546): The Earliest Welsh Printed Book', pp. 112–14.

Chapter Nine: A dictionary

1.　The privilege was not printed in the dictionary, but was included in a book of 1551, *Kynniver Llith a Ban*. From September 1545 until his death in January 1547, many everyday documents were signed on Henry's behalf with a facsimile, 'the dry stamp'. A list of these documents appears in SP4 in the NA. Salesbury's privilege is not on the list.

2.　Catherine's second book, *The Lamentations of a Sinner*, published after Henry's death, did not conceal her Protestantism.

3.　The conspiracy against Catherine Parr and Anne Askew is dealt with in many histories of Henry's life; Scarisbrick (pages 478–81) is particularly good.

4.　See J. E. Neale, *Queen Elizabeth*, p. 45.

5.　It is impossible to tell whether 'Reswm' (reason) is meant as a synonym of 'logic' or as 'cause', 'explanation' or 'justification'.

6.　Variations on Whaley's name include Waley and Whally.

7.　Mathias, for example, in 'William Salesbury a'r Testament Newydd' and in 'Cyd-ddigwyddiad Geiriadurol', *Taliesin*, 95.

8.　'William Salesbury a'r Testament Newydd', *Llên Cymru*, XVI, 1989. The Palsgrave (2/3) statistic is on page 98 of the *Taliesin*, 95, article.

9. Johnson's dictionary had approximately 40,000 entries.

10. From T. Arwyn Watkins in *Language and Linguistics* (ed. Elwyn Davies), quoted by Mathias in *Taliesin*, 95.

11. David Thomas, *Y Cynganeddion Cymreig* (1923), is an excellent introduction to the subject.

12. See *Gerard Manley Hopkins, Poems and Prose*, (ed. W. H. Gardner, Penguin, 1970), p. 250. See, also, Gweneth Lilly in *The Modern Language Review*, July 1943.

13. Example 1 is from 'I ofyn ffaling gan Niclas Ysnél gan Hywel Swrdwal' which appears in *Gwaith Hywel Swrdwal a'i Deulu* (ed. Dr Dylan Foster Evans), Cyfres Beirdd yr Uchelwyr (Aberystwyth, 2000). Examples 2, 3 and 4 are from 'Marwnad Wiliam Herbart Iarll Penfro' by Guto'r Glyn, lines 22, 26 and 75. (See *Gwaith Guto'r Glyn* (ed. Ifor Williams, Cardiff, 1939.)

14. The four examples of cynghanedd are *Cynghanedd groes rywiog* (1) and *Cynghanedd draws* (2, 3 and 4).

15. At the battle of Banbury, now renamed the battle of Edgecote Moor.

16. *Antiquae Linguae Britannicae, Nunc vulgo dictae Cambro-Britannicae, A suis Cymraecae vel Cambricae, Ab aliis Wallicae, et Linguae Latinae, Dictionarium Duplex*, London (1632).

17. This is a misprint for 'Kaer Gwydion'. Homer is 'Omer', Cato is 'Kato'.

18. *A briefe and a playne introduction.*

19. The sonnet's introduction is attributed to Thomas Wyatt, that of blank verse to Henry Howard, earl of Surrey (executed by Henry VIII in 1547).

20. 'Lunatic' had long been in use. It appears in the Lollard Bible.

21. Recorded in Boswell's *Life of Johnson*.

22. 'Less than a dozen' refers to the number of Latin words. Variations included by Salesbury, e.g. 'Kamberaec' (Welsh language), 'Kambry' (Wales), 'Kymbraes' (Welsh woman), 'Kymbro' (Welshman) increase the number to more than twelve.

23. The root of 'Cymry' is from the Brythonic word that means 'countrymen'. Intriguingly, although there is no connection to the Latin word 'Cambria', part of the Welsh-speaking kingdom of Rheged is now known as Cumbria.

24. In 'Gweithiau William Salesbury', *JWBS*, VII (1952), W. Alun Mathias lists eleven copies (NLW (1), Cardiff Central Library (1), British Library (3), Bodleian Library (1), Trinity College, Dublin (1), Belmont Abbey Library (1), Huntington Library (1), Folger Library (1), Newberry Library (1). In 'John Dee's additions to William Salesbury's Dictionary', the number of surviving copies is given as fourteen, but they are not listed.

25. The evidence that Salesbury ignored the plea to take Catrin back will be produced later in the book.

Chapter Ten: Proverbs, hope and further conflict

1. See the Introductory Note to J. Gwenogvryn Evans' reprint of 1902. The surviving copy of *Oll Synnwyr* is in the National Library of Wales.

2. Hill was a Dutchman, Nicholas Van De Berghe, who had become naturalised. His works for

Seres include *The Actes of the Apostles, translated into Englyshe metre* (1553) and *The Pandectes of Evangelycall lawe*, also 1553.

3. The documents and other information that help to date *Oll Synnwyr* appear towards the end of this chapter.

4. See MS Cardiff 6, which T.H. Parry Williams, on page lxxi of *Canu Rhydd Cynnar*, dates to 'circa 1551'. In a poem on page 291, taken from the manuscript can be found: 'rrwng', 'rrin' and 'rryfedd'. Yogh, thorn and dorn are three letters lost from the original English alphabet.

5. Tudur Aled took his name from the river that runs through Llansannan. He died in 1525, making it likely that both Salesbury and Gruffudd knew him in their youth. In *Gwaith Tudur Aled* there are two poems to Robert Salbri (Salusbury) (Senior), (pp. 20, 95). Gwenhwyfar, Salesbury's grandmother, is mentioned in the latter, his elegy. Salesbury's great-uncle, Ffwg Salbri (Foulk Salesbury) is the subject of the poem on page 92. Tomas Salbri Hen's elegy is on page 314. T. Gwynn Jones (editor) notes (p. xx) that Tudur refers to Gwenhwyfar as 'yn gares iddo' tr. 'a kinswoman to him', making Salesbury kin, too. Jones also refers on page 667 to a note in the margins of BL MS 14866 that Robert Salusbury (Salesbury's grandfather) had been a captain at the battle of Blackheath.

6. The original pages are in Welsh, of course.

7. Myrddin (Salesbury uses 'Merddin') is the original form of Merlyn/Merlin.

8. There is a misprint in the original and 'alit' appears as 'olit'. The lines are from Cicero's *Tusculanae disputationes*, written in 45 B.C.

9. The two lines are the closing couplet of 'Talu Dyled' [Paying a Debt].
   Ni ddeily cariad taladwy,
   Ni ddyly hi i mi mwy. [modern spelling]
   which is translated by Gwyn Jones in *Dafydd ap Gwilym his poems* as
   Worthy love extorts no fee:
   She has no further claim on me.
   Salesbury replaces the first two words with 'Cof am', so that the first line now reads, 'Memory of a worthy love'.

10. For the limited number of prose works available to Salesbury besides the Laws of Hywel Dda, historical chronicles and the lives of saints, see Chapter IV, 'Rhyddiaith', of Thomas Parry's *Hanes Llenyddiaeth Gymraeg Hyd 1900*.

11. The range of vocabulary is greater in Welsh as some of the words that represent large numbers, 'rhiallu' (100,000) and 'buna' (million) are not actually numerical in origin.

12. 'Maniffesto'r Dadeni Dysg a'r ddyneiddiaeth Brotestanaidd Gymreig' in *Efrydiau Catholig*, ii, 1947.

13. Brecon (Christ College) was founded in 1541, Abergavenny (King Henry VIII) in 1542 and Carmarthen in 1543 (re-established in the 1570s).

14. Letters that undergo nasal mutation are: c (ngh), p (mh), t (nh), g (ng), b (m), and d (n).

15. The NA reference is STAC 2/29/178. (It is reasonable to assume that the John Lloyd named

is John Lloyd of Llanarmon, a kinsman of Price; he married a Salusbury (Catherine Salusbury of Llanrhaiadr). See the entry on Evan Lloyd, his son and M.P. for Denbighshire in 1584, in *HP*.

16. Salesbury uses the words 'Kalan Mai', (May Day). Presumably he means the beginning of May or that they started/finished their journey on May Day.

17. Mathias, 'Gweithiau William Salesbury', p. 135.

18. See *WR*, p. 319.

Chapter Eleven: Building bridges

1. These books will be discussed in the next chapter.

2. In *Astronomical Thought in Renaissance England*, Francis R. Johnson describes *The descripcion of the Sphere or Frame of the Worlde* as the first science book in English.

3. Mathias, in his M.A. thesis, p. 14, argues that Salesbury returned to Wales.

4. The evidence for these connections will be produced in due course.

5. That the care of his estate and his children had been delegated to his mother and grandmother is an assumption. Both were alive in November 1546. Salesbury's eldest child would have been no more than 15 years old in 1550. Either Annes and Gwenhwyfar ran the estate in Salesbury's absence or a steward had been appointed.

6. NA ref: C 1/1316/9.

7. NA STAC 2/29/178.

8. The roll is written in Latin. This is the translation of the first third or so of the award, which appears on *Calendar of Patent Rolls, Ed VI, Index*, p. 208.

9. The most useful information on Sir John came from *HP*.

10. See H. E. Bell's *An Introduction to the History and Records of the Court of Wards and Liveries*, p. 16.

11. The bulk of the information used in the following pages to show the inter-connectedness of the leading Protestants of Edward's reign has been gleaned from the DNB. In addition, I have used Benjamin Woolley's *The Queen's Conjuror* (for John Dee), Winthrop S. Hudson's *John Ponet* and C. A. Bradford's *Blanche Parry, Queen Elizabeth's Gentlewoman* as well as more general books on the period.

12. Rich did not take over immediately. Paulet held the post for a few months after Wriothesley's dismissal.

13. *The baterie of the Popes Botereulx*.

14. The entry for Southwark starts on page 278 and finishes on page 279. (Volume 3 of *The Calendar of Patent Rolls, Edward VI*.)

15. The two books were *A briefe and a playne introduction* and *The Descripcion of the Sphere or Frame of the Worlde*.

16. Branches of the Poyntz family were closely linked to Tyndale.

17. The address appears in a work from 1547 by Philip Nicolles and dedicated to Peter Carewe. It is in the Lambeth Palace Library, bound with other works printed by Day and Seres and with Salesbury's *The baterie of the Popes Botereulx*.

18. The phrase 'ordained by Ridley' occurs often. It should not be assumed that this was the first time that the person had been ordained.

19. Foxe is the celebrated chronicler of the Protestant martyrdoms. His *Actes and Monumentes* was printed by John Day in 1563.

20. In *A briefe and a playne introduction*.

21. In 1567 Salesbury needed the signatures of the five Welsh bishops (St Davids, St Asaph, Bangor, Llandaf and Hereford). The bishops were not available and so Grindal, as bishop of London, signed instead.

22. See Letter XXXVI, *Original Letters relative to The English Reformation*, Vol. 1 (1846), pp. 71–3 (ed. Rev. Hastings Robinson). In this letter, to Henry Bullinger, Hooper writes, 'Tell my excellent friend, master Gesner, that there is on the road for him a Welsh dictionary, and some writings in the language of Cornubia, commonly called Cornwall.' (tr.) Gesner wrote a book on language which was published in 1555.

23. The quotation comes from Smith's DNB entry.

24. See Peter Lucas, 'Sixteenth Century English Spelling Reform and the Printers in Continental Perspective: Sir Thomas Smith and John Hart', *The Library*, 2000.

25. Another quotation from the DNB.

26. Stanley Wicken refers to the Bangor manuscript in 'William Salesbury and the Dutch Connection', *TDHS*, 46, pp. 52–8.

27. Blanche Parry became Elizabeth's nurse at the time of Ann Boleyn's execution (Elizabeth was three) and served her for the rest of her life, becoming Chief Gentlewoman of the Queen's Household.

28. For Thomas Parry's role in protecting Elizabeth, see Starkey's *Elizabeth*.

29. The evidence for Cecil speaking Welsh is that the deposed and exiled bishop Morris Clynnog wrote to him in that language. An extensive extract from this letter can be found in Chapter Four, 'Ysgol Milan', in *Y Traddodiad Rhyddiaith* (Gwasg Gomer, 1970), pp 108–9. A full version of the letter appears in *Rhyddiaith Gymraeg II* (1956), pp. 21–4.

30. NLW MS 3024. See Robin Flower, 'Richard Davies, William Cecil, and Giraldus Cambrensis', *NLWJ*, vol. 3 (1943), pp. 12–13.

31. The three 'favours' of Cecil and Grindal are dealt with in later chapters.

32. The two quotations come from page 21 and page 3 of *Llysieulyfr*: 'Yn y garddae y tyf y gwir acanthi. Ac velly y mae Mastr Turner yn doedyt yn gardd y Duc o Somerset yn Sion.' 'Y Wermod Pontic nid yw yn tyfu yn yr Ynys honn medd mastr Twrner.'

33. Turner's works on botany are: *Libellus de Re Herbaria Novus* (1538), *The Names of Herbes* (1548) and *A New Herball* (1551, 1562 and 1568 (parts 1, 2 and 3)).

34. In the archive of Longleat House: TH/VOL/II, 1542–1557, 3 a Ruthyn College.

35. Mathias notes in 'Gweithiau William Salesbury' (p. 136) that research by Mrs Olga Ilston points to Grafton rather than Crowley being the printer of *A briefe and a playne introduction*, although Crowley is acknowledged as such in the book.

Chapter Twelve: 1550; the year of four books

1. For the letter, see P. Heylyn, *History of the Reformation* (1849), pp. 201–6 and Glanmor Williams, 'William Salesbury's Baterie of the Popes Botereulx', *BBCS*, XIII, p. 147.

2. There are copies in the British Library and Lambeth Palace Library (the latter is bound with works printed by Day and Seres), the NLW and the Folger. The book is not paginated.

3. This copy must have been acquired by Lambeth Palace sometime after the death of Queen Mary in 1558.

4. See H. S. Bennett, *English Books and Readers*, Cambridge (1952), p. 157. Bennett gives a list of translations 1475–1560. There are two entries for Ovid (p. 311), only one of which is before 1550, an anonymous translation of his love poetry from 1513. Caxton's *The Metamorphoses of Ovid* (1480) is in prose. Book 7 contains a passage similar to the first of the passages used by Salesbury, in which Medea kills a black sheep (not a 'ramme') to rejuvenate Jason's father. The second volume of this manuscript by Caxton has 'Lumley' written on its first page; Salesbury's friend, Humphrey Llwyd, was librarian to the Lumley/Arundel family.

5. Just a few lines survive of this lost work by Ovid. The variation in line length between the first and second quotations might indicate two separate sources.

6. Ponet's insults can be found in *A Shorte Treatise of Politike Power*.

7. The controversy, including Salesbury's theological arguments for both sides, is outlined in Glanmor Williams' essay (see note 1).

8. The paintings of Walsingham and Sackville are in the National Portrait Gallery, London.

9. In exile, Ponet also wrote two responses to Thomas Martin's counter attack of 1554. Ponet's work of 1549 contains no reference to Wales.

10. There are two quotations at the bottom of the frontispiece: 'It is better to mary, than to burn.' (Corinthians, vii) 'The consent of the wyll, is this burning.' (St Ambrose) The page is bilingual, but the quotations are in English only.

11. The one doubt is Salesbury's use of the word 'text' in both versions.

12. The asterisk is in the text and in the margin next to it is printed, 'Thys was the eightenth auncestor from kinge Edward the syxtt.'

13. The twelve are named: 'Morgenewe the judge'; 'Kyfnerth his sonne'; 'Gweir vap Rufaun'; 'Gronoy vap Moridic'; 'Retwyd the judge'; 'Idic the judge'; 'Gwybery the olde, of lowe kenyn'; 'gurthnerth lhoyt his sonne'; 'Gwyn Vaer, he that was owner of Llantathun and of the house where they sate than in parliament'; 'Gogaune Divet'; 'Bledrus vap Bleydud'. 'Medwan ail Kerist' appears in the Welsh list, but not in the English. 'Of lowe kenyn' is the translation of 'o is kennen', Gwybery's address.

14. In the Welsh version the date is given as 909, Crowley putting 'viii' instead of 'xiiii'. Anastasius III was Pope from 911 to his death in 913. Presumably he gave his blessing to the legal code shortly before his death and it became law the following year after the Welsh party's long journey back from Rome.

15. See the 1850 edition of the work, edited by Henry Walter, p. 158.

16. Salesbury had already commented on the dispute in his dictionary (the definition of 'Wynwyn' (onion)) and in *Oll Synnwyr* (the anonymous reference to Elis Price).

17. In 'Ban wedy i dynnu: Medieval Welsh Law and Early Protestant Propaganda', *CMCS*, no. 27 (Summer 1994).

18. Ibid., p. 69.

19. Professor James records three copies of the laws which do not contain the words 'kanys yn erbyn dedyf y kahat': NLW Peniarth MS 38, BL Add. MS 22356 and NLW Peniarth MS 259B, which is in the Gwentian dialect. The Welsh of clause two, as it appears in *Ban wedy i dynny air*, is: 'Eil yw kymret gwreic o escolhayc o rod kenedyl ac odenya kemrat urdeu effeyryadaeth: ac ef yn effeiriat caffael map: Ny dyly y map a gaffat kyn yr urdeu keuran tir a map a gaffat wedy yr urdeu'. (Dafydd Ifans in *William Salesbury and the Welsh Laws* (1980), believes it possible that Salesbury worked from Llansteffan MS 116, which survives, though this particular section is missing. Salesbury's notes can be seen in the margins. Professor James makes the case (pp. 75–8) for Salesbury using a lost manuscript, of which a copy (NLW Peniarth MS 259B) by his friend, Richard Langford survives.)

20. The first Catholic book was Morys Clynnog's *Athrawaeth Gristnogawl* [Christian Teaching], which was printed in Milan in 1568. Catholic literature was either printed abroad or clandestinely, as with the press discovered in a cave on the Little Orme in 1587. Catholic exiles would not have had access to Welsh manuscripts and by 1568 the marriage of priests would not have been one of the prime subjects for debate.

21. The references are in Bodl. Cod. Seld. Supra 64, ff. 16, 124b, Bodleian Library, Oxford. See 'William Salesbury, Richard Davies, and Archbishop Parker', *NLWJ*, II, p. 14.

22. I recommend the work of this overlooked hero of English radical thought. He argued that if someone is ordered to do something morally wrong, he should 'leave it undone, for it is evil.' In an age when people believed in the divine right of kings, this was regarded as heresy.

23. The letter is CVII in *Parker Correspondence*.

24. The other copies are in the British Library and the NLW. It was reprinted in 1902 in the same volume as *Yny lhyvyr hwnn*. It is printed in black letter.

25. Corpus Christi MS 454. On f. 57b of the laws are written 'extracts from Denbigh court rolls of 15 and 7 Henry vi. This suggests that the manuscript came to Parker from one of the Denbighshire circle, in all probability from Salesbury himself who may well have inserted a copy of his printed pamphlet in it. A note on the second flyleaf of this MS. referring to Bale's *Scriptores*, 'claruit hic Howel da circa Domini 914 vide Baleum. Pag. 127,' is in Parker's hand.' These are the last seven lines of Robin Flower's article, 'Richard Davies, William Cecil, and Giraldus Cambrensis', *NLWJ*, 3, 1943. Bishop Ussher refers to Bale, 'Blegored' and the Corpus Christi Laws of Hywel Dda on page 468 of his 1654 book *Annalium Pars Posterior*.

26. In 'Gweithiau William Salesbury', Mathias notes (p. 136) his thanks to Mrs Olga Ilston for bringing the likelihood that Grafton was the printer to his attention. Grafton was Royal

Printer to Edward VI and Edward Whitchurch's business partner. In 1553, he printed a proclamation of the accession of Queen Jane (Lady Jane Grey) which led to his imprisonment. He survived and was elected M.P. for Coventry in the Parliament of 1563.

27. Will of Richard Kolynburn or Kolingburn of Llangollen, Denbighshire, 15.10.71. PROB 11/53/457.

28. The first quote is from Book 1 of the *Epistles*. The lines in Latin are 367–372 of *Epistle to the Pisones (Ars Poetica)*. I used *Horace, Epistles Book II and Epistle to the Pisones ('Ars Poetica')*, edited by Niall Rudd, Cambridge University Press. The earliest translation of Horace that I have found was by Thomas Drant in 1567. Drant was a child in 1550. Once again, the spelling suggests a fifteenth century source for the translation. Horace's poetry gives support to the linguistic philosophy of Erasmus and Salesbury, e.g. 'Words also, new and lately coined, will gain credit, if, slightly altered, they fall from a Grecian origin' and 'I struggle to be brief and I become obscure.'

29. For 'rh' Salesbury gives 'rr' as used in *Oll Synnwyr*.

30. Salesbury also uses the word 'deutche', but this appears to be a synonym for 'German' rather than a reference to 'Dutch'.

31. Although Salesbury's tone appears sceptical, he produces in the margin a verse by Guto'r Glyn, a fifteenth-century bard he respected, which summarises the bards' case:

Lhyfreu Kymry ai llofrudd

Ir twr gwyn ay than tar gudd

Ysceler oedd iscolan

Vwrw'r twr o lyfreu ir tan.

[The books of the Welsh murdered

They were hidden in the White Tower

Disgraceful [was it] that Ysgolan★

Threw a tower of books into the fire.]

★ Ysgolan was a mythical, destructive bard. The earliest reference to him comes from the thirteenth century. A similar character exists in Breton literature.

32. The line by Diogenes is 'O viri Myndi portas occludite, ne quando urbs vestra egrediatur' (O men of Myndum, close your gates lest your city leaves you). Myndum had huge city gates out of all proportion to its very modest size.

33. MS Peniarth 159 contains this anonymous couplet, but it is likely that Salesbury obtained it from a source that has not survived.

34. 'O rat un a thri' (from the grace of one and three) refers to God and the Trinity. 'Thri' is a mutated form of 'tri'.

35. The one surviving copy of this book is in the NLW. It is printed in black letter. I studied the Scolar Press 1969 facsimile of the book. Ellis's 1871 reprint was of Salesbury's edition of 1567, *A playne and a familiar Introduction*.

36. See Vincent Cronin, *The Flowering of the Renaissance* (1969), pp 180–3.

37. See Leland's *Itinerary*, Volume 3, p. 72. Leland is likely to have been referring to the John

Edwards who wrote a Latin grammatical tract in the 1480s (MS NLW 423). Salesbury's 'cosen' may have been the grandson of that John Edwards.

38. Someone, presumably Edwards himself, has written on the manuscript, 'John Edwards est possessor huius liber A[nno] 1551'.

39. Evidence for friendship with the first nine names on the list can be found in this book. Huw Dryhurst and Robert Huxley are amongst local gentry mentioned in Salesbury's herbal.

40. See 'Robert Wyer, printer and bookseller and "Some Rogueries of Robert Wyer"', H. B. Lathrop, *The Library*, no. 20, vol. v (1914), p 349.

41. See Francis R. Johnson, *Astronomical Thought in Renaissance England* (1937), p. 121 and p. 133. Bennet dismisses Andrew Borde's *Pryncyples of Astronomye* as a 'pamphlet', p. 118.

42. Salesbury uses Roman numerals. Wyer is unlikely to have had a set of Arabic numerals.

43. I studied the British Library copy. It is in black letter. Some woodblocks are diagrams, others are purely decorative. It is 47 pages long. The register of the Company of Stationers of London did not start until 1554, so putting the four books into chronological order is difficult, apart from *Ban wedy i dynny air* preceding *The baterie of the Popes Botereulx*, which would have appeared sometime in the latter half of the year but, given the urgency of the situation, as soon after May as possible. The sole surviving copy of the first edition of *The Descripcion of the Sphere* bears the date 11 February, suggesting it was the first book of the year, but it could refer to February 1551 (in the modern calendar). *A briefe and a playne introduction* is the most difficult to place. Salesbury speaks as if it was rushed into print, but it does not appear to have been. Did he wish to cash in on the success of *The Descripcion of the Sphere*? Ascertaining the correct order could shed light on the mystery of why *Ban wedy i dynny air* was anonymous and why Salesbury gave his address in only two of the books.

Chapter Thirteen: A prayer book by any other name

1. From Bindoff's *Tudor England*, p. 158.

2. The reference occurs in *A playne and a familiar Introduction* (Salesbury's second edition of *A briefe and a playne introduction*), which appeared shortly after the first official translation of the Prayer Book into Welsh. Mathias in his M.A. thesis (p. 140) states his belief that the draft petition is in Salesbury's handwriting.

3. In *Oll Synnwyr*, Salesbury had urged his countrymen to petition ('ddeisyf', mutated form) the King for the scriptures in Welsh (modern Welsh, 'deiseb' (noun), 'deisebu' (verb)).

4. Ninety per cent is my estimate. A few restricted areas of Wales (southern Pembrokeshire, the south of the Gower peninsula) were English speaking and some sectors of the urban population (towns of any size were few in number) might not have spoken Welsh, but the overwhelming majority of the population, up to and beyond the present day border, were Welsh speaking.

5. Worcestershire, along with Cheshire, Shropshire, Herefordshire, Gloucestershire and the city of Bristol came under the jurisdiction of The Council, which was based at Ludlow.

6.   The licence to Oswen can be found in *The Calendar of the Patent Rolls, Edward VI, 1547–8, Part 1*, p. 269, and is dated 6 January 1549.

7.   Cranmer's first Prayer Book did not appear before Convocation; Catholic bishops, such as Gardiner and Bonner, were still in office and might have prevented it gaining Convocation's approval.

8.   Even its full title, *Kynniver Llith a Ban or yscrythur lan ac a darlleir yr Eccleis pryd Commun* (A multitude of lessons and verses from the holy scripture to be read in church at the time of communion) avoids the words 'Prayer Book'.

9.   The verses quoted appear in Crowley's *Epigrams* (1550). The defence of the demands of the rebels appeared in *The Way to Wealth* (1550). It is possible that Grafton, rather than Crowley, was the printer. However, it is Crowley who is named as printer and that would have given Salesbury an element of protection.

10.   Surviving scriptural texts in Welsh that might have been available to Salesbury are: *Gwassanaeth Meir*, late fourteenth century, which Salesbury used (see later in the chapter); *Y Seint Greal*, fourteenth century, contains a small number of translations of verses and parables; *Y Groglith*, no earlier than the thirteenth century, quite possibly later, contains a translation of three verses of Matthew, 26, 27 and the first part of 28; *Llyvyr Agkyr Llandewivrevi*, fourteenth century, contains translations of the Lord's Prayer, the Ten Commandments, the Beatitudes, the in Principio and approximately 150 verses from both testaments; *Y Bibyl Ynghymraec*, from about 1300, which contains a list of the books of the Bible and other information, for example names and phrases, as well as a few quotations from Genesis.

11.   There were examples in medieval manuscripts of mutation not being shown, notably *Llyfr Du Caerfyrddin* [The Black Book of Carmarthen].

12.   Salesbury's description of Erasmus in *Oll Synnwyr*.

13.   The two translations here are from Tyndale's New Testament, Salesbury's rendering of the Titus is far more concise than Tyndale's.

14.   Holinshed made one error in his Welsh version, 'rhae' for 'rhac'.

15.   The wording is ambiguous. Does 'dwellynge in Elye rentes' refer to Crowley or Salesbury? I think the latter is the more likely, that quite possibly Salesbury had moved in with Crowley whilst the work was going through the press. In 1567, when his translations of the Prayer Book and the New Testament were being printed, he spent almost the whole year with Humphrey Toy, his publisher.

16.   The translation is John Fisher's from his 1930 edition of *Kynniver Llith a Ban*. There is an excellent Welsh translation of the letter in Ceri Davies, *Rhagymadroddion a Chyflwyniadau Lladin, 1551–1632* (1980). It is Davies who provides the information concerning the quotations from the *Adagia*.

17.   Arthur Bulkeley was the one native bishop.

18.   Salesbury does not mention the Gwentian dialect. Perhaps 'Demetian' is meant as an inclusive term for the whole of the south.

19.   'Not without Theseus' was a popular Athenian saying, uttered when starting a new venture. It reflected the iconic status enjoyed by the city's hero.

20. The words come from John Fisher's notes to the 1930 edition, p. xxxii.

21. For these comments on the sources used I have used the work of W. Alun Mathias (for *Gwassanaeth Meir*, see *Y Traddodiad Rhyddiaith*, pp. 70–1), John Fisher's notes on *Kynniver Llith a Ban* and Isaac Thomas (*William Salesbury a'i Destament* and, for the Old Testament readings, 'Yr Epistolau o'r Hen Destament yn Kynniver llith a ban', *NLWJ*, XXII (1982).

22. The first reading appears on page 147 of the 1930 edition, the second on page 155. The page numbers are those of Fisher's edition. The equivalent pages in the original are lxxiiii and lxxviii. In *Gwassanaeth Meir* the second reading is in verse: Salesbury uses / to denote line endings.

23. The seven readings from the Old Testament are: Proverbs xxxi, 10–31, Isaiah vii, 10–15, xl 1–11, l, 5–11, lxiii, Jeremiah xxiii, 5–8, Joel ii, 12–17.

24. Fisher also notes (p. xxxiv) Salesbury's use of some words that were starting to become obsolete. (cf. the King James Bible's 'hath', doth', etc.)

25. Similarly, 'pemped' appears for 'pumed' (fifth).

26. The English translations are mine.

27. Thomas's judgement is in *William Salesbury and his Testament* [William Salesbury a'i Destament], p. 55, Williams's in *WR*, p.178, and Parry's in *Hanes Llenyddiaith Gymraeg hyd 1900* [A History of Welsh Literature to 1900], p. 151. Parry finishes with the words, 'but that is not the unanimous opinion as regards orthography'. Salesbury's orthography is debated in a later chapter.

Chapter Fourteen: A book in manuscript

1. PROB 11/34/85. For Rhys Gruffydd marrying Salesbury's cousin, see his entry in *HP*.

2. MS Bangor Mostyn 1926, dated 1554 will be discussed in the next chapter.

3. Also in the next chapter.

4. NA E 134/38and39Eliz/Mich33.

5. See Mathias's 'Llyfr Rhetoreg William Salesbury' in *Llên Cymru*, Rhif 1 & 2 (1952).

6. Listed in Mathais's 'Llyfr Rhetoreg William Salesbury', *Llên Cymru*, Rhif 2 (1952), pp. 76–81. Mathias lists 15, including the original; the last from the end of the eighteenth century. There are 11★ surviving copies of the dictionary. Y Testament Newydd (1567) has more than 46 copies. No other surviving book reaches double figures. See Mathias, 'Gweithiau William Salesbury', p. 134. ★In 'John Dee's additions to William Salesbury's Dictionary', Gruffydd and Roberts state that there are 14 copies extant, but do not list them.

7. Wiliam Llŷn, Siôn Tudur and Siôn Philyp appear alongside Gruffudd in *OBWV*.

8. In Cardiff Library, MS Cardiff 21. The letter, of which nine copies survive, (see 'Llyfr Rhetoreg William Salesbury', *Llên Cymru*, Rhif 1, p. 261), is bound (pp. 467–72) as part of *Llyfr Rhetoreg* (pp. 475–527).

9. At St Guthlac's Priory, Hereford, and Wilton Abbey, Wiltshire.

10. 'British entertainment for a Welshman dwelling in England'.

11. Mathias states in his thesis (p. 79) that Salesbury used the 1529 Paris edition of Mosellanus.

12. The linguistic term for such a word is a 'calque'.

13. From *The Art of English Poesy, by George Puttenham. A critical Edition* (edited by Frank Whigham and Wayne A. Rebborn, 2007), p. 276. (Puttenham's book (printer Richard Field) was dedicated to William Cecil.)

14. See Geraint Bowen's *GGH*, p. lxxxvii. Note that Gruffudd is the only contemporary bard whose work is cited by Salesbury.

15. See Mathias's M.A. thesis, p. 89.

16. In 1579 Rhisiart ap Sion copied Simwnt Fychan's version. In 1593 Rhisiart made a second copy. (See 'Llyfr Rhetoreg William Salesbury', p. 77.)

17. Thomas Wiliems' unpublished Latin–Welsh dictionary was also incorporated into John Davies' dictionary of 1632.

18. Thomas Parry, *Hanes Llenyddiaith Cymru*, Thomas Parry, p. 160.

Chapter Fifteen: A Catholic Queen

1. Jane was born in either 1536 or 1537.

2. The authenticity of Edward's support for Lady Jane has been questioned. She was named in Henry's will as the future monarch in the event of Edward, Mary and Elizabeth dying heirless.

3. Jesus College MS 18, f 53. For Elis Price's role, see Glanmor Williams's 'Wales and the Reign of Queen Mary I', *Welsh History Review*, X, p. 335 and *WR*, p. 189.

4. From Rich's DNB entry. *HP* records that Strype called him a 'severe persecutor' of Protestants and that he initially supported Lady Jane.

5. See H. E. Bell's *An Introduction to the History and Records of the Court of Wards and Liveries*.

6. See Englefield's entry in *HP*.

7. Hudson gives an excellent account of Wyatt's Rebellion in *John Ponet (1516?–1556) Advocate of Limited Monarchy*.

8. Other worries were that John Bekinsau on whom Salesbury might have spied in 1539 was now an M.P. as was Thomas Martin who would soon be appointed to the Court of Chancery.

9. See *A Bibliography of Proclamations, 1485 to 1910* (ed. Steele), p. 460.

10. Details of Rogers' burial and entries for Smithfield, Church of the Holy Sepulchre and Southwark Cathedral (formerly St Mary Overie) are taken from *The London Encyclopaedia*.

11. Bishop Ferrar of St Davids was burnt in Carmarthen, William Nichol in Haverfordwest and Rawlins White in Cardiff. Ferrar had been in prison at the time of Edward's death and unable to flee.

12. Note that David Owen was named in Robert Salusbury's will of 1540 as one of the executors and curators.

13. The agreement continues: 'Attached: 1. Elyce Price of Spyttye, co. Denbigh, esq., Geoffrey Holland of Penant, co. Denbigh, gent., Richard ap John of Penmachno, co. Caernarvon, gent. Llewelyn ap John ap Madog of Llanelian, co. Denbigh, gent. and Thomas ap David ap

Llewelyn ap Howell of Garthgeuannethe, co. Denbigh, yeoman. 2. John Wyn ap Meredythe of Gwedyr, esq., David Owein of Maynan, clerk, Gruffuth Wyn ap John ap Gwedyr, gent. and Maurice Kyffin of Maynan, gent.'

14. See Lloyd's entry in *HP*.

15. See *PACF*, p. 228, p. 281, Bartrum's *Welsh Genealogies 1400–1500*, vol. 9, p. 1,573, and *Heraldic Visitations of Wales and part of the Marches between the years 1586–1613*, vol. 2, p. 160.

16. Will of John Wyn ap Maredudd (June 1559) PROB 11/42B/431.

17. See *HGF*, p. 48, 'Unkindnes and variance befalling betweene myself and my uncle Owen Wynne' over the 'caryinge of his haye from the kings meadowe in trevrew to his house at Caermelwr' which 'grewe to a great heate.' (The cause of the 1594 court case that mentions Catrin Salesbury.) See also John Gwynfor Jones, 'The Wynn Estate of Gwydir', *NLWJ*, XXII, p. 147.

18. The Maenan Mss (Bangor University Library) have some details of Kyffin's life. (His reports to Lord Burghley are preserved in the NA.) Whilst David Owen was conspiring against Salesbury, a case was brought (NA C 1/1390/41) alleging that he had obtained money 'under pretext of being collector of a clerical tenth and of an annuity due to the bishop of St. Asaph'. It is possible that Price reneged on the agreement after the court case of 1544/5 but, as will become clear later, Kyffin blamed neither Price nor ap Maredudd.

19. PROB 11/42B/431.

20. Gesner's version uses 'Santeiddier' and 'heddiw'. Salesbury would have written 'Sancteiddier' and 'heddyo' or 'heddio'. Nor is it Prise's translation.

21. See Robin Flower, 'Richard Davies, William Cecil, and Giraldus Cambrensis', *NLWJ*, 3, 1943, pp. 11–12: 'there is good reason to believe that the book belonged in 1554 … to William Salesbury who has annotated it throughout, one of the notes (p. 110) being clearly entered in that year.'

22. He appears as 'Sarisburie' and 'Sarisbury' in the Arundel Library catalogue, which contains his dictionary. See *Catalogue of the Library of John Lord Lumley*, (The Catalogue of 1609), British Museum, 1956.

23. The three 'new' children were Gwen, Marcelie and Elisau. See Cledwyn Fychan, 'William Salesbury a Llansannan', *TDHS*, 27.

24. Legislation outlawing Protestant and heretical texts referred to those written in English and Latin. Welsh had been overlooked.

25. Mary, Queen of Scots, the two surviving sisters of Lady Jane Grey and Margaret Clifford, Countess of Derby, also a granddaughter of Mary Tudor, Henry VIII's sister and a cousin of the Grey sisters. (The Grey sisters were the daughters of Frances Brandon, Margaret was the daughter of Eleanor Brandon. Frances and Eleanor were Mary Tudor's daughters.)

26. Cecil drew up Blanche Parry's will, which contains the following words, 'I do affirm that my cosyn, Mrs Blanche Apparye did confess this to be her last Will.' See C. A. Bradford's *Blanche Parry*, p. 26.

27. See David Starkey's *Elizabeth*, p. 222. For Parry's role in Elizabeth's life at this critical time, see pages 154–238. It is on page 236 that he calls Cecil and Parry 'distant cousins'.

28. See Chapter 11, note 34, for evidence of the Salusbury/Thynne contact.

29. Parry replaced Englefield as Master of the Court of Wards and Liveries and was succeeded by Cecil. See H. E. Bell's *An Introduction to the History and Records of the Court of Wards and Liveries* (1953), p. 17.

30. See letter CCVIII, *Parker Correspondence*. It was written to Bishop Richard Davies. Etiquette demanded that Parker first approach Davies (with whom Salesbury was staying) with the request, but there can be no doubt that Salesbury was the person he wished to carry out the work. Parker's copy of *A Certaine Case Extracte* is in the Corpus Christi College Library.

31. In addition to Welsh, English and the three classical languages, Salesbury spoke French (as mentioned in Gruffudd Hiraethog's poem to him), German and Spanish (both languages are frequently referred to in *A briefe and a playne introduction*). In his letter of 1567 to Richard Langford, Jenkyn Gwyn and Humphrey Llwyd, Salesbury refers critically to the standard of contemporary Breton and Cornish, indicating that these languages had also been mastered.

32. Details of Dee's life are taken from *The Queen's Conjuror* and from the DNB.

33. See *The Queen's Conjuror*, p. 52.

34. See 'John Dee's Library Catalogue', pp. 19–20. 'Tully' refers to Marcus Tullius Cicero.

35. Ibid.

36. See Simon Singh's *The Code Book*, in particular pages 26–7, which give details of the Atbash code and of Chaucer's interest in codes. The first record of a cryptogram in post classical Europe is the Bamberg Cryptogram, named after a monastery in Germany. A manuscript found there refers to a cryptogram at the court of Merfyn Frych ap Gwnad, King of Gwynedd, who died in 844. Its solution depends on the letters being transposed from Latin to Greek.

37. The two books are *Lliver Gweddi Gyffredin* and *A playne and a familiar Introduction*.

38. See E. J. Jones, 'Tra vo Lleuad', *NLWJ*, V, pp. 76–8 and Jones's article in *BBCS*, III, pp. 295–6 on 'Martial's Epigram on the Happy Life'. Not everyone agrees with Jones' interpretation.

39. Cynwal's elegy can be found in Rhiannon Williams, 'Cywydd Marwnad Wiliam Cynwal i wraig William Salesbury', *Llên Cymru*, IX, p. 228.

40. Elsbeth's will is NLW SA 3650003. It is not possible to tell from the will if Elsbeth's grandson John is the son of Reynald or William or of another son by then deceased. The 1667 will of Thomas Salusbury of 'Plas Issa' shows that the house was still in the family a century later.

41. Dee's continued friendship with Bonner seems perplexing. However, had there been a change of regime, and Elizabeth very nearly succumbed to smallpox in 1563, such a policy would have greatly aided his chances of survival. Note that Rich was also present at the examination of Philpot.

42. See *The Queen's Conjuror*, p. 59.

Chapter Sixteen: Campaigning re-joined

1. NA PROB 11/42B/431.

2. See J. Gwynfor Jones, 'The Wynn Estate of Gwydir', *NLWJ*, XXII (1981), p. 151.

3. See *HGF*, p. 48.

4. For his dealings with Robert Wynn and Katheryn Salusbury see 'The Wynn Estate of Gwydir', pp. 150–1. Jones gives NLW MS 9052E. 513 and NLW MS 9051E. 87 as his sources.

5. Katheryn was carrying her second son (the Salusbury who came to Shakespeare's aid) at the time of her first husband's funeral. Her fourth husband, Edward Thelwall, outlived her. Her portrait is in the National Museum of Wales. After her marriage to Morus Wynn, Katherine's eldest son, Thomas Salusbury, married one of Wynn's daughters. Thomas was arrested for his part in the Babington Plot and executed. His brother, John, inherited the title.

6. The bond forms part of NLW MS Gwysanau 27.

7. The will of Margaret vz (verch) John Pigot de Llanvair Dolhaiern. Margaret lived at Cae Du. ('De Llanvair Dolhaiern' refers to her father's birthplace.)

8. The document is Wiliam Cynwal's elegy to Catrin, which refers to 'Y Plas Isaf' (line 66).

9. The description comes from *A Tour in Wales* (1773), by Thomas Pennant (1726–98). Two centuries after his death few had anything positive to say about Price.

10. Details of Tomas Price, often referred to as Tomas Prys, are in the DWB.

11. For the background of these three people I have chiefly used: Starkey's *Elizabeth*; C. A. Bradford's *Blanche Parry*; the DNB and the DWB.

12. That Seymour behaved improperly towards the young princess is well-documented (see Starkey, pp. 70–8, for example). Seymour was forty and recently married, Elizabeth fourteen. His actions cost him his life.

13. For de Athequa and Skevington's (a possible early mentor of Salesbury) and absenteeism, see *WR*, pp. 43–4, for the Marian church, also pages 188–215, and for Elizabeth's early appointments pages 221–5. William Glyn, bishop of Bangor under Mary, was the much younger half-brother of John Glyn, dean of Bangor during Skevington's bishopric.

14. For the state of the Church in Wales, see *WR*.

15. In 1596, in a Lenten sermon before the Queen, Rudd quipped, 'O teach us to number our days that we may incline our hearts unto wisdom.' He was never forgiven.

16. Leicester's actions in Wales are well catalogued in *WR*, *Bywyd ac Amserau'r Esgob Richard Davies* and *Davies and Salesbury*. Davies, as bishop of St Davids, was Leicester's prime target and Herbert was the earl's chief ally.

17. 'Insatiable cormorants' refers to Leicester's local agents in west Wales. The description occurs in a letter (CCIV, 19 March 1566) to Archbishop Parker. See *Parker Correspondence*, pp. 265–7.

18. The sources for Davies's life are *Bywyd ac Amserau'r Esgob Richard Davies*, the DWB, DNB and *Parker Correspondence*.

19. Their times at Oxford might just have overlapped. Salesbury was familiar with the poetry of Davies's kinsman, Gruffudd ab Ieuan ap Llewelyn Fychan (d. 1553). *Detholiad o waith Gruffudd ab Ieuan ab Llewelyn Vychan* (edited by J. C. Morrice), contains a poem to Salesbury's great-uncle, Foulk, dean of St Asaph, but it could also be attributed to Tudur Aled. Salesbury refers to Gruffudd in a letter that accompanies his 1567 work, *Y Diarebion Camberaec*.

20. The Privy Council (13 April 1550) commanded that all priests appointed to livings during the reign of Edward VI were to preach a sermon before the king, those judged to be particularly able preachers would be given special licences to spread the Protestant message.

21. Pettie, now rarely read, was hugely popular in his day and influenced John Lyly, whose overblown style of writing was satirised by Shakespeare. Pettie lived in Oxfordshire, not so far from Burnham (Bucks.) His words may recall the time, thirty years earlier, when Davies was in residence there.

22. Richard Davies, *A Funerall Sermon [for walter Devereux, earl of essex]*, printed by Henry Denham, 1577.

23. See *Bywyd ac Amserau'r Esgob Richard Davies*, p. 22, which quotes Grindal's words as recorded in H. E. Jacobs's *The Lutheran Movement in England* (1908), p. 346.

24. For Llwyd's life I have used: R. Geraint Gruffydd, 'Humphrey Llwyd of Denbigh, some documents and a catalogue', *TDHS*, XVII (1968), pp. 54–107: D. J. Bowen, 'Cywyddau Gruffudd Hiraethog I Dri O Awduron Y Dadeni', *TCS*, 1974 and 1975, pp. 103–31; T. D. Kendrick, *British Antiquity* (Methuen, 1950); DNB and the DWB. For his kinship to Salesbury, see Bowen's article (above), p. 114: Salesbury's aunt, Marged, married Pirs ap Huw ap Ieuan Llwyd, from whom Humphrey Llwyd was descended.

25. See Kendrick, p. 87. Llwyd wrote equally vitriolic descriptions of William of Newburgh ('a greasie monk … more conversant in the kitchen than in the historie of olde writers') and Hector Boece ('a malicious falsifier'), both of whom had doubted Geoffrey's account of history. The descriptions can be found in Kendrick, pp. 136, 87 and 69 and in Twyne's translation of Llwyd's *Commentarioli Britannicae descriptionis fragmentum, A Breviary of Britain*.

26. The Bishop's Palace at St Davids was in ruins (Bishop Barlow had stripped it of its lead). Lamphey Palace had been acquired by the Devereux family, which left the Bishop's Palace of Abergwili, a mile from Carmarthen.

27. The information on parliamentary representation comes from *HP*.

28. The two Myddeltons contemporary with Salesbury who might have supported him were the brothers Richard and Robert. Robert lived in Llansannan and was a signatory of the bond of 1565. Richard had been M.P. in 1542. His son, Thomas, made his fortune in London and financed the publication of a Bible for domestic use. Thomas's mother had been a Dryhurst.

29. There is the fragment of an appeal or petition in MS Gwysanau 27 (a collection of papers belonging to Bishop Richard Davies) to 'traduct the book of the Lord's Testament into the vulgar Welsh tongue'. Mathias states in his M.A. thesis that the fragment is in Salesbury's handwriting. Williams in *WR*, p. 236, states his belief that the petition was sent to the Privy

Council in 1561 and refers to another historian who was of the same opinion. That is a possibility, but I have found no evidence to support it, certainly not in the relevant volumes of *Acts of the Privy Council of England* or *Correspondence to and from the Privy Council*. In *A playne and familiar Introduction* (1567) Salesbury refers to his 'long desired petition', which leads me to believe that it is a draft of the petition sent during the reign of Edward VI. Davies and Salesbury lived and worked together at Carmarthen from 1564/5, which is the likeliest explanation of how this fragment ended up in a collection of papers known to have been in the ownership of a descendant of the bishop, Robert Davies of Llanerch, in the eighteenth century.

30. See *A Transcript of the Registers of the Company of Stationers of London, 1554–1640* A.D. (edited by Edward Arber, 1875), p. 89. 'Recevyd of master wally for his lycense for pryntinge of the lateny in welshe … iiijd.' The date given is '22 July 1562 … 22 July 1563.' The Act of 1563 (see the next chapter) sanctions the temporary use of the Litany (which must refer to Salesbury's version) until the Prayer Book in Welsh is available. No copy of it survives.

Chapter Seventeen: The Act of 1563

1. A complete copy of the act, taken from *The Statutes of Wales* (ed. I. Bowen, 1908) p. 149, appears in the Appendix.

2. For the background to Parliament (1559 and 1563) and for statistics quoted, see J. E. Neale's *Elizabeth and Her Parliaments, vol. 1, 1559–1581* (1953).

3. Parliament opened on 12 January (p. 92, Neale); royal consent was given to bills on 10 April.

4. These references are made in *A playne and a familiar Introduction*.

5. The list of Welsh members (compiled from *HP*) appears in the Appendix. Eleven counties had two members (county and boroughs), Merioneth had one (county), Monmouthshire three (one county, two boroughs).

6. See *WR*, p. 220.

7. See Gerald Bray, *Records of Convocation*, p. 410 onwards. The last of the thirteen later sessions after 5 March was on 14 April. There were two later sessions, in October 1564 and May 1565. The next convocation was in 1567. Mr Peter Young and Ms Ruth Loughrey, archivists at York Minster have informed me that the Convocation of 1563 took place at York. For Davies's attendance at all the readings, see *Journal of the House of Lords*, (London, 1846), pp. 610–13. See also *WR*, p. 238.

8. See Neale, p. 41.

9. Cecil's letter is reprinted in T. Wright's *Queen Elizabeth and Her Times*, vol. 1 (Oxford, 1838), p. 127. It is fifteen paragraphs long. The quote regarding the pardon from the Pope comes from a footnote on page 127 of Wright's book. Note that Thomas Wilson M.P. and colleague of Cecil was the author in 1553 of *The Arte of Rhetorique* and that Richard Grafton, the printer, who may have collaborated with Salesbury and Crowley in 1551, was M.P. for Coventry.

10. For example, 'A.H.D.' who wrote his entry in *HP*.

11. See D. J. Bowen, *GGH*, p. 98. See also 'Cywyddau I Dri O Awduron Y Dadeni', *TCS* (1974, 1975) and Geraint Gruffydd, 'Humphrey Llwyd a deddf Cyfiethu'r Beibl i'r Gymraeg', *Llên Cymru*, IV. Gruffudd had used 'Perl mewn Tŷ Parlment' in his cywydd to John Prise.

12. This was the last parliament in which Cecil sat as an M.P.

13. See Stow's *Survey*, 1754 edition, vol. 1, pp. 138–9, 'The Bishop of St David's had his inn over against the north side of this Bridewell' and 'This place of the Bishop of St David's was granted in the time of Edward VI, it was granted in fee farm for a mark rent to Dr Huick the physician. Under which purchase the same was enjoyed long after.' My thanks to Mrs Nora Rees, sub-librarian at St Davids Cathedral Library, for her help in this matter. (Stow also states that 20,136 died in the 1563 outbreak of the plague.)

14. See Neale, pp. 122, 125.

Chapter Eighteen: The translation

1. Biographical details of the bishops are taken from *WR*, *Bywyd ac Amserau'r Esgob Richard Davies*, the DWB and the DNB (for Scory).

2. See *Parker Correspondence*, p. 265, letter CCIV. The 'request' refers to Davies's translating some of the O.T. books for the 'Bishops' Bible'.

3. Three pieces appear in this chapter. So few works survive, all brief and light in nature apart from the lines to Games, that a critical assessment is impossible.

4. From *A briefe and a playne introduction*.

5. See *WR*, p. 241. *Timothy 1* is the only one of the epistles that appear in Gwysanau 27 of which a version appears in the *Testament Newydd* of 1567. The other 1567 epistles by Davies were *Hebrews*, *James* and *Peter (1 and 2)*.

6. See Williams, *Bywyd ac Amserau'r Esgob Richard Davies*, pp. 50–4, 73–4.

7. Though others were involved in the translation, notably Gilby, Whittingham is generally credited as its chief 'author'.

8. See David Bellos, *Is That a Fish in Your Ear?*, p. 176.

9. There are just a handful of readings from the O.T. in the Prayer Book.

10. The text was *The Life of Gruffudd ap Cynan*.

11. It is possible that Salesbury went to Carmarthen as early as 1563; evidence produced later in this chapter makes 1564/5 more likely.

12. I have assumed that Llwyd's lost works, *An Almanacke and Kalender* and *De Auguriis* were not published.

13. The words are from Peter Betham's dedication to Sir Thomas Audley of his book, *The precepts of warre* (1544). See Bennet's *English Books and Readers, 1475–1557*, p. 174.

14. It is the county museum. Archbishop Laud commissioned the new building during his tenure as bishop.

15. Davies, '(Loving intirely the Northwales men) whom he placed in great numbers … kept an exceeding great post, Having in his service younger brothers of ye best houses in yt country,

to whom with his own sons … he gave ym good maintenance and education.' *HGF*, pp. 63–4.

16. The reference to Bowen comes in letter CCIV as does, 'Mr Doctor Aubrey and others, insatiable cormorants'. Aubrey was the grandfather of the diarist.

17. For the Llanddewi Brefi case, see *WR*, pp. 331–3 and *Bywyd ac Amserau'r Esgob Richard Davies*, pp. 58–62.

18. However heroically Essex fought, he would today be categorised as a war criminal, particularly for his slaughter of women and children on Rathlin Island.

19. See *Bywyd acAmserau'r Esgob Richard Davies*, p. 55.

20. Letter CCVIII of Parker's correspondence. Byron referred to Armenian's 'Waterloo of an alphabet' whilst trying, and failing, to learn the language. See Fiona McCarthy, *Byron, Life and Legend*, p. 32.

21. Salesbury's letter to Parker concerning the 'quire' is in the Corpus Christ College Library, Cambridge. It is partly reproduced in Robin Flower, 'William Salesbury, Richard Davies, and Archbishop Parker', *NLWJ*, II (1941).

22. 'Bishop Sulien, Bishop Richard Davies, and Archbishop Parker', *NLWJ*, no 3 (1948), pp. 215–19.

23. See *Bywyd ac Amserau'r Esgob Richard Davies*, p. 65, which contains details of the advowsons, the seals and the case brought by Hugh Price (NA C 3/57/6). For further corruption by Huet and Davies, see *WR*, p. 297. Note that Isaac Thomas is quite complimentary towards Huet's translation of Revelations, *William Salesbury and his Testament*, p. 99.

24. Davies's and Huet's contributions amount to approximately eighteen per cent of the text of the New Testament.

25. See Isaac Thomas, *William Salesbury a'i Destament/William Salesbury and his Testament*, p. 71.

26. NA C 3/177/93. The case against Leeke is in R. B. McKerrow, *Dictionary of Printers and Booksellers in England, Scotland and Ireland and of Foreign Printers of English Books* (TBS, 1910), p. 267. Elizabeth became queen in November 1558 and was crowned in January 1559. McKerrow gives the 'fifth year' as 1564.

27. See Joyce and Victor Lodwick, *The Story of Carmarthen*. In the will of Elizabeth Toy (Humphrey's mother), PROB 11/48/210, proved July 1565, there is a bequest to 'Robarte', 'the son of Humfrie Toye of Carmarthen'.

28. The letter is reprinted in W. Alun Mathias, 'Gweithiau William Salesbury', *JWBS*, 7 (1952).

29. See *The Life and Work of Davies and Salesbury*, pp. 5–8. The guarantors are Peter Salesbury of Penglogor, Ieuan ap John Pygot (Chwybren), Robert ap John ap Llewelyn (Deynant), Lewis ('Lodowicum') ap Meredydd (Penalet), Meredydd ap Thomas , Thomas ap Grono and Hugh ap David ap John, which Thomas counts as eight (he may have counted Thomas ap Rice Wyn, the lender, as a guarantor). It is possible the bond dates from just before Salesbury moved to Carmarthen.

30. See Mathias's M.A. thesis, p. 238.

31. Dwnn's englyn is in MS Hafod 26, p. 223. See also Thomas Parry, 'Tri Chyfeiriad at William Salesbury', *BBCS*, IX. Translating/interpreting the words is challenging; 'uchi' does not appear in a dictionary, nor in the list of archaic words used by Gruffudd Hiraethog; it may just be a variant of 'chi' (you). 'Wychaer' may be a variant of 'gwychr' (brave), which does appear in Gruffudd's vocabulary.

32. The date 22 September 1565 appears on the back of the first of the *englynion* that Salesbury wrote to Dwnn. The second bears the words, 'Wiliam Salsbri a'i cant 1566'. It could be that Salesbury's 'Farewell' ('Yn iach') indicates that he is leaving Carmarthen for London rather than that he has paid a second visit to Dwnn. The two poems appear in MS Llansteffan 133. They can also be found in G. H. Hughes's 'Y Dwniaid', *TCS* (1941), pp. 115–49. Dwnn's manuscripts would have provided valuable examples of vocabulary, constructions and idioms.

33. See Donne's entry in the DNB.

34. The poem is in the Appendix and on page 78 of *The Life and Work of Davies and Salesbury*. Games was High Sheriff in 1558 and M.P. for Brecon from 1542 to 1554. He appears in *HP*. Bindoff notes the absence of his name after 1564. Salesbury's poem is the only evidence of the year and the cause of his death (a fall onto a blade). Sir Roger Vaughan, M.P. for Brecon Boroughs in 1563, was his brother-in-law.

35. See *GGH*, p. xxiv.

Postscript

36. See Linne R. Mooney, 'Chaucer's Scribe', *Speculum* (January 2006), pp. 97–138.

37. See John M. Manley and Edith Rickert, *The Text of The Canterbury Tales*, Volume 1, Chicago (1940), pp. 279–82.

38. Elizabeth Done, born 1413, daughter of Elizabeth Done, neé Dutton, married Thomas Salusbury of Llewenni (date unknown). CR 72/Appendix A/84, dated 1542, is a marriage settlement in which Owynne Brereton, son and heir of John Brereton, agrees to marry Elizabeth, daughter of John Salusbury.

39. In 1859 the last of the Vaughans of Hengwrt bequeathed the manuscript collection to W.W.W. Wynne of Peniarth. That is why the collection is referred to as the Peniarth rather than the Hengwrt.

40. For Scribe B (Pinkhurst) being the Boece scribe, see Estelle Stubbs, 'A New Manuscript by the Hengwrt/Ellesmere Scribe?', *JEBS*, Volume 5 (2002), p. 161.

41. Salesbury's address to John Edwards in which he mentions his 'cousin's' ability with scientific instruments appears in *The Descripcion of the Sphere or Frame of the Worlde* (1550). Edwards' ownership of the manuscript is dated from 1551.

42. See 'The Merthyr Fragment', *NLWJ*, vol xxv, no. 1 (1987).

43. See *HP* (Bindoff), p. 463.

44. See Terry Jones, *Who Murdered Chaucer?*, pp. 330–5.

45. For the dangers involved, see Chapter 13 of Terry Jones's *Who Murdered Chaucer?*

46. See *The Text of The Canterbury Tales*, Manly and Rickert, p. 282. In 1404, Sir John Oldcastle captured Builth Castle from the Mortimer family, who had switched their allegiance to Glyndŵr.

47. Giraldus Cambrensis, NLW MS 3024; Roger Bacon, BL Cotton Tiberius C.V., ff 2-151; Vaughan wrote a 'Memorandum to enquire for the lyfe of St. Theulothoc alias Teulacus bishop of St Assaph sometime. Ex libro W. Salb.' (See Daniel Huws, *Medieval Welsh Manuscripts*, p. 302.)

48. Quotations from Jackson J. Campbell, *A New Troilus Fragment* (Publications of the Modern Language Association of America, 1958), p. 305.

49. Details of Warburton taken from the DNB.

Chapter Nineteen: A Godly enterprise

A 1567 Prayer Book survives in good condition in the John Rylands Library, Manchester. A facsimile edition was produced in 1965. For this chapter I have studied the facsimile and the two copies of *A playne and a familiar Introduction* held in the British Library.

1. The words are taken from a letter to Toy printed as the preface to *A playne and a familiar Introduction*, published on 16 May.

2. This section occurs in Salesbury's revamped letter to Colyngborne.

3. These two quotes, changed in their order, are taken from a passage in Salesbury's letter to Toy in *A playne and a familiar Introduction*. They occur after the sentence that starts, 'I knowe well M. Toy ...' 'What needed thys waste?' is a quote from Matthew 26, where Christ is anointed with precious (and expensive) ointment and Judas betrays him. Two groups might have had a personal grudge against Salesbury, Elis Price and his supporters and the Wynns of Gwydir, who had lost control of Plas Isa. However, Salesbury had taken Catrin back as his wife, thus satisfying Price's sense of family honour. What little evidence there is suggests the two men had reached some sort of accommodation. The Wynns might have pursued a vendetta, but there is no evidence and Sir John Wynn in his *HGF*, written during the 1620s, writes approvingly of Salesbury. The contemporary of Morgan quoted ('Could the devil ...') was Maurice Kyffin, who supported the cause of the Welsh Bible, but such was his animosity towards Salesbury (personally and towards his orthography) that he might well be regarded as a suspect.

4. There were approximately 800 parishes in Wales in 1567. See *WR*, p. 242. The words in inverted commas come from the 1563 Act.

5. Apart from these areas the country was Welsh speaking. When George Borrow toured Wales, it was not until he journeyed between Newport and Chepstow that he found people who could not speak Welsh. See *Wild Wales* (1862).

6. There are some precedents for this practice in ancient manuscripts and scholars such as Salesbury tended to revere examples from the past. Occasionally he forgets to obey his own rules: 'vym hecotau' (my sins) occurs on the first page.

7. Tolkien refers to Salesbury and c/k in 'English and Welsh', p. 165, printed in *The Monsters & the Critics* (1983). (An occasional 'k' creeps into Salesbury's text.)

8. The opening lines of Donne's 'Hymne to God my God, in my sicknesse' (1623).

9. See R. Geraint Gruffydd, 'The Welsh Book of Common Prayer', *Journal of the Historical Society of the Church in Wales*, vol. xvii (1967), p. 47. Cawood had been an overseer of Elizabeth Toy's will and Jugge a witness. The will of Robert Toy (Humphrey's father), PROB 11/37/549, proved March 1556, reveals that at the time of Toy's death, Jugge was living in a house owned by him. Jugge and Cawood are mentioned several times (John Whaley, printer of Salesbury's dictionary, is also mentioned) and Cawood is one of the four witnesses (as is Whaley).

10. In her will Humphrey Toy's mother left Erasmus Awdeley 'myne apprentice fortie shillings'. See E. J. Jones's 'Martial's Epigram on the Happy Life', *BBCS*, III, p. 296. Awdeley's *An Introduction for to lerne to recken with the pen, or with the Counters according to the trewe Cost of Algorisme* ... was printed in 1574. The work on navigation was *The Rutter of the Sea* by Pierre Garcie, translated by Robert Copland (1560) (originally printed by Copland half a century earlier). Two of his ballads are: *The Wonders of England* (1559), and *A godly ditty ... against all Traytours, Rebels and Papasticall Enemies*, 1569 (?). The sermon was *A Sermon made at the Gyllde Halle in London the xxix day of September 1574*. Robert Copland was a translator and printer from the early part of the sixteenth century. His *The hye way to the Spytlell hous* was the inspiration and a source for Awdeley's *Vacabondes*. It contained details of 'Thieves' Cant' the secret language of thieves, so coded messages, such as Salesbury's, are likely to have been of interest to him.

11. See E. J. Jones, 'Tra Vo Lleuad (Psalm 27)', *NLWJ*, vol. v, pp. 76–8. R. Geraint Gruffydd (The Welsh Book of Common Prayer, 1567, 1967) disagrees with Professor Jones's interpretation. Perhaps it is no more than a coincidence, but Denham printed 'At the sign of the star', Paternoster Row.

12. The English Prayer Book of 1662 was the first to include the Psalms.

13. The letter was copied by Thomas Wiliems in MS Peniarth 77, pp. 165–6 and is reprinted in *Report on Manuscripts in the Welsh Language*, Vol. I.

14. A copy of the statute can be found on page 512 of the volume named above. The copy sent by Salesbury is unlikely to have been an old one.

15. It was Toy who paid the 4d for the licence to print the book. See E. Arber, *Transcript of the registers of the Company of Stationers of London, 1554–1640* (1875–94).

16. The missing sections concern the ancient Britons, with a quotation from Lucanus, and a brief reference to the Queen.

17. There are a few, minor changes to the original letter, the most significant being in the sentence where Salesbury writes about his opponents. In 1550, he writes, 'cancred malicious checks of all those, who at all times ...' This is changed to, 'those, who most lyke filthie flies forsaking the sownde partes, feede only on the sores, at all times ...' The information on cynghanedd on the last page of the 1550 edition is dropped.

Chapter Twenty: The New Testament

Many copies of the N.T. survive. I studied one the British Library copies.

1. In C. A. Bradford's *Blanche Parry, Queen Elizabeth's Gentlewoman*, pp. 32–3, he writes, 'As the servant of a Queen who retained in her own private chapel the ornaments and symbols of the Church of Rome and was, therefore, thought to be personally favourable to the Old Faith, it may well be thought that Blanche was either Roman Catholic or at least what now might be termed 'High Church.' and '… since the young princess' ladies were mostly chosen for their Protestantism (for example, the well-known cases of Kate Ashley and Elizabeth Sands) the presumption is that Elizabeth's attitude toward church ceremonies may well have been due to Blanche's early influence.'

2. The quotations come from the Parker Correspondence: ccxi, 3 April 1566; ccxii, 4 April; ditto and ccxiii.

3. Hugh's will is in Cledwyn Fychan, 'William Salesbury a Llansannan', *TDHS*, 27.

4. 'Golaunt' should read as 'golauni'. The English version is Tyndale's (1526).

5. Cambria, presumably a Welsh version of Britannia; Martia is Marcia, who appears in Geoffrey of Monmouth as the wife of King Guithelin and the author of *Lex Martiana*; Bunduica, Boudicca; Claudia Rufina, a woman of British ancestry known to Martial and mentioned in explicit language in his *Epigrams* (XI; 53)★; Helena, Constantine's mother and claimed as British (mentioned by Camden in *Britannia* and Ussher in *Britannicarum Ecclesiarum Antiquitates*); St Ursula of Cornwall, went to settle Brittany with eleven thousand maidens, but ended up in Cologne where she and the maidens were executed. ★The 'explicit verses' arouses suspicion that Salesbury must be referring to another Claudia Rufina. If so, I have not been able to identify her.

6. Davies states that the only ancient scriptural translations into Welsh that he had seen had been in the collection of his kinsman, the bard Gruffudd ab Ieuan.

7. See D. Myrddin Lloyd, 'William Salesbury and Epistol E M at y Cembru', *NLWJ*, Vol. 2 (1941), pp. 14–16.

8. The Geneva Bible of 1560 was the first in English to have the chapters divided into verses. Following that precedent might not have pleased the Queen.

9. The copy of the letter is in NLW MS 6434. It is reproduced in Mathias's 'Gweithiau William Salesbury'.

10. Abyl i pop pethae boddlono
    Anhael pob cypydd
    Dewys or ddwy vachddu hwch
    Yspys y dengys pop dyn
    O ba 'raidd i vo i wreiddyn.

    [Able (is) everything that satisfies (?)
    Ungenerous is every miser
    Choose of two the small black sow (?);
    Clearly shows every man
    From what degree is his origin.]

11. It was common for a bard to liken his patron's hospitality to that of Nudd. I suspect that 'Sernan' is a misprint of 'Seruan'.

12. I have studied the fragments. However, the details concerning the book, its manuscript copy and the letter are taken from W. Alun Mathias's essay, 'Gweithiau William Salesbury'. It is research of the highest quality. One point not made by Mathias is that in 1566 Awdeley had printed *The golden Booke of Marcus Aurelius Emperour*. Salesbury's book contained translations of Marcus Aurelius.

13. Thomas Wynn does not appear to be a member of the Gwydir dynasty.

14. *Lloegr drigiant* is lost, but a copy (Peniarth 155) by Richard Phylip survives.

15. See Rachel Bromwich, 'William Camden and Trioedd Ynys Prydain', *BBCS*, XXIII, pp. 14–17. For Davies copying the two essays see page 133 of 'Gweithiau William Salesbury'. Vaughan's letter to Ussher is in MS Rawlinson Letters 89, ff. 101.

16. They may have come from Richard Morris's library, which was passed on to the British Museum in 1844.

17. Jenkyn Gwyn co-authored a poem with Dee. See F. G. Payne, 'John Dee and Jenkyn Gwyn', *RST*, vol. 31 (1961). See also F. G. Payne, 'A Letter by John Dee', *NLWJ*, vol. 1 (1939).

18. Llwyd's will is in the NLW (SA/1569/R1/116v).

19. See Lambeth MS 2003, f. 1.

20. See R. Geraint Gruffydd, 'The Welsh Book of Common Prayer, 1567', *JHSCW*, p. 53.

21. See Isaac Thomas, 'Sallwyr Llyfr Gweddi Gyffredin 1567', *NLWJ*, XXII, vol. 4 (1982), p. 401. 'Yn wir, po fwyaf y darllenir ar Sallwyr 1567, mwyaf yr eniller y darllenydd gan gyfaredd ei sain a'i synnwyr. Yn sicr, gwelir camp Salesbury fel cyfieithydd yr Ysgrythurau ar ei disgleiriaf yn y fersiwn hwn.'

22. The quotation comes from 'Yr Evangel, Y trydydd Sul yn Advent', p. xij. The English is Tyndale's of 1526.

23. Thirty-six years, if the 1563–7 use of *Kynniver Llith a Ban* (1563–7) is counted.

24. See MS Hafod 26, p. 204. Wiliems (a Catholic) later quarrelled with Salesbury over religion and scribbled out the passage. See 'Tri Chyfeiriad at William Salesbury', *BBCS*, XI.

25. The date of Salesbury's death is discussed in a later chapter.

26. Mathias's verdict of 'anwastad' comes from page 185 of his M.A. thesis.

27. See 'Dylanwad y Beibl ar yr Iaith Gymraeg' in *Y Gair ar Waith*, R. Geraint Gruffydd (ed.) (1988). The words mean: advent, mirthful, filth, non-beneficial, cleft, monstruous, hindrance, to forget, forgetful, unbelief, unacceptable, ill-matched, to disagree, re-birth, resurrection, imperfection, doubtful, impossible, unprofitable, manifestation, to breathe, unrepentant, un-renowned, greeting (address), unwilling, immortality, ungodliness, savage, untruth, ignorance, preposition, orator, to arm, to have dominion, impression, to print, to convince, fond of money, to give odour, dreadful, terrible/wonderful, guide, to confirm, remembrance, to rise again, prithee.

28. In the foreword to the 1939 reprint of Robert's Grammar, Professor G. J. Williams writes,

'Indeed, it can be inferred that it was observations by Salesbury in his book on the sounds of Welsh, *A briefe and a playne introduction* … that caused him [Gruffydd Robert] to start studying the Latin element in Welsh, one of the most notable sections in the Grammar.' Robert's Grammar has been reprinted by the Scolar Press, Menston. Cardinal Borromeo was the nephew of Pius IV (pope from 1554–65).

Chapter Twenty-One: Salesbury's last book

1. 'Dyma r naill ran yn barot, rhon a elwir y Testament newydd, tra vych yn aros (trwy Dduw ni bydd hir hynny) y rhan arall a elwir yr hen Testment.'

2. John Ballinger (ed.), *HGF* (1927), p. 64.

3. Ibid., p. 66.

4. Ibid., p. 64.

5. Ibid.

6. Ibid., p. 65.

7. Ibid., p. 64.

8. For Davies, see the DNB, the DWB and Glanmor Williams, *Bywyd ac Amserau'r Esgob Richard Davies*. For Morgan, see the DNB, DWB and *Y Traddodiad Rhyddiaith*.

9. Evidence to be produced in a later chapter.

10. The elegy appears in MS Mostyn 111, 96b and is reprinted in Rhiannon Williams, 'Cywydd Marwnad Wiliam Cynwal i Wraig William Salesbury', *Llên Cymru*, VIII. Ms Williams dates the elegy to between 1572 and 1573.

11. William Llŷn appears in the *OBWV*. His work was collected and printed in J. C. Morrice, *Barddoniaeth Wiliam Llŷn: A'i Eirlyfr Gyda Nodiadau* (1908).

12. In 1574, Salesbury made additions to Thomas Wiliems' copy (MS Hafod 26) of Wiliam Llŷn's *Geirlyfr* (book of voacabulary). See W. Alun Mathias, 'Gweithiau William Salesbury', *JWBS*, VII, p. 142.

13. See Evan J. Jones, 'Martial's Epigram on the Happy Life, Simwnt Fychan's Translation', *BBCS*, III.

14. The copy forms part of Simwnt's *Pum Llyfr Kerddwriaeth* [Five books of Minstrelsy], MS Jesus 9.

15. Cynwal's *Gramadeg* (MS Cardiff 38) contains notes on 'ffugrau' (figures of speech), but these can be traced to Gruffudd Hiraethog's oral lessons, not Salesbury's book. See 'Llyfr Rhetoreg William Salesbury I and II', *Llên Cymru*, I and II, p. 74 and J. T. Jones, 'Blwyddyn Marw Gruffydd Hiraethog a Dyddiad 'Ffugrau' Salesbury', *BBCS*, VIII.

16. See T. R. Roberts, *Barddoniaeth Edmwnd Prys* (1899). The *ymryson* took place during the 1580s.

17. Edmwnd Prys, clergyman and academic, mastered the art of *cynghanedd* independently of the bards. (Hence 'poet' rather than 'bard'.) Immeasurably more talented than Cynwal, he was the great-great-grandson of Rhys ab Einion of Llanrwst. Salesbury was Rhys's great-grandson. For Edmwnd being descended from Gwenhwyfar's half-brother, see

Gruffydd Aled Williams, 'Edmwnd Prys, un arall o Enwogion Llanrwst', *TDHS*, vol. 23.

18. Elisau Salesbury's will survives in the NLW. A copy of it appears in Cledwyn Fychan's 'William Salesbury a Llansannan', *TDHS*, 27. He bequeaths three sheep to 'Lowrie Salusburie my aunte'. I have been unable to identify this person, but it cannot be Catrin's sister, Lowri, as she pre-deceased her husband, Robert, who died in 1540. Note that the will of Siôn Wyn Salesbury's widow, Elsbeth (Elizabeth) has survived (NLW S/A 3650003). She died in 1625, leaving two sons (John and William), a daughter (Lowri) and a grandson (John). Nothing in the will or any other document suggests a weakness or fragility about her late husband.

19. Details of Thelwall's life are taken mainly from DWB and source 13 above.

20. Prise's will is reprinted in *NLWJ*, IX (1955), p. 255.

21. Bale's two books are *Index Britanniae Scriptorum* (1548–9) and *Scriptorium illustrium maioris Brytanniae Catologus* (1557–9).

22. The Martial broadsheet is reproduced in *BBCS*, III (see 13 above). There are copies of the *Defensio* and the funeral sermon in the British Library.

23. For the pirating of sermons, see Chapter Four, 'Reporting speech, reconstructing texts', of Laurie E. Maguire's *Shakespeare's Suspect Texts*.

24. See Mathias's *Llyfr Rhetoreg William Salesbury, II*, p. 77. In footnote 40 of the same page Mathias cites the evidence of Professor G. J. Williams. Mathias states that Simwnt copied the work before 1575, but Salesbury's additional notes might have been made some time later.

25. The two academics are Mathias, 'Llyfr Rhetoreg William Salesbury, II', *Llên Cymru*, II (p. 74) and, indirectly, J. Gwenogvryn Evans. Mathias cites the work of Evans and in footnote 24 refers to page 234 of the *Report on Manuscripts in the Welsh language, II*.

26. The date, '1574 : 17 February' appears on page 234 of MS Hafod MS 26. 'Phisicwr' on page 204.

27. The reference to radishes is in *Llysieulyfr*, p. 126. Salesbury calls the abbey a monastery, 'Vonachloc'.

28. The English translation of Dodoens' work is *A New Herball or historie of Plantes*, translated by Henry Lyte (1578), from the 1554 French translation, *Histoire des Plantes*, by Charles de l'Ecluse. The original work was *Cruydeboek* (1554). It did not appear in Latin until 1583.

29. Mathias's conjecture is in 'Astudiaeth o Weithgarwch Llenyddol William Salesbury', p. 222. Edgar discusses the dating of the herbal on pages xxiii–xxiv of *Llysieulyfr* and on page xviii demonstrates that Salesbury used a Paris edition of Fuchs' work.

30. Edgar writes about Morris and the history of the various copies in the introduction to *Llysieulyfr* (1997). Mathias discusses the herbal in 'Astudiaeth o Weithgarwch Llenyddol William Salesbury', pp. 214–222. There are elements of Gruffydd Robert's orthography in Morris's copy of the herbal. These are discussed in a later chapter.

31. Actually, there are 149, but 'Lupines' is not given a number.

32. Edgar (pages xv–xvii, *Llysieulyfr*) believes it is Morris who continues the work, Mathias (p. 224, 'Astudiaeth o Weithgarwch Llenyddol William Salesbury') that it is Wiliems. That

there are just sixteen additions points towards Morris. Wiliems is believed to have lived until 1622/3 (DWB).

33. See *Llysieulyfr*. Reference to birthplace, p. 7; Lancashire, p. 141; radishes, p. 126; 1555, p. 145.

34. See above. The pun is on page 10.

Chapter Twenty-Two: Salesbury's successors

1. The will is published in 'William Salesbury a Llansannan' by Cledwyn Fychan, *TDHS*, 24.

2. See *HGF*, p. 64, 'for ye Bishop lived 5 or 6 years after [the dispute] & Wm Salusbury about 24, but gave over writing (more was ye pity) for he was a rare scholar.' On the same page Wynn had stated that the two men were together 'almost Two years' in work on the Old Testament. Davies died in 1581, five years after the date given by Wynn.

3. See Fychan's article (above), note 11, p. 193.

4. Three copies of the 1586 Prayer Book survive in: Bangor University Library, (almost complete), Cardiff Library (condition poor) and the NLW (complete and well-preserved). For this part of the chapter I have made extensive use of 'Y Darnau Cyntaf o Ganu Rhydd i Gael eu Printio'?, William Linnard, *NLWJ*, XXVI. He is the academic referred to and the agricultural book was *Five Hundred Points of Good Husbandry* by Thomas Tusser (1573).

5. See T. H. Parry-Williams, *Carolau Richard White* (Cardiff, 1931), pp. 55–6. It is possible that Richard White (Gwyn), executed October 1584, wrote the poem, but many doubt it. Under the version which is found in MS Cardiff 23 is written, 'Mr White', which may refer to Richard White or to his fellow Catholic campaigner, Robert White.

6. Accounts of the dispute can be read in the DNB and *Y Traddodiad Rhyddiaith* (the chapter on Morgan by R. G. Gruffydd).
   To a great extent Morgan was the author of the troubles, having arranged for the daughter of a wealthy landowner to marry Robert Wynn of Gwydir, presumably Sir John Wynn's uncle. Maredudd's nephew had wished to marry the woman, Catrin ferch Dafydd Llwyd, and so profit from her father's estate. The dispute arose in the late 1570s and was not resolved until the early 1590s. A complicating factor was that Morgan's wife (she had been twice widowed) had been married to Maredudd's brother.

7. See the letter to the Queen that appears in the 1588 Bible.

8. From Salesbury's letter to Toy in *A playne and a familiar Introduction*.

9. Williams discusses the opposition in *WR*, p. 349.

10. Morgan also gives the arguments put by opponents of the Welsh Bible (that the Welsh should learn English rather than have the Bible translated for them), stating that before that could be achieved many would die of spiritual hunger.

11. For Catholic activity in Wales see 'The Romanist Challenge' in *WR*.

12. Possibly John Edwards's son. It is difficult to distinguish the generations.

13. *A Treatise Containing the Aequity of an Humble Supplication* (presented to Parliament); *An Exhortation unto the Governours, and people of Hir Maiesties Countrie of Wales* (presented to the

earl of Pembroke (Lord President of Wales) and *A Viewe of Some part of such Publike Wants and Disorders as are in the Service of God, within Her Maiesties Countrie of Wales* (presented to Parliament).

14. Penry's translation is 'I care not faith one [*sic*] for the father that cruel man, but the sonne is a good fellowe'. From *Three Treatises*, p. 34.

15. For the two quotations from Penry, *Three Treatises Concerning Wales*, ed. D. Williams, see pages 56 and 34. In modern orthography (very similar to Morgan's) Penry's sentence would be, 'Ni waeth gennyf ddim am y tad y gwr creulon hwnnw onid cydymaith da yw'r mab.' For the list of the failings of the clergy, see pages 62 and 63.

16. NA STAC 5/J22/2, 'Jenes v. Kiffin, Hoell'. See Williams, *WR*, p. 294. Kiffin [Kyffin] is likely to have been a member of the Kyffin clan, though not related closely to Maurice Kyffin.

17. The Prayer Book, Psalter and New Testament. Also *Kynniver Llith a Ban*.

18. 'Rhyddiaith gyntefig ymhob ystyr oedd rhyddiaith y *Mabinogion* … brawddegau sengl, syml, unrhyw oedd ynddo, addas i adrodd stori ond yn hollol anaddas i fynegi barn ar bynciau haniaethol neu i ddadlau pwnc.' From *Perl Mewn Adfyd* (1929 reprint), p. xxxiv.

19. See Philip Henderson's introduction to Spenser's *Shepherd's Calendar and Other Poems* (Everyman, 1932).

20. An examination of the 1567 Prayer Book shows that Salesbury used '-au' far more frequently than '-ae'. He also used '-e'.

21. For the differences between Morgan's and Salesbury's orthography, see the relevant chapters of *Y Traddodiad Rhyddiaith*.

22. Some believe Salesbury varied his spelling to promote copiousness, but he is more likely to have been following Tyndale's example: 'howe longe shall I be with you? howe longe shall y suffer you?' (Matthew, Chapter 27.)

23. See Brian Moynahan's *William Tyndale: If God Spare My Life*, p. 389.

24. See *HGF*, p. 66.

25. The first book of the Chronicle, which in Hebrew is called Difre Haiamim, and in Welsh The Stories (Histories) of Time. The Book of the Songs of Solomon, which in Hebrew is called Shir Hashirim and in Latin Canticum Canticorum. A part of the book of Esther, not being in Hebrew, (and) is not in Chaldean and in Greek starts in the tenth chapter. See *Y Traddodiad Rhyddiaith*, p. 173.

26. There is at least one copy of the 1588 bible in the British Library. Morgan's letter to the Queen is written in Latin. I have made use of Ceri Davies's translation of it into Welsh. (See *Rhagymadroddion a Chyflwyniadau Lladin, 1551–1632*.)

27. Details of Davies's life can be found in the DWB and DNB as well as the chapter 'Richard Parry a John Davies' in *Y Traddodiad Rhyddiaith*. The best book on his life and work is Professor Ceri Davies's *John Davies o Fallwyd*.

28. The quote regarding Davies working as Morgan's amanuensis comes from Ceri Davies's 'Two Welsh Renaissance Latinists: Sir John Prise of Brecon and Dr John Davies of Mallwyd'

in *Britannia Latina: Latin in the culture of Great Britain from the Middle Ages to the twentieth century*, editors Burnell, Charles and Mann (2005).

29. Huw Machno's words are quoted by R. Geraint Gruffydd on page 179 of his chapter on William Morgan in *Y Traddodiad Rhyddiaith*.

30. Morgan had been appointed bishop of Llandaf in 1595.

31. That, too, was Davies's work and was also published in 1620.

Chapter Twenty-Three: Post mortem

1. The quotation is from *HGF*, p. 17. Wynn names the half-sister as Lleucu, but Gruffydd Aled Williams identifies her as Annes. Note that Edmwnd Prys, the descendant of Gwenhwyfar's half-brother, Gruffudd, harboured no resentment towards Salesbury and praised his achievements.

2. 'Yr oedd cyfled llediaith a chymaint anghyfiaith yn yr ymadrodd brintiedig na alle clust gwir Cymro dioddef clywed mo naw'n iawn.' The most obvious difference between Richard Davies's and Salesbury's orthography is that Davies shows nasal mutation. He does, however, use 'Cembru', 'Cymbro', 'enwedic', caredic', 'ardderchawc', 'a ddanfonawdd', 'escop', 'ceremomiae' and many other formulations that bear Salesbury's hallmark.

3. Kyffin's English works were a defence of the execution of the Queen of Scots, a translation of Terence and *The Blessednes of Brytaine*. The first of these, dated 1587, was printed by John Windet, but any connection between Kyffin and the second edition of Salesbury's Prayer Book is improbable. Kyffin's will (1603) is in the National Archives, PROB 11/102/610

4. 'Yr hwn lythyr a scrifennodd y doededig Escob mewn Cymraec groyw, hyfedr, ymadroddus, a di-ammeu wneuthyr onaw lês mawr i bob Cymro a'i darllennodd.'

5. See W. Alun Mathias's 'William Salesbury a'r Testament Newydd', *Llên Cymru*, XVI (1989), p. 61.

6. See pages 62–3 of the above.

7. See pages 60 and 66 above.

8. See Ceri Davies, *John Davies o Fallwyd* (2001), pp. 80–1.

9. See Mathias's 'Llyfr Rhetoreg William Salesbury, II', *Llên Cymru*, vol ii (1952). The first, Simwnt Fychan's, can be dated to shortly before 1575. The last known is that of the dramatist, Twm o'r Nant.

10. From T. R. Roberts, *Barddoniaeth Edmwnd Prys*, (1899), p.75. At times I have translated the sense of the words rather than their literal meaning, e.g. 'wall mawr' (great failing/ defect/mistake) I give as 'silence'. The words can also be found on page 210 (Cywydd 48) of Gruffydd Aled Williams's *Ymryson Edmund Prys a Wiliam Cynwal*. Prys also praises Salesbury in Cywydd 23 (lines 67–74) and Cywydd 32 (lines 53–8). (Prys was not the first poet from the gentry. Dafydd ap Gwilym (fourteenth century) and Dafydd ap Edmwnd (fifteenth century), for example, were from well-connected families, but they never sought to undermine the authority of the bardic system. Edmwnd Prys, shaped by humanist values, did.)

11. See Gruffydd, R. G. and Roberts, R. J., 'John Dee's additions to William Salesbury's Dictionary', *TBS*, 2002.

12. See *Llysieulyfr*, pp. xxxi–xxxii.

13. See *Medieval Welsh Manuscripts*, p. 302.

14. It is possible that it was Egerton's son who acquired the Ellesmere.

15. See Richard Ovenden's 'Jaspar Gryffyth and his books', *British Library Journal*, vol. 20, no. 2 (1994). Note that Gryffyth was known to John Davies (see pages 32 and 34 of *John Davies o Fallwyd*) and that Davies's wife was the aunt of Robert Vaughan of Hengwrt (p. 43), which may indicate a route from Salesbury to Vaughan. From 1605 to 1614, Gryffyth was rector of 'the first part of Llansannan'. He wrote his name in Hebrew in *Llyfr Du Caerfyrddin*.

16. Even Morgan's Bible and Prayer Book (in the preface) contain the occasional Salesburian 'Camber-aec/g'.

17. Robert wrote a grammar, all three parts of which were printed in Milan, the first in 1567, two months before Salesbury's Prayer Book. (It is not a grammar in the Palsgrave sense of the word, more a guide to writing eloquent prose.)

18. Rhys's grammar was of the technical, Palsgrave sort. Commentators are critical of his 'shoehorning' of Welsh into a Latin template. Perri was the only author to use elements of his orthography.

19. See T. H. Parry-Williams, *The English Element in Welsh* (1923), p. 19. The student is referring to a poem either by Hywel Swrdwal or his son Ieuan. Parry-Williams gives the 'British Museum' (British library) Ms number as 14966.

20. See *Report on Manuscripts in the Welsh Language*, 1898–1910, p. 1,093.

21. They are: *Prifannau Sanctaidd, neu lawlyfr, o Weddiau a wnaethbwyd, yn dair rhan … Y trydydd agraphiad yn Saesonaeg, ar cyntaf yn gamberaeg o gyfieithiad Row: Vaughan.* Undated. *Pregeth dduwiol yn traethu am idion ddull, acagwedd gwir edifeirwch … a gyfieithiwyd yn Gamber-aec gan Robert Lloyd.* London 1629, author Arthur Dent. *Yr ymarfer o dduwioldeb: yn cyfarwyddo dyn i rodio fal y rhyngo ef Fodd Duw. Yr hwn lyfr a osodwyd allan yn season-sec o waith y gwir barcgedig dad Lewis Escomb Bangor, ac a gyfieithwyd yn gamber-aec o waith Row. Vaughan o gaergai o sir feirion wr bonheddig.* 1631, Lewis Bayly. *Hyfforddiadau Christianogol: yn dangos pa fodd i rodio gyda Duw ar hy[d] y Dydd/A osodwyd allan yn Saesonaec gan Tho. Gouge, gwenidog yr efengyl, ac yn Gamberaec gan Richard Jones o Ddinbich.* London, 1675, printer A. Maxwell. *Arweiniwr cartrefol ir iawn a'r buddiol dderbyniad o Swpper yr Arglwydd: Ym ha un hefyd, y mae'r ffordd a'r modd o'n hiechydwriaeth, wedi eu Gosod allan yn fyr, ac fal y bo hawdd eu deal … /gan Theophulus Dorrington; Ac a Gyfieithwyd i'r Gamberaeg, gan Ddafydd Maurice, DD.* Llundain (London), Argraphwyd gan J.H. dros B. Aylmer, 1700. *Testament y Dauddeg Padriarch, sef Meibion Jacob. A gyfieithwyd allan or Groeg gan Robert Grosthead, Esgob Lincoln ag yn awr yn Gamberaeg.* Dublin: ag a werth gan Cadwaladr Ellis yn y Bala yn Sur Meirionidd, 1700.

22. 'rhaid benthygio yn gyntaf gan y lladin, os gellir yn ddiwrthnyssig i gwneuthur yn gymreigiaidd: os bydd caledi yma, rhaid dwyn i nechwyn, gan yr eidalwyr, phrancod, ysphaenwyr, ag od oes geiriau saesneg wedi i breinio ynghymru ni wasnaetha moi gwrthod

nhwy, mal claim, acsiwn, sir hal, tentio tentasiwn' (I have not used Robert's dotted letters. The words are otherwise as they appear in *Gramadeg Cymraeg (Rhan Dau)*, which is discussed in 'Ysgol Milan' in *Y Traddodiad Rhyddiaith*, p. 97.)

23. Gwyn's book was the first to be printed in Wales (in a clandestine Catholic press set up in a cave on the Great Orme in Llandudno). Few copies were printed. Four survive.

24. Vaughan's work was *Yr Ymarfer o Dduwioldeb* (1629). Llwyd's work was *Llwybr hyffordd yn cyfarwyddo yr anghyfarwydd i'r nefoedd* (1630).

25. See Garfield H. Hughes, 'Llyfrau Samuel Pepys', *JWBS*, vol. 9 (1962), p. 135.

26. Lewis Morris was the finest poet of his time and a mentor to Owen and Evans. Richard moved to London, rose to a senior position in the Navy Office and founded the Honourable Society of Cymmrodorion. William was an antiquarian, naturalist and fossil hunter. Their correspondence is a fascinating record of their age.

27. Amongst the British Library books that I have studied that were once owned by Richard Morris are Robert's *Gramadeg Cymraeg* (1567), Morgan's Prayer Book of 1599 and Perri's *Egluryn Phraethineb*. The 1567 New Testament has 'Llyfr Rhis: Morris o'r Nafi Offis Llundain 1761' written on the title page. This post-dates his editions of the Bible and Prayer Book. Richard, the longest surviving of the brothers, joined his brothers' collections of books and manuscripts to his own. They were presented to the British Museum in 1841. The letter in which Richard informed his brother of the acquisition of the 'Salisbury [*sic*] Testament in morocco' and two other volumes, one wrongly attributed, is in *The Letters of Lewis, Richard, William and John Morris of Anglesey (Morrisiaid Mon) 1728–1765*, volume 2, p. 409. The reply (26 December 1761) is on page 427 'Gwyn eich byd chwi sydd yn cael meddianu llyfrau goreugwyr godigog, sef W Salbri, etc.'. 'You are so fortunate' does not convey the strength of 'Gwyn eich byd', literally, 'You are blessed'. William regularly used some aspects of Salesbury's orthography, notably 'aw' for 'o' and 'Iuddew' (see pages 247 and 272 above) in his letters.

28. In a letter (21 March 1761) to Richard Morris, Evans wrote, 'Mr Griffith Davies of Harwich has got some books of me ever since I have been there; viz Cyfraith Hywel Dda with Wotton's translation and notes; Lewis's History of Wales; two copies of Salesbury's translation of the New Testament into Welsh; and some other books I now forget.'

29. The couplet comes from 'The Love of our Country' (1772), one of the few poems that he wrote in English. (In a letter to Richard Morris (25 February 1764), Evans defends his use of 'i' for 'y' in the verb 'to be' (bod), for example, 'i mae e' for 'y mae e', he is.) Evans used this spelling in his correspondence and in *Some Specimens*.) The two letters mentioned in notes 27 and 28 can be found in *ALMA*, p. 523, p. 612.

30. For example, in Strype's *Historical and Biographical Works: The life and acts of Matthew Parker*, 1821.

31. The partial reprint of 1819 was by R. Saunderson. The 1850 edition was by Isaac Jones. See Mathias's 'Gweithiau William Salesbury', *JWBS*, VII.

32. Gabriel Goodman, from Rhuthun, was the dean of Westminster and was of great assistance

to Morgan. Edmund Prys also helped Morgan (and Davies) and translated the Psalms. In the nineteenth century John Davies's scriptural translations were widely and incorrectly attributed to Bishop Richard Parry.

33. The sculptor was Sir Goscombe John, R.A.

34. The biography was *The Life and Work of Davies and Salesbury* by D. R. Thomas. The editors of the new editions were J. Gwenogvryn Evans and John H. Davies, respectively.

Chapter Twenty-Four: Decline and fall

1. *OBWV*, p. 377.

2. He is in the DNB and the DWB. The Primrose Hill eisteddfod was in 1792.

3. Macpherson, Chatterton and Ireland are included in *The Oxford Companion to English Literature*.

4. All three are in the DWB.

5. *Palestina: sef, Hanes taith i ymweled ag Iuddewon Gwlad Canaan* (1860) and *Iuddewon Prydain* (1852). For 'Gamber-aeg', see *Y gwladgarwr: sef Cylchgrawn gwybodaeth, ysgrythorol, a chyffredinol*, p. 84.

6. Jones did not add the 'Morris' until later in life. He is in the DWB and DNB and this précis of his life is indebted to the latter.

7. The publication of the first edition of the *OED* lasted from 1884 to 1928.

8. *A Welsh Grammar* was published by the Oxford University Press. For 'Dynes', see page 223, for 'debased dialect', page 247.

9. 'fiction' appears on pages 257 and 303 and quite probably elsewhere. 'Mad' is on page 65. 'Spurious' is on page 367; 'fictitious forms' is from the preface.

10. *An Elementary Welsh Grammar* was also published by Oxford University Press. The sentence occurs on page iv.

11. Page 57.

12. The quote comes from page xxxix.

13. For discussion of Greg, see Laurie E. Maguire's *Shakespearean suspect texts; The 'bad' quartos and their contexts*, Cambridge. Interestingly, like Jones, Greg and his colleagues Pollard, McKerrow, Dover Wilson and Alexander, all had 'an interest in scientific and mathematical exactitude' (p. 29, Maguire). Greg wrote a book, *The Calculus of Variants*, and had a 'tendency to express textual issues in the form of an equation', yet his work is riddled with errors, contradictions and subjective opinion asserted as incontrovertible fact.

14. See Morris-Jones's 1913 work, p. 174.

15. See Ceri Davies, *John Davies o Fallwyd* (Gwasg Pantycelyn, 2001), p. 47.

16. 'Gweithgarwch' is singular, but here it translates better into English as a plural.

17. See 'William Salesbury a'r Testament Newydd', *Llên Cymru*, XVI (1989) (Palsgrave) and 'Gweithiau William Salesbury', *JWBS*, VII (1952), (*Y Diarebion Camberaec*).

18. The two academics were Melville Richards and, incredibly, Glanmor Williams. 'Facts' were lifted inaccurately from outdated sources. For example Salesbury's mother was named as

Elin Puleston (traceable to Thomas's book of 1902), when since the 1930s it was known to have been Annes verch Wiliam (ap Gruffudd ap Robin) of Cochwillan. Mathias's review appeared in *Llên Cymru* (1965), Volume 8, 3.

19. Published by Gwasg Gomer in 1970.

20. See page 98.

21. See *Bywyd ac Amserau'r Esgob Richard Davies*, p. 96.

22. See page 360.

23. Morgan is on the 18p (first class) stamp, Salesbury on the 26p, Bishop Richard Davies on the 31p and Bishop Richard Parry on the 34p. (Parry is credited for the work carried out by John Davies.) No contemporary portrait of Salesbury exists.

24. *Llysieulyfr*, Cardiff.

Epilogue

1. *A Compendious Dictionary of the English Language*, Webster (1806).

2. See *Yny lhyvyr hwnn* (not paginated).

3. Hart devised his alphabet between 1551 and 1570. For the quotation, see Peter Lucas, 'Sixteenth Century Spelling Reform and the Printers in Continental Perspective: Sir Thomas Smith and John Hart', *The Library*, 2000, p. 11.

4. See Vincent Cronin, *The Flowering of the Renaissance* (1969), p. 199.

5. From *The Faerie Queene*: Book 1: Canto1.

6. See *Y Traddodiad Rhyddiaith*, p. 68.

7. These spellings can be found on pages 119, 122, 123, 229, 118, 241, 135 and 155 of the British Library's 2000 reprint of Tyndale's New Testament.

8. See David Bellos, *Is That a Fish in Your Ear?* (2012), p. 98.

9. See 'An explanation of certaine wordes being quarrelled withall' in the preface to the Prayer Book of 1567.

10. From Salesbury's letter 'To my Loving Friende Maister Humfrey Toy' in *A playne and a familiar Introduction*.

11. The first translator of Y Gododdin, Evan Evans wrote, 'I do not absolutely understand above three parts in four of ... Aneurin.' (*The Percy Letters*, Vol. V, p. 159.) The literal, prose translation does not convey the majesty of the words. The Welsh word order sounds forced in English, but the word 'Gwenwyn' (poison) needs to retain its place or it loses its force. The poem celebrates an attack to regain Catraeth (Catterick) from the Saxons. All but one of the three hundred men were killed. That is why the mead they drank at the feast before the battle is described as poison.

12. The lines quoted, including the translation, are from Seamus Heaney's *Beowulf* (Faber and Faber, 1999).

Appendix

The Act of 1563

1. 'Whereas the Queen's most Excellent Majesty, like a most godly and virtuous Princess, having chief Respect and Regard to the Honour and Glory of God, and the Souls Health of her Subjects, did in the First Year of her Reign, by the Authority of her High Court of Parliament, chiefly for that Purpose called, set forth a Book of Common Prayer and Order of the Administration of Sacraments in the vulgar English Tongue, to be used throughout all her Realm of England, WALES and the Marches of the same, that thereby her Highness' most loving Subjects understanding in their own Language the terrible and fearful Threatenings rehearsed in the Book of God against the Wicked and Malefactors, the pleasant and infallible Promises made to the elect and chosen Flock, with a Just Order to rule and Guide their Lives according to the Commandments of God, might much better learn to love and fear God, to serve and obey their Prince, and to know their Duties towards their Neighbours: which Book being received as a most precious Jewel with an inspeakable Joy of all such her subjects as did and do understand the English Tongue, the which tongue is not understand of the most and greatest Number of all her Majesty's most loving and obedient Subjects inhabiting within her Highness Dominion and Country of WALES, being no small Part of this Realm, who therefore are utterly destituted of God's Holy Word, and do remain in the like or rather more Darkness and Ignorance then they were, in the Time of Papistry': Be it therefore enacted by the Queen our Sovereign Lady, the Lords Spiritual and Temporal, and the Commons, in the present Parliament assembled, and by the Authority of the same, That the Bishops of Hereford, Saint David's, Asaph, Bangor and Llandaff, and their Successors, shall take such Order among themselves for the Souls Health of the Flocks committed to their Charge within Wales, that the whole Bible, containing the New Testament and the Old, with the Book of Common Prayer and

Administration of the Sacraments, as is now used within this Realm in English, to be truly and exactly translated into the British or WELSH Tongue; and that the same so translated, being by them viewed, perused and allowed, be imprinted to such Number at the least, that one of either Sort may be had for every Cathedral, Collegiate and Parish Church, and Chapel of Ease, in such Places and Countries of every the said Dioceses where that Tongue is commonly spoken or used, before the First Day of March, Anno Dom. One thousand five hundred sixty six. And that from that Day forth, the whole Divine Service shall be used and said by the Curates and Ministers throughout all the said Dioceses where the WELSH Tongue is commonly used, in the said British or WELSH Tongue, in such Manner and Form as is now used in the English Tongue, and differing nothing in any Order or Form from the English Book; for the which Books so imprinted, the Parishioners of every of the said Parishes shall pay the one Half or Moiety, and the Parson and Vicar of every of the said Parishes (where both be) or else the one of them where there is but one, shall pay the other Half or Moiety: the Prices of which Books shall be appointed and rated by the said Bishops and their Successors, or by Three of them at the least; the which Things if the said Bishops or their Successors neglect to do, then every one of them shall forfeit to the Queen's Majesty, her Heirs and Successors, the sum of Forty Pounds, to be levied of their Goods and Chattels.

2. Be it further enacted by the Authority aforesaid, That every minister and Curate within the Dioceses before said, where the WELSH Tongue is commonly used, shall from the Feast of Whitsuntide next ensuing until the aforesaid Day of March, which shall be in the Year One Thousand five hundred sixty and six, at all Times of Communion declare or read the Epistle and Gospel of the Day in the WELSH Tongue, to his or their Parishioners in every of the said Churches and Chapels; and also once every Week at the least, shall read or declare to their said Parishioners in the said Churches the Lord's Prayer, the Articles of the Christian Faith, the Ten Commandments, and the Litany, as they are set forth in the English Tongue, in the said WELSH Tongue, with such other Part of the Common Prayer and Divine Service as shall be appointed by the Bishop of the Diocese for the Time being.

3. And one Book containing the Bible, and one other Book of Common Prayer, in the English Tongue, shall be bought and had in every Church throughout WALES in which the Bible and Book of Common Prayer in WESLH is to be had by Force of this Act (if there be none already) before the first Day of March which shall be in the Year of our Lord God One thousand five hundred sixty six; and the same Books to remain in such convenient Places within the said Churches, that such as understand them may resort at all convenient Times to read and peruse the same; and also such as do not understand the said Language, may by conferring both Tongues together, the sooner attain to the Knowledge of the English Tongue; any Thing in this Act to the contrary notwithstanding.

'Moliant William Salesbury o'r Plas Isaf', Gruffudd Hiraethog's poem to Salesbury, can be found in D. J. Bowen (ed.), *Gwaith Gruffudd Hiraethog* (Cardiff, 1990), pp. 83–5.

Dating the poem

Line 8, with its reference to Salesbury having been the second son but now being the first, clearly dates this poem to after 1540, the year of Robert's death, and as there are no references to Salesbury's books, it is reasonable to assume that it must date from before January 1547, when the dictionary was printed.

The arbitration document of November 1546 refers to Salesbury having 'put away' his wife. It is unlikely that Gruffudd would have included Catrin, Salesbury's wife (line 28), her family and lineage if that was still the case, which strongly suggests that there was a brief reconciliation between the date of the arbitration settlement and Elis Price's assault on Salesbury in January 1547. (The legal document of 1594 states that the estrangement lasted for 'x to xij years'. It may be that it was during this brief reconciliation, if a reconciliation occurred, that Gwen, their fourth child, was conceived.)

The opening four lines, which speak of the agreement bringing the sun to a place that was once cold, are further evidence of an outbreak of harmony, however temporary. Gruffudd would have seized this opportunity with great relief. He would have felt obliged to write a poem for his life-long friend, but would not have wished to alienate the powerful and extensive Price family and their many allies on whose patronage he was dependent. (Gruffudd wrote five poems of praise to Elis Price and others to family members and allies, such as John Wyn ap Maredudd.)

Details of Salesbury's life

The following facts, some of which are confirmed by other documents, can be gleaned from the poem: that he was living in Plas Isa (title and line 2); that he was the second son of Foulk (Ffwg) (line 13) and a grandson of Robert Salusbury senior (line 15); that Rhys ab Einion (Gwenhwyfar's father) was his great grandfather (line 18); that Annes was his mother (lines 19 and 20) (this is shown by mentioning Wiliam ap Gruffudd ap Robin (of Cochwillan); that he had married Catrin, who was the sister of Lowri, wife to his brother, Robert, and that the sisters' father was Robert ap Rhys (lines 27–32); that he had mastered Latin, Greek, Hebrew, Welsh, English and French (lines 39–44); that he was a determined character (lines 49 and 50); that he went to Oxford (line 54) and studied the 'seven arts' (Grammar, Rhetoric, Logic, Arithmetic, Geometry, Astronomy and Music); that he enjoyed puns and word-play (lines 73 and 74).

Bowen's notes in *Gwaith Gruffudd Hiraethog* are excellent and the chapter he wrote in the foreword concerning the friendship between Gruffudd and Salesbury is highly informative.

He wrote an excellent article ('Cywyddau Gruffudd Hiraethog i Dri o Awduron y Dadeni', *TCS*, 1974), in which this poem is one of three discussed in detail (the others being the *cywyddau* to Sir John Prise and Humphrey Llwyd). Bowen states (page 105) that the lines that include 'pen pob camp' and 'gair a mwys' can be interpreted as showing that Salesbury had gained access to the grammar books of the bards.

Bowen also demonstrates (page 114) that Salesbury was related, through the marriage of his aunt Marged to Pirs ap Huw ap Ieuan Llwyd, to Humphrey Llwyd.

A copy of the kynges moste gracious Privilege

Henry the eyght by the grace of God Kyng of England France and Ireland, defender of the faith and of the churche of Englande and Irelande in earth the supreme head. To all Printers and boke sellers, and to other officers, ministers and subjectes, we do you to understand that of our grace especial, we have graunted and geven priviledge and licence to our welbeloved subjectes William Salesbury and Jhon Waley to print or cause to be printed oure booke entitled a Dictionarie bothe in englyshe & welche, whereby our welbeloved subjects in Wales may the soner attayne and learne our mere englyshe tonge. And that no other person or persons of what estate degree or condicion so ever they be of, do prynte or cause the same Dictionarie to be printed or any part therof, but only the sayd William and Jhon, and eyther of them, and the assignes of anye of them duryng the space of seven yeres next ensuing the first printing of the sayd Dictionarie. And that none other person or persons of what estate, degre or condicion soever they be, do printe or cause to be printed any other booke or bookes which our sayde subjectes William and Jhon or eyther of them, hereafter do or shal first translate and setforth during seven yeres next ensuing the first printing of any such booke or bokes. Wherefore we wil, and straytly command & charge all and singular our subjectes, as well printers as bookesellers and other persons within our dominions, that they ne anye of them presume to print, or cause to be printed the sayde Dictionary or any part thereof, or anye other boke or bokes first translated and printed by the saide Wylliam and John or either of them contrary to the meanyng of thys our presente licence and priviledge upon payne of our high displeasure.

Geven at our Palace of Westminster the xiii day of December, in the xxxvii yere of our raigne,

The above privilege was not printed in the dictionary, but in *Kynniver Llith a Ban* (1551).

Printed books likely to have been found in Salesbury's library

From references in his works and other textual clues, it can be stated with some confidence that the following works would have been found on the shelves of Plas Isa during Salesbury's lifetime:

Most, if not all, of Erasmus's works, but certainly his Greek New Testament and his *Adagia*,

Palsgrave's *Lesclarcissement de la langue francoyse*,

The Proverbs of John Heywood,

Polydore Vergil's *Adagia* (compiled two years before Erasmus's first collection),

The works of Horace,

The works of Lucan,

The works of Ovid,

St Augustine's *Confessions* and *The City of God*,

Linacre's Latin translation of Proclus Diadochus's *De Sphaera*,

Works by Melancthon,

Works by Johann Hausschein,

Works by Johannes Aventinus,

Tyndale's New Testament,

Luther's New Testament and Old Testament,

The Great Bible,

Coverdale's Bible,

The Vulgate,

The Prayer Books of 1549 and 1559,

The Geneva Bible (English and French editions),

Beza's Latin translation of the New Testament,

Stephanus's Greek text of the New Testament,

Sebastian Munster's Hebrew Bible (and possibly his *Dictionarium trilingue*),

Petrus Mosellanus's *Tabulae de Scematibus et Tropis*,

Fuchs's *De Historiae Stirpium*,

William Turner's *Libellus de re Herbia*, *The Names of Herbes* and *A New Herball* (all three parts),

Dodoens' *Herball or Historie of Plantes* (French version).

List of the M.P.s for Welsh constituencies in the Parliament of 1563 (source: P. W. Hasler (ed.), *The History of Parliament: the House of Commons, 1558–1603* (1981):

Anglesey: Richard Bulkekley (county), William Price (borough) Merioneth*: Elis Price Caernarfonshire: Morus Wynn (c), John Harrington (b) Denbighshire: Simon Thelwall (c), Humphrey Llwyd (b) Flintshire: George Ravenscroft (c), John Conway (b) Montgomeryshire: Edward Herbert (c), John Price (b) Radnorshire: Thomas Lewis (c), Morgan Price (b) Breconshire: Rowland Vaughan (c) Sir Roger Vaughan (b) Cardiganshire: John Price (c) John Gwyn (b) Pembrokeshire: Sir John Perrot (c) William Revell (b) Carmarthenshire: Sir Henry Jones (c), John Morgan (b) Glamorgan: William Bassett (c), Henry Lewis (b) Monmouthshire*: Matthew Herbert, Thomas Herbert (c), Moore Powell (b).

* There was no borough seat for Merioneth, but two county seats for Monmouthshire.

Salesbury's *englynion* to Edward Games of Brecon

> Pemtheccant wylant o 'alar Gem Edward
> Gam ydoedd am 'wr gwar
> Ny phaid tr'ugain a phedwar
> Ac wylo byth o gael bar,

> [Fifteen hundred weep in grief for Edward Games
> (His death) was a mistake for a civilised man
> Sixty-four will never cease
> Weeping for him forever,]

> Mille et quingenti doctu' plorant Edvardum
> Sexaginta Gamu' Quatuor inde gemunt.

> [Fifteen hundred learned (men) lament Edward
> Sixty-four wail ever after.]

Pan las Edward Gams pen lain' yn athrist
Mae yn uthrach gan y rhain
Nyd Buchedd dda dra druain
A luddiai'r cwymp ladd wr cain.

[When Edward Games was killed the blade's point/
(was) sorrowful It is more awful for these
It is wretched that so good a life
Did not halt the fall that killed a cultured man.]

The poem can be found in NLW MS Cwrtmawr 3. It was printed on page 78 of *The Life and Work of Davies and Salesbury*. There is a reference to Salesbury as a poet in the British Library Add. MS. 14,872, but just a handful of lines have survived: a couplet in the dictionary, an englyn in *A briefe and a playne introduction*, a four-line verse in *Y Testament Newydd*, the *englynion* to Gruffydd Dwnn (NLW MS Llansteffan 133) and the elegy to Edward Games. There is a possibility that the English translations of Ovid and Horace that appeared in two of his books are his own.

Correspondence

Salesbury's letter to Gruffudd Hiraethog that accompanied his book on rhetoric is in Cardiff Library, MS Cardiff 21. A copy appears in Henry Lewis's 'Llythyr William Salesbury at Ruffudd Hiraethog', *BBCS*, ii, 2.

Salesbury's letter to those attending the eisteddfod of 1567 survives in a copy by Thomas Wiliems in MS Peniarth 77, which also contains a copy of the statute of Gruffudd ap Cynan. The letter was reprinted in the *Report on Manuscripts in the Welsh Language*, Vol. I, part II, pp. 165–6. The statute is on page 512.

A copy of Salesbury's letter that accompanied *Y Diarebion Camberaec* is in NLW MS 6434 and was reprinted in 'Gweithiau William Salesbury', *JWBS*, VII (1952).

All of Salesbury's other letters can be found in his books, apart from the one (consisting mostly of notes in English and Latin) that he wrote to Parker concerning the Armenian Psalter. It is in Corpus Christi College Library, Cambridge, alongside correspondence between Davies and Parker.

Hebrew Cryptogram:

The cryptogram, which can be read as 'by John Awdeley', appears in *A playne and a familiar Introduction* (17 May 1567) and in Simwnt Fychan's translation of Martial's *Epigram on the Happy Life* (1571). There are discreet references to it in *Lliver Gweddi Gyffredin* [The Book of Common Prayer] (6 May 1567).

Bibliography

Works by Salesbury in chronological order and with the name of the printer (as it appears in the book):

A Dictionary in Englyshe and Welshe, 1547, John Whaley.

Oll Synnwyr pen Kembero ygyd, 1547, Nycholas Hill.

A briefe and a playne introduction, teaching how to pronounce the letters in the British tong, 1550, Robert Crowley.

The baterie of the Popes Botereulx, 1550, Robert Crowley.

Ban wedy i dynny air/A Certaine Case Extracte, 1550, Robert Crowley.

The descripcion of the Sphere or Frame of the Worlde, 1550, Robert Wyer.

Kynniver Llith a Ban or yscruther lan, 1551, Robert Crowley.

Llyfr Rhetoreg, 1552, appeared in manuscript form only. There are many surviving copies; Salesbury's original is in Cardiff Library.

Lliver Gweddi Gyffredin, 1567, Henry Denham (includes the psalter).

A playne and a familiar Introduction, 1567, Henry Denham (a revised edition of the 1550 work).

Y Testament Newydd, 1567, Henry Denham.

Y Diarebion Camberaec (Crynodab or Diarebion sathredig), 1567, printer unknown (two fragments survive).

Y Llysieulyfr [Salesbury's herbal], produced in manuscript form, probably in the 1570s. The original manuscript has been lost. A copy (MLW MS 686) was printed in 1916. In 1997, *Llysieulyfr Salesbury*, the superior copy NLW MS 4581 appeared, edited and with notes and a commentary by Iwan Rhys Edgar. (Salesbury's translation of the Litany, printed in 1562 by John Whaley, has not survived.)

Other works:

Arber, Edward (ed.), *A Transcript of the Registers of the Company of Stationers of London, 1554–1640 A.D.* (Birmingham, 1875–94).

Awdeley, John, *The Fraternitye of Vacabondes: with Their proper names and Qualities*, printed by Awdeley (1575).

Bale, John, *Index Britanniae Scriptorum* (1548–9).

Bale, John, *Scriptorium illustrium maioris Brytanniae Catalogus* (1557–9).

Bartrum, Peter, *Welsh Genealogies 1400–1500*, volume 9 (Cardiff, 1983).

Bell, H. E., *An Introduction to the History and Records of the Court of Wards and Liveries* (Cambridge, 1953).

Bellos, David, *Is That a Fish in Your Ear?* (Faber and Faber, 2012).

Bennet, H. S., *English Books and Readers 1475 to 1557* (Cambridge, 1952).

Bindoff, S. T., *Tudor England (The Pelican History of England)* (Penguin, 1950).

Bindoff, S. T. (ed.), *The History of Parliament; The House of Commons, 1509–1558.*

Bowen, D. J., *Gwaith Gruffudd Hiraethog* (Cardiff, 1990).

Bowen, Geraint (ed.), *Y Traddodiad Rhyddiaith* (Llandysul, 1970).

Bowen, I. (ed.), *The Statutes of Wales* (London, 1908).

Bradford, C. A., *Blanche Parry, Queen Elizabeth's Gentlewoman* (privately printed, 1935).

Bristow, Adrian, *Doctor Johnson and Mrs Thrale's tour in North Wales* (Bridge Books, 1995).

Bruce, John (ed.), *Matthew Parker, Correspondence*, Parker Society (Cambridge, 1853).

Byrne, Muriel St Clare (ed.), *The Lisle Letters* (University of Chicago Press, 1981).

Caxton, William, *The Metamorphoses of Ovid* (1480, British Library facsimile of the original manuscript).

Cogan, Thomas, *The Haven of Health*, 1584.

Cronin, Vincent, *The Flowering of the Renaissance* (Collins, 1969).

Crowley, Robert, *Epigrams* (1550).

Davies, Ceri, *John Davies o Fallwyd* (Gwasg Pantycelyn, 2001).

Davies, Ceri, *Rhagymadroddion a Chyflwyniadau Lladin, 1551–1632* (Cardiff, 1980).

Davies, Ceri, 'Two Welsh Renaissance Latinists: Sir John Prise of Brecon and Dr John Davies of Mallwyd' in *Britannia Latina: Latin in the culture of Great Britain from the Middle Ages to the twentieth century*, editors Burnell, Charles and Mann (2005).

Davies, John, *Antiquae Linguae Britannicae … Dictionarium Duplex* (printed by Robert Young, 1632).

Davies John (translator), *Llyfr Gweddi Gyffredin* (printed by Bonham Norton and John Bill, 1620).

Davies, John (translator), *Y Bibl Cyssegr-lan* (printed by Bonham Norton and John Bill, 1620).

Davies, John H., *The Letters of Lewis, Richard, William and John Morris of Anglesey (Morrisiaid Môn) 1728–1765* (1907, 1909).

Davies, Richard, *A Funerall Sermon [for Walter Devereux, earl of Essex]* (printed by Henry Denham, 1577).

Dobson, E. J., *English Pronunciation 1500–1700* (Oxford, 1957).

Drabble, Margaret, *The Oxford Companion to English Literature*.

Ekwall, Eilert, *Place-names of Lancashire* (Manchester University Press, 1922).

Erasmus, *Praise of Folly*, translated by Roger Clarke (One World Classics, 2008).

Evans, J. Gwenogvryn (ed.), Salesbury's *Oll Synnwyr* (1902 edition).

Evans, J. Gwenogvryn, *Report on Manuscripts in the Welsh Language* (London, 1898–1910).

Febvre and Martin, *The Coming of the Book* (tr.) (London: New Left Books, 1976).

Foster Evans, Dr Dylan (ed.), *Gwaith Hywel Swrdwal a'i Deulu* (Aberystwyth, 2000).

Gairdner, James (ed.), *Letters and Papers, Foreign and Domestic, Henry VIII* (1885, the volumes from 1530 to 1546).

Gardner, W. H. (ed.), *Gerard Manley Hopkins, Poems and Prose* (Penguin, 1970).

Geoffrey of Monmouth, *The History of the Kings of Britain*, translated by Lewis Thorpe (Penguin Classics).

Gesner, Conrad, *Mithridates de differentis linguis* (1555).

Greenblatt, Steven, *Will in the World* (Jonathan Cape, 2004).

Griffiths, J. E., *Pedigrees of Anglesey and Caernarfonshire Families* (1914).

Gruffydd, R. Geraint (ed.), *Y Gair ar Waith* (Cardiff, 1988).

Hasler, P. W. (ed.), *The History of Parliament: the House of Commons, 1558–1603*.

Heaney, Seamus (translator), *Beowulf* (Faber and Faber, 1999).

Henderson, Philip (ed.), *Shepherd's Calendar and Other Poems* (Everyman, 1932).

Heywood, John, *A dialogue conteyning the number in effect of all the proverbes in the englishe tongue … set foorth by John Heywood* (1546).

Holdsworth, William, *A History of English Law*, vol. 2 (Methuen).

Holinshed, Raphael, *Chronicles of England, Scotland and Ireland* (1587).

Hudson, Winthrop S., *John Ponet (1516?–1556) Advocate of Limited Monarchy* (includes Ponet's *A Shorte Treatise of Politike Power*) (University of Chicago Press, 1942).

Hughson, David, *A History of London*.

Huws, Daniel, *Medieval Welsh Manuscripts* (University of Wales Press, 2000).

Ifans, Dafydd, *William Salesbury and the Welsh Laws*, Pamphlets in Welsh Law series (Aberystwyth, 1980).

Ives, Eric, *The Life and Death of Anne Boleyn* (2004 edition).

Johnson, Francis R., *Astronomical Thought in Renaissance England* (Baltimore, 1937).

Jones, G. Lloyd, *The Discovery of Hebrew in Tudor England: a Third Language* (Manchester University Press, 1983).

Jones, Gwyn, *Dafydd ap Gwilym his poems* (Cardiff, 2001).

Jones, T. Gwynn (ed.), *Gwaith Tudur Aled* (Cardiff, 1926).

Jones, Terry (and others), *Who Murdered Chaucer?* (Methuen, 2003).

Kendrick, T. D., *British Antiquity* (Methuen, 1950).

Kerrigan, John (ed.), *The Sonnets and A Lover's Complaint* (Penguin, 1995).

Knowles, David, *The Religious Orders in England,* vol. iii (Cambridge, 1959).

Kyffin, Maurice, *Deffyniad Ffydd Eglwys Lloegr* (1671 reprint).

Lewys, Huw, *Perl Mewn Adfyd*, ed. W. J. Gruffydd (Cardiff, 1929).

Lodwick, Joyce and Victor, *The Story of Carmarthen* (St Peter's Press, 1994).

Maguire, Laurie E., *Shakespearean Suspect Texts* (Cambridge, 1996).

Manley, John M. and Edith Rickert, *The Text of The Canterbury Tales*, vol. 1, (Chicago, 1940).

McCarthy, Fiona, *Byron, Life and Legend* (John Murray, 2002).

McConica, James, *The History of the University of Oxford* (OUP, 1986).

McKerrow, R. B., *Dictionary of Printers and Booksellers in England, Scotland and Ireland and of Foreign Printers of English Books* (Bibliographical Society, 1910).

Meyrick, S. R. (ed.), *Heraldic Visitations of Wales and part of the Marches between the years 1586–1613, Lewys Dwnn*, (volume 2) (1846).

Morgan, William (translator), *Llyfr Gweddi Gyffredin* (printed by Christopher Barker, 1599).

Morgan, William (translator), *Y Beibl Cyssegr-lan* (printed by Christopher Barker, 1588).

Morrice, J. C. (ed.), *Detholiad o waith Gruffudd ab Ieuan ab Llewelyn Vychan* (1910).

Morris-Jones, John, *A Welsh Grammar* (Oxford, 1913).

Morris-Jones, John, *An Elementary Welsh Grammar* (Oxford, 1921).

Moynahan, Brian, *William Tyndale: If God Spare My Life* (Little, Brown, 2002).

Neale, J. E., *Elizabeth and her Parliaments, Vol. 1, 1559–1581* (Jonathan Cape, 1953).

Neale, J. E., *Queen Elizabeth* (Jonathan Cape, 1934).

Owen, Hugh, *Additional Letters of the Morrises of Anglesey (1735–1786)*, (Y Cymmrodor, 1947, 1949).

Palsgrave, John, *Lesclarcissemente de la langue francoyse* (reprinted by Menton Press, 1969).

Parry, Thomas, *Hanes Llenyddiaeth Cymru hyd 1900* (Cardiff, 1944).

Parry, Thomas (ed.), *The Oxford Book of Welsh Verse* (Oxford, 1962).

Parry-Williams, T. H., *Carolau Richard White* (Cardiff, 1931).

Parry-Williams, T. H. (ed.), *Rhyddiaith Gymraeg, II* (Cardiff, 1956).

Parry-Williams, T. H., *The English Element in Welsh* (Cardiff, 1923).

Pennant, Thomas, *Tours of Wales* (London, 1810).

Perri, Henri, *Egluryn Phraethineb* (printed by John Danter, 1595).

Ponet, John, *A Defence for Mariage of Priestes by Scripture and Aunciente Wryters* (1549).

Prise, John, *Historiae Brytannicae Defensio* (printed by Henry Binneman, 1573).

Pryce, Arthur Ivor, *The Diocese of Bangor in the Sixteenth Century* (Jarvis and Foster, 1929).

Richards, Thomas, *Antiquae linguae britannicae thesaurus* (1815).

Robert, Gruffydd, *Dosparth Byrr ar y rhan gyntaf i ramadeg cymraeg* (and the subsequent two parts) (Milan, 1567).

Roberts, T. R. (ed.), *Barddoniaeth Edmwnd Prys* (Caernarfon, 1899).

Robinson, Rev. Hastings (ed.), *Original Letters relative to The English Reformation*, Vol. 1 (Cambridge, 1846).

Rudd, Niall, ed., *Horace, Epistles Book II and Epistle to the Pisones ('Ars Poetica')* (Cambridge).

Scarisbrick, J. J., *Henry VIII* (Yale University Press, 1997).

Sears, Jayne and Francis R. Johnson (eds), *The Lumley Library, The Catalogue of 1609* (British Museum, 1956).

Simwnt Fychan, *Epigram on the Happy Life* (1571).

Singh, Simon, *The Code Book* (Fourth Estate, 1900).

Smith, L. T., *Leland's Itinerary in England and Wales* (Centaur Press, 1966, reprint of 1906 edition).

Smyth, Rhosier, *Gorsedd y byd* (Paris, 1615).

Starkey, David, *Elizabeth* (Chatto and Windus, 2000).

Steele, Burt Franklin (ed.), *A Bibliography of Proclamations, 1485–1910* (New York, 1910).

Stein, Gabriele, *John Palsgrave as Renaissance Linguist: A Pioneer in Vernacular Description* (Oxford, 1997).

Stow, John, *Survey of London,* ed. C. L. Kingsford (Oxford, 1971).

Thomas, D. R., *The Life and Work of Davies and Salesbury* (Oswestry, 1902).

Thomas, Hugh, *A History of Wales, 1485–1600* (Cardiff, 1972).

Thomas, Isaac, *William Salesbury and his Testament* (Cardiff, 1967).

Thomas, Isaac, *Y Testament Newydd Cymraeg 1551–1620* (Cardiff, 1976).

Tolkein, J. R. R., *The Monsters and the Critics and other essays* (George Allen and Unwin, 1983).

Trevelyan, G. M., *English Social History* (Longmans, 1944).

Tyndale, William (translator), *The New Testament* (British Library, 2000).

Weinreb, Ben and Christopher Hibbert (eds), *The London Encyclopaedia* (Macmillan, 1983).

Whigham, Frank and Wayne A. Rebborn (eds), *The Art of English Poesy, by George Puttenham. A critical Edition* (Cornell University Press, 2007).

Williams, David (ed.), *Three Treatises Concerning Wales* (Cardiff, 1960).

Williams, David H., *The Welsh Cistercians* (Bridge Books, 2001).

Williams, Glanmor, *Bywyd ac Amserau'r Esgob Richard Davies* (Cardiff, 1953).

Williams, Glanmor, *Wales and the Reformation* (Cardiff, 1999).

Williams, Gruffydd Aled, *Ymryson Edmwnd Prys a Wiliam Cynwal* (Cardiff, 1986).

Williams, Ifor (ed.), *Gwaith Guto'r Glyn* (Cardiff, 1939).

Wood, Anthony, *Athenae Oxonienses* (1691, reprint New York, 1967).

Wood, Anthony, *The History and Antiquities of the colleges and halls in the University of Oxford* (1786).

Woolley, Benjamin, *The Queen's Conjuror, The Life and Magic of Dr. Dee* (HarperCollins, 2001).

Wright, T., *Queen Elizabeth and Her Times,* vol. 1 (Oxford, 1838).

Wynn, Sir John of Gwydir, *The History of the Gwydir Family* (Cardiff, 1927).

Wynne Jones, Robert and R. Ellis, *Hanes hen furddynod plwyf Llansannan* (1910).

Standard Works of Reference:

DWB, ed. Sir John Edward Lloyd (The Hon. Soc. of Cymmrodorion, 1959).

Oxford DNB (2004).

Calendar of the Patent Rolls, Edward VI, 1547–8, Part 1.

Articles in Academic Journals:

Bowen, D. J., 'Cywyddau Gruffudd Hiraethog i Dri o Awduron y Dadeni', *TCS*, 1974.

Bowen, D. J. and Cledwyn Fychan, 'Cywydd Gofyn Gruffudd Hiraethog i ddeuddeg o wŷr Llansannan', *TDHS*, volume 24.

Bromwich, Rachel, 'William Camden and Trioedd Ynys Prydain', *BBCS*, Vol. XXIII, Part 1, 1968.

Campbell, Jackson J., 'A New Troilus Fragment', *Publications of the Modern Language Association of America*, 1958.

Flower, Robin, 'Richard Davies, William Cecil and Giraldus Cambrensis', *NLWJ*, vol. 3, 1943.

Flower, Robin, 'William Salesbury, Richard Davies and Archbishop Parker', *NLWJ*, II, 1941–2.

Fychan, Cledwyn, 'William Salesbury a Llansannan', *TDHS*, 27.

Gruffydd, R. Geraint, 'Humphrey Llwyd a Deddf Cyfiethu'r Beibl i'r Cymraeg', *Llên Cymru*, IV, 1956–7.

Gruffydd, R. Geraint, 'Humphrey Llwyd of Denbigh, some documents and a catalogue', *TDHS*, XVII, 1968.

Gruffydd, R. Geraint, 'The Welsh Book of Common Prayer', *JHSCW*, XVII, 1967.

Gruffydd, R. Geraint, 'Yn Y Lhyvyr Hwnn (1546); The Earliest Welsh Printed Book', *BBCS*, vol. XXIII, 1969.

Gruffydd, R. G. and R. J. Roberts, 'John Dee's Additions to William Salesbury's Dictionary', *TCS*, 2002.

Hughes, G. H., 'Llyfrau Samuel Pepys', *JWBS*, vol. 9, 1962.

Hughes, G. H., 'Y Dwniaid', *TCS*, 1941.

Huws, Daniel, 'The Merthyr Fragment', *NLWJ*, vol. xxv, no. 1, 1987.

James, Christine, 'Ban wedi i dynny: Medieval Welsh Law and Early Protestant Propaganda', *CMCS*, 27, 1994.

Jones, E. J., 'Martial's Epigram on the Happy Life', *BBCS*, III.

Jones, E. J., 'Tra Vo Lleuad', *NLWJ*, V, 1947.

Jones, Evan D., 'William Salesbury a'i Deulu', *BBCS*, VII, 1933–5.

Jones, J. Gwynfor, 'The Wynn Estate of Gwydir: Aspects of its Growth and Development c.1500–1580', *NLWJ*, XXII, 2, 1981.

Jones, J. T., 'Blwyddyn Marw Gruffydd Hiraethog a Dyddiad "Ffugrau" Salesbury', *BBCS*, VIII, 1935.

Ker, Neil R., 'Sir John Prise', *The Library*, 1955.

Lathrop, H. B., 'Some Rogueries of Robert Wyer', *The Library*, no. 20, vol. v.

Lewis, Henry, 'Llythyr William Salesbury at Ruffudd Hiraethog', *BBCS*, II.

Lewis, Saunders, 'Maniffesto'r Dadeni Dysg a'r Ddyneiddiaeth Brotestanaidd Gymreig', *Efrydiau Catholig*, ii, 1947.

Linnard, William, '"Y Darnau Cyntaf o Ganu Rhydd i Gael eu Printio'?', *NLWJ*, XXVI.

Lloyd, D. Myrddin, 'Epistol E M at Y Cembru', *NLWJ*, II, 1941.

Lucas, Peter, 'Sixteenth Century Spelling Reform and the Printers in Continental Perspective: Sir Thomas Smith and John Hart', *The Library*, 2000.

Mathias, W. Alun, 'Cyd-ddigwyddiad Geiriadurol', *Taliesin*, 95, 1996.

Mathias, W. Alun, 'Gweithiau William Salesbury', *JWBS*, VII, 1952.

Mathias, W. Alun, 'Llyfr Rhetoreg William Salesbury', *Llên Cymru*, Rhif 1, Rhif 2, 1952

Mathias, W. Alun, 'William Salesbury a'r Testament Newydd', *Llên Cymru*, XVI, 1989.

McConica, James, 'The Recusant Reputation of Thomas More', *CCHA*, Report 30 (1963).

Mooney, Linne R., 'Chaucer's Scribe', *Speculum*, January 2006.

Ovenden, Robert, 'Jasper Gryffyth and his books', *British Library Journal*, 1994.

Parry, Thomas, 'Tri Chyfeiriad at William Salesbury', *BBCS*, IX.

Payne, F. G., 'John Dee and Jenkyn Gwyn', *RST*, vol. 13, 1961.

Plomer, H. R., 'Robert Wyre, Printer and Bookseller', *TBS*, 1897.

Roberts, Julian and Andrew G. Watson, 'John Dee's Library Catalogue', *TBS*, 1990.

Roberts, Julian and Andrew G. Watson, 'John Dee's Library Catalogue: Additions and corrections', *TBS*, November 2009.

Roberts, Peter, 'The Welsh Language, English Law and Tudor Legislation', *Transactions of the Hon. Soc. of Cymmrodorion*, 1989.

Stubbs, Estelle, 'A New Manuscript by the Hengwrt/Ellesmere Scribe?', *JEBS*, Volume 5, 2002.

Thomas, Isaac, 'Fersiwn William Morgan o'r Hen Destament Hebraeg', *NLWJ*, XXIII, no. 3, 1984.

Thomas, Isaac, 'Sallwyr Llyfr Gweddi Gyffredin 1567', *NLWJ*, XVII, no. 4, 1982.

Thomas Isaac, 'Yr Epistolau o'r Hen Testament yn Kynniver Llith a Ban', *NLWJ*, Vol. XXII, 1982.

Wicken, Stanley, 'William Salesbury and the Dutch Connection', *TDHS*, 46.

Williams, Glanmor, 'Bishop Sulien, Bishop Richard Davies and Archbishop Parker', *NLWJ*, no. 3, 1948.

Williams, Glanmor, 'William Salesbury's Baterie of the Popes Botereulx', *BBCS*, XIII, 1948–50.

Williams, Glanmor, 'Wales and the reign of Queen Mary', *Welsh History Review*, X.

Williams, Gruffydd Aled, 'Edmwnd Prys, un arall o Enwogion Llanrwst', *TDHS*, vol. 23.

Williams, Rhiannon, 'Cywydd Marwnad Wiliam Cynwal i Wraig William Salesbury', *Llên Cymru*, IX.

Unpublished thesis:

Mathias, W. Alun, 'Astudiaeth o weithgarwch llenyddol William Salesbury', M.A. (University College, Cardiff), 1949.

Index of principal historical figures and locations

ap Maredudd, John Wyn 69, 75, 162, 167, 181–5, 193, 195, 261, 351, 375

ap Rhys, Robert 10, 61–3, 266, 334–5, 375

Askew, Anne 91, 109, 120, 131, 155, 247, 339

Awdeley, John 193, 240, 243, 251, 268–9, 276–7, 380

Bale, John 66, 73, 91, 118, 120, 123, 125–7, 137, 179, 186, 191, 232, 269, 294, 336, 345, 364

Bekynsaw, John 71–3, 337–8

Boleyn, Anne 47, 57, 67, 179, 199, 333, 343

Bonner, Edmund (bishop of London) 91, 109, 130, 179, 191, 194, 348, 352

Brereton, William Sir 41, 56–7, 59, 67, 230, 333–4

Calais 50, 71–2, 82, 337–8

Carmarthen 66, 71, 205–6, 219, 221–2, 227, 229, 232–3, 263, 265, 268, 271, 331, 341, 348, 350, 354–8, 378

Cecil, William Sir 32, 118, 120, 123–7, 138, 152, 188–93, 203, 210–11, 213–14, 225–6, 231–3, 235, 247, 269, 296, 343, 345, 350–2, 355–6

Chaucer, Geoffrey 33, 38, 126, 147, 192, 229–32, 320, 352, 358–9

Colyngborne, Richard 138–9, 144–5, 245, 359

Cranmer, Thomas (archbishop of Canterbury) 37, 51, 73, 90–1, 109, 119, 128, 153–4, 157, 161, 179–80, 348

Cromwell, Thomas 19, 40–1, 50, 56–7, 61–2, 65–7, 70, 73, 78, 162, 333, 335, 337–8

Crowley, Robert 118, 120, 123–8, 132, 135, 138, 149, 155–6, 160, 162–3, 179, 191–2, 203, 232, 240, 246–7, 333, 343–4, 348, 355

Cynwal, Wiliam 169, 175, 193, 265, 271, 292–3, 328–9, 352–3, 363, 367

Davies, John 100, 103, 175, 253, 258, 260, 274, 286, 288, 291, 293–4, 297, 299–300, 303, 306, 312–13, 324, 350, 366–8

Davies, Richard (bishop of St Davids) 125, 134–5, 148, 179, 188, 201–6, 210, 213, 215, 217–26, 229, 232–3, 249–51, 254, 261–4, 270, 276, 278, 281–2, 285–6, 290, 294, 300–3, 306, 311, 315–16, 336, 339, 343, 345, 351–8, 361–3, 365–7, 370–1, 379

Dee, John Dr 85, 104, 124, 126, 186, 191–2, 194, 232, 254, 293–4, 340, 342, 349, 352, 362, 368

Denham, Henry 192–3, 239–40, 243, 248, 251, 269–70, 354, 360

Devereux, Walter (earl of Essex) 203, 223, 232, 264, 270, 354

Dudley, John (earl of Warwick, duke of Northumberland) 124, 152–5, 162, 167, 177–8, 187, 190, 212–13, 270

Dudley, Robert (earl of Leicester) 162, 197, 205, 212, 220, 223, 225, 232, 264, 353

Dwnn, Gruffudd 148, 228–9, 233, 246, 268, 301, 358, 379

Elizabeth I 14, 44, 124–5, 132, 138, 179, 185–6, 188–94, 198–201, 206, 208–15, 220, 235, 246, 248–9, 262, 281, 298, 339, 343, 350, 352–3, 355, 357, 360–1, 365, 372–3

Elyot, Thomas 29, 53, 92, 102, 116, 173, 236, 311, 314

Edward VI 14, 34, 67, 87, 90, 109–10, 112, 116, 121–2, 154, 162, 166, 168, 180–1, 190–1, 199–200, 203, 275, 331, 342, 346, 348, 354–6

Edwards, John 66, 147–8, 192, 230, 232, 275, 279, 336, 346–7, 358, 365

Erasmus 21–30, 38–9, 42, 46, 50–1, 64, 87, 91, 93–4, 99, 105, 109, 111–13, 115–16, 129, 131, 139, 158, 160–1, 163, 168, 220, 236, 257, 311, 313–14, 318, 330, 335, 338, 346, 348

Foxe, John 91, 123, 125, 137, 192, 278, 331, 343

Frankfurt 147, 191, 203, 206

Gardiner, Stephen (bishop of Winchester) 73, 91–2, 109, 179–80, 191, 194, 348

Geneva 20, 203, 220, 226, 248, 262, 298, 361

Gesner, Conrad 123–5, 180, 185–6, 272, 343, 351

Grafton, Richard 127, 138, 339, 343, 345, 348, 355

Grey, Jane Lady 177–9, 203, 346, 351

Grindal, Edmund (bishop of London, archbishop of Canterbury) 123–5, 127, 203, 206, 213, 240–1, 247, 256, 343, 354

Gruffudd Hiraethog 31, 37, 64, 78, 80, 82–3, 105–6, 110, 115, 117, 138, 145, 148, 168–71, 174–5, 205, 214, 229, 242, 247, 252, 265, 327–9, 334–5, 352, 354, 358, 363, 374–5, 379

Henry VIII 19, 23, 33, 39, 47, 49–50, 57, 67, 73, 79, 81–4, 86–7, 89–91, 94–5, 100, 109, 117, 119, 121, 123, 127, 131–2, 155, 177, 191, 197, 200, 248, 327, 339–41, 351

Herbert, William Sir (earl of Pembroke) 40, 79–83, 91, 98, 123–4, 139, 153, 155, 172, 177–9, 190–1, 199, 212, 220, 223, 225, 232, 270, 338–9, 353

Heywood, John 26, 108, 111

Hooper, John (bishop of Gloucester and Worcester) 118, 123–5, 180, 186, 343

Huet, Thomas 225–6, 251, 257, 303, 357

Jones, John Morris 306–12, 315, 318, 370

Kyffin, Maurice 180–4, 289, 295, 299, 311, 351, 359, 366

Lancashire 13–14, 18–21, 47, 274, 328, 331, 338, 365

Leland, John 64–6, 72–3, 79, 147, 191, 199, 232, 336, 338, 346

Llanrwst 9, 12–13, 16, 20, 44, 64, 68, 74–6, 147, 180, 183–4, 202, 241, 261–2, 265, 267, 285, 295, 330, 337, 363–4

Llansannan 10–11, 13, 16, 59, 64, 66, 68, 75, 147, 184–7, 196, 205, 242, 267, 274, 303, 327–9, 334, 336, 341, 351, 354, 361, 364–5, 368

Llwyd, Humphrey 9, 19, 66, 148, 159, 204–5, 210–12, 214–15, 221, 229, 254–5, 269, 282, 344, 352, 354, 356, 362, 375

Llŷn, Wiliam 169, 175, 242, 265, 271, 349, 363

London 13, 17, 20, 31, 35, 39–40, 42–6, 49, 54, 57–60, 64, 71, 73, 78, 80, 91, 95, 106, 109–10, 116–24, 126–8, 130, 133, 141, 144, 147, 160, 162, 167–8, 172, 177–80, 183–5, 187, 190–1, 193–4, 203, 206, 213–15, 218, 226–7, 229, 232–4, 239–41, 246–9, 255, 257, 268–70, 278–9, 299, 304, 324, 332–4, 337, 343–4, 347, 350, 354–5, 358, 360, 368–9

Ludlow 35, 59, 78, 220, 227, 229, 255, 275, 278–9, 281, 333, 335, 347

Luther, Martin 33, 38–9, 218, 220, 257, 309, 331–2, 354

Mary I 12, 44, 73, 87, 91, 124–5, 153, 168, 177–80, 184–6, 188–95, 198–9, 200–1, 213, 216–18, 232, 261, 332, 344, 350

More, Thomas Sir 22–3, 34, 39, 45–7, 50–1, 55, 58, 67, 134, 247, 330, 334

Morgan, William 18, 201, 211, 235, 237, 247, 256–8, 260, 262–4, 276, 278, 280–91, 295–8, 300–3, 306, 310, 312, 314–16, 318, 324, 329, 359, 363, 365–71

Owen, David 41, 68–9, 75, 180, 183, 337, 350–1

Oxford 13, 17, 20–1, 23, 30–1, 33, 35–40, 42, 51, 59, 64–5, 71–3, 78, 95, 116, 123, 131, 138, 147, 165, 190, 202, 217, 232, 287, 296, 306–8, 312, 314, 329–31, 345, 354, 375

Palsgrave, John 49–54, 84, 92–3, 95–6, 98–9,
116, 142, 260, 313, 332, 339, 368, 370
Paris 22, 25, 49, 53, 71–3, 275, 296, 337–8,
349, 364
Parker, Matthew (archbishop of Canterbury)
138, 189–92, 206, 217, 220, 222, 224–5,
246, 249, 262, 301, 336, 345, 352–3,
356–7, 361, 369, 379
Parr, Catherine 80, 90, 98, 109, 339
Parry, Blanche 125, 189, 199, 246, 342–3,
351, 353, 361
Parry, Thomas Sir 125–6, 175, 189, 199–200,
231, 343, 352
Penry, John 280–1, 290, 366
Perri, Henry 175, 289, 291, 296, 368–9
Philip, King of Spain 80, 91, 178–9
Pole, Reginald (archbishop of Canterbury)
130, 179, 194
Ponet, John (bishop of Winchester) 125, 130,
132, 137–8, 187, 190, 342, 344, 350
Price, Elis Dr 9, 41–2, 61–3, 68–70, 72–7,
100, 104, 116–17, 119–20, 132, 135, 147–
8, 156, 162, 167, 170, 177, 180–4, 187,
196–7, 205, 210–12, 217, 225–6, 229,
242–3, 266–7, 335–8, 342, 345, 350–1,
353, 359, 374–5
Prise, John Sir 64–6, 73, 78–87, 101, 103,
111, 127, 142, 154, 158–9, 172, 190, 198,
206, 209, 232, 260, 269, 277, 318, 336,
338–9, 351, 356, 364, 366, 375
Historiae Britannicae Defensio 79, 269
Yn y lhyvyr hwnn 83–8, 106, 154, 158,
206, 277, 318, 345

Prys, Edmwnd 265, 285–6, 291–3, 300, 303,
329, 363–4, 367, 370
Puleston, John Sir 119–20, 162, 167, 174,
181, 183
Rich, Richard Sir 55, 57–9, 71, 73, 91, 109,
119–22, 128, 131–2, 162–3, 166, 178,
191, 247, 333–4, 342, 350, 352
Ridley, Nicholas (bishop of London) 37,
118–19, 123–5, 127–9, 132, 156, 168,
179–80, 278, 343
Robert, Gruffydd 260, 295, 298, 318, 363–4
Robinson, Nicholas (bishop of Bangor) 201,
221, 225, 256
Rogers, John 123, 127, 180, 236, 350

Salesbury, William:
Act of parliament (1563) 125, 207–15,
326
Arbitration 9, 17, 60, 74–5, 104, 117,
181, 184, 328, 334, 374
Assault (upon him) 116–17, 132, 243,
267, 374
Broadgates Hall 13, 31–2, 39–40, 42
Cae Du 11–12, 170, 184–6, 193, 196,
263, 327
Classical translations (possible) 129–30,
140
Court cases 10, 16, 57, 59, 116, 119, 227
Early career 55–60
Espionage (possible) 121, 188–94
King's privilege (1547) 83, 89, 118, 154–
5, 327, 339, 376
Marriage 10, 59–60, 62–5, 70, 168, 187,
333–5, 353, 375
Old Testament, The 163, 219, 229, 233,
249–50, 257, 261–5, 267–71, 280,
284–7, 324, 349, 365
Orthography 84–5, 87, 101, 116, 126,
132, 141, 147, 163–4, 171, 186, 211,
218–19, 222, 235–6, 241, 245, 249,
254–5, 257–8, 273, 278, 280, 282–3,
285, 290, 295–7, 300, 305–6, 308–11,
313–14, 317–18, 320, 323–5, 349,
359, 364, 366–9
Petition, The 110, 153, 347, 354–5
Plas Isa 11–13, 15, 17, 64, 75–6, 170,
183–5, 193, 195, 197, 218, 226, 261,
271, 295, 328, 335, 353, 359, 374–6
Relations with the bards 64–5, 80, 96–8,
106, 111–12, 144–7, 167–75, 222,
229, 242–4, 253–4, 260, 265–6, 291–
2, 310, 324, 328, 350, 361–3, 367, 375
Reputation (posthumous) 238, 289–303,
304–16
Seizure of his estate 69, 179–85
Thavies Inn 13, 31, 40, 42–3, 47, 57–9,
116, 122–3, 127, 131, 138, 143, 180,
215, 332, 337
Year of birth 10, 327
Year of death 31, 35, 170, 175, 257,
276–8, 293, 296–7, 362

Works by Salesbury

A Dictionary in Englyshe and Welshe 11, 83–4, 92–104, 115, 118, 141, 175, 332

A briefe and a playne introduction 138–46, 156, 161–2, 169, 174, 235, 243, 260, 316, 332–3, 339–40, 342–3, 347, 352, 356, 363, 379

A playne and a familiar Introduction 193, 243, 301, 346–7, 352, 355, 359, 365, 371, 380

Ban wedy i dynny air/A Certaine Case Extracte 132–8, 141, 303, 345, 347

Kynniver Llith a Ban 154–66, 171, 180, 187, 198, 206, 209, 220, 226, 238–9, 259, 264, 282, 311, 339, 348–9, 362, 366, 376

Lliver Gweddi Gyffredin 211, 234, 237–9, 241, 243–5, 257–8, 276–8, 352, 380

Llyfr Rhetoreg 167–76, 289, 364

Y Llysieulyfr (The Herbal) 10, 18, 100, 126, 170, 271–5, 327, 329–30, 336–7, 343, 364–5, 368, 371

Oll Synnwyr 105–17, 137, 141, 158, 168–9, 243, 252–3, 303, 311, 330, 334, 339–41, 345–8

The baterie of the Popes Botereulx 118, 124, 128, 131–2, 134, 140, 160, 178, 247, 275, 331, 333, 342, 347

The Descripcion of the Sphere 146–51, 156, 235, 299, 329, 332, 347, 358

Y Diarebion Camberaec 251–5, 261, 293, 313, 354, 370, 379

Y Testament Newydd 11–13, 211, 219, 248–51, 255, 258–9, 271, 339, 349, 363, 379

Salesbury Family, The:

Annes (mother) 13, 16–17, 70, 75–6, 182, 328–9, 342, 371, 375

Catrin Llwyd (wife) 10, 60–4, 76–7, 104, 167–8, 181, 185, 187, 193, 197, 247, 265–7, 335, 340, 351, 353, 359, 364, 374–5

Foulk (father) 9, 16–17, 74–6, 329, 336

Foulk Sr (great-uncle) 9, 14–15, 40–1, 56, 62, 333, 336, 341, 354

Gwen and Elen (nieces) 9, 68–70, 75–7, 119, 167, 180–3, 247, 262, 289

Gwenhwyfar (grandmother) 9, 15–17, 63–4, 70, 75–6, 119, 182, 184, 289, 329, 336–7, 341–2, 363, 367, 375

John Wyn (son and heir) 9, 60, 76, 193, 266, 276, 295

Lowri (sister-in-law) 61, 64, 69, 336, 364, 375

Robert (brother) 13, 15–17, 20, 60–1, 64, 68–71, 74–6, 80–1, 119, 136, 168, 180–1, 183–4, 289, 330, 337, 350, 364, 374–5

Robert Sr (grandfather) 9, 14–16, 75–6, 184, 329, 333, 336, 341, 375

Salusbury Clan, The

John, Sir of Llewenni (d. 1612) 14–15, 63

Katheryn (of Berain) 15, 196, 211, 353

Thomas (founder) 9, 14

Thomas (conspirator) 14–15, 201, 279

Thrale, Hester 15, 328

Seymour, Edward (duke of Somerset) 121–2, 124–6, 152–3, 162, 166, 188, 190, 213, 231, 275

Sidney, Henry Sir 57, 202, 204, 224, 255, 269, 279, 286, 336

Simwnt Fychan 169–71, 175, 265, 268, 271, 299, 350, 363–4, 367, 380

Shakespeare, William 14–15, 27–9, 42, 44, 54, 101, 108, 139, 150, 159, 220, 240, 312, 319–21, 330, 353–4, 364, 370

Skevington, Thomas (bishop of Bangor) 57–9, 200, 262, 327, 334, 353

Smith, Thomas 34, 91, 124, 152, 213–14, 318, 331, 343, 371

Sydley, John 57–9, 334

Thelwall, Simon 211, 268–9, 364

Toy, Humphrey 226–7, 229, 233–6, 239–40, 243–5, 251, 256–7, 269–71, 276, 278, 348, 357, 359–60, 365, 371

Turner, William 118, 123–6, 203, 272–5, 299, 343

Tyndale, William 25, 44–7, 86, 88, 93–4, 107, 113, 116, 127, 134, 144, 157, 162, 209, 218, 236, 257, 274, 284–5,

291, 303, 311, 316–17, 320, 322, 332,
  342, 348, 361–2, 366, 371
Vaughan, Robert 175, 230, 232, 253,
  293–5, 299, 335, 358–9, 362, 368–9
Vergil, Polydore 78–9, 111, 204, 320,
  338
Whaley, John 83, 92, 100–1, 106, 117,
  149, 206, 339, 360
Whitchurch, Edward 83, 85, 101, 127,
  339, 346
Whitgift, John (bishop of Worcester,
  archbishop of Canterbury) 57, 235,
  278–81, 286, 298, 334
Wiliems, Thomas 148, 257, 263, 271,
  273–5, 293–4, 327, 350, 360, 362–5,
  379
Wolsey, Thomas 23, 35, 39, 46–7, 49–
  51, 58, 61
Wriothesley, Lord 91, 121, 342
Wynn, John Sir 195–6, 261, 270, 276,
  284–5, 359, 365
Wynn, Morus 182, 185, 196, 210–11,
  329, 353, 378

William Salesbury is just one of a whole
range of publications from Y Lolfa. For a full
list of books currently in print, send now
for your free copy of our new full-colour
catalogue. Or simply surf into our website

www.ylolfa.com

for secure on-line ordering.

TALYBONT CEREDIGION CYMRU SY24 5HE
e-mail ylolfa@ylolfa.com
website www.ylolfa.com
phone (01970) 832 304
fax 832 782